AF568155

Waqai-i Manazil-i Rum
Tipu Sultan's Mission to Constantinople

Waqai-i Manazil-i Rum
Tipu Sultan's Mission to Constantinople

KHWAJA ABDUL QADIR

Edited by
MOHIBBUL HASAN

Introduced by
IRFAN HABIB

Waqai-i Manazil-i Rum
Tipu Sultan's Mission to Constantinople

First Published 1968
Reprinted with a new Introduction by Irfan Habib 2005
Reprinted 2022

ISBN 978-81-8787-956-5

Published by
AAKAR BOOKS
28 E Pocket IV, Mayur Vihar Phase I, Delhi 110 091
E-mail : aakarbooks@gmail.com

Printed at
Sapra Brothers, Noida.

TO THE MEMORY OF MY MOTHER

CONTENTS

INTRODUCTION

—Irfan Habib*

The late Professor Mohibbul Hasan put all students of the history of Tipu Sultan in his debt not only by his standard biography of that ruler (Calcutta, 1951; second ed., 1971), but also by his edition (now being reprinted) of a diary of Tipu Sultan's mission to the Ottoman court, the *Waqa'i'-i-Manazil-i Rum*, unfortunately extant only in part, covering the period from 17 November 1785 to 9 January 1787.[1] The diary ends at the point when the embassy was just leaving Basra, the Ottoman port on the Persian Gulf, for Baghdad, on its way to Constantinople ('Islambol' in the Diary). The diary was presumably written by the secretary to the mission, Khwaja 'Abdu'l Qadir. Professor Mohibbul Hasan carefully edited the text, based on a single manuscript, and provided a historical introduction as well as a summary of the diary which brings out the bulk of the significant material contained in it.

One notable relevant published addition since Professor Hasan's edition of the *Waqa'i'* has been the translation of the instructions by Tipu Sultan issued in November 1785 to the same mission, which was originally expected to visit Constantinople, France and, possibly, England in that order. The text of these instructions is preserved in the library of the Asiatic Society, Calcutta (MS No.1677), the very collection where the manuscript of the *Waqa'i'-i Manazil-i Rum* is also preserved, and has been translated (2001) by Iqbal Husain, with the necessary annotation.[2] These instructions are important for understanding what Tipu Sultan's objects were in the despatch of his embassy to Constantinople.

A major misconception these instructions dispose of is the one which Professor I.H. Qureshi had propounded in 1945: that Tipu's project was "directed towards gaining recognition for his newly independent title of an independent monarch." He aimed to get it from the Sultan of Turkey, "as the foremost power of political Islam", when he could not make the Mughal Emperor at Delhi, then under the control of the Marathas, confer it on him.[3] In a recent work Dr Kate Brittlebank tells us that Tipu Sultan's ambassadors were "*instructed* to seek the Ottoman ruler's confirmation, *in his role as Caliph*, of legitimacy of Tipu's claims and his rule of Mysore."[4] Since the instructions

* Irfan Habib is formerly Professor of History, Aligarh Muslim University, Aligarh.

actually exist, it can now be seen that solicitation for recognition of any kind from Constantinople was no part of the envoys' brief. Moreover, nowhere is the Turkish Sultan recognized as Caliph. He is usually referred to simply as Khondkar, or Qaisar or Sultan; and Tipu continuously asserts an implicit equality or parity with him. His envoys were, indeed, instructed to underline his own power and resources, and it was on this basis that he wished to seek an alliance, not a diploma of recognition, from the Porte.

It is clear from the instructions issued to the envoys, which included a brief for negotiations with the English court (the opportunity for which never arose) that Tipu Sultan at the end of the Second Mysore War (1784) was left with a sense of great self-confidence, and a number of grievances. The self-confidence arose from the fact that, despite the Marathas' withdrawal from the war (1782), followed by that of the French (1783), he had been able to stand up to the English on his own. The English East India Company was, in his eyes, his major enemy, so that it was worth exploring, especially after the conduct of the French in the latter part of the late war, whether Turkey could not replace France as a military ally. Yet Turkey was a still untried power, and its reaction to the warlike proposals could not have been confidently predicted. Tipu Sultan's instructions for negotiations with the French Government showed that he thought it still feasible separately to try for a French alliance, without reference to Turkey, and entice the French into a common war against Britain with the prospect of a share in the British possessions in India. Finally, the instructions for the mission in England were so framed as even to dream up a military alliance with England, if the fort of Trichnopoloy was 'returned' to Mysore. France is altogether forgotten here. What we have is, therefore, a set of three alternative schemes, which, Tipu thought, could be explored by his mission, first with Turkey, failing which with France, and, then, finally, with England. As it turned out, the mission to the Ottoman court could not go on to France, and so a separate embassy had to be sent directly to France in 1788. But the French reports indicate that this embassy pursued the same brief there as the one given to the embassy stalled at Constantinople.[5]

While these military projects occupied a large space in Tipu Sultan's vision for the future, he was also unique among Indian potentates in seeing a close relationship between economic strength and military power. He, therefore, assigned to the mission to Constantinople the task of opening up trade between Mysore and the Ottoman Empire. Mysore had products to export, chiefly, textiles, sandalwood and pepper; and all of these could reasonably be expected to have markets in West Asia and south-eastern Europe, accessible to Mysore through the Persian Gulf. Tipu Sultan's embassy to Constantinople was, therefore, not only a diplomatic mission, but also a significant commercial enterprise. It had been given a large amount of merchandise that was to be carried in a fleet of vessels, all to be sold on the state's account. In return were to be secured what today would be called industrial and technology imports. The French had probably been Tipu Sultan's source of knowledge about coal. He directed that 'stone-coal' (*sang-*

i angisht) be brought back by the mission from Turkey in ships as ballast.[6] While proud of the muskets he was himself manufacturing in Mysore, he asked that the Sultan of Turkey be requested to let the mission recruit from his dominions "better craftsmen to manufacture muskets, cannon-pieces, clocks, glass, chinaware and mirrors". It was their superiority in the manufacture of these articles that had enabled "the Christians" to obtain dominance over India, the Sultan was to be told.[7] Further, an effort was to be made to secure from Turkey as well as France the services of "good carpenters and ironsmiths" for constructing ships.[8] Silk-worms too were to be looked for within the Ottoman dominions;[9] and we must remember that sericulture as an industry in Mysore owes its initiation to Tipu.

Characteristically, even in commercial matters Tipu Ṣultan dreamt big; and he was already thinking of Basra as a port given over to the control of Mysore! In the draft of a possible agreement with the Sultan of Turkey, it was proposed that the port of Basra be taken on lease, the amount of hire being directly paid to the Sultan, while the latter could similarly lease a port in Tipu's dominions.[10]

There are numerous indications in the text of Abdu'l Qadir's diary or report (henceforth cited as *Waqa'i'*) that the instructions that the envoys had with them were precisely the ones that have come down to us. As prescribed in the latter, the mission was placed under four persons, G͟hulam 'Ali K͟han, Nurullah K͟han, Lutf 'Ali K͟han and Ja'far K͟han, who were always to act in concert. The *Waqa'i'* styles them chiefs (*sardars*) and 'the K͟hans' (*k͟hawanin*), with their meetings treated almost like 'council' meetings among the English. The bickerings and disagreements that inevitably took place at these meetings are narrated in cold detail in the *Waqa'i'*. Uptill the time the extant part of the report was completed at Basra, the mission was still under the impression that it was to proceed to France and England from Turkey, as laid down in the instructions. It informed the French factors at Basra of the mission's projected journey to France,[11] and gifts intended for England were also cleaned and repaired at Basra.[12] Similarly, the plan to excavate a canal at Najaf at Tipu's expense, proposed in the instructions,[13] is duly referred to in the *Waqa'i'*.[14] When the Turkish governor of Basra asked them for particulars of the port of Mangalore (Koriyal), the envoys were immediately led to the conclusion that the Sultan of Turkey wanted information about Mangalore in order to compare its condition with that of Basra,[15] obviously having in their own mind Tipu's suggestion that an exchange of ports to be mutually leased should be raised with the Sultan.

The way the *Waqa'i'* is composed and the subjects it covers indicates that its writer was aware of Tipu Sultan's injunctions in regard to the kinds of reports he wanted:

> The particulars of every stage of journey and leading officials of each of the three States [Turkey, France and England], with indications of the status of the said leading officials and descriptions of their affairs as discovered (by you) and the industries and rarities of each city and territory and the account of the affairs of the cities, should be written down..[16]

The *Waqa'i'*, therefore, is not only a narrative of the experiences of the mission, its commercial and diplomatic transactions, its internal feuds, etc., but also includes fairly detailed and accurate accounts of physical geography, lay-out of towns, conditions of housing and clothing, local products, qualities of markets, detailed lists of prices, shipping, nature of local administration, etc., at all points of the voyage from Musqat to Basra. The *Waqa'i'*, indeed, offers an admirable administrative and commercial profile of the Gulf and Oman in the 1780s, though it is not clear if its value as a source of information about the region, has been as yet fully appreciated.

The details of the voyage and transactions of the mission in the *Waqa'i'* are given in a cool and detached manner so unlike what was expected by the conventions of the Persian style of the day. The author's restraint is all the more remarkable since the report actually had to deal with a series of accidents that spoilt what were seemingly most carefully laid plans and arrangements. First, the four elephants, one each intended for the three kings to be visited, and one for reserve, all perished before the fleet anchored at Musqat, in the very first part of the voyage.[17] Later, soon after arriving at the Basra estuary the ship *Nabi Bakhsh* caught fire and sank with much loss of life and merchandise.[18] Then, when the Ottoman authorities did not allow the full military complement of the embassy to proceed further, and the remaining two vessels, the ship *Fath Shahi Mu'izzi* and the galliot *Surati*, lifted anchor to carry back the returning personnel, both were overwhelmed by a storm and sank in the Basra estuary, taking down most of the people aboard.[19] These three losses must have been a stunning blow to Tipu Sultan's endeavours to build a fleet for commerce with the Gulf.

The style of the *Waqa'i'*, as we have just said, is unemotional, so that even quite stressful occasions do not seem to affect the dull tone of its simple narrative. But sometimes a human touch is provided. At one place we are told:

> Lutf Ali Khan [one of the four leaders of the mission], sitting in a palanquin wandered about the lanes and bazars of Basra. Setting down his palanquin at this place and that, he engaged in buying small cornelian stones, etc., thus throwing to the wind all respect for his status of a chief, his palanquin and the good name of this Government.
>
> Previously too, he twice went about in lane and bazar, visiting every shop, and arguing with each shop-keeper and grocer over every copper coin.[20]

Or a laconic comment on the doings of an apparently spiteful subordinate member of the mission:

> The French chief factor was deeply hurt and remarked privately: "what kind of men these four chiefs of the [Mysore] mission are and how they make their dealings, I have now learnt from Muhammad Bhatu."[21]

Professor Mohibbul Hasan is probably right in attributing the authorship of the report to the Secretary (*munshi*) of the mission, 'Abdu'l Qadir whose signatures appear on the fly-leaves of the manuscript. But in the report itself he is always referred to by his name, just like other persons. Since some incidents described do not go to the credit of one or the other of the mission's chiefs, or even of the first chief, Ghulam 'Ali Khan,[22] it is difficult to believe that it was drafted on behalf of the chiefs of the mission and had their unanimous approval. Was, then, the authorship concealed so that the author might be able frankly report to Tipu Sultan whatever actually transpired, without being exposed to later personal enmities? It is likely that this was what Tipu himself had prescribed. A more extensive exploration of the Tipu Sultan archives, now so widely dispersed, could possibly tell us whether other reports that he received on the doings of his officials were also similarly composed. This is one reason among many other weightier ones why the kind of work that Professor Mohibbul Hasan undertook by editing the *Waqa'i'* needs to be followed up and a most valuable store of evidence that the Tipu archives are be not allowed to remain unexposed.

NOTES

1. I accept the dates as converted from dates given originally in Tipu Sultan's official calendar, by Professor Mohibbul Hasan.
2. Iqbal Husain, 'The Diplomatic Vision of Tipu Sultan: Briefs for Embassies to Turkey and France, 1785-86' in: Irfan Habib (ed.), *State and Diplomacy under Tipu Sultan*, New Delhi, 2001, pp.19-65. The documents translated include a brief also for negotiations with the King of England (pp.49-51).
3. *Journal of Indian History*, Madras, XXIV (1945), pp.77-84.
4. *Tipu Sultan's Search for Legitimacy: Islam and Kingship in a Hindu Domain*, Delhi, 1997, p.70 (italics ours).
5. For these reports see S. Venkatesh (transl.), *The Correspondence of the French During the reigns of Hyder Ali and Tipu Sultan*, Vol.III, Bangalore, 1998.
6. Iqbal Husain (transl.), 'The Diplomatic Vision of Tipu Sultan...', op.cit., pp.33, 53. Tipu Sultan's belief that there was "plenty of stone-coal" available in the Ottoman Empire, does not seem to have been justified.
7. Ibid., p.42. See also ibid., p.37.
8. Ibid., p.36.
9. Ibid., p.53.
10. Ibid., pp.36, 41.
11. *Waqa'i'*, pp.50-51.
12. *Waqa'i'*, pp.65-66.
13. 'The Diplomatic Vision of Tipu Sultan', op.cit., p.81.
14. *Waqa'i'* , p.48.
15. Ibid., pp.149-50.
16. 'The Diplomatic Vision of Tipu Sultan...', p.29.
17. *Waqa'i'*, pp.2-3.
18. Ibid., pp.40-41, 59-60.
19. Ibid., pp.99-101.
20. Ibid., p.88.
21. Ibid., p.52. Muhammad Bhatu, because of his uncontrolled tongue, was ultimately sent home by the mission.
22. See, for instance, the account of a crisis Ghulam 'Ali Khan created at Basra (ibid., pp.135-137).

EDITOR'S NOTE

It is my pleasant duty to express my gratitude to Mr. Zia Ahmad, formerly Professor of Persian in the Aligarh Muslim University, for help in preparing the Persian text. I am also thankful to Dr. G. J. Alder of the Public Relations Department, Esso Petroleum Company, London, for introducing me to Mr. A.H. Kamal and Mr. William E. Mulligan of the Iraq Petroleum Company, who very kindly identified a number of obscure place-names which were plaguing me. I am indebted to Mr. Victor Kiernan of Edinburgh University for reading through the introduction and making useful suggestions. My thanks are also due to Prof. Bernard Lewis of the School of Oriental and African Studies, University of London, for various useful suggestions and for drawing my attention to Mr. Abu Hakima's unpublished thesis entitled *The Utbi States in Eastern Arabia in the Second Half of the 18th Century*, which proved to me of incalculable help. I am obliged to Mr. Ubaid ul-Haq of the Jamia Millia for preparing the map showing the route followed by the envoys. I should also like to acknowledge here my gratitude to the French Government and the British Council for arranging my visit to Paris and London which enabled me to collect material not only for this work but also for revising my *History of Tipu Sultan*, a second edition of which is expected to be published soon. Lastly, I must thank my old colleagues, Professors Nurul Hasan and K.A. Nizami, for arranging the publication of this work.

Owing to certain technical difficulties,—oriental words could not be transliterated. However, those wishing to find out the correct spellings of such words are referred to the Persian text and its index. For the spelling of place-names I have mostly based myself on Lorimer's *Gazetteer of the Persian Gulf, Oman and Central Arabia* and Razmara's *Farhang Jughrafiya-i Iran*. But for well-known towns like Basra, Mecca and Madina their common spellings have been retained.

M. H.

INTRODUCTION

In 1786 Tipu Sultan of Mysore (1782—99) sent an embassy to Constantinople. It was required, in the first place, to establish commercial relations with the Ottoman Empire. "The object of the embassy," as Manesty, the English agent at Basra, reported, "is to obtain *firmans* to establish factories in the Turkish dominions for selling the produce of his kingdom." In the second place, it was required to secure confirmation of Tipu's title to the throne of Mysore from the Caliph. This was necessary because Tipu had failed to secure an investiture from the Mughal Emperor and was regarded as an usurper. The third main object of the embassy was to obtain military assistance from the Ottoman Sultan against the English who were Tipu's most formidable enemies. In addition to achieving these objects, the ambassadors were instructed to land at Masqat in order to strengthen the trade and friendly relations which already existed with Oman, and, on their way up the Persian Gulf, to touch Bushire and obtain commercial concessions from the Shah of Persia.

The embassy consisted of Ghulam Ali Khan, Nurullah Khan, Lutf Ali Khan and Jafar Khan, with Sayyid Jafar and Khwaja Abdul Qadir as secretaries. Ghulam Ali Khan, the leader of the delegation, was one of the most important and trusted officers of Tipu. A resident of Arcot, he had entered the service of Tipu's father, Haidar Ali, when the latter had captured the town in November 1780. Later Tipu made him *Mir Sudur* (Inspector General of forts). However, since he was looked upon as a skilful diplomat, he was entrusted with this mission to Constantinople. On his return from there he was appointed by Tipu to negotiate a treaty with the English (1792), and was afterwards deputed to accompany the hostage princes to Madras. Again, in 1797, he was selected as one of the members of the embassy to proceed to Mauritius and negotiate an offensive and defensive alliance with the French. Although he was not able to go, he, as First Lord of Admiralty, welcomed Ripaud, the French emissary from Mauritius, and sent him to Seringapatam with an escort. After the fall of Seringapatam in 1799, he was given a handsome pension by the English, and he passed the rest of his days in Mysore.

Very little is known about the other members of the embassy. Nurullah Khan, who was a Sayyid of Persian origin, had been sent by Haidar Ali to Shiraz in 1770 in order to get military help from Karim Khan-i

Zand. It was because of this experience that he was now selected for this mission. He was the most active member of the embassy, though in rank he was next to Ghulam Ali Khan and was placed in charge of the financial side of the mission. Lutf Ali Khan (Mirza Lutf Ali Beg) was a military officer who had served Haidar Ali in his wars, and had also, for a short time, held the important post of an Admiral. Under Tipu Sultan also he was sent on various military campaigns. From a reference by Wilks, it appears that he was still alive after the fall of Seringapatam. As regards Jafar Khan, the fourth and least important member of the embassy, we know nothing. Nor do we have any information about Sayyid Jafar and Khwaja Abdul Qadir, the two secretaries of the embassy.

The present work entitled *Waqai Manazil-i Rum* is a diary of this embassy, and was kept by order of Tipu Sultan, who wanted information about the countries of the Middle East with whom he was trying to establish friendly and commercial relations. It is a unique copy, and was found among the papers of Tipu on the capture of Seringapatam. It was sent to Fort William, Calcutta, and thence found its way, along with some other papers and books of Tipu, to the Asiatic Society of Bengal (Ivanow 1678). The earliest mention of it is in Wilks, History of Mysore, ii, 362, though he never utilized it and is wrong in stating that Sayyid Jafar was the author of the journal. It was actually written by Khwaja Abdul Qadir, and the present copy bears his signature (*Waqai* pp. 4, 7). The work is also known as *Diary of Ghulam Ali Khan* (Ibid, pp.1, 3), because Ghulam Ali Khan was the leader of the embassy. But there is no evidence to show that it was either written or dictated by him. The personality that emerges from the journal is that of a man who is irritable, proud, egoistical and tired, having little control or influence over his colleagues and the members of his staff. Surely, if he had been the author of the journal, he would have shown himself in a better light by glossing over his faults and exalting his virtues.

The *Waqai* contains an account of the activities and experiences of the embassy from the time it left Seringapatam until its departure from Basra to Constantinople. The remaining portion of the diary, describing the journey from Basra to the Ottoman capital and back to India, is no longer extant. The *Waqai* throws light on Tipu's commercial ambitions in the Persian Gulf and on certain aspects of his administration. It also describes the position of the Indian merchants in the Persian Gulf and the part they played in its economic life. It further shows that, in spite of the efforts of Haidar Ali and Tipu Sultan to build a mercantile marine and a navy, the Mysorians were still lagging far behind the Europeans in the technique of shipbuilding and the art of navigation. For, of the four boats which left the shores of India carrying the envoys, only one returned, the rest were wrecked in the Shatt ul-Arab, causing considerable loss of life and property. The *Waqai* is also valuable for an understanding of the Persian Gulf territories at the end of the 18th century, and is thus a useful supplement to the European accounts of the period. It depicts the character and administration of the Imam of Oman and the social and economic conditions of Masqat. It gives a detailed account of the buildings, history and economic life of Kharag Island. It also makes brief, but interesting, observations about the other islands in the Persian Gulf. Its account of Abu Shahr, though scrappy, provides valuable information about the prices prevalent in the Abu Shahr market. Particularly interesting are the descriptions of buildings, administration, and the social, economic and political conditions in Basra. We find here, for example, a very vivid description of the scars which the recent Persian invasion of Basra had left on the town. We also get here a valuable picture of the corruption and inefficiency of the Ottoman government of Basra, the insecurity of roads in Iraq and of the rebellion of Shaikh Suwaini in the Basra area and of Sulaiman al-Shawi in the neighbourhood of Baghdad. Furthermore, the diary shows that the Jewish community was commercially very prosperous, and one of its members named Abdullah was not only a rich merchant but exercised considerable political influence in Basra.

In describing his experiences Abdul Qadir enjoyed certain advantages denied to most of the European travellers. In the first place, he was not unfamiliar with the peoples and the culture he came across. In the second, he was conversant with Persian and Arabic, the two languages spoken and understood in the Persian Gulf area. Moreover, wherever he went he was received cordially, and came into friendly contact with all classes of people. At the same time it is necessary to point out that, despite these advantages, Abdul Qadir never cared to sift the evidence, but noted down indiscriminately whatever was related to him. The result is that there are occasional lapses and inaccuracies in his narrative, and important facts have been left out. In the description of Oman no mention is made of the authority wielded by Hamid, the son of Imam Said. References to Zubarah and Kuwait and their rulers have been made, but their commercial importance has not been commented upon. Nor is there any allusion to the Wahhabis, although they were rapidly becoming an important force in the northern part of the Persian Gulf. The conquest of Kharag Island from the Dutch by the notorious corsair, Mir Muhanna, has been explained in accordance with the local legends. Moreover, he is said to have been killed on the way to Basra, although in actual fact he was put to death at Basra by order of the Pasha of Baghdad. In the account of Basra the

Janissaries are not even once mentioned, and generally the Indo-Persian instead of Turkish administrative terms have been used for Ottoman officials. In his itinerary he sometimes misplaces the order of towns and does not always give their correct locations.

It is always difficult to edit a manuscript when only one copy is available ; it is specially so in the case of this work on account of its peculiar orthographical features. The style of the *Waqai* is extremely careless and loose. Its constructions are long and involved. No care has been taken to make the verbs agree with the subjects, while the importance of the order of words and their location in a sentence has been ignored. The language of the *Waqai*, too, is very defective. Archaic words and forms of spelling have been commonly employed, and instances are not wanting of words incorrectly spelt. Moreover, the dots are often misplaced. Copious use has also been made of words of Portuguese, Tamil, Kannada, Marathi and Hindi origin. All this makes the sentences obscure and their understanding difficult.

No attempt has been made by the present editor to effect any considerable changes in the text, for this would have destroyed some of the special features of the work. Alterations have been made only where it has been deemed absolutely necessary. In a few cases archaic forms of spelling have been replaced by modern ones, and uniformity has been maintained in the spellings of proper names, for in the original the same word has been spelt in different ways. Names of persons and places have been identified and annotated as fully as possible in Appendix B, while technical terms, allusions and words of non-Persian origin have been explained in Appendix C. In the second part of the Introduction a summary of the *Waqai* has been given, but important portions, particularly those relating to Masqat, Abu Shahr, Basra and some of the islands of the Persian Gulf have been translated in full. Since the journal does not narrate the progress of the embassy beyond Basra, it has been felt necessary to give in Appendix A a short account of the subsequent events connected with it, along with a brief analysis of its success and failure. A fuller treatment of this will be found in my forthcoming revised edition of *History of Tipu Sultan*.

The chief sources used in the preparation of this work are :

Factory Records :—*Persia and the Persian Gulf* (India Office No. 18).

Public Record Office, London : *British Foreign Office Records*, 7/8-1786. 78/8-1787, 78/9-1778.

Archives Nationales : *Affaires Étrangères*, B Nos. 176, 177, 197 (*Correspondance Consulaire*)—Bassorah 1743-91 ; B 448 (*Correspondance Consulaire*)—Constantinople (1787-90).

Hukum-namah, Asiatic Society, Calcutta, M.S.1677.

Husain Ali Khan Kirmani, *Nishan-i Haidari.* Bombay 1307/1890.

Salil b. Razik, *History of the Imams and Seyyids of Oman from* 661 *to* 1856. Translated from Arabic by G. P. Badger. London, 1871.

Kirkpatrick W., *Select Letters of Tippoo Sultan.* London 1811.

Neibhur, C., *Voyage en Arabie et en d'autres pays circonvoisins.* 2 *vols.* Translated from German. Amsterdam 1776-80.

Longrigg, S. M., *Four Centuries of Modern Iraq.* Oxford 1908.

Abu Hakima (Ahmad Mustafa), *The Utbi States in Eastern Arabia in the Second Half of the* 18*th century* (Unpublished thesis, 1960 London University).

Lorimer, J. G., *Gazetteer of the Persian Gulf, Oman, and Central Arabia.* 2 *Vols. Calcutta* 1908-15.

Wilson, H. H., *A Glossary of Judicial and Revenue Terms and of Useful Words Occurring in Official Documents Relating to the Administration of the Government of British India.* London 1855.

HISTORICAL BACKGROUND TO THE EMBASSY

The Mughals

The decline of the Mughal Empire began during the last years of Aurangzeb's reign. Bahadur Shah, his son and successor, tried to check this process, but his efforts were cut short by his death. After him, owing to the incompetence of his successors, and the greed, selfishness and rivalries of the Mughal officers, the empire continued on its downward course; and with the deposition and assassination of Alamgir II in 1758, it virtually ceased to exist. It is true that the facade of imperial greatness remained till the end of the eighteenth century and the Mughal Emperor continued to enjoy great prestige. He was still acknowledged as Emperor in many parts of India. Coins were struck and the *Khutbah* was recited in his name. Indian princes and European trading companies eagerly sought to obtain titles and privileges from him; but he wielded no power or authority beyond a small area around Delhi.

Owing to the collapse of the central government, one by one the different provinces slipped out of the imperial control. Kabul was occupied by Nadir Shah in 1739 and the Punjab by the Afghans in 1754. Bengal, Bihar and Orissa became independent under Alivardi Khan in 1750, and similarly Gujarat and Sindh cut themselves off from the empire in 1750. Oudh also fell away under Saadat Khan, an immigrant from Khorasan. His descendants ruled a kingdom comprising more or less the modern Uttar Pradesh until 1848.

The Nizam

In the Deccan, Mir Qamr ud-Din Chin Qilich Khan, better known as Nizam ul-Mulk, laid the foundations of the kingdom of Hyderabad. He was able, energetic, far-sighted, and died after a long and successful career at the age of 90 on 21 May, 1748. Nasir Jung, his second son, at once proclaimed himself ruler. But his claim was disputed by Muzaffar Jung, Nizam-ul-Mulk's daughter's son. In the war of succession, Muzaffar Jung, supported by the French, worsted his rival and declared himself *Subadar*. But while being escorted by the French from the Carnatic, which was the scene of the war, to his capital, he was assassinated by some of the disaffected nobles. Salabat Jung, the third son of Nizam ul-Mulk, was thereupon made the *Subadar*. He was weak, incompetent and irresolute, and was able to maintain himself in power only with the help of Bussy, the French general. But on 6 July, 1762, his more vigorous brother, Nizam Ali Khan, seized the government and threw him into prison. Nizam Ali Khan, though not possessing the courage, wisdom and statesmanship of his father, was shrewd and resourceful, and during his reign of forty-one years gave stability to his kingdom. Faced as he was by powerful neighbours like the English, the Marathas and the new rulers of Mysore, he was able to maintain his position by playing these powers against one another, and in the end, realizing that the star of the English was in the ascendant, he established a firm alliance with them and became their tributary.

The Marathas

The foundations of the Maratha kingdom were laid in Western India during the second half of the seventeenth century by Shivaji, who successfully defied Aurangzeb. But after his death the Mughal Emperor suppressed his successors. However, taking advantage of the disintegration of the Mughal Empire, which followed Aurangzeb's death, the Marathas revived their power and, between 1714 and 1761, succeeded in establishing an extensive kingdom. They began to raid the suburbs of Delhi, and in 1738 compelled the Mughal Emperor, Muhammad Shah, to cede to them Malwa. They then occupied Orissa and started raiding other parts of the Empire, collecting *Chauth* and *Sardeshmukhi* and looting and plundering wherever they went. Invited by Alamgir II to drive out Ahmed Shah Abdali from the Punjab, they occupied Lahore in 1758 and began to dream of establishing a Maratha Empire in the North. And for a time it seemed that the mantle of the Mughal Empire would fall on them. But they threw away the opportunity by a total lack of statesmanship and by administrative incompetence, for except to the heart of their kingdom, they failed to give political and economic stability to other areas which they occupied, while their plundering raids in Bengal, Malwa, Rajasthan and other provinces kept the inhabitants in a state of constant fear and anxiety. That is why, when they were routed by Ahmad Shah Abdali at Panipat in 1761, many people breathed a sigh of relief at their good riddance.

From this shattering blow the Marathas never really recovered. Although the Peshwa Madhava Rao, the son and successor of Balaji Rao, tried to revive the Maratha power and rally the different chiefs under his leadership, his premature death in November 1772 once again threw Maratha affairs into confusion. Wars of succession for the office of Peshwa, and rivalries among the Maratha chiefs, who had carved out separate kingdoms for themselves and were engaged in self-aggrandizement, greatly weakened the central government at Poona. Their internecine conflicts were taken advantage of by their greedy and powerful neighbours.

The English and the French

The English and French East India Companies which were, by the early part of the eighteenth century, well established in Bengal and on the eastern and western coasts of India, could not remain mere passive spectators of this drama of political disintegration and struggle for power that was being enacted before their eyes. They realized that, because of their better organization and superior military and diplomatic skill, they need not confine their activities merely to trade, but, that profiting from the conditions in India, they could make a bid for political power.

It was Dupleix, the French governor of Pondicherry, who first conceived the plan of interfering in the internal disputes of Indian princes and thereby acquiring political control over large territories by reducing their rulers to the status of puppets. Dupleix was resourceful and courageous, and possessed a fertile mind. But he was over optimistic and did not always understand the realities of the situation. He failed to realize that the English, who were the rivals of the French, would not allow him a free hand. Accordingly, when he took up the cause of Chanda Sahib against Muhammad Ali for the Nawabship of the Carnatic and of Muzaffar Jung against Nasir Jung for the *Subadari* of the Deccan, the English decided to support Muhammad Ali and Nasir Jung. In the conflict which ensued, Dupleix failed to defeat Muhammad Ali and the English. This was due partly to his own mistakes, for he failed to realize his limitations, and partly because he was not supported by the Company and the government in France. Dupleix, however, was successful in setting up Muzaffar Jung, his own candidate as *Subadar* of the Deccan. In reward for this he received Masulipatam and the Northern Sarkars and was made governor of all India south of the Kistna by the Mughal Emperor. Muzaffar Jung demanded some French troops to accompany him to his capital and help him consolidate his power. Dupleix made the mistake of sending with him Bussy, his best officer, leaving the Carnatic in the hands of incapable men. He failed to realize that although the French influence might be established in Hyderabad, it could be wiped out by French disasters in the Carnatic.

After the assassination of Muzaffar Jung (1751), Salabat Jung, another son of the Nizam ul-Mulk, became the *Subadar* ; and since he lacked both courage and self-confidence, Dupleix sent Bussy to escort him to Aurangabad. Bussy for four years protected the kingdom against the encroachments of the Marathas, the intrigues of Nizam Ali Khan and Basalat Jung, the other two rivals for the *Subadari*, and the intrigues of the nobles against himself. But all his work was undone when the Seven Years' War broke out and he was recalled by Lally to help him in the Carnatic against the

English. At first the French achieved success and occupied all the English posts in the Carnatic, except Madras and Trichinopoly. But from the time Madras was besieged, the tide of war turned against the French. In the battle of Wandiwash Bussy was taken prisoner, and owing to the mistakes of Lally and D'Ache, the French naval commander, all the French possessions in the Carnatic were occupied by the English, including Mahé on the west coast. Although by the Peace of Paris (1763) the French got back Pondicherry, yet henceforth, beyond carrying on intrigues with the Indian powers against the English and making grandiose plans for establishing an empire in India, they never made any serious military efforts to realize their ambitions.

While the Carnatic wars were going on the English provoked a conflict in Bengal. Learning from the experiences of Dupleix and Bussy in the south that the Indian powers were militarily and politically weak, the English felt that the time had come for them to establish their political power in Bengal. Accordingly, when Alivardi Khan died on 10 April, 1756 and his grandson Siraj ud-Daula succeeded him, they plotted the latter's overthrow in favour of the faction of Ghasita, which they hoped to dominate. As soon as Siraj ud-Daula found his position secure, he demanded from the English the surrender of those of his subjects to whom they had given protection ; and learning the lesson of what had happened in the Carnatic he demanded the demolition of their new fortifications. He also abolished the unjust trade privileges of the English which were causing great loss of revenue to him.[1]

The English were not prepared to accept any of Siraj-ud-Daula's demands, and so it led to war. At first they were defeated, but when Clive arrived in Calcutta, he by all kinds of methods, fair and foul, won over the Hindu bankers of Bengal, who had a common interest with the English, and some of the Muslim nobles who were greedy for power. The result was that because of treason in his camp, when on the morning of 23 June, 1757, Siraj ud-Daula met the English at Plassey, he was easily routed.[2] This battle virtually meant the establishment of English rule over Bengal and Bihar. By 1763, with the defeat of the French in the Seven Years' War, the Carnatic also passed under their control. Then a year later, the defeat of Shuja ud-Daula at Buxer brought Oudh too into their sphere of influence. All this greatly increased their resources and power, and they became strong enough to cross swords with any Indian power.

Haidar Ali

Another state that rose into prominence during the second half of the eighteenth century was Mysore, a tiny kingdom situated in South India at the junction of the Eastern and Western Ghats. About the middle of the eighteenth century it was in an unsettled state. Chikka Krishnaraja, its ruler,was a puppet of the two brothers Devraj, his commander-in-chief, and Nanjaraj, his finance minister. But he chafed under their domination and was anxious for their overthrow. Meanwhile, the ambition of Nanjaraj had led him to futile military adventures in the Carnatic, which resulted in the financial bankruptcy of the state and the loss of his prestige. At the same time the kingdom was threatened by the Marathas and the Nizam, both of whom claimed obedience and tribute from it. These conditions paved the way for the rise of Haidar Ali, a man of extraordinary abilities and a born leader of men, who knew how to take advantage of opportunities.

Haidar Ali, the son of Fath Khan, a soldier of fortune, was born in 1721. He enlisted in the Mysore army at an early age and secured a small command. But by distinguishing himself in wars both in Mysore and in the Carnatic, where he was sent by Nanjaraj ; by establishing law and order in Dindigul of which he was made *faujdar* in 1755 ; by repelling the Maratha invasions and by discharging the arrears of pay of the soldiery, Haidar Ali, within a short period, made himself the most powerful man in Mysore. Devraj had already retired from public affairs in 1757 due to old age and differences with his brother, and now Nanjaraj, faced with disaffection in the army and financial bankruptcy caused by his rash military adventures in the Carnatic, was compelled to retire. Haidar Ali, who was only waiting for this opportunity, quietly stepped into his shoes. He infused vigour into the administration, improved the finances, and not only defended Mysore against external attacks but also extended its territories. He organized a fine army, established law and order and promoted agriculture. He tried to build a strong navy, and in order to promote trade and commerce, he entered into relations with the rulers of Oman and Persia and established a factory at Masqat.[3]

Haidar Ali's abilities, energy and ambition aroused the jealousy of his neighbours, the Marathas, the Nizam and the English, who were, like him, greedy for power and territorial aggrandizement. Anxious to bring the whole of south India under Maratha rule, the Peshwa Madhava Rao invaded Mysore thrice between 1764 and 1772, occupying some of its districts and realizing large sums as tribute. What he really wanted was the complete subversion of Haidar Ali's power, but, fortunately for Mysore, he died in 1772, and his death was followed by a war of succession for the office of Peshwa. This was taken advantage of by Haidar, who not only recovered the possessions which he had lost to Madhava Rao, but also occupied all the Maratha territories south of the Kistna (1774-78). These conquests were confirmed first by Raghunath Rao, the claimant to the Peshwaship, and later by Nana Phadnavis, the prime minister at Poona. But despite this, the Marathas could not reconcile themselves to the loss of their territory. That they could not do anything about it at the time was due partly to their internecine dissensions and partly to their war with the English.

The English who had gained the virtual control of the Carnatic, could not tolerate the existence of a powerful neighbour like Haidar who possessed a strong army and a large kingdom and was allied with the French, their rivals. They were, accordingly, anxious for the reduction of his power ; and they were encouraged in their hostile designs by Nawab Muhammad Ali, the ruler of the Carnatic. Violently detesting Haidar and ambitious to extend his territories, Muhammad Ali never ceased instigating the English to invade Mysore. The result was that in November 1766 they formed an alliance with the Nizam to attack Haidar. However, the latter succeeded in detaching the Nizam, and with him invaded the Carnatic. Thereupon, the English, chagrined at this betrayal, set out to invade Hyderabad. When the Nizam found that his capital was threatened, he left his ally. The Anglo-Mysore War, however, continued until Haidar dictated peace to the English at the very gates of Madras (April 1769).

According to a clause of this treaty the English Company agreed to support Haidar against any attack from his enemies. But when two years later he was attacked by the Marathas, the Company remained indifferent to his requests for help. This made Haidar angry. Nevertheless for about six years, from 1769 to 1775, he made all possible efforts to secure the friendship of the English, but without success. In February, 1780, therefore, he entered into a coalition with the Marathas, who were already engaged in a war with the English. He also drew closer to the French, who supplied him with military stores, and decided to attack the English. The latter's attack on the French port of Mahé, which Haidar had declared to be under his protection, furnished him with a *casus belli*, and on 20 July, 1780, with a large army of 90,000 men he swept through the pass of Changama into the Carnatic. This was the beginning of the Second Anglo-Mysore War. However, Haidar failed to crush the English. This was partly because of the failure of the French to fulfill their promise of assistance, and partly because the Marathas withdrew from the conflict and made peace with the English by the Treaty of Salbai,(May 1783), while the Nizam who had also joined the coalition remained only a passive spectator. Despite this Haidar continued to wage war until his death in December, 1782.

Tipu Sultan

After Haidar's death his able and energetic son and successor, Tipu Sultan, continued the war, and it was only after the withdrawal of French support owing to the conclusion of the Preliminaries of Peace at Versailles (9 February, 1783) between England and France that he signed the Peace of Mangalore. But this treaty left the English dissatisfied and frustrated. Unlike the other treaties which they had concluded with the Indian powers, this had not brought them any accession of territory. Moreover, far from reducing Tipu's power it had increased his prestige, while the manner in which it had been concluded had made the English lose face. That is why Hastings had called it a "humiliating pacification,"[4] and many of the Company's officers regarded the treaty as only a truce.[5] The English also could not forget the serious reverses which they had suffered at the hands of Haidar and Tipu, and so were eager for a trial of strength to avenge themselves.

The Marathas, too, were anxious for a war with Tipu. We have seen that owing to their internal dissensions and their conflict with the English, they had not been able to direct their attention to the recovery of their territories annexed by Haidar. But after concluding the Treaty of Salbai, they demanded their restoration. Haidar Ali reminded them that his claims had been confirmed by both Raghunath Rao and Nana Phadnavis, and so he was not prepared to part with them. After Haidar's death Nana pressed the demand on Tipu, but he, too, gave the same reply. Nana, thereupon, concluded a treaty with the English on 28 October, 1783, for the recovery of these lands. But nothing came of it because of the signature of the Peace of Mangalore in 1784 which ended the war between Tipu and the English.[6]

However, in 1786, Nana entered into an offensive and defensive alliance with the Nizam, who also was anxious to recover his territories occupied by Haidar, and together they invaded the Mysore kingdom. Nana also asked the English for help. Macpherson, the Governor General, in violation of the Treaty of Mangalore, agreed to send troops for the defence of the territories of the Nizam and the Marathas.[7] But this was disapproved by the Home Government, which desired to adhere to a policy of non-interference.[8] When, therefore, Cornwallis arrived in India as Governor General, he withdrew the offer of help, not because he was wedded to a policy of peace, but because he found neither the Company's armies nor its finances in good condition. But after he had been able to reorganize them, he turned his attention to making plans for the subversion of Tipu whom he regarded as more dangerous to English ambitions than either the Nizam or the Marathas. Moreover, he realized that the time had come to set the stage for another expansion of the English territories in India.

He turned his eyes towards Tipu's kingdom, and particularly towards his Malabar possessions, which were rich in spices, sandalwood and pine trees and possessed a number of fine ports. Their acquisition, he felt, would be some compensation for the loss of the thirteen English colonies in America.[9]

But it would not be correct to say that the English, the Marathas and the Nizam alone were anxious for self-aggrandizement while Tipu's policy was one of peace. In reality, he too was ambitious and keen to extend his influence and territories. That is why, not long after the conclusion of the Treaty of Mangalore, he began to negotiate an alliance with the French in order to drive out the English from India. Having failed to obtain such an alliance with the French in India, he decided to negotiate directly with the French government in Paris by sending an embassy to France.

It is against this background that the significance of the embassy which Tipu sent to Constantinople can be understood.[9a] Owing to his own ambition and because he was surrounded on all sides by unscrupulous and greedy enemies, Tipu thought he might be able to get military aid from outside. Moreover, since his father had secured 1000 troops in 1775 from Shiraz, he too expected to get some assistance from Turkey.[10]

Tipu and his Commercial Activities in the Persian Gulf

From the beginning of the sixteenth century Malabar's trade with the Persian Gulf had been controlled by the Europeans to the partial exclusion of the Indian and Arab merchants who had hitherto, since times immemorial, held the monopoly of this trade. But Haidar Ali, on conquering Malabar in 1765, and after him his son Tipu Sultan, placed great restrictions on the European trade with Malabar,[11] and thereby gave great encouragement to the Indian and Arab merchants. Moreover, the preferential treatment given to these traders at Masqat and the Mysore ports also gave great fillip to their business. Thus, while the Europeans had to pay a duty of 5%, the Indian 8% and the Arabs and Persians 6½%, merchants belonging to the Mysore kingdom paid only 4%[12]. Similar privileges were also given to the Imam and his subjects at the Mysore ports. But it must be remembered that the traders from Masqat were not all Arabs. A few like Seth Mao, Jiwan Das and Ratanji were of Indian origin and had settled in Masqat, and were the subjects of the Imam. They were very wealthy, owning trading vessels and having establishments at important ports in the Persian Gulf.[13] Similarly there were a large number of Indians who lived in Basra, Abu Shahr and other commercial centres and carried on trade with the Gujarat and Malabar ports.

At the beginning of 1774, Haidar Ali sent an envoy to the court of

Karim Khan-i Zand at Shiraz with the request for a trading settlement in the Persian Gulf. Karim Khan offered Bandar Abbas, but it seems that Haidar Ali was not able to take advantage of the offer.[14] However, the relations that were established with the Imam Ahmad of Oman led to more fruitful results. In July 1775, the Imam despatched an envoy to Mangalore to find out why the export of rice to Masqat had been prohibited. The envoy was well received by Haidar's representative at Mangalore, who explained the non-shipment of rice to foreign ports. Next year Haidar sent a return envoy to Masqat with instructions to sign a convention with the Imam and to remain there permanently as his agent. A house was built for this agent known as *Bait-ul-Nawwab*.[15]

Tipu Sultan took even greater interest than his father in promoting the trade and commerce of his kingdom. He therefore not only kept a *wakil* permanently at Masqat, which was an important emporium of trade between India, the Red Sea and the Persian Gulf, but in addition, he established a factory there in 1785.[16] Tipu also wanted to establish factories at Abu Shahr and Basra, but owing to his constant wars with his neighbours, his plans did not materialize.

Tipu's factory at Masqat was very important, because it was through this that exports from his kingdom were distributed over the Persian Gulf, and imports from the Persian Gulf were brought into Mysore. The exports were timber, sandalwood, silk, cardamoms, pepper, rice, ivory and cloth. The imports were saffron-seeds, silkworms, horses, pistachio-nuts, raisins, rock-salt, pearls, sulphur, copper, dates and coarse chinawares. The silkworms were required to promote the silk industry. Horses were meant for the army and sulphur was imported for the manufacture of gunpowder. Among the exports rice was an important article, for whenever its export from Mangalore was withheld, it caused great hardship to the people of Oman. Malabar teakwood was used in the Persian Gulf for the construction of boats, and was mostly exported from Calicut.[17] The cloth exported was of different varieties, some of which was manufactured in Mysore, while others were obtained from different parts of India.[18]

The organization of the factory at Masqat was based on that of the English and French factories. At the head of the factory was a *darogha*, and under him were *mutasaddis* (writers) and *gumashtas* (agents) and a body of troops. The buying and selling was done either directly by the *darogha* himself or through a broker. Tipu Sultan's chief broker at Masqat and Abu Shahr was Seth Mao. At Basra, his chief broker was Abdullah, a Jew, and a confidant of the *Mutesellim*.[19] Tipu maintained a brisk correspondence with the *darogha* at Masqat, giving him detailed instructions about buying and selling transactions and various other matters relating to trade and the organization of the factory. In one of the letters, for example, Tipu informs Mir Kazim, his *darogha* at Masqat, that the pearls which he had purchased were expensive, and that he should buy them at a cheaper rate from Bahrain. Since the price of sandalwood and pepper was low at Masqat, they must not be sold until the rates become favourable. The *darogha* is asked to send ten shipwrights for the construction of dhows.[20] In a subsequent letter the Sultan fixes the price at which sandalwood is to be sold. The first quality is to be sold at 120 pagodas per candy ; the second at 100 pagodas per candy ; the third at 90 pagodas per candy ; and the fourth quality at 80 pagodas per candy.[21] In another letter the Sultan instructs the *darogha* to obtain silkworms and their eggs from Qishm Island and send them to Seringapatam, including a few men acquainted with the art of rearing them.[22] Similarly there are letters in which the *darogha* is ordered to buy saffron-seeds and sulphur from Persia and date-palms from Masqat. Furthermore, he is required to send pearl divers from Bahrain to help establishing a pearl-fishery on the Malabar coast.[23]

No figures are available of the volume of Mysore exports to and imports from the Persian Gulf. From the letter of a broker at Masqat, addressed to the Governor of Bombay, it appears that about five or six vessels, laden with goods, arrived annually at Masqat under Tipu's colours.[24] In addition, there were a large number of smaller vessels and dhows and dinghies, belonging to Indian and Arab merchants, which plied between the Malabar coast and the Persian Gulf.

Tipu Sultan had established a state monopoly in sandalwood, teakwood, black pepper and coconut, but in other articles he not only permitted private trade, but even encouraged it. Thus writing to certain Armenian merchants in January 1787, he observes that all goods brought by them to Mysore ports will be exempted from duty, that they will have complete freedom to buy and sell, and that they will be provided with a suitable place of residence and permitted full freedom of movement.[25] Tipu, however, placed great restrictions on the trade of the European Companies with Malabar. In consequence, the trade of the English settlement of Tellicherry and the French settlement of Mahé greatly declined.

The Persian Gulf

The Persian Gulf covers an area of about 97,000 sq. miles. Its length from the Oman coast to the head of the Persian Gulf is about 500 miles. Its breadth varies from 180 miles at the widest part to a minimum of only 29 miles at the straits. On either side of the Persian Gulf are situated the great plateaux of Persia and Arabia.

The Persian Gulf, considering its large area, is very shallow. The

Gulf of Oman is deep, in the middle the depth being of about 1,800 fathoms. Inside the Persian Gulf the soundings range from 40 to 50 fathoms. The Persian coast is mountainous, and, with deep water close to it, is safe for ships to approach. The Arabian shore, however, with the exception of the western side of the Oman Peninsula, is exceedingly low and is full of reefs and shoals, and so the ships passing up and down the Gulf always keep close to the Persian coast. Throughout the Gulf there is a great scarcity of fresh water. It is dotted by a large number of islands. The winds blow with great force. The *shamal*, from the north-west, blows about nine months in the year, during which the navigation is risky. During the winter months the south-easter called *qaus* or *sharqi* blows. This too is regarded as dangerous, and hence has a bad reputation.[26]

Oman and the Saidi Dynasty

The Persian Gulf has been dominated in turn by the Persians, Arabs, Turks, Portuguese, Dutch and English. In the second half of the eighteenth century it was divided into a number of independent or semi-independent principalities. On the Arabian coast, the territory from the entrance of the Persian Gulf to the neighbourhood of Ras Sajar opposite Saqotrah, and inland as far as the confines of Ruba al-Khali or the Great Desert, was called the kingdom of Oman. It was ruled by the Saidi dynasty which was founded in 1749 by Ahmad b. Said, a shipowner and merchant. He made himself strong by establishing a navy and promoting commerce and giving the country a good administration. He died in 1783, and was succeeded by his second son Said who was weak and incompetent. His position was therefore challenged by his brothers. However, his eldest son Hamid defeated them and acted as his Regent, governing the kingdom with ability from his capital of Masqat until his death on 13 March, 1793. After him his uncle, Sultan, succeeded him, and exercised all political power. Said, however, remained the Imam and continued to perform the spiritual duties of his office from Rustaq until his death in 1812.[27]

During this period, owing to the wise policies of the Saidi rulers, Oman was in a prosperous state. Sultan b. Ahmad conquered the islands of Qishm and Hormuz from the Bani Main, and obtained a concession from the Persian Government to farm the revenues of Bandar Abbas (1794), and this part of the Persian littoral remained a dependency of Masqat for nearly three quarters of a century.[28] In addition, the mercantile marine of Masqat was in a flourishing state and was very important. Most of Masqat's trade was with India, and more than half of Indian imports at Basra and Abu Shahr and the bulk of those into Bahrain came through Masqat. In the last decade of the eighteenth century the proportion of the Persian

Gulf trade that passed through Masqat was equal to 5/8 of the whole, or one crore of rupees.[29]

The Qawasim and the Pirate Coast

The Trucial coast known to the Arabs as the Oman Coast extends from the base of the Qatar peninsula in the west to the Musandum promontory of Ruus ul-Jabal in the north-east at the entrance of the Persian Gulf. This was formerly known as the Pirate Coast. It was inhabited by the Qawasim, a branch of the great Huwala clan, who were engaged in piracy.[30] They extended their depredations along the southern coast of Arabia, and even to the shores of India and the Red Sea. Ras ul-Khaimah, formerly known as Julfa, was the residence of the most noted of their chiefs. The Qawasim became very active after Nadir Shah's death in 1747. They obtained a footing on the island of Qishm, then held by the Main tribe, and at Lingeh and Shinas. They were expelled in 1763 when Karim Khan established his rule over Persia. Towards the end of the century, inspired by the Wahhabis, they again became active and began to attack not only Arab vessels but also those belonging to the English. It was not until the early part of the nineteenth century that they were crushed by the joint efforts of the English and the Imam of Masqat.[31]

The Bani Khalid

Beyond the Trucial coast lay the kingdom of al-Hasa ruled by Bani Khalid in the eighteenth century and extending from Qatar in the south to Basra in the north and parts of Najd in the east. Bani Khalid controlled the trade of central Arabia ; al-Qatif and al-Uqair being the ports through which sugar, coffee, spices and textiles from India found their way to central Arabia. Kuwait participated in this trade, but did not gain importance till the second half of the eighteenth century.[32] The power of Bani Khalid began to decline after the death of their Shaikh, Sulaiman b. Muhammad, in 1752. This led to the declaration of independence by the Utub at Kuwait and Zubarah, and Āl-Musallam in Qatar.[33] Arar b. Dujayn, who succeeded Sulaiman, died in 1774 and was succeeded by Butayn. But in 1777 he was murdered by his brothers, Dujayn and Sadun. Sadun soon after poisoned Dujayn and became the Shaikh of Bani Khalid, ruling until 1785. He was a strong ruler and checked the Wahhabi aggression. But incited by Abdul Aziz, the Wahhabi chief, one of the Khalidi chiefs defeated Sadun, who had to take refuge with the Wahhabis. He was succeeded by Abdul Muhsin and his nephews, Duwayhis and Muhammad (1785-89). Next came Urayir (1789-93). Eventually al-Hasa was occupied by the Wahhabis in 1795 and the Khalidi rule came to an end.[34]

The Utub

The decline of the power of Bani Khalid in the middle of the eighteenth century led to the rise of the Utub. Originally from Aftaj in Najd, the Utub established their first settlement in the early years of the eighteenth century in Kuwait, where they lived under the protection of the Shaikh of Bani Khalid.[35] But taking advantage of the decline of the Bani Khalid power in the middle of the eighteenth century, the Utub of Kuwait declared their independence, and, in 1750, chose as their chief Shaikh Sabah b. Jabir, the ancestor of the present Shaikh of Kuwait. Sabah was succeeded in 1762 by his son Abdullah, who ruled Kuwait until 1812. It was during his early rule (about 1766) that the Āl-Khalifah division of the Utub emigrated to Qatar, where they established Zubarah, the second Utbi settlement.[36] The chieftain of Āl-Khalifah was Khalifah b. Muhammad, whose name the family bore. In 1768 they built their fort of Zubarah, situated on the west coast of the Qatar promontory.[37] Zubarah under them became a flourishing town and drew away much of the trade of al-Qatif and al-Uqair.[38] In 1782 Shaikh Ahmad b. Khalifah conquered Bahrain from the Persians while his father was absent on a pilgrimage to Mecca. Khalid died im 1783 and was succeeded by his son Ahmad. The latter died in 1796 and was succeeded by his son, Salman, who ruled until 1825.[39]

Throughout the second half of the eighteenth century, it was mostly the Utbi fleet along with that of Masqat which held the monopoly of the freight from India to Masqat and the Gulf. The Utub were good merchants and had commercial relations with the Persian coast, Masqat and Basra. They carried merchandise to various ports in central and northern Arabia, and, on account of their possession of Kuwait, also shared in the commerce between the Gulf and Aleppo. Ships owned by the Utub of Kuwait, Zubarah and Bahrain and those of the Arabs of Masqat almost monopolised the conveyance of goods in the Gulf.[40] The siege and occupation of Basra by the Persians had very favourable consequences for the Utub. For owing to Basra's misfortunes, Kuwait and Zubarah became rich. Kuwait became the centre for all caravans carrying goods between Basra and Baghdad and Aleppo during the years 1775-79. Kuwait also became the centre of the desert mail of the English East India Company. The prosperity of the Utub naturally provoked the jealousy of Shaikh Nasr of Abu Shahr, the Kaab and the Shaikh of Bandar Rig. But the Utub were ready to defend themselves. The struggle led to the conquest of Bahrain by the Utub and the collapse of the power of the Arabs of Abu Shahr.[41]

However, towards the end of the eighteenth century the Utub were subjected to a very serious threat. This was from the Wahhabis who occupied their port of Zubarah in 1798. The Utub of Kuwait continued to resist, but by 1800 they had recognized the Wahhabi suzerainty.[42]

Basra

To the north-west of Kuwait lay Basra, the chief port of Iraq. It was an *eyalet* of the Pasha of Baghdad and was governed by a *Mutesellim*. Until 1773, when a most violent plague effected Basra and the neighbouring areas, the trade of Basra, mostly monopolised by the Europeans and the Muslim merchants of Surat, had flourished.[43] After the plague came the Persian invasion led by Sadiq Khan, brother of Karim Khan. Basra resisted the Persians, but after a siege of about a year it surrendered in April 1776. The extortions and injustices of the Persians led merchants to leave Basra, which, in 1779-80, looked a depopulated and ruined city.[44] But from 1780, when the Persian rule ended, trade revived, and British vessels and those of the Indian merchants again began to frequent the port of Basra. But the town did not become as prosperous as it had been before 1773. This was due to a number of reasons. In the first place, duties on merchandise brought into Basra were heavy, and as a result merchants diverted their goods intended for the Aleppo market from Basra to Kuwait.[45] Then there was a scarcity of specie both in Persia and Iraq. This was partly due to the non-production of exportable goods sufficient to balance imports, and also, in part, to hoarding, consequent upon political insecurity. Karim Khan forbade the export of specie, and as a result the balance of trade became much more favourable. However, the balance of trade was again upset, and about 1790, nine-tenths of the merchandise imported into Persia from India was paid for in bullion.[46]

Another cause of the decline of trade of Basra was that the Khazail were in a state of revolt, and interrupted communication between Basra and Baghdad by the Euphrates route. Merchants were, therefore, compelled to send goods by the longer and more expensive Tigris route.[47] Then at the end of 1785 Sulaiman al-Shawi, chief of the Ubaid, revolted against Sulaiman Pasha. He hovered around Baghdad and kept the roads connecting the town unsafe. But in the end, afraid of the Ottoman troops, he fled to Shaikh Suwaini.[48]

Shaikh Suwaini, head of the Muntafiq, had been loyal to the Basra government, but taking advantage of the weakness of the Turks he decided to occupy Basra. He advanced on Zubair and seized Ibrahim Beg, the *Mutesellim*, and other members of his government, and then occupied Basra. It was not until October, 1787, that Suwaini was defeated and Basra reoccupied by the Ottoman troops. But the trouble was not over ;

for Mustafa Agha, the *Mutesellim*, joined Suwaini and revolted. However in February, 1788, the rebels were defeated by forces sent from Baghdad.[49]

Persia and the Persian Gulf

Like the Indian Mughals, the Safavids of Persia also began to decline at the end of the seventeenth century, and in 1722 they were overthrown by the Afghans, who ruled Persia until 1730. But in the same year Tahmasp Quli, better known as Nadir Shah, drove out the Afghans, and became *de facto* ruler of Persia. In 1736 he usurped the throne and declared himself Shah, ruling Persia with firmness and ability. Nadir Shah built a Persian navy in order to establish his mastery over the Gulf. In 1736 Nasir Khan, governor of Abu Shahr, and later Nadir's commander of the Persian Gulf fleet, occupied Bahrain, which remained a Persian possession until it was seized by the Utbi Arabs. Nadir Shah also occupied certain islands off the Persian coast, including Qishm, which under weak Persian kings had been seized by the Masqat Arabs. Moreover, Nadir overran Oman in 1737 and it remained under Persia until 1744.[50]

In 1747 Nadir Shah was assassinated. In consequence, Persia was plunged into chaos until 1750, when Karim Khan-i Zand, chief of a small nomad tribe of west Persia, rose to power and made himself master of the greater part of the country. In 1769 he took Kharag Island from Mir Muhanna, a predatory chief of Bandar Rig, who had seized it from the Dutch. He then sent a large force under his brother Sadiq Khan to capture Basra, which, as we have seen, put up a brave resistance, but surrendered after undergoing a siege of about a year. Under Karim Khan Persia became strong, achieved peace and prosperity, and revived her sea power. However, on his death in 1780 Persia was torn by internal dissensions and so ceased to play any important part in the affairs of the Gulf.

The Persian Coast

The Persian coast was also in the eighteenth century under Arab domination except when, as already mentioned, Persia was under the strong rule of Nadir Shah and Karim Khan. The Arabs of the Huwala stock inhabited the southern parts of the Persian shore and the islands of Qishm, Qais, Hormuz and other small islands of the Persian Gulf. But the political power was exercised by the Shaikh of a small tribe called Bani Main. Towards the end of the century these islands and this part of the Persian littoral, including Bandar Abbas, were held by the Imam of Oman. The Persian coast from Bandar Abbas to Ras Berdistan was occupied by the Qawasim, a branch of the Huwala clan. Further to the north-west lay

Abu Shahr, which, owing to the decline in the importance of Bandar Abbas, became the chief port of Persia in the latter half of the eighteenth century. It was under the Bani Mazkur Arabs, whose Shaikh was Nasir Khan. He occupied Bahrain in 1736 and was the commander of Nadir Shah's Persian Gulf fleet.[51] On his death in 1776 his son Shaikh Nasr succeeded him as governor of Abu Shahr and, like him, held the command of the Persian Gulf fleet. He died on 11 April, 1789. He and Karim Khan did a great deal to promote the trade of Abu Shahr.

Thirty-one miles to the north-west of Abu Shahr lies the port of Rig, which was ruled by Mir Muhanna of the Bani Saib who were of Omani origin. His grandfather had established the rule of the family at Bandar Rig and also occupied Kharag Island in 1753. He was strangled by his cruel son Mir Muhanna in 1758. The latter refused to acknowledge the authority of Karim Khan. He drove the Dutch from Kharag in 1765 and carried out acts of piracy in the Persian Gulf, several times defeating the combined forces of the English and Persians. In the end, hard pressed by Karim Khan, he fled to Kuwait. From there he went to Basra, where on 21 March, 1769, he was seized and strangled by order of the Pasha for his past cruelties.[52]

Europeans and the Persian Gulf

The Portuguese dominated the Persian Gulf all through the 16th century. But in the early part of the 17th century they had to face the competition of their two European rivals, the Dutch and the English, who by the middle of that century succeeded in destroying their power. Next started the struggle between the Dutch and the English. In this at first the Dutch were successful, and they remained superior to their English rivals during the greater part of the 17th century. Their commercial superiority lasted till about the middle of the 18th century. But by 1753 they withdrew from Basra, and soon afterwards they closed down their factory at Abu Shahr. They retained possession of Kharag Island until 1765, when they were driven out from it by Mir Muhanna. This was the end of their ascendancy in the Persian Gulf.[53]

The English extended their influence throughout the 18th century. They had their factories at Ispahan, Bandar Abbas and Abu Shahr, and were given commercial concessions by the Persian rulers. In 1750, however, they closed down their factory at Ispahan for good. The factory at Bandar Abbas was also abandoned after it had been burnt and its staff taken prisoner by a French squadron on 15 October, 1759. They next established their factory in 1763 at Basra which was recognized by the Ottoman Sultan as a Consulate under the Capitulations. In 1763, they were permitted by

Karim Khan to establish a factory at Abu Shahr, and given rights of trade to the exclusion of all European merchants.[54] Towards the end of the 18th century the English had attained a position in the Gulf to which none of their competitors could lay claim. They joined Karim Khan in driving out Mir Muhanna, one of the most notorious pirates of the Persian Gulf, from Kharag Island. They also co-operated with the Turks in attempting to suppress the Kaab, though without any success, for the Kaab continued their piratical activities in the Persian Gulf, and remained for a long period a thorn in the side of the Turks, the Persians and the English in turn. Throughout the second half of the 18th century the English went on improving their position. They established their influence over the *Mutesellim* of Basra and the Pasha of Baghdad,[55] and in 1798 entered into commercial relations with Said Sultan, the Imam of Oman.[56] Despite this it must e remembered that both politically and commercially the Arabs remained important until about the end of the 18th century. Oman was in a prosperous condition, and its mercantile marine the most important among all the statesof the Gulf ; and together with the Utub it monopolised the greater portion of the trade with India.

REFERENCES

1. Gupta, *Sirajuddaulah and the East India Company*, pp. 50-3.
2. Ibid., p. 121.
3. See p. 14, *infra*.
4. *Cambridge History of India*, v, p. 333.
5. Innes Munro, *A Narrative of the Military Transactions on the Coromandel Coast*, 1780-84, p. 370.
6. Mohibbul Hasan Khan, *History of Tipu Sultan*, pp. 90-91.
7. Secret Proceedings, National Archives of India, February 14, 1786, Consultation No. 4.
8. Secret Despatches from England, National Archives of India, July 21, 1786, Vol. 1 pp. 32-5.
9. Mohibbul Hasan Khan, *History of Tipu Sultan*, p. 148.

9a. See for details regarding the aims of the embassy, Mohibbul Hasan Khan, *History of Tipu Sultan*, pp. 132-35.

10. Rice, *Mysore and Coorg*, i, p. 268.
11. The Tellicherry and Pondicherry records are full of complaints of these restrictions.
12. *Waqai Manazil-i Rum*, pp. 25-6 ; see also p., 28 *infra*.
13. Kirkpatrick, *Select Letters of Tippoo Sultan*, No. 146. From the *Waqai* also it appears that these Indian merchants were prosperous and carried on considerable business.
14. *Selections from State Papers*, Bombay, No. ccv, Henry Moore at Basra to Governor in Council at Bombay, April 23, 1774.
15. Salil b. Razik, *History of the Imams and Seyyids of Oman*, trans. G.P. Badger, pp. 170-71 and n.1.

16. *Selections from State Papers*, Bombay, No. cclvii.

17. Hourani, *Arab Seafaring in the Indian Ocean*, pp. 89-90; see also *Selections from the Records of the Bombay Government* (New Series), No. 24, p. 613.

18. The different varieties of cloth are mentioned in the *Waqai*. *Shila*, thin white muslim, was probably obtained from Dacca. *Khadi Nirmali*, a thick coarse cloth, was obtained from Nirmal, Adilabad district.

19. It is with the help of these brokers that the envoys sold the goods which they had brought with them. In the *Waqai* their names are constantly mentioned. See for Abdullah and other brokers Appendix B, s.v.

20. Kirkpatrick, *Letters of Tippoo Sultan*, No. cc.

21. Ibid., No. ixxii.

22. Ibid., No. clv.

23. Ibid., No. cclviii.

24. *Selections from State Papers*, Bombay, No. cclvii, p. 337.

25. Kirkpatrick, *Letters of Tippoo Sultan*, No. ccccxxv.

26. Wilson, *The Persian Gulf*, pp. 2-6; see also Constable and Stiffe, *The Persian Gulf Pilot*, pp. 1-8.

27. Salil b.Razik, *History of the Imams and Seyyids of Oman*, trans. Badger, pp. 176-88; Kelly, *Sultanate and Imamate in Oman*, p.5.

28. Bertram Thomas, *Arab Rule under the Ali Bu Said Dynasty of Oman*, p. 15. The Imam of Masqat held by lease from the Persian Government the islands of Qishm and Hormuz, as well as Bandar Abbas, at a yearly rental of 6000 *tumans*. (Adamiyat, *Bahrein Islands*, p.32).

29. Saldanha, *Selections from State Papers*, p. 409; Parsons, *Travels in Asia and Africa*, p. 207; It must be remembered that Masqat was not of any great commercial importance until the Portuguese captured the town in 1509, and made it into an intermediate port where their ships might revictualize themselves on the way between India and Hormuz, which they had occupied.

30. In English they were called Jawasim. See for their history *Selections from the Records of the Bombay Government*, No. 24, New Series.

31. Wilson, *The Persian Gulf*, pp. 199 ff.

32. Abu Hakima, *The Utbi States*, pp. 78-9.

33. Ibid., p. 130.

34. Ibid., 227 ff.

35. Ibid., 93 ff.

36. Ibid., 115.

37. Ibid., 121.

38. Ibid., 133.

39. Ibid., 204, 272; also Tweedy, *Bahrain and the Persian Gulf*. It appears from *The Selections from the Records of the Bombay Government*, No. 24, pp. 29; 364-66 that the claim of the Arabs and English that the Utub exercised sovereign authority, over Bahrain is not tenable, for they paid tribute to Persia from time to time.

40. Abu Hakima, *The Utbi States*, pp. 295-97.

41. Ibid., 171-90; 317.

42. Ibid., 272, 292.

43. Niebuhr, Ives and others who visited Basra about the middle of the 18th century describe about the prosperity of Basra.

44. *Selections from State Papers*, pp. 412-13.

45. Ibid., 411.

46. Ibid., 413-29.

47. Foreign Department, Miscellaneous 5, para (National Archives of India) ; also Longrigg, *Four Centuries of Modern Iraq*. pp. 201-01.

48. Ibid., 203-04.

49. Ibid., 204-06; also Foreign Dept., Misc. 5, para 163.

50. Lokhart, *Nadir Shah*, pp. 182-96, 212-22; also Lokhart, *The Navy of Nadir Shah*, pp. 6, 13.

51. Adamiyat, *Bahrein Islands*, p. 34.

52. Wilson, *The Persian Gulf*, pp. 181-82.

53. Ibid., 164-81; *Selections from the Records of the Bombay government*, pp. 31-2.

54. Wilson, *The Persian Gulf*, pp. 176-78.

55. Sulaiman Agha had become Pasha of Baghdad through the efforts of Latouche, the English Resident at Basra; and later, when the news spread of the appointment of Sulaiman al-Shawi in his place, Sulaiman Pasha wrote to the British ambassador in Constantinople to intercede on his behalf with the Sultan. Thus Manesty, the English Resident at Basra, refers "to the very extensive influence which the English enjoy and the very extensive friendship which without exception they now are in with every person of consequence in the country." *Selection from State Papers*, p. 323). Manesty also informs the Court of Directors that "Sulaiman Pasha is partial to the English." (Factory Records, India Office No. 18), f. 29 la.

56. Wilson, *The Persian Gulf*, p. 232.

III

SUMMARY OF THE WAQAI

The ambassadors left Seringapatam on 17 November 1785,[1] and sailed from Tadri,[2] a small port on the Malabar coast, on the night of Wednesday, 9 March 1786, in four ships named *Ghurab-i Surati*, *Fakhurul-Marakib*, *Fath-i Shahi Muazi* and *Nabi Bakhsh*. They were accompanied by a huge staff of about 900, comprising secretaries, interpreters, attendants, sweepers, cooks and soldiers, and carried with them considerable quantities of cloth, sandalwood products, spices, gold and silver coins of Mysore, rich dresses, jewellery and four elephants. Some of these articles were to serve as advertisements for the products of Tipu's kingdom and be sold at various ports of call. The remaining articles were intended as presents to the nobles, high officials and rulers of Oman, Persia, and Turkey.[2a] As regards the elephants, one was to be presented to the Ottoman Sultan, and the other was to be sold to realize the expenses of the journey, while the other two were meant for the kings of France and England, where the envoys were required to proceed after fulfilling their assignment in Constantinople.[3]

On leaving Tadri, the ships headed straight for the Arabian coast. On 15 March the sea became very stormy, and the *Fakhrul-Marakib*, which had Ghulam Ali Khan and Nurullah Khan on board, was seriously damaged. The passengers fell into a panic, and raised an uproar. Ghulam Ali tried to quieten them, but in vain. Luckily the vessel was repaired. After a few days there was again a storm, and as a result three of the elephants fell ill. One of them later died, but the other two recovered. Early on the morning of 6 April, the flotilla sighted the island of Masira. On the 8th it passed the Rasul-Had, and on the 11th anchored in the port of Masqat.

Masqat

The envoys were received by the Khalfan, governor of Masqat, and his two sons. They then proceeded to the town, and put up in houses rented for them. Nurullah called on the Khalfan and gave him two letters, one of which was addressed to him and the other to the Imam of Oman. Since the latter was at Rustaq, his capital, the letter was sent to him. In the course of their conversation, the Khalfan enquired from Nurullah about Tipu Sultan's kingdom. The Indian envoy replied that the extent of his kingdom was equivalent to a distance of three months' journey, and that his army consisted of 60,000 cavalry, 15,000 *jaish* and 30,000 infantry, excluding garrisons in the various forts.[4]

Meanwhile, on 26 April the Imam himself arrived in Masqat. On hearing of this Nurullah paid him a visit. The Imam inquired from him about the position of the English in India, and instructed the Khalfan to take a personal interest in the affairs of Tipu.

On 7 April various articles were disposed of. Different varieties of cloth and shawls were sold to Maoji Seth, an Indian broker at Masqat. Sandalwood was sold through him at 571 *hun haidari* per candy, and cardamoms weighing 4½ candies were sold at the rate of 15½ *huns* per *ratl*.[4]

On the 12th Ghulam Ali and Nurullah sent a despatch via Bombay to Tipu about the progress of the mission. On the afternoon of the 13th three *jawans* escaped in a dinghy which was proceeding to Bombay. The next day a guard was placed at the port to prevent further desertions. Nevertheless, after three days a water-carrier escaped.

On 22 and 23 April, when the salaries of the *sazawals* and the *asad ilahi* troops were being distributed, a deduction was made of the amount already paid to the men of their units who had run away. This was according to the Sultan's instructions that if any one deserted after receiving his pay, the sum was to be recovered from his officer. The *juqdars* and the *sarkheils* protested against this, and requested the envoys that, since they were proposing to make a representation to the Sultan, no deduction should be made from their salaries until his reply came. The envoys agreed to this.

The envoys, having hired two dhows for Rs. 5,100, embarked early on the morning of 25 June and sailed in the afternoon. They were seen off by the Khalfan and his sons. At Matrah, which is close to Masqat, Maoji Seth proposed to buy all the 500 sacks of black pepper at the Basra rate. But Muhammad Hanif, who was in charge of these transactions, demanded a higher price. Maoji was prepared to buy at the rate of 44 *huns* per candy. Still the bargain did not come off. The sacks of black pepper were, therefore, left with the broker to be sold when the rates became favourable.

Description of Masqat

The extent of the Imam's kingdom is 31 days' journey, covering the area of the highlands, which extend from Masqat to the Nizwa fort, a distance of 13 days' journey, and the lowlands, which extend from Ras ul-Had to Suhar and Khor Faqqan, a distance of 16 days' journey.

The entrance of Masqat from the sea is guarded by four forts, each

Plan of the Town of Masqat reproduced from *Voyage en Arabie et en d'autres pays circonvoisins*, Vol. II, facing page 68.

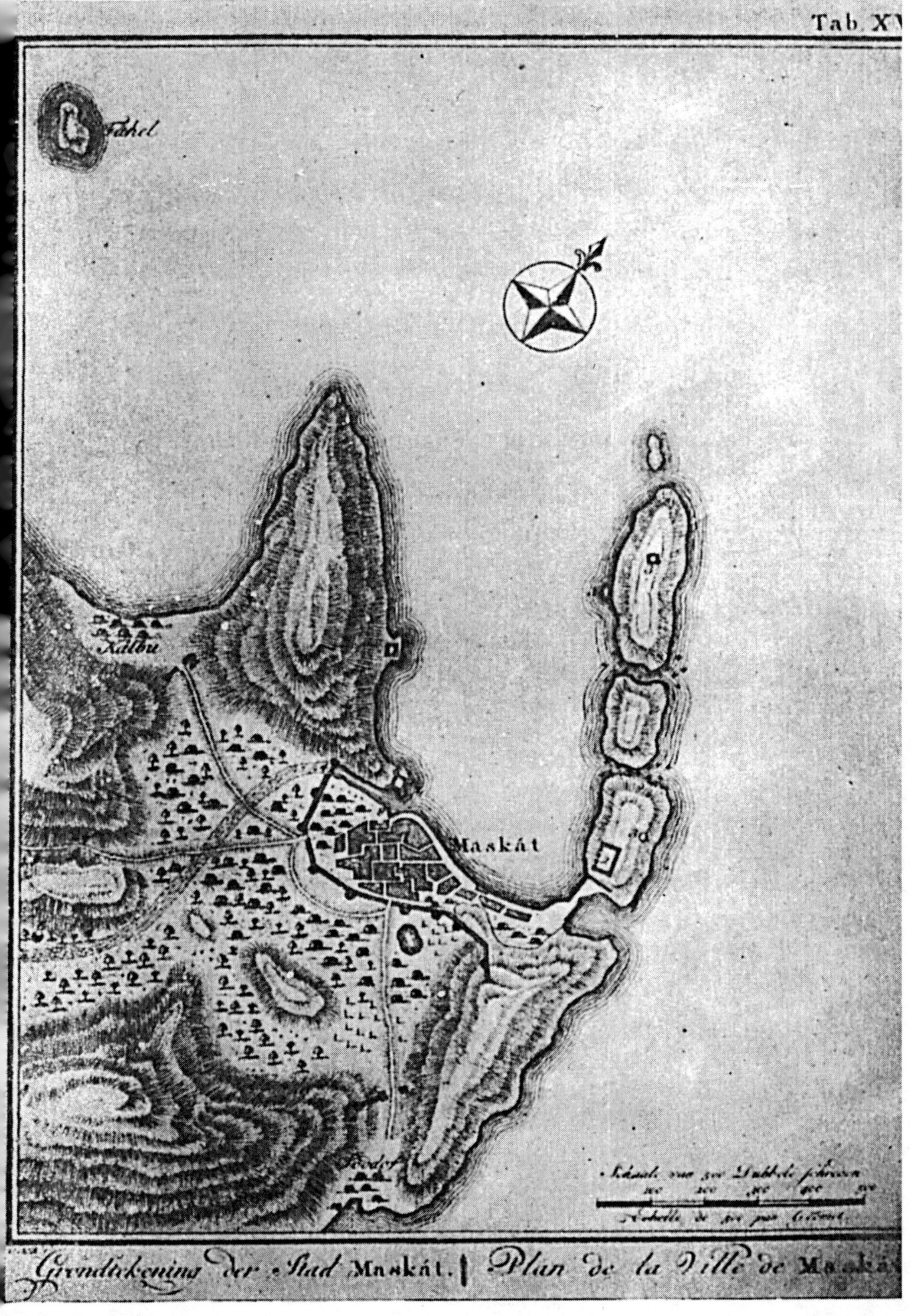

1. Mirani (Kaptani)
2. Jalali
3. Batteries and towers (Jurra-i-Kalan and Jurra-i-Khurd)
4. Town wall

5, 6, 7. Exits leading to Sidab, Kalbuh and Matrah

8. Well which gives water to the town of Masqat

under a commandant. Two of these forts are situated on the right, the other two are on the left, as one enters the harbour. Of the two forts on the right, one is called Jurra-i Kalan, and the other, which is near the town, is called Jalali. Of the two forts on the left, one is called Jurra -i Khurd, and the other, which is near the town, is called Kaptani.[5] The breadth of the sea between the forts of Jalali and Kaptani is 370 yards, and that between the forts of Jurra-i Klan and Jurra-i Khurd is 301 yards. The high tide near Masqat rises about 15 yards, while the ebb tide falls by about 3½ yards.

Masqat is surrounded on the north by the sea, and on the other three sides by hills. Between these hills and the town wall are some orchards and the houses of common people—water-carriers, washermen and Afghans. To the east of Masqat, separated by hills and gardens, lies the port of Matrah. To the south, between the sea and the mountainous area, is situated Sitab. The town of Rustaq, where the Imam resides, lies to the west of Masqat at a distance of six days' journey. Tipu's factory is situated to the west of the port of Masqat.

Masqat has four gates. Two of these are towards the sea-front, on the north. In between the two gates are situated a depot for sale and purchase and a customs-house (*firdah*). The other two gates are on the south side at the foot of the hills. There are three more gates called Sidab, Riyam and Kalbuh, which are situated on the hills to the south, west and north-west respectively.[6] Below the fort of Jalali there is a dockyard, where small boats are made and repaired, but there is no provision for either the making or repairing of large vessels.

The inhabitants of Masqat are clean, but its streets and lanes are in bad condition and extremely narrow. The houses of the Imam, the Khalfan, the nobles and the rich Arab merchants are double-storeyed. Wooden planks are laid over the four walls and covered with lime and earth ; the second storey is built in a similar way. The houses of the common people and the Indian merchants are roofed over with twigs and date-palm leaves laid close together, both lengthwise and breadthwise, over beams, and then covered up with earth. The houses of the poor, situated outside the town, are just huts made of plam leaves. The houses of the nobles number 45, those of brokers and *banyas* number 97 and have to pay taxes.[7] The remaining houses belong to the Arabs and number from 1,500 to 1,700. The palm-leaf huts, which are outside the town, number 2,000.

The dress of the Arab Shaikhs consists of a pair of pyjamas, a shawl or a *lungi* which covers the head, a coat or cloak (*jubbah*) and over it a coarse woollen garment. The dress of the Arab soldiers and common people consits of a *lungi* tied round the head, and a *lungi* covering the lower part of the body with a cloak (*jubbah*) over it. Women's dress, which is generally black, consists of a pair of trousers, a cloak, and a black mantle (*chadar*) for a veil.[8]

The food of the poor consists of dates, dry or fresh, fish and some rice. The food of the rich consists of wheat-bread, dates, rice and fried fish ; they eat dates and fish in abundance.[9]

The Imam Said has four brothers called Qais, Sultan, Saif and Talib, each of whom has a fief.[10] Thus Qais is in possession of Suhar ; Sultan of Samail ; Saif of Numan ; and Talib of Sur. The Imam has two sons. The eldest, Ahmad, is the governor of Barkah, and the second son, Hamid, is in charge of Suwaiq.[11] Khalfan b. Muhammad, the governor of Masqat, has five sons : Sulaiman, Muhammad (the son of the Imam's sister), and Ali. The names of his two other sons are not known.

The Imam possesses four ships. Three of them are large ; they are called *Rahmani*, *Kaba-Ras* and *Nasiri*. The fourth is a small ship named *Baz*. The Imam has also eight men-of-war and eight dhows. Maoji Seth, the broker of Masqat, owns 14 dinghies.[12]

The income of the Imam amounts to Rs. 400,000 annually. One half of it is derived from the duty on exports and imports, and the other half from land revenue, including income from the date-palm groves and other fruit-gardens. The Imam also derives his income from the ships and dinghies which he personally owns. The income from the tax on tobacco is spent on the repair of forts and other government buildings. Customs duties are levied on goods imported, but no duties are imposed on goods taken out of the country. The English, French and Portuguese pay a duty of 5 per cent ; the Arabs and Persians pay 6½ per cent ; Indian merchants generally pay 8 per cent, but goods belonging to the Mysore State only 4. The Indian businessmen, who live in Masqat, have to pay 15 *ghaz* per month.[13] The income from this source is distributed among the disabled and the poor. The administration of the kingdom is carried on by the Khalfan in the name of the Imam. The latter lives mostly in Rustaq, in ease and luxury. It is only occasionally that he visits the different parts of his kingdom.

The salary of the Imam is Rs. 50 a month ; of the Khalfan Rs. 20/- a month ; of the broker Rs. 7, a month ; of a soldier Rs. 3 a month, but in time of war the soldier gets, in addition to his pay, 5 *qiyas* of dates and 2 *ghaz* in the morning, and a quarter of a *seer* of rice in the evening.

The names of the four seasons are retained in Masqat, although it is warm all the year round. It is hot from the beginning of June till the end of August, and the season is called *rabi* (spring), during which dates, grapes, mangoes, figs, melons and peaches ripen. September, October and November, which mark the beginning of cold weather, are autumn months (*kharif*), during which pomegranates, oranges, sweet and sour lemons and vegetables grow. The next three months represent winter (*shita*), during which sugar-cane is grown. March, April and May are the summer months (*saif*), when apples and other fruits, roses and foodgrains grow.

The following are the crops raised in Masqat : dates, grapes, figs, pomegranates, lemons, melons, water-melons, mangoes, sugar-cane, apricots, peaches, raisins, radish, onions, pumpkins, spinach and greens, rice, barley, wheat, various kinds of pulses, coconut and betel-leaves.[14]

The prices of different articles at Masqat on 18th April 1786 were as follows: Sandalwood scent Rs. 10 per *seer* (ordinary); sandalwood 57.8 *hun haidari* per candy ; cardamom 15 *hun haidari* per *man* ; cloves Rs. 110 per *man* ; mace Rs. 220 per *man* ; nutmeg Rs. 115 per *man* ; sugar Rs. 9 per *man* ; saffron Rs. 10 per *seer* (ordinary) ; musk 3 *mahmudis* per *misqal* ; raisins Rs. 4 per *man* ; *cinnamon* Rs. 4 per *man* ; poppy Rs. 6 per *man* ; lump sugar (or fresh sugar) Rs. 80 per candy ; candied sugar Rs. 160 per candy ; almonds Rs. 52 per candy ; pistachio Rs. 120 per candy ; filbert nut Rs. 200 per candy ; walnut Rs. 1⅓ per 1000 ; fresh dates a*nnas* twelve per *man* ; dried dates Rs. 15 per candy ; ghee Rs. 7 per *man* ; rice (first quality) 22 *mahmudis* per sack ; rice (second quality) 20 *mahmudis* per sack ; rice (third quality) 18 *mahmudis* per sack ; *cytisus cajan* Rs. 1 per *man* ; seasame oil Rs. 4½ per *man* ; cotton Rs. 5 per *man* ; silk Rs. 132 per *man* ; anise seed Rs. 2 per *man* ; betel leaves Rs. 2 per *man* ; soap Rs. 2 per *man* ; salt Rs. 2 per candy ; fuel 2½ *ghaz* per *man-i masqat* ; crimson dye Rs. 86 *annas* 12 per *man-i masqat* ; sulphur Rs. 32 per candy; saltpetre Rs. 40 per candy ; lead Rs. 100 per candy ; dry ginger Rs. 18 per candy ; iron Rs. 18 per candy ; copper Rs. 240 per candy; brass Rs. 11 per *man* ; assafoetida Rs. 30 per *man* ; black pepper 43 *hun haidari* per candy ; wheat 4 *mahmudis* per *man-i masqat* ; tamarind (Masqat) 1.8 *mahmudis* per *man* ; millet 12 *ghaz* per *man-i masqat* ; phaselous mungo Rs. 2 per *man-i dehli* ; curd 2 *ghaz* per *qiyas* ; meat 3 *mahmudis* per *qiyas* ; onion 3 *mahmudis* per *man-i masqat* ; garlic 1¼ *mahmudis* per *man-i masqat* ; turmeric 1¼ *mahmudis* per *man-i masqat* ; unground coffee 12 *mahmudis* per *man-i masqat* ; tin 24 *mahmudis* per *man-i masqat* ; ivory (first quality) Rs. 800 per *candy* ; ivory (second quality) Rs. 700 per *candy* ; ivory (third quality) Rs. 600 per *candy*.

(1 *hun bahaduri*=20 *mahmudis* (silver) ; 1 rupee=5 *mahmudis* ; 1 *riyal*=11½ *mahmudis* ; 1 *mahmudi*=20 *ghaz* (copper) ; 1 *man-i masqat*=24 *qiyas* ; 1 *qiyas*=Rs. 14 weight ; 1 candy=20 *mam-i masqat*).

Islands and Ports of the Persian Gulf :

The following is a list of the islands and ports, along with their rulers, where pearls and precious stones are found in large quantities : The ports of Sharjah, Zulfar and Umm ul-Qaiwan and the island of Humrah are ruled by Shaikh Rashid b. Matar, a Sunni, of the Qawasim tribe. The ports of Zubarah and Bahrain are ruled by Ahmad al-Khalifah, a Sunni, of the Utbi tribe. The port of Kuwait and Failakah island are ruled by Abdullah b. Shaikh Sabah, a Sunni of the Utbi branch. The port of al-Uqair and Qatif, which are in the Hasa Oasis, are ruled by Shaikh Butayn b. Urayir b. Khalid, also a Sunni.[15]

The latitude and longitude of Masqat, Basra and other places are follows :[16]

Masqat : 26°45′N, 82°3′E. Lima : 25°49′N, 79°39 E.
Zulfar : 25°28′N, 78°E. Qais : 30° 15N, 70°E.
Basra : 30°50′N, 70°E. Surat : 21° 15N, 36°E.
Lahari (Larry Bandar) : 24°30′N, 0°40′N. Jusk : 25° 17N, 81°E.
Hormuz : 27° 27′ N, 70° 35′E. Abu Shahr: 25° 15N, 73° 52′E.
Khor Musa : 29°55′N, 52° 39′E, Khor Basra : 30°N, 71°35′E.

The envoys left Matrah early on the morning of 27 June. The dhow of Ghulam Ali and the *Ghurab-i Surati* reached Rumais, which belonged to the Imam, in the afternoon. Here fire-wood was obtained. While they were waiting for the arrival of other boats, a strong gale sprang up, and therefore they had to weigh anchor. On 28 June, after sunset, the dhow entered the roadstead of Suhar, which also was part of the Imam's kingdom. It was a very picturesque place, having a pleasant climate and beautiful trees and gardens. Nurullah went ashore and purchased mangoes, while the boats obtained water, fire-wood, and other necessary things. They left Suhar on the night of 1st July and reached the island of Mama Salamah, where violent winds always blow, at midday on the 5th. They arrived in the evening at the island of Larak, which has large quantities of salt and sulphur. It is situated opposite the island of Qishm and the port of Qishm, Behind it is the island of Hormuz ; on the right are situated Bandar Abbas and Bandar Khamir, where sulphur is found in considerable quantities. On the 6th some men were sent to Larak Island to obtain sheep and drinking-water, but were unsuccessful, though they tired themselves out in the search. On the 7th they resumed their voyage. The next morning Shaikh Ismail, who had been keeping watch during the night owing to the danger from the pirates, accidentally struck his hand against the trigger of his loaded gun, which went off, and the bullet grazed the shoulder of Abd un-Nabi, an attendant, passed across his breast without seriously hurting him.

In the afternoon, on account of a storm, the ships anchored in the

Qishm harbour. On the morning of 8 July they sailed, but after three or four *krohs*, owing to the strong *shamal*, which sprang up, they anchored at Qishm Island at sunset. On the 9th they again sailed, but owing to strong winds they had to cast anchor after a few *krohs* in the afternoon near the village of Suzeh, situated on Qishm Island. Men were sent to the village, and they brought drinking water and 5 sheep at 5 *riyals* each. They set out on the 11th and reached the island of Hanjam the next day. Here the *Fakhr ul-Marakib* was anchored to obtain water. Meanwhile, Nurullah, Abdul Qadir and other members of his staff went ashore to visit the tomb of Sayyid Muhammad, son of the Imam Ali Musa Raza, situated on the sea-shore. They left Hanjam on the 13th, and after a few miles cast anchor at the island of Qishm in the evening. They resumed their voyage and in the evening reached the end of Qishm Island opposite Tunb, which had flocks of deer, but was deserted. On Friday the 15th the boat again sailed and after travelling for 8 *krohs* it reached a point in the night with the islands of Kung and Lingeh to the right and the island of Nabiyu to the left. But the same night the *qaus* started blowing, so the boat had to weigh anchor. The dhow of Muhammad Hanif reached Bustaneh, which belonged to Persia, on the 16th. Fire-wood was obtained there. The dhow of Ghulam Ali passed close to the island of Farur, which was deserted except for flocks of deer. On the 17th morning it reached the island of Qais. Men were sent there to bring drinking water and buy sheep, oil and other articles. The ship next stopped at Kungoon which is 21 *krohs* from Qais. It then passed Nakhilu, which is 20 *krohs* from Kungoon, and cast anchor at the island of Khan on the evening of the 20th. It sailed the same night and reached Abu Shahr on the 23rd.

The envoys sent the captain of the ship and a clerk to Shaikh Nasr,[16a] the ruler of Abu Shahr, with their greetings. They returned with Nasr's good wishes and a message that he would send his own representative to the envoys. Accordingly, on the 25th Shaikh Nasr's son and his agent, Abul Hasan, came with a message of welcome and presents consisting of 3 water-melons, 3 hampers of grapes, 1 hamper of peaches and 9 sheep. Abul Hasan requested them on behalf of their master to disembark in order to rest and transact their business, adding that arrangements for their accommodation had been made in the town. The envoys expressed their gratitude, but told him that they could not disembark, because they had to leave within a few days and reach their destination with the utmost speed. Abul Hasan then informed the envoys that Shaikh Nasr intended to send a mission to Mysore in order to seek Tipu Sultan's permission to set up a factory at Mangalore, in return for allowing him to have one at Abu Shahr. The envoys were requested to recommend these proposals to Tipu. Ghulam Ali and Nurullah, accordingly, prepared despatches with their recommendations and gave them to Abul Hasan to be sent to the Sultan.

Abu Shahr

Abu Shahr has factories belonging to the English, the Khalfan, and Maoji Seth, the broker of Masqat. The town has a small but prosperous population, and the bazaar is full of articles of various kinds for sale. However, it has no water, and this has to be obtained from a distance of two miles.

The envoys inquired from the agents of the Khalfan and Maoji Seth, who have their respective factories in the towns, about the rates of various articles, and showed them the sample of goods which they wished to sell. But as the rates in the Abu Shahr market were not favourable, no transactions were effected.

The following were the prices at Abu Shahr on 26 July, 1786 : Sugar 7½ *mahmudis* per *man-i tabriz*; candied sugar 17 *mahmudis* per *man-i masqat*; sandalwood 25 *maumudis* per *man-i tabriz* ; black pepper 90 *mahmudis* per *man-i tabriz* ; tin 23 *mahmudis* per *man-i tabriz* ; copper 19 *mahmudis* per *man-i tabriz* ; turmeric 4 *mahmudis* per *man-i tabriz* ; dry ginger 6 *mahmudis* per *man-i tabriz* ; cinnamon (Mangalore) 8 *mahmudis* per *man-i-tabriz* ; cinnamon (Ceylon) 40 *mahmudis* per *man-i tabriz* ; Basra stone 12 *mahmudis* per *man-i tabriz* ; rice (first quality) 30 *mahmudis* per sack ; rice (second quality) 25 *mahmudis* per sack ; wheat 1 *mahmudis* per *man-i tabriz* ; phaselous mungo 3 *mahmudis* per *man-i tabriz* ; assafoetida 32 *mahmudis* per *man-i tabriz* ; gram 2 *mahmudis* per *man-i tabriz* ; ghee (boiled butter) 30 *mahmudis* per *man-i tabriz* ; seasame oil 8 *mahmudi* per *man-i tabriz* ; cloves 190 *mahmudis* per *man-i tabriz*; nutmeg 220 *mahmudis* per *man-i tabriz* ; mace 600 *mahmudis* per *man-i tabriz* ; cotton 10 *mahmudis* per *man-i tabriz* ; onion 8 *mahmudis* per *man-i tabriz* ; garlic 4 *mahmudis* per *man-i tabriz* ; dry coriander seed 4 *mahmudis* per *man-i tabriz* ; walnut 6 *mahmudis* per *man-i tabriz* ; pistachio 8 *mahmudis* per *man-i tabriz* ; almonds 3 *mahmudis* per *man-i tabriz* ; salt 4 *mahmudis* per *man-i tabriz* ; fenugreek 3 *mahmudis* per *man-i tabriz* ; dried potatoes 4 *mahmudis* per *man-i tabriz* ; dried figs 3 *mahmudis* per *man-i tabriz* ; raisins 7 *mahmudis* per *man-i tabriz* ; dates 1 *mahmudi* per *man-i tabriz* ; poppy 5 *mahmudis* per *man-i tabriz* ; dried rose flowers 5 *mahmudis* per *man-i tabriz* ; rose of Shiraz 9 *mahmudis* per *man-i tabriz* ; vinegar 4 *mahmudis* per *man-i tabriz* ; musk melon ½ *mahmudi* per *man-i tabriz* ; water melon ½ *mahmudi* per *man-i tabriz* ; grapes ¾ *mahmudi* per *man-i tabriz* ; thick tailed sheep 15 *mahmudis* each ; tobacco (first quality) 6 *mahmudis* per *man-i tabriz*; tobacco (second quality) 4 *mahmudis* per *man-i tabriz* ; brinjal ½ *mahmudi* per *man-i tabriz*. (3½ *man-i tabriz*=1 *man-i mangalore* ; 1 *man-i tabriz*=16 *qyias-i masqat*).

On Friday the 28th July, which was the day of the *Id ul-Fitr*, the envoys left Abu Shahr, and after sailing for a few *krohs* through stormy weather they touched the picturesque villages of Banu Tamim Ansari, which lay on a river and grew wheat and other foodgrains which they exported to Abu Shahr and Basra.

On the night of the 28th the dhow resumed its voyage, but after half an hour, owing to the strong winds coming from the opposite direction, it had to cast anchor. Early on the morning of the 30th it weighed anchor, and the same night the dhow and the *Nabi Bakhsh* reached the island of Kharag.

Kharag Island

The next morning Nurullah disembarked and proceeded to the fort of Jauza, which had been unoccupied for ten years. It is 650 yards long and 590 yards broad. It has six towers of which four are situated on the four corners, and the others are over the two gates facing the sea. One of these is closed. There are two more gates, one looking out on the sea and the other opening on to the town. Inside the fort there are inns, houses, a bazaar with roofed shops, a mosque and a factory which once belonged to the Dutch. There is also a well of sweet water and a fourteen-door house, adjacent to the towered gate overlooking the sea. This house, being vacant, was occupied by the envoys.[17]

The island possesses some orchards, but it is sparsely populated and some of the houses are in ruins. There are also a number of sanctuaries.[18] The tomb of Ibn Hanafiya is situated outside the fort to the left on a hillock. It has a tiled minaret and was constructed in 730 A.H./1329 A.D. Previously there was only a small sanctuary, but a Persian architect, named Sayyid Ali b. Husain al-Bukhari, added a twelve-door structure to it. His grave is situated outside the tomb. Over the cave, which Ibn Hanafiya is supposed to have entered, there is an iron box 7 yards in length, 4 yards in breadth, and 1½ yards in height, with verses of the Quran inscribed on it. The mausoleum also has the grave of the tutor of Ibn Hanafiya, on which Quranic verses are inscribed, and anyone who visits the place recites them. There are also a number of graves both outside and inside the four walls of the tomb. Outside the fort to the right is the tomb of Abdullah b. Omar, and to the left is the tomb of Muhammad b. Abu Bakr. In addition there is a walled area where Khwaja Khizr had performed *chilla kashi*.

It is said that Khizr came to the island with a large army and killed all the infidels. But his own followers were also slain. After this, while he was sitting in an isolated place, seven boats carrying troops, including a tall, strong, wicked woman, who was a witch, arrived on the island. The commanders of the army pleaded that they lacked courage to attack Khizr. The witch, thereupon, told them that they should follow her without fear. If the Khwaja was really a saint he would not approach a naked woman. If he was a wizard he would use his witchcraft against her. The woman then stripped herself, and, with the infidel army following her, went to the Khwaja. The latter came out of his cell, and, seeing a naked woman, prayed to God to turn them into stone. His prayer was answered, and the woman and the soldiers were all turned into stone. The Khwaja then with his spear struck the ground, which caved in, and he entered the opening. The cave was covered by a large iron box to represent his grave, and over that a tomb was constructed. Traces of the fleet and army, which were turned into stone, still exist. At two places the marks of the Khwaja's feet and of the hoofs of his horse on the stone can be seen. It is said that the Khwaja struck the ground with his spear at three different places, at some distance from the tomb, and, as a result, three wells of sweet water emerged. Besides these, the island has many other wells of sweet water.

On the *Id* day in the sanctuary food is distributed to the poor. The tomb has 4 small golden minarets erected on the four corners of the box, like cupolas, by Mir Muhanna, who ruled the island after the Dutch. He had his own name and that of the Khwaja inscribed on the minaret. Four mirrors were fixed on the minarets, towards the inside. In addition a few mirrors were fixed on the walls of the sepulchre.

On occupying Kharag Island the Dutch built a fort. They imposed a customs duty and invited merchants and brokers to come and settle there by giving them assurances of safety.[19] But since they began to raise pigs, and one of the pigs strayed into the sanctuary of Khizr, the saint ordered Mir Muhanna, who belonged to the Kaab tribe, to drive out the Dutch. Mir Muhanna succeeded in this and became ruler of the island. After sometime he started oppressing the inhabitants, so Khizr advised the islanders to put him to death. Mir Muhanna, having got this news, fled towards Basra, but was assassinated on the way. The island has remained sparsely populated ever since.[20]

Mir Ali, the governor of the island, was absent on a campaign with Shaikh Nasir, so on his behalf Shaikh Salman, the *mutawalli* of the tomb of Khizr, welcomed the envoys and presented one sheep each to Ghulam Ali and Nurullah and two sheep to their staff. When the envoys visited the sanctuary they presented 20 *qurs rumi* to Shaikh Salman and his nephew Nasir and distributed money and wheat among the beggars.

On the night of 5th August, a rumour spread that 400 Arabs and Persians were on their way to kill and plunder the visitors. The embassy staff were alarmed and ran to the ships for safety. Ghulam Ali, Nurullah and Jafar Khan, however, did not lose courage, and remained on the island.

On the afternoon of Sunday 6 August, the agent of Maoji Seth, who came to buy 5 candies of cardamoms and the bags of black pepper, brought the information that the *Fathi-i Shahi* would soon be arriving. The next day the envoys sent some of their staff on board to find out the cause of their late arrival, and to tell the troops that they should visit the sanctuaries, and that after revictualing the ship they must be ready to leave that very night.

The prices in the Kharag market on 6 August 1786 were as follows, rice 3 *mahmudis* per *man-i tabriz* ; wheat 1½ per *man*; flour 2½ per *man* ; ghee Rs. 16 per *man*; *erveun lens* 3½ per *man* ; dates 3 per *man*; fresh clover 2½ per *man* ; water melon 2 per *man* ; sheep 15 each; chicken 1 each; firewood 8 *ghaz* per *man* ; brinjal 1½ per *man*.

On the night of 7 August the dhow and the *Fath-i Shahi*, along with 16 or 17 other vessels, all sailed together from Kharag Island for fear of the Kaab pirates who infested the route to Basra. They anchored off the island of Khargu, which produced everything except rice and firewood, and had 25 date palm trees and a few wells of sweet water. They left Khargu on the 11th, touching the next day, on the way to Basra, the ports of Dilum, Banak and Bahragan. They then entered the Khor Musa.

The Envoys enter the Shatt ul-Arab

Henceforth the progress of the squadron was very slow owing to bad weather and the *shamal*. The latter was so violent that the *dao saif* lost two of its sails, and after it had entered the Khor Bahmanshir, it twice came into the shallows, where it ran aground and had to be dragged off with considerable difficulty. On the morning of the 17th they entered the Khor Basra. To its right is the desert which is the territory of the Kaab, who formerly waylaid travellers, but now, owing to the strictness of the Basra government, have become peaceful. To the left of Khor Basra are the sugarcane plantations. The same day the ships entered the boundaries of Minohi, which possesses palm plantations. To the right of Minohi, also, is the Kaab territory.

After proceeding one *kroh* the boat had to cast anchor owing to the violence of the *shamal* and low tide. On the night of the 20th it reached the frontier of Chabdah, which has a large population, a number of palm plantations, two sanctuaries and many islands. It was intended to buy from Chabdah the necessary supplies. But meanwhile the *qaus*, which had disappeared for the last ten days, suddenly sprang up, and so the anchors were weighed. But immediately the *qaus* subsided and the *shamal* took its place. Thereupon the sails were hauled down, and the boat was towed as far as Shattait and Bawairdeh. To these villages men were sent to purchase provisions. Shaikh Salim, the proprietor, sent to the envoys trays full of fresh dates and three chickens as a present.

The envoys had already sent a messenger to Ibrahim Agha, the *Mutesellim* of Basra, informing him of their arrival ; so after they had passed through the villages of Shabanah, Khast, Saihan, Baraim, Nahr ash-Shaikh, Mutawa, Zain, Mahallah, Hadd, Muhammareh and Derbend situated on either side of the Shatt ul-Arab, they were received by Haji Muhammad Effendi *Defterdar* and Haji Jawwad, the Kaptan Pasha, who had come with 8 boats to welcome them and escort them to Basra owing to the danger of attack from the Kaab pirates. The Turkish officers left two of their boats for the protection of the *dao saif*, and set out with the rest to protect the other ships of the embassy which were following behind. Shortly afterwards a certain Hamda, an inhabitant of the village of Zain, brought 4 trays full of dates. On the night of the 19th the *dao saif* weighed anchor and sailed escorted by the two Turkish boats. The same night, while he was sleeping on the edge of the deck, Rustam, a servant of Muhammad Omar *Chobdar*, having turned over, fell into the river and was drowned. The fast current of the river (Euphrates) carried away the body so swiftly that no trace of it could be found. The *dao saif*, having passed through the villages of Faiyazi, Abu Ibgai, Abul Khaseeb, Khumaiseh, Nahr Amir, stopped in order to wait for the others which were left behind.

Meanwhile, news arrived that on the night of Friday 18th August the *Nabi Bakhsh* had caught fire and sunk, causing the death of 50 men. However, the remaining persons were saved owing to the efforts and timely help of Jafar Khan, one of the envoys.[20a]

The Envoys arrive in Basra

On the arrival of the *Fath-i Shahi* and the *Ghurab-i Surati*, the *dao saif* raised anchor and together they reached Basra on 22 August. Haji Muhammad and other officials came on behalf of the *Mutesellim* to express sympathy on the sinking of the ship and the loss of goods, and gave assurances that every effort would be made to salvage what could be saved. They presented the envoys with several hampers of fruits and vegetables. Accommodation had been arranged for the embassy in the houses belonging to the Dutch and French factories. Some houses had also been rented outside the Dutch factory. The envoys, escorted by their troops, rode in palanquins through the streets of Basra to their lodgings. Sumptuous food was sent to them by the *Mutesellim*.

On 24 August Ibrahim Agha, accompanied by the high officials of Basra, called on the envoys. He expressed his regret for the sinking of the *Nabi Bakhsh*, and asked for details of the articles intended as presents to the Ottoman Sultan which had been lost in the ship, and those which were still with them, so that a statement could be prepared and sent to Sulaiman Pasha at Baghdad. Ibrahim Agha was entertained with coffee, sherbet, betel, cardamom and jam. On his return to his residence, he sent the envoys 10 sheep. At the same time Shaikh Suwaini, head of the Muntafiq group of tribes, sent them 10 sheep, 10 baskets of dates and 4 baskets of grapes.

The envoys gave Haji Muhammad a list of the articles which Tipu had sent for the Ottoman Sultan. These consisted of 11 pieces of jewellery, 2 elephants with silver canopied howdahs, a sandalwood bedstead, 5 *mans* of sandalwood scent, and 33 dresses. Altogether the presents consisted of 202 articles, excluding 200 *hun haidari*, 100 gold mohurs, 500 *haidari* silver coins and 36 *khilats* for the ministers of the Sultan. All these articles, including the 11 pieces of jewellery, were lost when the ship was wrecked, while the two elephants had died on account of the heat during the journey. However, 9 pieces of jewellery, which were the property of the envoys, were shown to Haji Muhammad *Defterdar*, and he was told that if these were approved, they could be included in the list of the presents.

On 25 August Ghulam Ali Khan and Nurullah Khan each addressed a letter to Jafar Khan, Shah of Persia, saying that their master was anxious to establish commercial relations with Persia, and desired that Persian merchants should visit his ports for the purpose of trade. They had been sent by Tipu Sultan to make a pilgrimage to the shrines and arrange for the construction of a canal to Najaf.[21] The envoys also sent letters to Sulaiman Pasha informing him of their arrival at Basra, and that they would at once set out for Baghdad on receiving his reply.

On the 27th Shaikh Abdullah, the *Shaikh ul-Islam* of Basra came to see the envoys. Later, five agents of the English East India Company, including Khoja Petrus Mellick, Antony and Kemball, called on the envoys.[22] They pointed out that two years ago there had been a conflict between the English and Tipu Sultan, but that now after the Treaty of Mangalore friendly relations existed between them.[23] From his side Ghulam Ali reciprocated these sentiments. The envoys, with the exception of Jafar Khan who was unwell, with some of their staff went to the residence of Ibrahim Agha, the *Mutesellim*, for lunch. They were served with about a dozen varieties of dishes.

In the evening Sieur Moustier and Monsieur Edouard, accompanied by two priests and two French merchants connected with the French factory at Basra, came to see the envoys, and brought a letter from Moniseur Rousseau, the French Consul at Baghdad. The letter welcomed their arrival, recalled the friendly relations which had always existed between the French and Tipu, and suggested that, considering these bonds of amity, if they stood in need of anything they could obtain it from the French factory at Basra. The envoys agreed that friendship had existed between Mysore and France since the time of Haidar Ali, and observed that there could be no ground for misunderstanding. They further stated that they had come prepared to proceed to France, and would do so as soon as they had completed their mission in Constantinople.[24] They promised to reply to M. Rousseau the next day. The French were entertained with sherbet and tea.

On the 29th Ghulam Ali and Nurullah discussed with Lutf Ali the question of expenses connected with the sanctuaries at Najaf, Karbala, Baghdad and other places. Lutf Ali reminded them that since the 65,000 *hun haidari* that had been sanctioned for the mission's three years stay abroad were insufficient, they could not incur any further expenses. If, however, a *ghilaf* had to be taken to Najaf, it could be made out of one bale of *shila*. Both Ghulam Ali and Nurullah were amused by this droll suggestion. On the 31st Ghulam Ali withdrew Rs. 12,000 to cover expenditure on the sanctuaries. Out of this Rs. 4,000 were to be spent as offerings in cash and Rs. 8,000 on coverings for the graves, to be made out of brocaded broadcloth. This, it was felt, would redound to the prestige and good name of Tipu Sultan. Lutf Ali accepted the proposal with reluctance.

On 2 September Ghulam Ali purchased 12 bales of broadcloth at 3 *qurs rumi* per Basra yard. Later he returned this cloth, having purchased through Isa Yahudi, one of the Basra brokers, 12 bales of cloth at 2 Rs. 2 as. per Basra yard. The French factors were annoyed at this erratic behaviour of the Indian envoys.

On the 6th Ghulam Ali wanted to pay the salaries of his staff at the rate of exchange of 1 *hun*=20 *mahmudis* (*masqati*)=3 *qars rumi*=3½ *mahmudis* that was current from Masqat to Kharag Island. The army officers agreed to this rate, but Lutf Ali argued that at Basra one *qurs rumi* was equal to 5 *mahmudis* (*masqati*), and therefore the balance of his salary of two months should be paid at this rate of exchange. Hearing of this the officers were disturbed ; brought information from the bazaar of Basra that 1 *hun* was equal to a little over 4 *qurs rumi*, and 1 *qurs rumi* was equal to 15 *mahmudis* (*masqati*), and demanded that they should be given their pay on the basis of this rate of exchange. Ghulam Ali agreed, but at the same time got a written statement from them that in future, at Baghdad or elsewhere, they would accept their salaries at the lower rate.

On 8 September Haji Jawwad, the Kaptan Pasha, came to the envoys along with Murad Khan, Muhammad Shafi and Shams ud-din, and described the burning and sinking of the *Nabi Bakhsh* and the loss of lives and baggage. They reported that four guns and some unimportant articles of iron had been salvaged by the divers; of the 263 persons who were on board, 94, including women and children, had been burned to death or drowned, the rest had been saved by the courage and resourcefulness of Jafar Khan.

On the 11th Sayyed Ali, a *pir* attached to the Mysore army, who had come to Iraq at the invitation of Ghulam Ali to make a pilgrimage to the holy places, celebrated the anniversary of his ancestor, Khwaja Banda Nawaz of Gulbargah. Many people of Basra came to see the ceremonies and the profuse illuminations that had been made. On the third day again there was illumination. On this occasion the notables of Basra also came at the invitation of the envoys and greatly enjoyed the sight.

On the night of 22 September Muhammad Ali Bhatu and Muhammad Omar *Chobdar* went along with an interpreter to the house of a Jew and got drunk. They then thrashed the interpreter, who went to the house of Ghulam Ali at midnight and loudly complained of his treatment. Ghulam Ali was angry, and gave him a shoe-beating. The next morning all three were called into the presence of the envoys and rebuked for having got drunk.

On the 23rd Ghulam Ali and Nurullah prepared a despatch containing an account of their experiences from Masqat to Basra, and sent it by a dinghy belonging to the English factory at Basra to the broker at Masqat to be forwarded to Tipu.

In the evening an interpreter speaking Arabic, Turkish and English was employed at Rs. 30 a month (36 days) with victual.

On 3 October two letters from Ahmad, *Diwan* of Sulaiman Pasha, were received by the *Mutesellim* in reply to those of Ghulam Ali and Nurullah. Ahmad welcomed their arrival, stating that Sulaiman Pasha had issued orders to the *Mutesellim* that he should send them in state to Samawah, where sufficient horsemen would be waiting to escort them. They should then visit the sacred places and come to Baghdad whence, after resting for some time, they should continue their journey.

When Ghulam Ali and Nurullah had written to Sulaiman Pasha, Lutf Ali had objected that the letters did not bear his signature. In consequence there had been great altercation, and he had himself addressed a letter to the Pasha and had also put his signature to the letter written by Ghulam Ali. These letters had been sent to Baghdad through the *Mutesellim*.

However, replies only to the letters of Ghulam Ali and Nurullah had been received. Lutf Ali enquired why no reply to his letter had come, and was suspicious of Nurullah having a hand in the matter. When, therefore, the *Mutesellim* came to dine with the envoys, Lutf Ali broached the subject. Ibrahim Agha, who was only in name the ruler of Basra, for the real power was wielded by Ali Agha, Haji Muhammad *Defterdar* and Abdullah Yahudi, could not give any explanation. He only said that he had forwarded two letters of the envoys to Sulaiman Pasha. This confirmed Lutf Ali in his suspicions, and on making inquiries from Haji Muhammad he was told that he had sent three letters, including one from him, to Baghdad. He would be able to ascertain the facts on reaching Baghdad, and if he discovered that any incorrect statement had been made, he could complain to Sulaiman Pasha and have him dismissed.

The *Mutesellim*, accompanied by his cortege of twelve notables of Basra and one hundred attendants, came to dine with the envoys. After the banquet, which he greatly enjoyed, he requested the envoys to dine with him one day. They gladly accepted the invitation.

On 10 October Abdullah came to Nurullah, and after looking at different varieties of cloth pointed out that white cloth, and still more so, black cloth was both expensive and of poor quality, and was not worth 12 as. per *anga*. Besides Abdullah other merchants held the same opinion. In the end Abdullah suggested that all the goods should be left with him, and he would try to sell them gradually without loss. They should not be sold while prices were low. The envoys agreed with this.

The next day, however, Nurullah informed Abdullah that if he was prepared to buy white cloth and other articles at the rates quoted by Murad Khan, well and good, otherwise the stuff would be loaded on the ships and sent back to Mysore. He also warned Abdullah that when the envoys reached Constantinople they would report to the Sultan the treatment meted out to them. Hearing this the Jew became alarmed and went to Murad and told him that not a single bale of cloth should be sold to anyone else, for he would take all.

After a few days Abdullah came and wanted to buy white cloth at 12 as. per *anga* : but Nurullah demanded R. 1-4 as. After a great deal of haggling, Abdullah agreed to buy the white cloth of Muslipatam at Rs. 11 per bale and black cloth at 13 as. per 100 *angas*.

On 14 October Husain Agha came and informed the envoys that three boats belonging to the Basra government were at their disposal and inquired when they proposed to leave. Ghulam Ali replied that he would be dining with the *Mutesellim* next day, and would consult him about it.

On the 16th Ghulam Ali, Nurullah and Lutf Ali in their respctivee palanquins, followed by Jafar Khan and Sayyed Ali *pirzada* on horseback and others on foot, proceeded to the residence of the *Mutesellim.* First they were offered jam and coffee, and then different sorts of dishes were served. In the course of conversation Nurullah asked the *Mutesellim* when they would be able to set out for Baghdad. He was told that they could leave by the 2nd of Moharram/26 October.

The envoys had hired one large boat named *Bashtardeh* and two small ones for 2,035 *qurs rumi* through Husain Agha and Abdullah. But since these were not sufficient to meet their requirements, one extra boat was hired for Rs. 800 through Isa Yahudi. The amount was to be paid when the embassy reached Baghdad.

On the 23rd answers to the two letters which Ghulam Ali and Nurullah had sent to M Rousseau, French Consul at Baghdad, were received. Rousseau complained that in spite of the friendly relations which had prevailed between France and Mysore since the time of Haidar Ali, the envoys had not made any purchases from the French factory at Basra.

On the 31st (7th Moharram) some boys came to Ghulam Ali, lancing their arms and mourning the death of Husain, and received from him 4 *qurs rumi.*

On 2 November Abdullah called and complained that the coarse cloth he had purchased was old and defective, and that its price was higher than that of the specimen shown to him. He wanted to return it ; Nurullah replied that he should have examined the bales before taking them to his house, and for him to return them now would be very irregular. There was great controversy over this question. In the end Nurullah took back the cloth, but warned the broker that the matter would be reported to the Ottoman Sultan, since the goods belonged to the Mysore state.

On 3 November (10th Moharram) all the men and women of Basra who were friends of "the People of the House" of the Prophet, gathered at Maqam Ali, making recitations and mourning the death of Husain. Some of the Arabs carrying lances and swords inflicted wounds on their bodies. Some of the Persians were weeping bitterly and beating their breasts. The Persian and Arab women had thrown a sheet over a cradle representing the dead body of Asghar, and were wailing and beating their breasts. And from one jujube tree blood was spouting. In fact this always happened on the anniversary of the martyrdom of Husain. This blood, applied to the eyes of the blind, restores sight.

On the 14th the envoys sent a letter to Maoji Seth of Masqat that they had received 20,000 *hun haidari* from Prem and Sewa, his agents at Basra, on account of the goods which he had purchased at Masqat.

On the 16th some of the bales of coarse cloth and the *pamri* chintz which Abdullah had returned, were purchased by Ahmed Chelebi, the *Mehmandar*, and Husain Agha on condition that the money was to be paid in Baghdad. Ishaq Yahudi, who supplied provisions to the *asad ilahi* troops, also made purchases. He had already bought cloth for 2,500 *qurs rumi* at 13 as. per *anga*, and now he bought cloth worth 4,000 rupees and sandalwood oil.

Abdullah paid a visit to Nurullah and told him that, since the 160 bales of cloth, which he had purchased, were defective, their price ought to be reduced. Nurullah replied that this was highly improper, for the price had been settled and the goods taken away. But despite this, if Abdullah insisted, he would take them back, for they could be sold to other merchants at a higher price. Realizing that he would not succeed in his bargaining, he kept the bales. In all he had purchased cloth worth 13,000 *qurs rumi*, and he gave Nurullah a bill of exchange for the amount on a banker at Baghdad.

When later the envoys sent a despatch to Tipu Sultan, Abdullah also addressed a letter to him, stating that all the goods which the envoys had brought had been disposed of, and requesting that in future he should be entrusted with all the transactions of the Mysore kingdom.

On 19 November Nurullah came to Ghulam Ali and suggested to him to tell Lutf Ali not to go about in the bazaars of Basra purchasing chalcedony and other articles, for this got them a bad name. Ghulam Ali replied that he did not care much for loss of prestige, for their reputation had already suffered much owing to lack of money. Nurullah suggested to Ghulam Ali that he should fix from Rs. 2,000 to Rs. 10,000 for such purchases, and withdraw the amount from the *tosha-khana*. He himself could not do this without his consent and permission. It would not be proper if Ghulam Ali showed indifference and threw all the responsibility on his shoulders. Ghulam Ali felt piqued at this reply, and observed that he had been interested until then in the question of giving presents, but henceforth he would leave it to Nurullah to decide. This led to serious argument between them. Meanwhile Lutf Ali arrived. Nurullah enquired from him where he had gone yesterday, and said that people were talking about it. He replied that he had gone to Maqam Abbas, and, having seen a precious stone in the bazaar, had purchased it. There was nothing wrong in this. He had then visited the tomb of Yahya b. Imam Musa Raza.

Muhammad Rafiq, the adopted son of the late Muhammad Hanif, claimed from Ghulam Ali one thousand rupees which he owed his father.[25] Ghulam Ali told Muhammad Murad that he would give some bales of broadcloth at Rs. 5 per yard, which he should take with him to Mangalore and after selling them pay the proceeds to Rafiq. If there was any loss he would pay the balance on his return. Murad replied that he would take the cloth at Rs. 3½ per yard, provided that Hanif took the responsibility for both profit and loss. Since the matter could not be settled Hanif requested Nurullah to intervene. Accordingly, the latter went to Ghulam Ali and suggested that he should give the cloth at Rs. 5 per yard, and send instructions to the broker at Mangalore to sell it, whether there was profit or loss, and give the money to Rafiq. Ghulam Ali accepted his advice and gave 250 yards of broadcloth, which he had borrowed from the French factory at Basra, to Muhammad Rafiq. He also gave two letters to him: one was addressed to the broker, Kishore Das, and the other to the *amil* at Mangalore, with instructions not to demand any duty from Rafiq.

Jafar Khan had saved a slave girl and a male slave when the *Nabi Bakhsh* had caught fire and sunk, and kept them himself. When later Murad Khan and others demanded them, he returned the male slave, but retained the girl. Murad Khan however persisted in demanding her, and sent twenty-eight rupees for the board of the two slaves which he thought Jafar Khan must have spent on them. Jafar Khan took only five rupees and returned the slave girl.

On 25 November Jiwan Khan, a soldier, came and surrendered. He had escaped at Masqat, and having secured employment on a ship had arrived in Basra. The envoys decided that he must be shot in accordance with the punishment prescribed for such offences in the *Fath ul-Mujahidin*, which Tipu had given them for their guidance.[26] However, it was felt that if such a punishment were inflicted it would injure their reputation. It would therefore be better if Jiwan Khan were taken with them in shackles, and dealt with in accordance with the rules laid down for them in some desert place on the way to Baghdad.

On the 26th Husain Agha brought to Nurullah a letter, which he had received from Shaikh Suwaini, saying that the envoys should wait for five or six days until his return to Basra, for otherwise, owing to danger on the route to Baghdad, they would come to grief. Nurullah was very angry to hear this, and, sending for Abdullah and the *Mehmandar*, informed them of the contents of the letter, pointing out that since their attitude was extremely unhelpful and undesirable, they would like to return to Masqat and thence proceed to Constantinople via Jeddah.

On the 30th Husain Agha came to the envoys with a message from the *Mutesellim* and Abdullah that a messenger had arrived from Baghdad with a letter from Sulaiman Pasha to the effect that there was no danger on the way, and that the envoys should start on the 14th Safar 1201, the 13th being an inauspicious date.

On 2 December the news spread that two of Tipu Sultan's ships had been wrecked by a severe storm on the night of Tuesday, 29 November, at Dawasir in Khor Basra. Meanwhile Ahmad Chelebi, the *Mehmandar*, also brought the tragic news of the sinking of the ships. He suggested that the envoys should send one of their men along with his in order to obtain correct information. The envoys deputed three persons to proceed with Ahmad Chelebi's servant to the scene of the tragedy.

Later, two gunners belonging to the two ships came and described how their boats and one *batela* belonging to a monk of Masqat had been wrecked. The *Ghurab-i Surati* had been swept away by the tide in the Shatt ul-Arab and disappeared in the sea. Having lost everything, they were returning by road to Basra.[26a]

Meanwhile, the three men who had been sent returned with news about the ships. They said that the *Ghurab-i Surati* had disappeared, but the *Fath-i Shahi*, with its guns and other equipment, was visible. Nurullah went to the *Mutesellim* and described all this to him and asked him about the date of their departure for Baghdad. The *Mutesellim* fixed 17 Safar, 1201/9 December, 1786, for this, and promised to send the passengers of the wrecked ships to Masqat after their cargo had been salvaged.

On 7 December Husain Agha came to Nurullah and told him that the *Bashtardeh*, which was armed with 14 guns, did not possesses any ammunition ; and since the route was dangerous, he should ask the *Mutesellim* for some gunpowder. Accordingly, Nurullah made this request to him, but he procrastinated. Nurullah therefore purchased gunpowder through Abdullah.

The Envoys leave for Baghdad

On the 8th the envoys with a retinue of 300 men sailed in four boats.[26b] Stopping about two miles from Basra, near the English factory,[27] they discovered that the *Bashtardeh* had been left behind. This was because the *asad ilahis* had refused to embark on the ground that all the space was taken up by the *sazawals*. Ghulam Ali and Nurullah were greatly perturbed to hear this. The latter at once sent one of his men to the *asad ilahis* to embark, and then he himself sent to the *Bashtardeh* to enquire into the matter. He also wrote to Jafar Khan to obtain one boat from Husain Agha and at once proceed. In the end Jafar Khan hired one boat and obtained another from the Turkish authorities, and then, with the *assad ilahis*, sailed towards Qurnah.

Meanwhile, a strong gale started blowing, and Nurullah's boat and the *Bashtardeh*, which had by now come up, had to weigh anchor and sail. When Nurullah reached the camp of Suwaini, who was encamped at a distance of four *krohs* from Basra, he went to Ghulam Ali's boat and proposed that, since Suwaini was encamped in the neighbourhood, they should present him with a *khilat* and meet him before going further, for the route was full of danger from the Bedouins. Ghulam Ali agreed with him, and Nurullah called on Suwaini. The latter was glad to see him, and entertained him to a good dinner which he had ordered a few hours be-before, having heard that the envoys would be visiting him. Suwaini advised Nurullah that, since there was likelihood of a strong wind and storm, he must without delay start for Qurnah. The envoys therefore sailed at once, and reached Qurnah on 13 December.

Qurnah has a town wall which is in a dilapidated condition. A mosque, an inn and some coffee-houses were deserted, but a few houses, cloth and tailoring shops and coffee restaurants were open. Meat, oil, wheat, rice and barley were available in small quantities. However, Qurnah had large date plantations. It is here that the Euphrates and Tigris meet, and near the junction is the place of the Prophet Abraham.

From Qurnah the route leads to Hillah via the Euphrates, and from Hillah it goes to Najaf, Karbala and Baghdad, which are distant a few days, journey. From Qurnah to Hillah takes eleven days via the Euphrates, but by the Tigris route it is over two months' journey. There is great danger from the Khazail on the Euphrates route, but the Tigris route is safe.

The controversy over the allotment of accommodation again revived. Nurullah proposed to Ghulam Ali that the *asad ilahis* should be embarked on the *Bashtardeh*, with the consent of the *sazawals*. In case there was any shortage of space, some of the *sazawal* men should be transferred to another boat. Ghulam Ali's reply was that he was unwell, and since the *asad ilahis* had no respect left for any of the chiefs, he had no desire to interfere. It would be better if Nurullah, by inspiring awe and fear among them, should get them to travel in the *Bashtardeh*. If required he should take the help of Jafar Khan and Lutf Ali. But in spite of all his efforts, Nurullah failed to persuade the *sazawals* the leave the boat. They gave him insolent replies; Muhammad Imam, their officer, for example, said: "If you desire that a *juq* of *sazawals* should leave the *Bashtardeh*, not even the angels, if they were to come down to earth, would be able to get it done."

The result of the recalcitrant attitude of the *jawans* was that the departure of the embassy to Baghdad was delayed. Meanwhile Jafar Khan, after discussing the problem with the *asad ilahis*, found out that what they really wanted was that Ghulam Ali and Lutf Ali should leave their boats and embark on the *Bashtardeh*, while the *asad ilahis* and the *sazawals* should each be given a boat thus vacated. The envoys felt disgusted at the behaviour of the soldiers, but finding no alternative, accepted the proposal.

On 16 December Nurullah wrote to the *Mutesellim* that they had reached Qurnah, and he should ask Husain Agha to expedite their departure for Baghdad, and further, that he should help in the recovery of goods from the wrecked ships and in sending his men to Masqat. A similar letter was addressed to Abdullah, who was further asked to bring with him 100 maunds of rice and 3,000 *qurs rumi*.

On the 20th a messenger came from Shaikh Suwaini to the agent of Husain Agha with a letter stating that all the boats which had reached Qurnah must return to Basra. The agent replied that this could not be done without the order of Husain Agha, who was at the moment in Basra. When Nurullah heard of the letter he was angry, and inquired from the agent the cause of Suwaini's highhanded behaviour. The agent explained that the latter wanted customs-dues on the articles which the envoys were carrying, and unless these were paid, he would not allow them to proceed to Baghdad.[28] But the agent assured Nurullah that there was no need to worry, for Husain Agha would soon meet Suwaini and settle everything, and then, within two or three days, they would be able to continue their journey. The same evening the agent brought information to Nurullah that the *Mutesellim* of Basra and Shaikh Suwaini had received messages from Baghdad that the Turkish Sultan had confirmed Sulaiman Pasha in his post for a term of seven years,[28] and had ordered him to send the Indian envoys with due honours to Constantinople. Accordingly, Sulaiman Pasha had despatched six *bairaqdars* and some horsemen to receive the envoys, and also issued instructions to the *Mutesellim* and Suwaini to expedite their departure. Nurullah was pleased to hear this news.

Shortly after, Nurullah received answers to the letters which he had sent to the *Mutesellim* and Abdullah. The *Mutesellim* wrote that the *Ghurab-i Surati* had disappeared, while the *Fath-i Shahi* was visible during low tide; that owing to the constant effort and labour which his men had been undergoing for the last month in salvaging the cargo, they had become tired out ; and that, because of the cold winds, it had now become difficult for the divers to do their work efficiently. Already between two to three thousand *qurs rumis* had been spend, but only two guns and one anchor had been found. There was no hope of the recovery of any other articles.

The letters from Husain Agha and Abdullah stated that they would be reaching Qurnah on 21 December and then together they would continue their journey. They further stated that they were prisoners of Suwaini, who said he had written to Baghdad about the envoys, and on receipt of a reply would permit them to resume their journey.

On the night of 21 December news came that the Sultan of Aleppo had written to Suwaini that Sulaiman Pasha had been dismissed, and that Suwaini, therefore, wanted the envoys to return to Basra. The next day a letter came from Suwaini addressed to Nurullah urging him to return at once to Basra. Husain Agha also arrived from Suwaini's camp, and he too gave Nurullah the same advice. He further said that Suwaini would soon be going to Basra, and the envoys could then, in a week's time, leave for Baghdad. Nurullah felt helpless; so, as soon as there was low tide, he raised anchor and sailed towards Basra.

On the 23rd the boats reached Maqam Mehdi, which had one tomb and a tall minaret. Nurullah went to meet Suwaini, who was encamped in the neighbourhood, but was told that the Shaikh was away. Later, Husain Agha informed Nurullah that Suwaini was actually present at the time, but did not wish to meet the envoys in order to avoid an embarrassing situation. Husain Agha pointed out, however, that Suwaini had asked him to reassure the envoys that they would soon be able to resume their journey. To this Nurullah replied that he and his colleagues were tired, and it would be better if some of them could leave even if the route was not safe. On the afternoon of the 24th, the boats anchored beyond the English factory, which was close to Basra. They then set out again, and reached the port of Basra in the night.

The Envoys Return to Basra

The next day Ibrahim Agha sent a message to Nurullah that the envoys must remain on their boats for four or five days, after which Suwaini would arrive in Basra, and then they could leave. But during the night Husain Agha came and informed Nurullah that Abdullah had come from Suwaini's presence and brought the news that the Shaikh would be proceeding in a day or two against an enemy to a place about twenty stages distant from the town of Zubair ; hence, in his absence, the envoys could set out for Baghdad without any fear of molestation.

In the meantime, Abdullah came with news that Suwaini was to arrive in Basra in a day or two, and then the envoys could leave. The news from Baghdad was also favourable. Moreover, it was likely that the Shaikh might, within five or six days of his arrival, march with his forces to a distance of over twenty stages against a man who was claiming to be God. In that case the envoys could set out on their journey without any fear. Furthermore, a letter dated 24 Safar, 1201/ 16 December, 1786, had come from the *Kahya* of the *Diwan* of Sulaiman Pasha addressed to Abdullah, stating that 500 horsemen were being sent from the village of

Bani Lam so that the envoys might be under escort and their baggage safely carried from Qurnah to Baghdad. The letter also discounted the false rumour of the dismissal of the *Mutesellim* of Basra and of Sulaiman Pasha.

Nurullah told Abdullah that if their departure did not take place within four or five days, he would hire a small boat, and with Jafar Khan and a few other persons would leave for Baghdad. On arriving there he would arrange for the recall of the others. He informed both Husain Agha and the *Mutesellim* about his programme. They, of course, tried to dissuade him from this course of action, assuring him that the departure of the embassy would soon be arranged. Suwaini would be coming to Basra, and the matter would be discussed with him; and besides, favourable reports had already arrived from Baghdad.

But Nurullah was not satisfied with these explanations. He knew that the *Mutesellim*, Husain Agha and Abdullah were preoccupied with their own affairs, and so were procrastinating. He went to Ghulam Ali and informed him that on 14 Rabi I, 1201/4 January, 1787, he would leave for Baghdad with the help of Abd ur-Rahman, a merchant, who had promised to provide him with a boat. Ghulam Ali assented, but argued that it would be better to wait until Suwaini came to Basra. If he proved unhelpful, then Nurullah could act as he thought fit.

On 31 December some boats belonging to the Turkish navy arrived in Basra. Their crew brought the news that 7 guns, 31 rifles, 2 anchors and a few other articles had been recovered. The two silver-canopied howdahs could not be salvaged because they were in the hold of the *Fath-i Shahi*.

As the date of the embassy's departure was not fixed, Ghulam Ali disembarked and went to a house near Maqam Ali, which he rented for two *qurs rumi* per day. Similarly Lutf Ali took a house near Maqam Ali at 15 *qurs rumi* a month. Nurullah wanted a bigger house in order to accommodate the troops and baggage. The *Mutesellim* sent for Petrus Mellick, an agent of the English Company and the owner of the house which the envoys had occupied before leaving for Qurnah, and asked him for his house. Petrus Mellick refused, saying that the previous rent had not been paid. In the end Ishaq Yahudi, who supplied provisions to the *asadilahis*, arranged for a large house at a rent of 40 *qurs rumi* per month.

On 2 January Nurullah went to the house of Ghulam Ali in order to meet Abd ur-Rahman and discuss with him his departure for Baghdad. He found Haji Jawwad also present there. While they were talking, a Bedouin came and told the Haji of the arrival of a *juqdar* with letters and good news from Baghdad. Haji Jawwad thereupon went to the *juqdar* named Sulaiman Agha, and made inquiries from him. The *juqdar* replied that Sulaiman Pasha had been confirmed in his office ; that a *Mehmandar* had arrived in Baghdad from Constantinople ; and that all arrangements for the reception of the envoys had been made. Sulaiman Pasha had sent 500 horsemen to Basra to escort them to Baghdad, and these would soon be arriving. After this the *juqdar* went to see Nurullah, who, together with him and Haji Jawwad, went to Ghulam Ali and informed him of the news. The envoys rewarded the *juqdar* with a turban and rich cloth. After this Nurullah went to the *Mutesellim* to see the letters which he had received from Baghdad. The *Mutesellim* congratulated Nurullah, and after showing him a copy of the *firman*, confirming Sulaiman Pasha in the government of Baghdad, assured him that now all problems would be duly solved.

Nurullah went from the residence of the *Mutesellim* to Ghulam Ali and informed him that Muhammad Imam wanted one extra boat. Ghulam Ali observed that since the present four boats did not provide enough space, another must be obtained. To this Nurullah replied that he did not want to spend the money of the government unnecessarily; but in case all the four members of the mission thought that an extra boat was required, he would have no objection. Ghulam Ali retorted that he saw no reason why all the four chiefs should be brought in ; he was the leader, and his opinions must be regarded as final. This led to sharp arguments. Ghulam Ali got excited and abused Nurullah, who in turn abused him. Ghulam Ali thereupon said that he would no longer go to Baghdad, and any one who asked him to would get a slap in the face. When Jafar Khan came to know of this, he went to Ghulam Ali along with Sayyid Ali *pirzada* and spent the whole day trying to persuade him to change his mind, but Ghulam Ali remained angry and obstinate. He even hired a camel to go to Najaf and Karbala by himself. Lutf Ali was present during the meeting, but remained silent. In fact, he was ready to accompany Ghulam Ali to Najaf. Later, however, he joined others in trying to pacify Ghulam Ali, but without success. It was therefore decided that Ghulam Ali be left behind, while the rest should continue their journey to Baghdad without him.

On 8 January Nurullah and Jafar Khan went to the *Mutesellim* and told him that they had hired a few boats through Abd ur-Rahman, and wanted his permission to proceed to Baghdad by the Euphrates route. Ibrahim Agha replied that the route was still unsafe, all the more because the envoys were known to be carrying large quantities of jewellery, gold and money; and if anything happened to them, the blame would fall on him. Nurullah replied that in that case he would follow the Tigris route up to Kut, and from there go to Baghdad. He no longer needed the boats arranged by Husain Agha, who was a liar and had been postponing their departure day after day. The *Mutesellim* replied that the *Bashtardeh* and two other boats belonging to the Turkish government were at their disposal. A few more could be hired, and then they could leave on 22 Rabi I, 1201. He swore in the name of God that he was speaking the truth and would not break his promise. He also said that it was mentioned in the copy of the Turkish Sultan's *firman* to Sulaiman Pasha, which had been sent to him Tipu's *wakils* were respectable and trustworthy and, having come to discuss the question of exchange of Mangalore with Basra and other matters, should be at once sent to Constantinople. He then put various questions about Mangalore, and noted down the replies. Nurullah informed him that the income of Mangalore was Rs. 80,000. The number of villages, large and small, belonging to it amounted to 750. Sandalwood, cardamoms, pepper, fine rice, coconut, iron and white cloth were produced there. The town of Mangalore had numerous wells of sweet water, and there were also many streams of sweet water outside the town. The Commandant had at his disposal 1,700 *jaish*, and 300 horse, while the *amil* had 1,000 infantry. There were 28 forts belonging to Mangalore, each with over 100 foot soldiers. A large number of vessels were made at Mangalore. To reach Masqat from Mangalore ships took from a week to forty days.

On 9 January Sayyid Jafar went to Nurullah and told him that Ghulam Ali had proposed that the four members of the delegation should agree to decide matters either in accordance with the special instructions given to them by Tipu or by agreement among themselves. It was therefore necessary that Nurullah should visit Ghulam Ali, and everything would be settled.

Abdullah came to Nurullah and told him that if they did not go with Husain Agha, he would arrange for two extra boats, besides the three belonging to the Ottoman government. Nurullah sent for Husain Agha and inquired whether or not he was prepared to start on 24 January. Husain Agha replied that he would set out on the day already fixed. Nurullah thereupon asked Abdullah to persuade him to start earlier. Abdullah replied that he would go to the *Mutesellim* and tell him that if Husain Agha did not start soon, he would hire two extra boats and arrange for the departure of the embassy. Abdullah did go to the *Mutesellim*, who told him that he would send for Husain Agha the next day and settle the matter so that either he or Abd ur-Rahman could accompany the envoys.

A despatch containing a detailed account of the mission was prepared, and after being signed and sealed by the envoys was handed over to Sayyid Wali to be taken to Seringapatam and presented to Tipu Sultan. A letter was also written to Maoji Seth that 90 men, survivors of the wrecked vessels, were being sent on a boat belonging to Sultan b. Haji at a fare of 5 *qurs rumi* per head. Sultan had been paid 270 *qurs rumi*, and the remaining 180 *rumis* were to be paid by Maoji when the boat reached Masqat. Maoji was further asked to arrange for the passage of the men from Masqat to Mangalore. The men were given two *rumis* each for the expenses of their journey.

The departure for Baghdad was fixed for 15 or 16 January.

Description of Basra

Basra[29] has a town wall on three sides ; the fourth side, towards which the ships anchor, is protected by a fort. The length of the wall is about 14 miles, and it is thickly studded with 131 mud towers with a large number of guns, many of them unserviceable. The town wall and the towers are in a dilapidated condition and in need of repair. The length of the town is 9 miles and its breadth is 3 miles.

Basra has four gates, the Baghdadi, Zubair, Siraji and Majmua, each guarded by 20 Arab soldiers. There is also a smaller gate called Bab ul-Rabat. The Baghdad Gate was fortified with a number of batteries, some of which were destroyed by Sadiq Khan, brother of Karim Khan of Persia, who entrenched himself before this gate when he besieged Basra. It is from this gate that the highway to Baghdad starts. There are no houses beyond the gate, but at a distance of about two miles on the road to Baghdad is situated the English factory in pleasant surroundings.[30] Towards the Bab ul-Rabat Gate there are some houses and a mosque. Outside the town wall towards the west and south-west there is a large canal which feeds smaller canals inside the town.

Beyond the Zubair Gate are the ruins of a mosque.[31] It was built by the Caliph Ali near the scene of the *jang-i jamal* (the Battle of the Camel), but now only two of its pillars and some crumbling minarets are left standing. Near the mosque, on the left, is a small vault with a wooden coffin 4½ yards long, 2 yards wide and 1½ yards high containing the body of Talha. There are also in the neighbourhood a large number of graveyards. The village of Zubair lies at a distance of one mile from the mosque. It used to be thickly populated, but now is in a deserted state. It has about 100 shops, two or three coffee houses, and a large mosque. To the right of the mosque's puplit, at the back, is the gate of Zubair's tomb; and to the right of the mosque, at the base, there is a small cupola containing the grave of one of Zubair's relations. To the left of the mosque, within the compound, there are 5 to 6 graves of the merchants of the Chelebi family from Surat. Inside the tomb of Zubair, at a distance of about two feet from the grave, a

Chelebi merchant had constructed an ornamented wooden lattice 4½ yards long and 3½ yards broad and 3 yards high.

The tomb of Hasan al-Basri is situated to the south of Zubair at a distance of a few bowshots. It has two cupolas: one containing the grave of Hasan al-Basri himself, and the other that of Ahmad, the architect of the tomb. Within the compound of the tomb are the graves of 14 martyrs. Near the tomb are many graveyards and also the graves of the officials of Basra. There are also the ruins of a mosque built by Hasan al-Basri. The latter's grave is over 2½ yards and 2 *grah* in length, 1 yard and 2 *grah* in breadth and 1½ yards and 2 *grah* in height. The tomb of Anas b. Malik is situated in a waterless waste, about 10 miles from the tomb of Hasan al-Basri.[32]

Maqam Ali is situated near the Shatt ul-Arab, at the end of the town wall. It contains a large minaret, near which is a mosque. Ali's footprint is impressed on the marble floor of the mosque, signifiying that he used to live in Maqam Ali. The mosque has a roofed pulpit. The date of its construction, which is inscribed over the gate, is 1067 A.H. (?). Maqam Ali, Maqam Zain ul-Abidin, Maqam Abbas, Maqam Ali Musa Raza, the tomb of Yahya, b. Musa Kazim, the tomb of Sharif b. Āli and Maqam Ali b. Musa Raza lie within the town. The tomb of Sayyid Shaaban is situated outside the town to the south. The tomb of Shams ud-Din also lies outside the town to the north.

Basra has many gardens, both inside and outside the town wall. They produce roses, grapes, pomegranates, figs and vegetables. The gardens inside the town wall run from the Siraji Gate to the town wall, from the Zubair Gate to the canal near Maqam Ali, and from the latter to the bank of the river. The gardens are situated in between the town wall and the houses, which are at a distance of a few bowshots from the former.

The English, the French, Saleh Chelebi, a merchant from Surat, Maoji Seth, the Imam of Masqat, Shaikh Ahmad, broker and merchant, all have their business establishments in Basra. The town has two customs-houses: a maritime one, protected by three guns, on the canal which traverses the town, and a landward one inside the town.

Basra is inhabited by Arabs, Turks, Persians, Jews, Armenians and Christians.[33] They all wear the Arab dress, which consists of from two to four cloaks (*qaba*) made of *shila*, broadcloth or coarse cotton or woollen cloth, depending on the status of the person, pyjamas, made of broadcloth or coarse cotton cloth, and leather shoes. The headgear consists of a cap made of broadcloth, which is covered by a shawl or a piece of cloth depending on the wearer's status. The number of Bedouins is very large, and the dress of their Shaikhs consists of a cloak (*aba* or *qaba*)

Plan of the town of Basra reproduced from *Voyage en Arabie et en d'autres pays circonvoisins* vol. II, facing page 171.

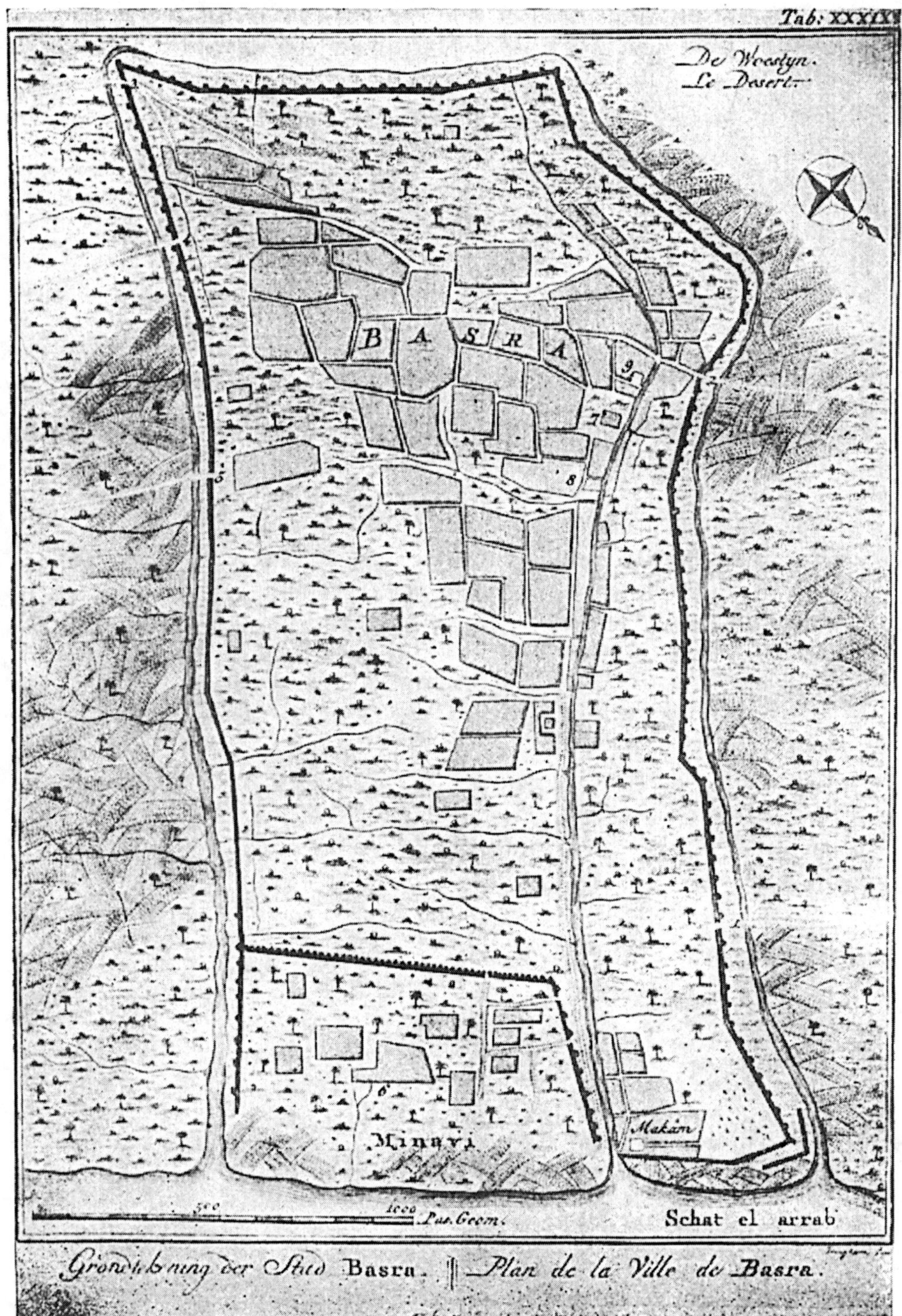

For details see back page

1. Bab-ul-Rabat
2. Darwaza-i Baghdadi
3. Darwaza-i Zubair
4. Darwaza-i Siraji
5. Darwaza-i Majmua
6. Near 6 is the house of Kaptan Pasha
7. Near 7 is the house of the *Mutesselim*
8. Near 8 is the English factory
9. Near 9 is the French factory

made of broadcloth or coarse woollen cloth and drawers. Over the head is placed a folded piece of cloth round which is tied a shawl or something similar. Poor people cover their heads with a large handkerchief and wear one or two cloaks made of coarse woollen cloth. The dress of the Arab and Persian women consists of one or two tunics, pyjamas and leather shoes. They cover themselves with a *chadar*. The Bedouin women wear only a tunic and a *chadar*.

The food of the rich in Basra, both of Arabs and Persians, consists of wheat bread, cheese, *kababs* and dates. In the morning they take bread, *kababs* and coffee. At midday they eat bread, *kababs*, cheese, rice and some dates. At night also they take the same food. The food of the poor consists of bread and dates, and sometimes of onion or radish, *kababs* or fried meat.

The bazaars of Basra remain open from morning till the midday prayers, and then close for the day. Every bazaar and quarter of the town is guarded by watchmen from evening till the next morning.

The duty on the goods belonging to the Imam of Masqat is realized at the rate of 3 per cent. This concession is given to him because he helped the Turks when the Persians besieged Basra.[34] The English, the French and the Chelebi merchant also pay 3 per cent, and the same amount is charged on goods from Mysore. But all other merchants have to pay 8 per cent.[35]

The *Mutesellim* is the ruler of Basra only in name, for the real power is exercised by Haji Muhammad, Ali Agha and Abdullah Yahudi. He sends 1500000 *rumis* annually to Baghdad, and the rest is appropriated by Shaikh Suwaini,[36] who virtually rules the *vilayet*, Ali Agha, Haji Muhammad and Abdullah. The income of the Basra port is not fixed, for the expected amount is never realized. In this *vilayet* there are no proper rules and regulations.[37] The practice is, after deducting the expenditure on the army and administration, to send the balance to Baghdad.

The Turkish navy in Basra comprises eleven large ships and two small ones. In addition to these there are two or three trading vessels. Basra also has a number of boats belonging to the different merchants.

The following were the quotations in the Basra market on 4 October 1786: Sugar 42 *mahmudis* per *man-i attar*; white candied paper 85 *mahmudis* per *man-i attar*; red sugar 70 *mahmudis* per *man*; black pepper 77½ *mahmudis* per *man*; cardamoms 500 per *man*; cloves 800 per *man*; turmeric 15 per *man*; dry ginger 25 per *man*; cinnamon (Ceylonese) 200 per *man*; cinnamon (Mangalore) 45 per *man*; camphor 120 per *man*; incense of aloes wood 115 per *man*; tin 100 per *man*; copper 90 per *man*; Basra stone 60 per *man*; lead 50 per *man*; sandalwood 80 per *man;* tobacco 25 per *man*; crimson dye 1,300 per *man*; gall or oak apple 35 per *man*; blue tutti 60 per *man*; nutmeg 1,200 per *man*; saffron 4 per *tola*; alum 22 per *man*; filbert-nut 130 per *man-i basra*; iron 120 per *man-i basra*; cotton 140 per *man-i basra*; almonds 95 per *man*; walnuts 15 per 1,000; pistachio 300 per *man-i basra*; raisins 90 per *man*; musk 15 per *misqal*; silk 1,300 per *man*; unground coffee 90 per *man*; meat 1½ per *waqiya*; dates 14 per *man-i basra*; grapes 2 per *waqiya*; pomegranates 2 per *waqiya*; cucumber 2 per *waqiya*; rice (first quality) 50 per *man-i basra*; rice (second quality) 32 per *man*; *rice* (third quality) 28 per *man*; wheat 31 per *man*; wheat flour 36 per *man*; *phaseolus mungo* 40 per *man*; millet 18 per *man*; loba (a kind of pulse) 30 per *man*; erveun lens 30 per *man*; beans 30 per *man*; per gram 60 per *man*.

Finer quality of rice of the Mysore variety is not available in Basra. The prices of the various articles do not remain constant, but fluctuate day to day.

1	*man-i-attar*	=	24 *waqiya*
1	*waqiya attar*	=	112 *misqal*
1	rupee	=	2½ *misqal*
1	*waqiya*	=	45 Rs. weight
1	*man-i basra*	=	24 *waqiya basra*
1	*waqiya basra*	=	3½ *waqiya attar*.

The crops raised in Basra are as follows: dates, grapes, quince, pomegranates, wheat, rice, peaches, beans, different kinds of pulses, figs, apricots, different varieties of oranges, sweet and sour lemons, brinjal, white pumpkins, fenugreek, purslain, *hibiscus belmoschus* (lady's fingers), cumber, raddish, petha (a kind of gourd), onions, dry and fresh coriander, *rubia manjith*, *soya*, rozella, apples, mulberry fruit, millet, gram, and garlic.

The crows of Basra are black and white or just black. Unlike Indian crows they do not live near human habitations but in the desert.

The names of the quarters of Basra are : in the south Mishraq, Kawazi, Manakh, Maidan ul-Abid; in the west Qiblah, Sharabati, Mohallat ul-Zahab, Sif, where the *Mutesellim* lives, and Majmua; in the north Nazran, Ras ul-Jisr, Mohallat ul-Jisr. Mohallat uz-Zajjah, Majmuah, Minavi and Maqam Ali; in the east Jisr ul-Abid, Muhallah Murad Pasha, Muhallah Hush ul-Pasha, Muhallah Khan ud-Dohn, Simar and Jisr ul-Khauz.

The following are the names of the bazaars of Basra: Suq ul-Mazarah, where broad-cloth and other requirements of the soldiers are sold; Suq ul-Qazzazah, for silk and materials for embroidery; Suq ul-Bazazah, where white cloth and other things are sold; Khan Shustariyya, for cloth and other things and where caravans from Shustar arrive here; Suq ul-Pahpahaniyya for tailors; Suq ul-Mishraq, where everything, except cloth, can be purchased; Suq ul-Hidaratiyya, where knives, pens, caps and iron goods are sold; Suq us-Safafir, for copper; Suq ul-Shabatiyya, for earthenware vessels; Suq ul-Himarah for camels, horses and sheep; Suq uz-Zahab, for fish, poultry, vegetables and greens; Suq us-Sif, near the residance of the *Mutesellim*, for wheat and other grains; Suq ul-Attatir, for scents; Suq us-Simar, where every article except cloth is sold; Suq ul-Qattan, for cotton; Suq Jisr ul-Abid, for everything; Suq ul-Hindi, ditto; Suq ul-Hindi is situated to the west of the town on a canal, and some Indians live there.

The names of the notables of Basra are. The *Mutesellim*, the *Qazi*, the *Mufti*, the *Naqib Ashraf*, Ibrahim Agha, Shaikh Ahmad, Sayyid Mahmud, Shaikh Maruf, Haji Muhammad, the *Defterdar*, Ali Agha, Mustafa Pasha (Haji Jawwad), the Kaptan Pasha, Ismail Agha, the customs officer, Ahmad Chelebi and Abdullah Yahudi.

Basra has ten large and innumerable small mosques.[38] It has 89 coffee-houses which are open and 34 unoccupied. The number of Turkish baths is 9 and that of the barbers' shops 35. There are also a large number of tombs. The number of large and small houses is 100,000. From the Zubair Gate to the canal many houses are in ruins. In the whole town over half of the houses are in a dilapidated state.[39]

The *Waqai* ends with the departure of the embassy from Basra to Baghdad. But from a letter of Ali Raja of Cannanore, addressed to Tipu Sultan, which is appended to the *Waqai*, we are told that the envoys left Constantinople happily with robes of honour and letters, and proceeded to Madina: There Nurullah was detained because of his illness. But the others took ship from Jeddah, for Masqat, and were expected to reach Mangalore soon. After the departure of the envoys, Sultan Hamid died and was succeeded by Sultan Mahmud. On Friday, in the month of Shawwal, while the *khutbah* was being recited, an Indian assassinated the preacher. However, he was himself killed by the congregation. In Arabia, from the beginning of the month of Rabi I till the end of Shawwal, Luban, Abu Arish, Mocha, Huwaizah and other places were subjected to severe earthquake shocks which caused great human suffering and destruction of buildings.

Notes and References

1. The dates given in this work are according to Tipu Sultan's calendar which he introduced between January and June 1784. In the year 1787 he again reformed the calendar and gave it the name of *Mauludi* era. These changes were made by him because the *Hijra* years, being lunar years of twelve months each, were administratively inconvenient. Tipu mainly adopted the Hindu calendar in common use in Mysore, which had a cycle of 60 years, and gave new names to the cycle years and months (see for details, Henderson, *The Coins of Haidar Ali and Tipu Sultan*, also Mohibbul Hasan Khan, *History of Tipu Sultan*, Appendix D).

2. For notes on place-names and names of persons see Appendix B, and for notes on technical and non-Persian words see Appendix C.

2(a). *Hukm-namah* 1677 gives details of the staff of the embassy and of the different articles which were intended for presentation or for sale.

3. The envoys were required to proceed to Paris and London in order to persuade the kings of England and France not to help the Marathas and the Nizam against Tipu Sultan (Secret Proceedings, January 5, 1787, No.3).

4. The strength of the cavalry here appears to be exaggerated. See details for the strength of Tipu's army at different periods, Mohibbul Hasan Khan, *History of Tipu Sultan*, p. 28 n. 140 and pp. 351-52.

4(a). According to Manesty 200 candies of pepper and some piece-goods were sold at Masqat (I.O. Factory Records, Manesty to Court of Directors, 5 Sept. 1786, f. 248b).

5. This is the Mirani fort situated to the west of the Masqat harbour. Both the Mirani fort and the other fort known as Jalali are perched on rocks about 150 ft. above sea-level. They were built by the Portuguese to command the town and protect it both from the landward and seaward sides. The distance between these forts is about half a mile. Two other subsidiary defences were also constructed by the Portuguese and have been referred to in the *Waqai* as Jurra-i Kalan and Jurra-i Khurd.

6. The Waqai refers to the three gates of Masqat. Rimam (modern Riyam) is situated midway between Masqat town and Matrah. The ordinary land-route between Masqat and Matrah passes through Riyam. Shitab (modern Sidab) is about a mile south of Masqat. There is also a village bearing the same name. Kalbuh is about a quarter mile north-west of Masqat.

7. Wellsted, *Travels in Arabia*, vol. i, p. 18, writing in 1838 says that there were 1, 500 *banyas* in Masqat. He seems to have made the mistake of regarding every Indian there as a *banya*. The Hindus had a small temple in Masqat and enjoyed perfect freedom to observe their customs and religious rites and held almost an exclusive monopoly of pearl trade. The *banyas* were very prosperous. They also dealt in grain and textiles which they brought from India (Wellsted, *Travels in Arabia*, i, pp. 18-9; 21).

8. Compare this with Wellsted, *Travels in Arabia*, i, pp. 348; 351-52.

9. Ovington, *A Voyage to Surat in the Year 1689*, pp. 426-27, says: "The inhabitants of Muscat eat fish, meat (beef, mutton and camel's). . They grow abundant wheat, which might be properly made use of for their bread, but the dates are so plentiful, so pleasant and admired that they mix them with all their food and eat them instead

of bread, through all these parts of Arabia, with their fish and meat. See also Wellsted, *Travels in Arabia*, i, pp. 349-50.

10. The *Waqai* says that Ahmad had five sons, but Salil, *History of the Imams and Seyyids of Oman*, p. 188, adds two more names, Hilal and Muhammad, Hilal being the eldest and Muhammad the youngest.

11. When Said succeeded Ahmed in 1783, it resulted in a war of succeession with his brothers. But they were defeated by his eldest son, Hamid, who became the *de facto* ruler, and governed the kingdom from his capital of Masqat. Said however continued as Imam.

12. The statement in the *Waqai* of Said's naval strength is confirmed by Niebuhr, *Descriptions de l'Arabie*, p. 265. But in addition to the 4 large vessels and 8 men-of-war, the *Waqai* also mentions that the Imam possessed 8 small boats. These were, probably, employed for trade in the Persian Gulf and with the Malabar coast.

13. *The Waqai* refers to the import duties at Masqat which seem to have been determined on religious and national grounds. The Hindu merchants had to pay 8%. But those Hindus who had settled at Masqat paid 15 *ghaz* per month. Tipu Sultan received preferential treatment and paid 4%. The English, French and Portuguese merchants paid 5%, while the merchants from Persia and Arabia had to pay 6½%. Compare this with Niebuhr, p. 264, who says that the European merchants paid 5%, Muslims 7½% and *banyas* and Jews 9%. But Niebuhr does not refer to the duty on goods imported from Mysore because, when he wrote his work, trade relations had yet not been established between Haidar Ali, who was then ruler of Mysore, and Oman.

14. Compare with Wellsted, *Travels in Arabia*, i, pp. 288-91.

15. According to the *Waqai* Butayn was ruling Lahsa at that time. But this is incorrect. When Urayir, the Bani Khalid chief, died in 1774, he was succeeded by his eldest son, Butayn. The latter, however, was strangled by his brothers, Dujayn and Sadun. Then Sadun soon poisoned Dujayn and became Shaikh of Bani Khalid and ruled until 1785. But he was in turn defeated by one of the Bani Khalid chiefs, and, as a result, Abdul Muhsin and his nephews, Duwayhis and Muhammad, became rulers (1785-89). See Abu Hakima, p. 227ff.

16. These figures are inaccurate. I have not been able to find out on what basis the latitude and longitude has been calculated in the *Waqai*. The correct figures of latitude and longitude are:

Masqat: 23° 45′N 58° 35′E; Basra: 30° 31′N 47° 45′E;
Surat: 21° 2′N 72° 50′E; Lahari (Larry Bandar): 24° 55′N 67° 0′E;
Jusk; 24° 50′N 54° 50′E; Hormuz (Ormuz); 25° 0′N 55° 30′E;
Abu Shahr: 29° 0′N 50° 50′E; Khor Musa: 30° 29′N 48° 15′E
Khor Basra: 30° 30′E 47° 46′N;

16a. The *waqai* wrongly calls him Nasir. It was Nasr and not his father Nasir who was ruling Abu Shahr at this time.

17. Driven by the Turks from Basra, the Dutch came to Kharag where Baron Kniphausen built a fort of 4 bastions, each mounting 10 guns (*Selections from State Papers*, Bombay....1600-1800, No. ixix, pp.90-91 also Niebuhr, pp. 277 ff.).

18. The monuments at Kharag are not genuine, but were erected in memory and honour of the Imams and saints, though none of them is buried there. Some of the chur-

ches which the Portuguese built during the period of their rule were converted into tombs (Ives, *A Voyage to India in the year 1754* etc., p. 208).

19. The Dutch made the island of Kharag prosperous, but after their departure, owing to the cruelties of Mir Muhanna, it lost its trade, became impoverished and deserted.

20. Mir Muhanna was not assassinated on his way to Basra, but was put to death by order of the Pasha of Baghdad (see *supra*, p. 21.)

20.(a). Manesty says that between 40 and 50 persons perished. In addition 400 candies of pepper, a small quantity of sandalwood and other articles were also lost. The articles which remained with the envoys were 600 candies of pepper, 50 candies of sandalwood and 15 candies of cardamoms (I.O. Factory Records, Manesty to Court of Directors, 5 Sept. 1786, f. 248b).

21. Nawwab Asaf ud-Daula (1775-97), ruler of Oudh, planned to construct a canal known as Nahr-i Hindia or Nahr-i Asafi in order to bring water from the Euphrates to Najaf, the burial place of Ali. The canal remained incomplete (*Travels of Abu Talib*, p. 339). Now Tipu Sultan wanted to finish the work, and his envoys were required to secure the permission of the Turkish Sultan for this.

22. See Appendix B s.v. for notes on these persons. It is strange that Manesty is not even once mentioned in the *Waqai*, although he was British Resident in Basra at this time and held that office until 1810, playing an important role in the politics of the province.

23. War between Haidar Ali and the English began in July 1780 with his invasion of the Carnatic. Haidar died on 7 December 1782, but the war was continued by his son and successor, Tipu Sultan. It ended with the conclusion of the Treaty of Mangalore on 11 March, 1784. In history this conflict is known as the Second Anglo-Mysore War.

24. The envoys were required to proceed to France from Constantinople, but as they took a long time reaching the Ottoman capital, another mission was sent direct from Mysore to France (for details of this embassy, see Mohibbul Hasan Khan, *History of Tipu Sultan*, pp. 132-38). Moreover, the French government did not want that these envoys should visit France, so they were recalled from Constantinople (see Appendix A).

25. Muhammad Hanif was in charge of the sale of goods which the envoys had brought. He died of fever in Kharag Island.

26. *Fath ul-Mujahidin* was written by Zain ul-Abidin Shushtari, a courtier of Tipu Sultan.. It deals with the rules, regulations and organization of the Sultan's army. The envoys were carrying the book by order of the Sultan for their guidance, MSS of this work are scattered in various libraries of India and Europe.

26. (a). Manesty says that a violent gust of wind destroyed the boats, and with them the principal part of the crew perished (I.O. Factory Records, Manesty to Court of Directors 20 Dec. 1786. f. 266a).

(b). Manesty also says that the envoys left with 300 men. But he gives the date of their departure as 7 December instead of 8 Dec. (Ibid).

27. This refers to the British Consulate which was situated on the right bank of the Shatt ul-Arab, a little below the mouth of the creek, Nahr ul-Ashar (see map of Basra).

28. This refers to the rebellion of Haji Sulaiman al-Shawi, the chief of the Ubaid and head of the Shawi family. He was on friendly terms with Sulaiman Pasha, but was jealous at the advancement of Ahmad Agha, a Georgian, whom Sulaiman

Pasha made his *Kahya.* Meanwhile, Ahmad Agha succeeded in turning the Pasha against the Shawi chief. As a result the latter's property was seized, and he was ordered to leave Baghdad. The Shawi chief fled to his tribe and rose in revolt. He defeated the troops of the Pasha, and hovered around Baghdad ready to attack it. Meanwhile, a sudden rumour spread that he had been appointed Pasha of Baghdad. For a time Sulaiman Pasha believed it (Longrigg, *Four Centuries of Modern Iraq*, pp. 203-04). It is to this rumour that reference is made in the *Waqai*. The conditions of half-blockade and insecurity continued around Baghdad, and that was one of the reasons why the progress of the embassy was delayed.

29. The original city of Basra was built on the site of modern Zubair by the Companion of the Prophet, 'Utba b. Ghazwan in 17/638. It was abandoned in the 13th century due to the Mongol invasion and conquest of Iraq. The new city of Basra was gradually transferred to another site 12 miles further east (see *Encyclopaedia of Islam*, s.v).

30. This refers to the residence of the English agent.

31. The *Waqai* gives a vivid description of the mosque built by Ali. The Arabic historians attribute the Great Mosque not to Ali but to Ziyad, Muawiya's governor. According to al-Harawi the minaret and south wall only were ascribed to Ali (Gibb, *Ibn Battuta*, ii, p. 275 n. 19).

32. All these graves are today three miles distant from the town.

33. The *Waqai* does not mention here the Indian merchants of Basra. But later it says that some Indians lived in Suq ul-Hindi. According to Niebuhr, ii, p. 180, there were Hindu *banyas* and about one hundred Indian families in Basra.

34. When Karim Khan's forces, which were sent under his brother, Sadiq Khan, besieged Basra in 1775, the Imam Ahmad b. Said set out with his navy composed of the *Rahmani*, on which he himself embarked, 70 galleots and trankies and 50 dhows full of men. The Imam having failed to compel the Persians to raise the siege of Basra, returned to Masqat at the end of 1775 (Miles, *The Countries and Tribes of the Persion Gulf*, ii, p. 272).

35. The *Waqai* says that owing to the friendly relations existing between the Turks and the Imam of Oman and because of the help he gave them against the Persians, his goods imported into Basra paid 3 per cent. The goods belonging to Tipu also paid at the same rate. But other traders paid 8½ per cent. The report of the English Company's agent at Basra, however, does not make any reference to the preferential treatment given to Tipu or the Imam. It mentions that the finer goods imported from Baghdad and by sea paid 7 per cent, while the gruff goods paid 8½ per cent. But goods belonging to the English Company and individual English men paid an import duty of only 3 per cent because of the special privilege granted by the Ottoman government. (*Selections from State Papers*, Bombay, Appendix F, p. 411) This was in 1790. But Niebuhr for the earlier period gives different figures. According to him European merchants trading in Basra who brought goods from India paid 3 per cent. All other nations paid 7 per cent (Niebuhr, ii, p. 92).

36. Suwaini was very powerful at this time. In 1785 he had captured Basra and imprisoned the *Mutesellim*, Ibrahim Beg. A 'loan' of 6,000 *tumans* was demanded from the inhabitants of Basra. It was not till late October 1788 that Ṣuwaini's forces were defeated by the troops sent from Baghdad, and Basra was re-occupied. Mustafa Agha, a Kurd, was appointed *Mutesellim* (Longrigg, *Four Centuries of Modern Iraq*, pp. 204-05).

37. The *Waqai* refers to the chaos prevailing in Basra during this period. There was

great inefficiency and corruption in the administration. Most of the revenue went into the pockets of officials or Suwaini. Life and property were unsafe, and there was no political stability. These facts are all corroborated by the contemporary accounts.

38. According to Niebuhr, ii, p. 172, there were 9 large mosques and 40 small ones.

39. The number of deserted houses was so large because of the insecurity caused by the Persian occupation of Basra and the tribal incursions. Niebuhr, who visited the town during its days of prosperity, says that it had 70 *mohallas* or quarters, some of them having 300 or 400 houses and others 10 to 20 only. The total population of Basra, according to Niebuhr, was 50,000. Rousseau, p. 32, also gives the same figure. Ives, p. 231, who visited Basra in 1758-59, says that the town contained between sixty and seventy thousand inhabitants.

APPENDIX A

The envoys left Basra by the Tigris route on 10 February, 1787,[1] with a retinue of 400 men, including 200 sepoys trained in the European fashion. The three hundred thousand rupees and the rich presents which they carried had created a sensation in the country. When they reached Baghdad on 25 April, escorted by 500 horsemen who had been sent to meet them at Samawah, they were received by Sulaiman Pasha with great honour. From Baghdad they went to pay visits to Najaf and Karbala, and returned after twenty days.[2] They set out from Baghdad on 29 May, escorted by the *qapji bashj* sent by the Sultan from Constantinople. They travelled overland via Mosul and Diarbeker and reached Scutari on the 1st September. They entered Constantinople on the 25th, and were lodged in one of the palaces of the city. On the 1st October the Grand Wazir granted them a public audience, but received them without any extraordinary ceremony. They presented to him rich dresses, jewellery and 70,000 Venetian sequins. In return they received robes of honour.[3] Later, the Grand Wazir gave a magnificent fete in their honour at the village of Kelhana, where first the Turkish soldiers performed their exercises, and then "the Indian sepoys went through the European exercises with great regularity and quickness." All the high officials were present at the function, and the Sultan himself was also there incognito.[4]

On 5 November the Sultan received the envoys with honour and invested them with sable furs, and the two secretaries with ermine furs.[5] Meanwhile plague had broken out in Constantinople, and many persons belonging to the embassy died. The severe cold weather, to which the Mysorians were not accustomed, also took a heavy toll of their lives. So that by the end of January 1788, out of their retinue of 400 men, only 70 had survived. Ghulam Ali Khan was dangerously ill. For a change of climate, therefore, the envoys moved to Scutari on the Asian coast.[6]

It has been mentioned in the Introduction that the envoys were required to proceed from Constantinople to France and thence to England. Accordingly, after their arrival at the Ottoman capital, they began to press the French ambassador to make arrangements for their journey to France.[7] Meanwhile Tipu had sent a mission directly to France. It had stayed there for over five months and cost the French exchequer a large sum of money. The French government was therefore not prepared to receive another mission, particularly in view of the worsening economic situation in the country. Moreover, the French government had changed its policy in India, and it looked upon a second embassy from Tipu not only serving no purpose, but likely to involve it in an embarrassing position *vis-a-vis* England to whom it had assured not to give any cause of provocation.[8] Le comte de Montmorin, therefore, advised the French am ba ssador in Constantinople to dissuade Tipu's envoys from proceeding to Paris. But if they insisted in coming, they were to be informed that they would be treated like the envoys of any other foreign power, and that no special treatment would be shown to them as had been done in the case of the first embassy.[9] Owing to these reasons the envoys gave up the idea of going to France and decided to return to India. Meanwhile Tipu had also sent instructions to them to return.

On 4 March the envoys had a farewell audience of the Sultan,[10] and at the end of the month they sailed for Alexandria. From there they proceeded up the Nile to Cairo, and thence crossed to Suez. From Suez they sailed to Jeddah, and then went to Mecca and Madina to make the pilgrimage according to the instructions of Tipu Sultan.[88] After this they set out on their homeward journey from Madina via Jeddah and reached Calicut on 29 Decenber, 1789. They arrived at Tipu's camp in the neighbourhood of the Travancore Lines early in January 1790.

The embassy had cost the Mysore state a huge sum of money, and in addition the envoys had suffered all kinds of privations in the course of their journey. Three of the four boats in which they had travelled to Basra had been wrecked, causing great loss of life and property. Many of their retinue had died of dysentery, fever, cold and plague, Out of about 900 men, who had left the shores of Malabar, only a handful returned to their homes.

Despite the enormous expense, great suffering and loss of life, the embassy had been able to secure from the Ottoman Sultan only the letters patent, which gave Tipu permission to assume the title of an independent king, and the right to strike coins and to have the *khutba* read in his name. The envoys were also given for Tipu friendly letters and *khilats* from the Caliph and his *Wazir*, and a sword and a shield studded with precious stones as presents.[12] But the embassy failed to obtain either any commercial privileges or military help. This was due to two reasons. First, Turkey was not in a position to give any assistance, because she was fighting for her very existence against Russia and Austria, who had entered into an agreement with each other in 1787 to partition the European provinces of the Ottoman Empire. Secondly, the Sultan could not accept the proposals of the envoys because of his anxiety not to displease the British, who were his allies. The contemporary sources do not throw much light on the British attitude towards this embassy. But judging from their relations with Tipu Sultan, it could not have been anything but hostile. Manesty, the English agent at Basra, writing to the Court of Direction on 5 September, 1786, observed : "The *Wakil*s want to obtain *firmans* to establish factories in Turkish dominions for selling the produce of his kingdom. We think this is a circumstance very material for the Honourable Court of Directors to be acquainted with, as we apprehend it precludes all hopes of your servants at Tellicherry being able to provide pepper for your homeward ships."[13] It is obvious from this statement that the British could not have watched with complaisance the activities and plans of the ambassadors. On the contrary. they must have done their best to frustrate them with the help of the influence which they commanded both at Baghdad and Constantinople.

References

1. *Factory Records* (India office), *Persia and the Persian Gulf*, No. 18 ; Manesty to Court of Directors, 15 March, 1787, f. 286.
2. *Affaires Etrangeres* Bl 107 (Archives Nationales, Paris), Rousseau to Castries, 25 April, 1787, No. 39 ; also British Foreign Office Records (cited hereafter as F.O.) 78/8-1787, Robert Ainslie to Carmathian, 9 June, 1787, f. 96b.
3. Ibid., 20 Oct., 1787, ff. 216b-17a.
4. Ibid. 25 Oct., 1787, f. 235a.
5. Ibid. 10 Nov., 1787, f. 241a.
6. Ibid., 78/9-1788, 25 Jan., 1788, ff. 22a-b.
7. *Affaires Etrangeres* Bl 448, *Correspondance Consulaire—Constantinople*-1787-90 (Archives Nationales, Paris), Choiseul-gouffier to de la Luzerne, 30 Oct., 1788.
8. F.O. 27/29, Dorset to Carmathian, 7 Aug., 1788, No. 55.
9. *Affaires Etrangeres—Turquie* (Archives Nationales, Paris), Montmorln to Choisieul-gouffier, 22 Aug., 1788, vol. 178. f. 44a.
10. F.O. 78/9-1788, 8 March, 1788, f. 63b.
11. Ibid., 15 and 25 March, 1788, ff. 68a, 76b.
12. *Waqai*, f. 123a ; also Kirmani, *Tarikh Saltanat-i Khudadad*, p. 328.
13. *Factory Records* (India Office), Manesty to Court of Directors, 5 Sept., 1786, No. 18, f. 249a.

APPENDIX B

NOTES ON PERSONS AND PLACE-NAME OCCURRING IN THE PERSIAN TEXT

Abbadan, also called Jazirat ul-Khizr from a shrine near its centre, is an important island enclosed by the Karun river, the Shatt ul-Arab, the Persian Gulf and the Bahmanshir.

Abdullah was the son of Shaikh Sabah, the founder of the family's greatness. He succeeded his father in 1762 and ruled as Shaikh of Kuwait until 1812.

Abdullah, the Jewish banker, played a very important part in the economic and political life of Iraq at this time. He enjoyed the confidence of both Ibrahim Agha and Sulaiman Pasha.

Abdullah, the son of Umar, the second Caliph, was a prominent personality of the first generation of Muslims. But he was not energetic and remained aloof from politics. He died in 73/693 (see for details E.I., s.v.)

Abu 'Arish, 16° 57′N, 42° 50′ E, lies about 25 miles inland.

Abu Mughaireh, a village on the right bank of the Shatt ul-Arab.

Abu Silal, a place outside Basra.

Abul Khasib, a large town in 'Iraq, on the south side of the Shatt ul-Arab, midway between Basra and Muhammareh.

Ahmad al-Khalifa, the son of Khalifah of the Utbi tribe, was ruling Bahrain and Zubarah at this time. It was Ahmad who conquered Bahrain in 1782 from the Persians, while his father was away on a a pilgrimage to Mecca. He succeeded to the Shaikhdom on his father's death in 1783 and ruled until his death in 1796. He was succeeded by his son Salman who ruled until 1825. (see A. Hakima, p. 204)

'Ammiyah, a wide canal south of Basra with many gardens on both sides.

'Ali al-Raza, the eighth Imam of the Shias, also called Musa Raza the was, son of Musa al-Kazim, and was born in 765 or 770 in Madina. The Caliph al-Mamun, while at Merv, summoned him, nominated him his heir, and gave him the title of al-Raza. Ali al-Raza died suddenly at Tus in September 818, having been poisoned by al-Mamun. His mausoleum (*mashhad*) has given its name to the town, supplanting the old name of Tus. (see E.I., s.v.)

Ali Asghar was the youngest son of Husain, the son of the Caliph Ali. He was only six months old when he was killed in the arms of his father by an arrow from Hurmula, a soldier in the army of Yazid I. His tragic death is celebrated every year during the first ten days of the month of Muharram.

Anas b. Malik (d. 710) was, as a young boy, the personal servant of the Prophet Muhammad, and the last survivor of the Companions (see E. I., s.v.).

Bahmishir is a natural mouth of the Karun. Locally it is called Bahman-shīr or Bahmānshīr. The channel between the mouth of the river and the open sea is called Khor Bahmanshir.

Bahrgan, in lat. 30°′ N, Long. 40° 30′ E, is on the coast of Persia.

Bait Hindi lies near Hudayyidah.

Bait ul-Qasr lies near al-Hudayyidah, 14° 48′ N, 42° 57′ E.

Baljaniyah. a populated place at 30° 26′ N, 48° 06′ E.

Banak is on the Shibkuh coast of Persia, situated three miles off Kangun, and 2 miles inland.

Bandar Luban or Bandar Itab lies nearly halfway between Qishm and Sayhut on the southern coast of Arabia. "It is a slight blight which affords some shelter from the north easterly winds. "(*Sailing directions, Red Sea and Gulf of Aden*, Hydrographic Office, U.S. Navy, H.O. Pub. and 157, p. 279)

Bani Lam, a numerous and important Arab tribe found chiefly in Iraq, but also to some extent in Khuzistan. The Bani Lam country proper is the plain between the Persian hills (or Pusht-i kuh) and the left bank of the Tigris from a point opposite Shaikh Saad down to Amarah town. In Iraq, however, parties of the tribe are found scattered elsewhere also.

Banu Tamim Ansari, a large and powerful Arab tribe of Muntafiq origin who live in tents in the drier parts of the country between the Karun, Shatt ul-Arab and Tigris rivers. In their mode of life they differ from the other Arab tribes of Khuzistan. Their territory in southern Khuzistan includes mostly the right bank of the Karun river (*Gazetteer, of the Persian Gulf* vol. ii, p. 5)

Baraim is a village situated on the west shore of Abbadan island from the confluence of the Karun river and the Shatt ul-Arab to the sea.

Baraziah, a village on the right bank of the Shatt ul-Arab not far from Basra.

Barkah, a large town on the Batinah coast of the Oman Sultanate, lying west by north of the Oman Sultanate.

Bhongir, a town in Nalgonda district, is the headquarters of the *taluq* of the same name, and an important centre of trade. In the Nalgonda district coarse cotton cloth is made and cotton fabrics are exported. The cloth made in Bhongir was called *bhongiri.*

Boonbai is modern Bombay, as known to Europeans, and Bumbai, as called by the Indians. Various versions have been given by English and Portuguese writers about the origin of the name Bombay. But none of them is correct, Bombay or Bumbai is derived from the shrine of Mumba Devi, patron deity of the earliest inhabitants of the island. (*Gazetter of Bombay City and Island,* pp. 19-21 Vol. 9. Bombay 1909).

Buchabdah or Bukabdah is, probably, Kabdah point 30° 10′N, 48° 25′E.

Bustaneh is not an island but a cape. The diary usually identifies an island with a cape. The village of Bustaneh is situated 15 miles west by south of Lingeh town.

Chabdah or Kabdah, a village belonging to the Dawasir district on the west coast of the Shatt ul-Arab (see for more details, *Persian Gulf Pilot*, pp. 290 ff.)

Chaab or Kaab ('K' being softened in speech) are the largest and most important tribe in south Khuzistan. They are Arabs but they have become greatly Persianised. They form almost the entire population of the Fallahiyah district, and occupy the greater part of the Abbadan island. They live in Fao on the left bank of the Bahmanshir. The original home of the Kaab is said to have been Najd, from where they made their way to Arabistan in the seventeenth century, and occupied settlements of the Afshar Turks. Their power increased rapidly and, in the middle of the eighteenth century, they seized Dauraq and Fallahiyah from the Afshars. Their success was mainly due to the energy and ability of their chief, Shaikh Sulaiman, who maintained his virtual independence by playing off the Turks and Persians against one another. The Kaab became a great source of trouble to the Turks, Persians and English. The Kaab pirates were active in the Shatt ul-Arab and the Persian Gulf. On account of their activities in the Basra region they remained a source of trouble to the *Mutesellem* of Basra till the end of the eighteenth century. (Niebuhr, *Descriptions de l' Arabie*, page 276 ; Niebuhr, *Voyage en Arabie*, ii, pp. 151, 186 ; also Iongrigg, *Four Centuries of Modern Iraq*, page 78 and n. 1).

Chelebi. According to Professor Gibb, Chelebi was a title applied to Sufi leaders in Anatolia as well as to princes and high officials. (Gibb, *Ibn Battuta*, ii, 424 n.46). But at Surat the Chelebis were members of an influential and wealthy family of foreign merchants. In the English Factory Records of the 17th and 18th centuries, there are constant references to this family. A mosque called Chalibini Masjid and another building known as Darya Mahal, which were built by the Chelebi family, still exist at Surat. (see Forrest, *Selections..in the Bombay Secretariat*, Home Series, vol. I, pp. 241 ff ; J. J. Modi, *Rustam Manek and the Persian Qisseh*, in J.B.B.R.A.S., vol. VI (New Series) pp. 38-40.

Daaiji, a large village situated on the right bank of the Shatt ul-Arab, about 2½ miles up a great creek the mouth of which is nearly 11 miles from Basra.

Dawasir, a village near Kabda (see for details, *Persian Gulf Pilot*, 292).

Dilam, situated about 85 miles north-north-west of Abu Shahr, was a Dutch trading port in the 18th century, but is now an unimportant fishing village.

Fah is probably Fao or al-Faw, situated near the mouth of the Shatt ul-Arab, 20° 58′ N, 48° 29′ E.

Failakah, an island lying on the northern side of the entrance to the Kuwait bay.

Faiyazi is in the Muhammareh *boluk;*.

Bagi is Abu Ibgai, a tract situated on the right bank of the Shatt ul-Arab, reaching from the Abul Khasib creek to a point 1½ miles further down stream.

Farur, an island, 20 miles south of the Shibkuh port of Mughu. To the English navigators it was at one time known as "Polior."

Ganava or Ganaveh is not an island, as described in the diary, but a small port. It comprises a group of three villages on the coast of the Persian district of Hayat Davud, 15 miles north-west of the town of Rig. (*Gazetteer of the Persian Gulf*, ii, 563). To the East of Ganaveh are the ruins of Jannabah which in the middle ages was an important port (see also *Geog. Hand Book Series—Persia*, Sept. 1945 Naval Intelligence Division, p. 124).

Gardilan, a creek and large village on the left bank of the Shatt ul-Arab at Basra.

Hadd, a small village on the left bank of the Shatt ul-Arab in the Muhammareh *boluk*.

Haji Jawwad was the Kaptan Pasha and an important personality of Basra at this time.

Hamdan, a town on the south side of the Shatt ul-Arab about 2/7 of the way from Basra to Muhammareh town.

Hamrah, an island and village, 12 miles south-west of Ras ul-Khaimah town in Trucial Oman.

Hanjam, an island situated off the south coast of Qishm Island. After rain, some water can be had from the ruined reservoirs at the north end, and there is a well of fairly good water near the village, about ¼th of a mile from the south-east point of the island (*Persian Gulf Pilot*, 213). The diary refers to the drinking water that was obtained from the island.

Hasan al-Basri, the son of a Persian *Mawla*, was born in 21/642. He was a great theologian, and had a reputation for piety, learning and eloquence. He exercised great influence on the development of Sufism. He died on 1st Rajab, 110/10 October, 728 (for details see E.I., s.v.).

Hillah ('the settlement') was founded by the Shia Arab, Shaikh Sadaqa b. Mazyad, in 1102, as the capital of a minor Arab principality in lower Iraq. Thanks to its bridge, it became an important station on the route from Baghdad to the Hijaz (Gibb, *Ibn Battuta*, ii, p. 324, n. 174).

Hormuz or Ormuz, an island situated south-east of Bandar Abbas. It was captured by the Portuguese from the Persians in 1507, but was recovered by the latter in 1622 with English help. Hormuz, which had been enjoying great prosperity for several centuries, began to decay after 1522. Shah Abbas, the Persian ruler, tried to divert the trade and population of Hormuz to the small fishing village of Gombrun to which he gave his own name. (see Wilson, *The Persian Gulf*, pp. 116 ff.).

Husain, the son of Ali and of Fatimah, the daughter of the Prophet, was the third Shia Imam. He refused to pay homage to Yazid I, and so was cruelly slain, along with many of his relations and companions, at Karbala in 61 A.H.

Huwaizah or Hawizah lies in a marshy plain, seventy miles north of Muhammareh (Khurramshahr).

Ibrahim Agha became the *Mutesellim* of Basra in 1785. He was imprisoned by Suwaini who occupied Basra on 6 May, 1787. Ibrahim Agha, with the principal Basra officials, was later released by Suwaini on receiving a large sum of money, which was advanced bythe English Company's agent, Manesty. Ibrahim Agha went away to Abu Shahr (Factory Records. I. O. vol. 18, ff. 356a, 318b).

Imam Said belonged to the Saidi dynasty of Oman which was established in 1749 by Ahmad b. Said, a merchant and shipowner, after he had overthrown the Yaarabi dynasty. Ahmad b. Said was a powerful ruler. He died in 1785 and was succeeded by his second son, Said, who was weak and incompetent. As a result there was confusion and anarchy in the country and an attempt was made to set up his brother Qais on the throne. However, his eldest son, Hamid, defeated his rivals. He acted as Regent and governed the kingdom with firmness and ability from his capital of Masqat until his death on 13 March, 1792. His father, Said, however remained an Imam and continued to perform the spiritual duties of his office from his capital of Rustaq until his death in about 1821 (see for details, Miles, *Countries and Tribes of the Persian Gulf*, i, 265-66 and ii, 282 ff).

Jafar Khan was the son of Sadiq Khan, brother of Karim Khan. He occupied the throne of Persia in 1785 and ruled until his assassination on 23 January, 1789.

Jalali was built by the Portuguese and is situated at the south-eastern corner of the Masqat harbour. Jalali fort is now used as a local jail.

Jang-i Jamal was the famous battle of the Camel, so called because of the Camel on which Aishah, the widow of the Prophet Muhammad, rode, and which was the rallying-point for the insurgents against Ali's forces.

Jask or Jashk, a small port 140 miles south-east of Bandar Abbas, is situated on the Makran coast. It was the original Gulf station of the English East India Company.

Jazira-i Tawil is the Qishm island, which is thelargest island in the Persian Gulf. The Arabs call it Jazira-i Tawilah and the Persians Jazira-i Daraz (Ousley, *Travels*, ', p. 162 fn.).

Kangun is the northernmost of the Shibkuh ports of the Persian coast in the province of Fars.

Karbala, a town in Iraq, 10 miles south-south-west of Baghdad. It is celebrated as the scene of the martyrdom of Husain and the place of his shrine. Shias from all over the world make their pilgrimage to it.

Karim Khan-i Zand, chief of a small tribe in Western Persia, rose to power in 1750. He occupied practically the whole of Persia except Khurasan, and made Shiraz his capital. He, however, did not assume the title of king, but called himself *Wakil* of the blind Shahrukh, Nadir Shah's grandson. In 1775 his brother Sadiq Khan, besieged Basra, which surrendered in 1776. It remained under Persian rule until his death in 1779. Under his rule Persia achieved peace and prosperity.

Kemball, Lt. was British Assistant Resident in the Persian Gulf.

Khain is Khaiyain, a village marking the boundary between Iraq and Iran. It is on the right bank of the Shatt ul-Arab in the Muhammareh *boluk*.

Khamir, a large village situated on the coast of Bastak district of Persia. Three miles north-west of Khamir are mountains which have deposits of sulphur to which reference has been made in the diary.

Khan is really a shoal situated between the islet of Nakhilu and the Persian coast. It is an excellent haven for native boats and is used as such by the people of the nearest mainland villages.

Kharabeh, a small village on the Shibkuh coast of Persia, quite close to Dastur.

Kaus or Qaws, a populated place, 30° 25′ N, 48° 06′ E.

Kazimain, a town near Baghdad, one of the most celebrated of Shia places of pilgrimage. It means "the two Kazims." This refers to Musa al-Kazim and Muhammad al-Jawwad, the seventh and ninth Shia Imams who are buried there. (see E.I., s.v.).

Kharij, modern Kharag, an island. The Arabs call it Kharij. The Europeans called it Karrack, Kharrak or Carrack. (*The Island of Kharag*, Asiatic Journal, Sept.-Dec. 1838). The Persians call it Khark (Razmara, vii, p. 61). It has been occasionally referred to in the diary as Jazira-i-Mubarak because of the numerous monuments erected there in remembrance and honour of the Imams and saints, (Ives, *Voyage from England to India*, 208). It is situated about 34 miles north-west of Abu Shahr and is of some importance in the Persian Gulf. The

Dutch in 1753, having been driven out of Basra by English intrigues with the Ottoman government, established themselves on this island. The Dutch factor, Baron Kniphausen built a fort here and made the island very prosperous. But in January 1766 the Dutch were driven out by the Arab corsair, Mir Muhanna. (see for details Niebuhr, *Description de I' Arabie.* 277 ff).

Khast is a village situated on the river about midway between the two ends of the Saihan tract.

Khawarij, modern Khargu, is an island. The Arabs call it Khawairij, and the Persians Kharku (Razmara, vii, 61) It is a very low, white sandy island, situated north of the Kharag island.

Khazail, a large tribe which occupied an area extending from Kufa to Samawah and a portion of the adjoining Shamiyah desert. They are strong and warlike, and are all Shiites. They were a great source of trouble to the Turkish government because they interrupted communications between Basra and Baghdad by the Euphrates river. (*Description du Pachalik de Baghdad*, 59 ; *Bombay Selections* (1600-1800) p. 324).

Khizr or al-Khazir, literally "the green one", is the immortal wandering saint of the Muslim legend. He is supposed to have discovered and drunk of the fountain of life. He is regarded by many Muslims as a Prophet. (See E.I., s.v.).

Khoja Petrus Mellick, a broker of the English East India Company at Basra.

Khor Faqqan is modern Khor Fakkan, a town on the Oman coast with a good harbour and protected by two small islets. It is 75 miles north of Suhar.

Khor Musa is situated 20 miles east of Bahmanshir. It is a deep channel about 12 miles wide in the tidal flats. It winds inland for 50 miles.

Khumaiseh, a small village on the right bank of the Shatt ul-Arab in the Muhammareh *boluk*.

Khwajah Bandah Nawaz, a Chishti saint who was born in Delhi on 2 Rajab 721/ 30 July 1321. His real name was Sadr ud-Din Husaini, but he is commonly known by the title of Gisu Daraz (one with long locks of hair) which his *pir*, Shaikh Nasir ud-Din Chiragh Dehlvi, had given him. He migrated to Gulbargah from Delhi during the reign of Sultan Firuz Shah-Bahmani. He died in 825/1422 and was buried in Gulbargah, where Ahmad Shah Bahmani built a beautiful tomb over his grave. Gisu Daraz is said to have been the author of 105 books (see E.I. (New) s.v.).

Kut ul-Ju, a village about 3½ miles from Basra on the left bank of the Shatt ul-Arab.

Labani, a small village on the right bank of the Shatt ul-Arab, about 12 miles by water from Basra.

Lahsa, Hasa or al-Ahsa oasis is about 36 miles long from north to south and its breadth is about 20 miles The eastern boundary of the oasis approaches within about 30 miles of the Persian Gulf coast of Oqair. (see for details Le Strange, *Lands of the Eastern Caliphate*, 87 ff ; also *Gazetteer of the Persian Gulf*, Vol., ii, 642).

Laja is probably Umm Lajj, 25° 05 'N, 42° 13′ E.

Lajir is al-Ojair or al-Uqair, 25 32′ N, 50 12 'E, a port about 6¼ miles south—west of Qatif town.

Larak is a barren island in the Persian Gulf, 20 miles south-east of Bandar Abbas.

Lima is near cape Musandam (Forster, *Historical Geography-of Arabia*, ii, 226 n.).

Linga is Lingeh, a town on the Persian coast, situated 96 miles south-west of Bandar Abbas.

Machhli Bandar, now Masulipatam, headquarters of Kistna district in Andhra Pradesh. It is a small seaport and was an early European settlement.

Machira, now Masirah, is a large island, 40 miles long and 10 miles broad, situated off the south-eastern coast of Oman. A chain of hills traverses Masirah longitudinally, while shorter spurs protrude in different directions. It is to these hills and spurs that the diary refers.

Mahallah, an island near the larger village of Harta.

Mama Salamah of the Arabs and Persians is the Ras (or cape) Mussendom of Euorpean sailors (Ousley, *Travels*, i, 154 m.). It is an island adjoining the north-eastern tip of the Ruus ul-Jibal promontory, from which it is separated by a narrow strait. At its north end Musandam terminates in a cliff, the celebrated cape, Ras Musandam.

Manavi, a large village suburb of Basra.

Manyuhi, a stretch of date plantations extending 15 miles along the Shatt ul-Arab on the west shore of the Abbadan island.

Maqam Ali, a quarter of Basra.

Matrah is situated on the south-west side of the Matrah Bay and is about 2 miles west of Masqat town. It is commercially an important town in Oman.

Mir Muhanna, belonging to the Bani Saab, who were of Omani origin, was a chief of the coastal district north of Abu Shahr with his headquarters at Bandar Rig. He strangled his father to death in 1758. His relations with the Ottomans were good. But he refused allegiance to Karim Khan of Persia and gave him a great deal of trouble. Brave but extremely cruel, he interrupted communications between Shiraz, Karim Khan's capital, and Abu Shahr, and carried on acts of piracy in the Persian Gulf. He was attacked by the combined forces of Karim Khan and the English in Kharag, the which he had seized from Dutch. He defeated his enemies several times, but in the end, pressed by Karim Khan, he fled to Kuwait where he was given refuge by the Utub. From there he went to Basra. He was received kindly by the *Mutesellim*, but on account of his past cruelties he was seized and strangled by order of the Pasha on 21 March 1769 (Parsons, *Travels in Asia and Africa*, 96-98; also Abu Hakima, 146 ff).

Moustier, Sieur, was a French dragoman at Basra.

Muhaijaran, a village two miles up a creek of the same name, situated on the Shatt ul-Arab.

Muhammad, the son of Abu Bakr, the first Caliph, was a partisan of Ali. He played an important part in the movement against Osman. He was Ali's governor of Egypt and was killed in 38 A.H./658 A.D. when Amr b. al-As, the partisan of Muawiya, invaded Egypt to occupy it on behalf of Muawiya.

Muhammad Hanif b. Ali is the same as Muhammad b. al-Hanafiya, a son of Ali and Khawwla, a woman of the tribe of Banu Hanifa. He was born in 16 A.H./637 A.D. He was of a retiring and quiet disposition. After the tragedy of Karbala, he was regarded by some as an Imam in succession to Husain. He died in about 81/700 (see E.I., s.v.).

Muhammad b. Khalfan, belonging to the influential family of the Al-Bu-Said, was made governor of Masqat by the Imam Said. He was able and ruled Masqat with severity tempered with justice.

Mukha or Mocha is a port in Yemen on the Red Sea. It was a great centre of trade in ancient times. (see Hitti, *History of Arabs*, 49).

Musa al-Kazim, the seventh Imam of the Shias. Son of Jafar b. Muhammad al-Sadiq, he was born about 745 A.D. in Madina, where he remained until his father's death. Though he was not interested in politics, yet the Caliph al-Mahdi imprisoned him. Harun al-Rashid had him brought to Baghdad where he died in prison in August-September 799.

Mutawa or Mutawaiyah, a tract which begins below Zain from which a creek divides it, and from this creek known as Mutawa creek it extends down the bank for 1½ miles.

Nabivah is the Nabiyu Tunb, a small uninhabited island without water, situated 8 miles west of the island of Tunb.

Nahr Amir, a canal in Basra. It was dug by the Caliph al-Mansur (see Yaqut's *Mujam al-Buldan*).

Nahr Khauz, also called Nahr Khaus, is a village on the right bank of the Shatt ul-Arab, 2 miles up a creek of the same name.

Nahr Shaikh is Nahr ush-Shaikh, a canal on the left bank of the Jarrahi. The settlement also bears the same name as the canal.

Nahr Yusuf is situated on the left bank of the Shatt ul-Arab and is in the Muhammareh *boluk*.

Najaf, a town in Iraq close to Baghdad. It is a place where Ali,the first Shia Imam, was buried, and is a great centre of pilgrimage for the Shias from all over the world.

Nijwa, modern Nizwa, a town of Oman, is situated near the fort of Jabal Akhdar. It had a fort which was one of the most important ones in the country.

Nirmal, a fortified town and headquarters of the same name in the Adilabad district. The weavers of the Adilabad district made coarse cloth (*Hyderabad Gazetteer*, 192-93) which was named as *nirmali* after the town.

Numan, a village near Barkah having a fort.

Qais, an important island, situated 11 miles off the coast of the Shibkuh district. The English formerly called it "Kaeese", "Ghes" or "Kenn" ; the Persians called it Kish (Le Strange, *Lands of the Eastern Caliphate*, 257 ; *Gazetteer of the Persian Gulf*, vol. ii, 147).

Qasim or Qawasim are a branch of the great Huwala clan and occupy the Persian coast from Bandar Abbas to Ras Berdistan. They got their name from Shaikh Qasim, the grand-father of Shaikh Rashid b. Matar, who was ruling at this time. Shaikh Rashid was succeeded by his son, Saqr. (Abu Hakima, 199).

Qatif, chief town in the Qatif Oasis on the coast of Eastern Arabia, is 36 miles north-west of the nearest part of Bahrain Island. It was an important centre of trade during this period.

Qism is Qishm, the chief town in Qishm island, is situated on its easternmost extremity.

Al-Qurain is the modern town of Kuwait.

Qurnah is a village situated at the junction of the Euphrates and Tigris rivers.

Rimam or Riyam, a village midway between Masqat and Matrah.

Rousseau, of Genevese origin, was born in Ispahan. He knew Arabic, Persian and Turkish. He joined the French East India Company at Basra and rendered valuable service. When, therefore, M. Tirault left for France in 1732 on leave, he nominated Rousseau in his place as the Company's agent. On May 1, 1733, Tirault died and so Rousseau became permanent. In 1784, Rousseau was transferred to Baghdad as French Consul. (Archives Nationales, *Affaires Etrangères* B[1] No. 197, *Correspondance Consulaire*—Bassorah).

Rumais, a small port in the Gulf of Oman about 32 miles east of Masqat.

Rustakh is Rustaq. It was the capital of Oman until 1793 when it was replaced by Masqat. It lies 90 miles west of it.

Sabiliyat, a village on the right bank of the Shatt ul-Arab, about 10 miles from Basra.

Sadiq Khan was the brother of Karim Khan. It was he who occupied Basra and ruled it for four years until his brother's death in 1779. He ruled Persia for a short time and was put to death with his sons, except Jafar, in March 1782.

Saihan is a village situated on the right bank of the river from Muhammareh to Fao.

Samail. This is Hisn Samail, an important place on the bank of Wadi Samail in Oman Sultanate.

Samarrah, a town in Iraq, situated on the left bank of the Tigris, 70 miles north-north-west of Baghdad. The 17th century mosque with its golden dome is sacred to the Shias.

Samulat is modern Samawah (31° 18 N, 45° 17 E), an important town in Iraq, situated on the Euphrates.

Saraji, a village on the right bank of the Shatt ul-Arab on the way from Basra to a point opposite the mouth of the Karun, a distance of 22 miles.

Sayyid Muhammad, the son of Imam Musa Raza, the ninth Shia Imam, was born in Ramazan 195/June 811. He married the daughter of the Caliph al-Mamun, called Umm al-Fazl. The Shias believe that he was poisoned by his wife at the instigation of the Caliph al-Mutasim. He was buried in Hanjam. (see E.I. s. v.).

Shaikh Nasr al-Mazkur, son and successor of Nasir Khan, belonged to the Matarish Arabs of Oman (Abu Hakima, p. 133) and ruled Abu Shahr at this time. He paid tribute to Karim Khan, Shah of Persia, and was the admiral of his Persian Gulf fleet. He occupied Bahrain in 1753, but lost it to the Utub in 1782. He died on 11 April, 1789. (*Factory Records*, vol., 18 No. 1520).

Shamartah is situated on the left bank of the Shatt ul-Arab on the way between the Persian Gulf and Basra (see Niebuhr, 168).

Shariat is near Basra and is situated on the left bank of the Shatt ul-Arab.

Sharjah is the capital of a shaikhdom of the same name situated on the Trucial coast. It used to be the commercial centre of the Trucial coast, but from the latter half of the last century it lost its trade to Dubai due to the silting up of the Sharjah creek.

Shatait, a village situated on the west shore of Abbadan island from the confluence of the Karun river and the Shatt ul-Arab to the sea.

Shitab is the same as Sidab. It is a village situated at the foot of a bay which is 1 mile south of Masqat town.

Shuza is modern Suzeh, a village on the south coast of the Qishm island, 12 miles north-east of Ras Khargu.

Suhar, an important town and port on the Batinah coast of the Oman Sultanate and the seat of government of the whole western half of Batinah. It is 125 miles north-west of Masqat.

Sulaiman Pasha was a Georgian freedman of Hasan Pasha, Wali of Baghdad. On account of his abilities he received promotion under successive Pashas and, in 1765, was appointed as *Mutesellim* of Basra. When the Persians invaded Basra, he defended it bravely. But Basra was captured and he was sent as prisoner to Shiraz. He was allowed to return to Basra after 4 years. In July 1780 he became Pasha of Baghdad and held that office until his death on 7 August, 1802 at the age of 86. He was one of the greatest Pashas of Baghdad. Longrigg, *Four Centuries of Modern Iraq*, 187-220 ; Olivier, *Voyage dans l' Empire Ottoman*, iv, 143 ff).

Sur, an important town on the coast of Eastern Hajar, situated 17 miles from west of Ras ul-Hadd and 74 miles south-west of Masqat.

Suwaini al-Abdullah succeeded Shaikh Samir as head of the Muntafiq group of tribes in 1779. For six years he remained loyal to the Turkish government, and, in 1784, he even helped the Turkish government to suppress the Chaab. But in 1785 he occupied Basra. He wanted to become its governor and so wrote to the Sultan to be confirmed in that post. But in late October, 1787, he was defeated by the forces of the Pashalik and fled. Thereupon, Hamud al-Samir was appointed Shaikh in his place. But Suwaini remained a source of trouble to the Iraq government. In 1792, however, he was pardoned, and in 1797 restored to his rank and home. But early in July 1797 he was assassinated by a negro slave (Longrigg, *Four Centuries of Modern Iraq*, 195 ff.) It was during the period of Suwaini's revolt against the Turks that Tipu's ambassadors arrived in Basra. Since he dominated the route to Baghdad, he had to be won over, if the ambassadors were to proceed on their journey.

Talhah the son of Ubaidullah, the Quraish, was a Companion of the Prophet. He wanted to become Caliph, and so organised a movement against Osman and then against Ali. He was killed in the battle of the Camel (36 A.H.) near Kufa and was buried at Basra. His tomb is near the Great Mosque.

Tamar is in the Muhammareh *boluk*.

Tarpatri is in the Anantapur district and is situated on the southern bank of the Pennar river. It has always been an important weaving centre or cotton and silk cloth (*Anantapur Gazetteer*, pp. 63-64, 202).

Tum is the island of Tunb, formerly pronounced in English as Tomb. It lies south of the south-west point of the Qishm island.

Umm ul-Qaiwain, a small town on the coast of the Trucial Oman about 18 miles north-east of Sharjah town and the capital of a Shaikhdom of the same name.

Umm Nakhilah is the low islet of Nakhilu, half a mile in diameter and situated six miles off the Persian coast of Dashti.

Utbi, Utub, Bani Utba, Uttoobee or Attaba belong to Anaza, an Adnani Arab tribe inhabiting Najd and North Arabia. They established themselves in Kuwait during the first half of the 18th century, and in about 1750 chose as their leader Shaikh Sabah, after whom the present family is called. He was succeeded by his son Abdullah in

1762. It was in about 1766 that the Āl-Khalifah branch of the Utub emigrated to Qatar, where they established *Zubarah*.

The Utub were good merchants, having commercial relations with the Persian coast and with Masqat and Basra. They carried merchandise to various parts of central and northern Arbia. Their vessels also sailed to India and brought goods to the Utbi ports and to Basra. Their fleet was next in importance to that of Masqat and throughout the latter half of the 18th century they remained powerful and prosperous. While the Khalifah branch of the tribe controlled Bahrain and Qatar with its port of *Zubarah*, the Sabah branch ruled Kuwait. Bahrain is still being ruled by the Khalifah branch of the Utub. (Abu Hakima, 115, 295-97 ; also Parsons, 207 ; *Selections from Bombay Records*, 409).

Yahudi, a village 1½ miles up a tortuous creek, situated on the right bank of the Shatt ul-Arab from Muhammareh to Basra.

Yusifan, a settlement on the river bank near the Muhaijaran creek.

Zain, a tract lying immediately below Faiyazi and extending for one mile down stream to the Mutawa creek.

Zain ul-Abidin, the son of Husain, is the fourth Imam of the Shias. He was with his father at Karbala but was saved because of his illness. However, he was subjected to sufferings and indignities at the hands of Yazid's officers and was taken in chains to Damascus. He was allowed to return with the members of his family to Madina, where he died in about 711 and was buried there.

Zubair, the son of al-Awwan, was a Companion of the Prophet. He married Asma, the daughter of Abu Bakr, the first Caliph. Anxious to become Caliph, he joined *Zubair* and Aishah, the wife of the Prophet, in organizing opposition to Ali, but was slain in the Battle of the Camel (36 A.H.) His tomb is in the town named after him.

Zubarah, a ruined and deserted town on the west side of the Qatar Promontory, about five miles south of Khor-Hassan. It was founded by the Āl-Khalifah division of the Utub in 1766 and a fort was built in 1768. It became a very flourishing commercial town on account of its policy of free trade. It was occupied by the Wahhabis in 1798.

Zulfar was the port of the Qawasim.

APPENDIX C

NOTES ON NON-PERSIAN AND TECHNICAL WORDS OCCURING IN THE PERSIAN TEXT

Ahl-i Bait-i Rasul, "people of the House of the Prophet Muhammad." These, according to the Shias, include Ali, the cousin and son-in-law of the Prophet, Fatimah, the daughter of the Prophet, and their two sons, Hasan and Husain. The Sunnis, however, add to this list the wives of the Prophet as well.

Ashurah is the 10th of Muharram 61 A.H./10 October, 680, on which Husain, his relatives and companions were cruelly slain by the forces of the Ummayad Caliph, Yazid I.

Akrot (Hindi); Urdu *Akhrot*; Persian *Akhrot.*

Ambara or Anbara (Hindi), the esculent plant *Hisbiscus cannabinus* commonly called rozella.

Angah, Anga (Telugu), a stride or pace of about 3 ft., i.e. a yard (Wilson, *Glossary*, 26).

Ank, a mark or a number on the cloth. It has also been used in the diary in the sense of rate (see Wilson, *Glossary*, 26).

Armad is derived from the Portuguese word, 'armada' meaning fleet, royal navy, squadron. Here it is used in the sense of royal navy. The official in charge of this navy was called *darugha armad* in Mysore. In the Ottoman Empire he was called Kaptan Pasha.

Asad ilahi : Tipu continued his father's practice of forming the prisoners of war into separate battalions. Haider had called them *chelas*, but Tipu gave them the name of *asad-i ilahi* or *ahmadi* troops.

Amil or amildar, the head of a district in Tipu's kingdom. He was required to maintain law and order, collect revenues, look after the welfare of the peasants and supply the commandants of the forts with provisions and military stores. (See for details Mohibbul Hasan Khan, *History of Tipu Sultan*, pp. 338-32).

Bhatta, a Hindi word meaning extra pay or allowance given to public servants or soldiers employed on special duties or in distant places.

Bhindi, the vegetable *Hibiscus a belmoschus*, commonly called in India "Lady's finger".

Baikh manjith is the root of the drug *Rubia manjith* which yields a red dye.

Bajra, a kind of millet (*Panicum spicatum*) which is the food of the poorer classes.

Bani is from the Hindi word *banya*, meaning a grain-seller, a merchant. Hindu merchants settled either as agents or principals at the chief trading centres in the Persian Gulf or Red Sea are known by this term.

Baqilah (Hindi and Urdu) ; Persian *baqila'*. A bean (*Faba sativa*).

Batel, Marathi *batela*, a boat from 50 to 500 candies' burden (Wilson, *Glossary*, p. 67).

Batti (Hindi *Batta*). Rate of exchange.

Bayeb (Sanskrit Vayavya), meaning north-west.

Bora (Hindi), a sack for holding rice, spices etc.

Barg-i Tambul, betel leaf. The Perso-Arabic word is *tambul* derived from the Sanskrit name of the betel shrub, the common European term betel being derived from the Malayalam language through Portuguese (Yule's *Marco Polo*, ii, 371, 374 ; also *Hobson-Jobson*, s.v.).

Canteroy, a gold coin formerly used in south-eastern part of Madras territory. It was worth three rupees. Properly *Kanthiravi hun* (or pagoda) from Kanthirava Raya who ruled in Mysore from 1638. (*Hobson-Jobson*, p. 121).

Chashm (Persian), meaning eye ; here used in the same sense of "*ank*" for in Dakhini Hindi the word for *Chashm* is *ank*.

Chaulai, a species of pot-herb, *Amaranthus polyganous*, having two varieties : one red and the other green.

Chhint (Hindi), Persian *Chit*; English chintz. It is a cotton cloth printed with flowers or other designs in various colours and usually glazed.

Chillah-kashi, the practice of retiring for forty days to a lonely spot or cell for prayer or contemplation. Sometimes a circle is drawn by the devotee and is not crossed until the forty days are over.

Chobdar, a mace-bearer ; herald ; a servant whose business it is to announce the arrival of visitors.

Chutia (Hindi), a term of abuse.

Dahliat (Hindi), shield-holder; Persian *siphah-bardar*.

Dallal, an agent between buyer and seller, a broker.

Daw or *dao*, a term of Swahili origin, corrupted by European writers as 'dhow' and applied by them to Arab sailing vessels, specially in the Red Sea and Indian Ocean (Hourani, *Arab Seafaring in the Indian Ocean in Ancient and Early Medieval Times*, p. 89 and n).

Defterdar was the chief revenue and treasury officer of a province in the Ottoman Empire. For the *defterdar* at the centre see Gibb, *Islamic Society and the West* vol. I, part I, pp. 128 ff.

Dinar : 100 *dinars*=1 *mahmudi* (one Bombay rupee=5 *mahmudi*)
200 *dinars*=1 *abbasi*.
1 *abbasi*=2 *mahmudis*
=4 *shahis*

Dingi, a small vessel employed in the trade between the Malabar coast and the Arabian and Persian coasts. In Bengal and in Northern India small boats or skiffs plying in the rivers are also called dongi or dongya.

Doriya (Hindi), a kind of cloth both in cotton and silk. It has stripes which run along the length of the *than* i.e. in warp threads (see *Hobson-Jobson*, s.v.).

Dubashi, one who speaks two languages, an interpreter.

Dushala, a pair of shawls. Since a single shawl is too thin, a pair is usually worn.

Dupatta, a piece of cloth in which there are two breadths and is thrown loosely over the shoulders. It is also the name given to a piece of cloth measuring 2 yards or more with which women in northern India cover their head and the upper portions of their body.

Effendi, a Byzantine term meaning Lord, used by the Turks also to describe men of religious learning. In the Arab lands of the Near East, other than Iraq, and most of Arabia, it is now the normal word for Mr. Here also it is used in this sense. (See *Handbook of Oriental History*, p. 16).

Falam, a small silver coin formerly current in South India and called in English Fanam. 123 Fanams were worth 1 rupee.

Faqir Muhrram ul-Haram : In memory of Husain sometimes Muslims in India and Persia assume the role of beggars on one of the ten days of Muharram, and beg in the name of Husain in fulfilment of some vow.

Firda, poll-tax. Here it is used in the sense of customs-house In the Ottomon Empire the customs dues were called *gumruk* and customs house *gumrukleri*.

Gandhakh, Sulphur.

Gaz-i Shahi ; The following is a table of the lineal measure on the Persian coast :

4 *gireh*=1 *chaharak*
4 *chaharak*=1 *zara* or *gaz-i shahi*
4 *gaz*=40½ inches (English).

Garha (Hindi), a kind of coarse, thick cotton cloth.

Gernal (Dakhini), short piece of ordnance for throwing shells.

Ghari, measure of time, being one sixtieth part of a day and night i.e. 24 minutes. In common use it has come to mean a watch.

Ghaz, a small coin that used to be worth 1/10 of a *shahi*, which itself was worth 1320 of a *qran*.

Gudi, a sort of dry dock, a place made by the side of a river or sea for repairing and caulking boats.

Gumashtah, an agent.

Harkarah, a running footman, courier, messenger.

Hazri, an offering of food made to a saint or an Imam by reciting verses from the Quran. After the ceremony, guests partake of the food.

Hing (Hindi and Urdu), asafoetida.

Hun was a gold coin current in south India ; also called *pagoda*, usually about 50 grains in weight but varying in standard and value according to the place where coined. *Hun Haidari* or *bahaduri pagoda* was named after Haidar Ali (see *Hobson-Jobson*, 498-99 ; and Wilson, *Glossary*, 221).

Jaish, a term used for Tipu Sultan's regular infantry.

Jali, (Hindi and Urdu). Trellis-work.

Jam, is the same as *gam* ('g' having been softened). *Gam* means a step, a pace. Here *du gam* has been used in the sense of close proximity.

Jawan, a term used for a common soldier in the army of Tipu Sultan. The Indians who were employed by the English East India Company were called sepoys, a distortion of the Persian word sipahi. Sipahi was the term used by the English for an Indian soldier after the Mutiny. Since 1947, however, the word *jawan* is in common parlance.

Juar, Indian millet (*Andropogen sorghum* or *Holcus gorghum*).

Jughrat, sour or coagulated milk.

Juqdar (Captain) was the head of a *juq* (company) of infantry in the Mysore army. A *Juq* was a sub-division of a *risalah* or *kushoon*.

Kahya, the Turkish version of the Persian *Kat-khuda*, literary "lord of the house" or "Major-domo". Here it means the chief minister in a provincial government under the Pasha. (Longrigg, *Four Centuries of Modern Iraq*, p. 354 ; Gibb, *Islamic Society and the West*, vol. I, part 1, p. 200 ; also vol. 11, part 2, pp. 86, 226)

Khadi, a thick, coarse kind of cloth woven by hand.

Khandi, (Marathi). In English candy. A measure of weight and capacity commonly termed candy from the Tamil spelling *kandi*. Its value varies in different places. (see for details Wilson, *Glossary* pp. 277, 278).

Khurfa, Pursain (*Portulaca Oleracea*).

Kirani or *karrani* "is a writer who keeps the accounts of the ship" (*Ain-i Akbari* tr. Blochmann, i, 290). Ibn Battuta also uses the term in the same sense (see Gibb, *Ibn Battuta*, i, 383). It is in this sense that the word has been used in the diary. In modern times *kirani* has been used in the sense of a clerk (generally of mixed European and Indian descent), also a convert to christianity but used in a derogatory sense.

Kothi (Hindi), a warehouse, a mercantile firm or factory. Tipu had a factory at Masqat for the purpose of trade between his kingdom and the Persian Gulf.

Lobah (Persian) ; *lobia* (Urdu). A kind of pulse.

Lungi (Hindi), a piece of cloth covering the lower part of the body. It is also used as a scarf or a large handkerchief.

Machhwa, Portuguese *Manchua* ; Marathi *Machva*. A cargo-boat with one mast and a square sail varying from five to 30 tons. The coasting *machvas* are much larger than the river *machvas*. Here the *machva* is employed to drag the ship towards or away from the harbour. (see *Gazetteer of Bombay Presidency, Kanara*, pp. 62 ff.).

Mahmudi, 1 *mahmudi*=100 *dinars*
200 *dinars*=1 *abbasi*
1 *abbasi*=2 *mahmudis*
=4 *shahis*
1 *rial*=13 *shahis*
1 *shahi*=4 pence
(*Selections from State Papers, Bombay, regarding Persian Gulf* (600-1800, p. 459).

Maithi is the plant fenugreek.

Mashru, a kind of cloth of silk and cotton mixed. The word is no longer in vogue now.

Mehmandar, a superintendent and purveynor assigned to look after foreign ambassadors or other important visitors.

Man-i Masqat = 8 lb. 14 oz.

Man-i Tabriz : One Tabriz md=$6\frac{1}{4}$ lbs. to $6\frac{3}{4}$ lbs.
1 seer=4297
2 maunds (*man*)=srs=28 $\frac{14}{100}$ lbs.
1 candy=20 maunds (Buchannan, III, 26).

Misqal : 1 *misqal*=$74\frac{1}{4}$ grains English.

Muharram, the first month of the Islamic year. Here it is used in the sense of the first ten days of the month observed in connection with the martyrdom of Husain, the grandson of the Prophet Muhammad. These ten days are observed by Muslims, in particular by the Shia Muslims, as a period of mourning. While celebrating it they beat their breasts, cut themselves with lancets, and inflict tortures on their bodies in various ways as a remembrance of the sufferings of Husain.

Muli, radish.

Mung, a kind of pulse (*phaseolus mungo*).

Mutesellim was deputy governor of a *sanjak* or of an *eyalet* when more than one were under the rule of one Pasha. The *Mutesellim* of Basra was under the Pasha of Baghdad.

Niyaz or *Nazr*, an offering of food or sweets made in the name of a saint by reciting verses from the Quran. After this ceremony the offering is distributed among friends and relations.

Nania (Kannada), coin, money.

Naqib Ashraf (*Naqib ul-Ashraf*) or Marshal of *Sharifs*. *Sharif* was one of the terms applied to the descendants of the Prophet, enjoying a special respect and forming a separate and privileged corporation in the Ottoman Empire. The *Naqib* was the chief executive officer of this corporation and his duty was to see that there were no imposters who called themselves *Sharif*. (See *Gibb*, *Islamic Society and the West* vol. 1, part ii, p. 93).

Padak (Dakhini), name of an ornament for the neck.

Pallu (Hindi), the hem or border of a garment.

Pasha, a Turkish title dating from the 13th century. It was formerly the highest title of honour in the Ottoman Empire. It was abolished by the Turkish Republic under Mustafa Kemal.

Pethha'i (Hindi and Urdu), a kind of gourd.

Phitkari (Hindi and Urdu), alum.

Pichhauri (Hindi), diminitive of *Pichhaura*. A sheet or cloth woven round the waist or thrown carelessly over the head.

Pir-zadah, a Persian term meaning son of a *pir* or sufi saint.

Pitara (Hindi), a large basket (generally of cane or wicker work); a box (for clothes). It is used in the latter sense here.

Qiyas, a weight used on the Persian coast. 48 *misqals*=1 *qiyas*, 16 *qiyas* =1 *man*=73/4 lbs.

Qaus or sharqi, the winds in the Persian Gulf which alternate with the north westers. They blow strong from December to April. The *qaus* is generally accompanied by thick, gloomy weather, with hard squalls, rain, thunder and lightning and is disliked by all (*Persian Gulf Pilot*, p. 8; also Wilson, *The Persian Gulf*, p. 6).

Qurs rumi : 1 *qurs rumi*=7 *mahmudis*
5 *mahmudis*=1 Bombay rupee.
(Ives, *A Voyage from England to India etc*, p. 232).

Ragi is *Eleusine coracana*, a species of grain commonly called raggy, much cultivated in South India.

Ratl, a unit of weight, varying greatly in value with time, place and the material weighed.

Risalah, a body of cavalry equivalent to a regiment. Its commander is called *Risaldar*. The term *risalah* was also sometimes applied to infantry, and occasionally to a mixed corps of horse and foot. (Kirkpatrick,p. 57 n. 1)

Rahmani, name of a large frigate built for the Imam Said at Zanzibar. (*Gazetteer of the Persian Gulf*, vol. I, p. 412).

Rial, a unit of money.

1 *rial*=13 *shahis*
1 *shahi*=about 4 pence

Sarpech, an ornament of gold, silver or jewels, generally placed in front of the turban.

Sazawal were a kind of bailiffs or duns employed to collect revenue from the defaulters. They were maintained, while employed, at the expense of the defaulters (Kirkapatrick, No. 48). They also acted as sentries or guards. Here the term has been used both in this sense and in that of a common soldier.

Shahi see *rial*.

Shal-i Tus, *tus* is a Kashmiri word which means fine, superb and *Shal-i Tus* is a species of fine, soft Kashmiri shawl woven from the wool imported from Tibet and Ladakh. It is of a drab or grey colour and very expensive. (Moorcroft, i, 349).

Shamal, the prevailing wind in the Gulf, blowing about 9 months in the year in its northern half. During a *shamal*, after rain, the air is so loaded with dust that the navigation becomes dangerous (see for more details Constable, *Persian Gulf Pilot*, p. 6).

Shanari, This was the venetian zecchino, cecehino or sequin, a gold coin long current on the shores of India. In the early part of the 15th Century, Nicolo Conti mentions that in some parts of India Venetian ducats i.e. sequins were current. Sequin is from sikka. The sequin was sometimes called in South India "shanar cash" because the Doge with his sceptre is taken for the shanar or toddy-drawer climbing the palm tree. Sometimes the term venetian was used for sequin and was equal to 4½ Arcot rupees. (*Hobson-Jobson*, Art., *cash* and *chik*.

Shilah, a kind of cloth. According to Buchannan, ii, 240, it was thin white muslin, 22 cubits long and 2½ or 2¾ cubits broad. It was very coarse and sometimes striped and then *dupattas* were made out of it which were sold from about three shillings to 10 shillings a piece.

Sonth (Hindi), dry ginger.

Soya, (Hindi) pot-herb of *Eennel*, *Anethum sowa*.

Tadri, a small port in the Kanara district, situated at the mouth of the Tadri river.

Tarakari (Hindi and Urdu), vegetables. In Persian the word for vegetables is *tarabi*, and *tarakari* means the sowing of vegetables.

Tarkankri, fresh cucumber.

Thhan (Hindi), Persian *dast* or *taqah*; cloth in piece.

Tur, a species of pulse (*Cytisus cajan*).

Tutia (Hindi and Urdu), Persian *tutya*; sulphate of copper, tutty.

Waqiyah was the unit weight current in Turkish Iraq.

1 *waqiyah*=lb 2 oz. 3-2 dr. English.

Yazak : Tipu's regular horse was divided into four *cutchehries* (brigades) each *cutchehry* was divided into five *mokums* (regiments); each *mokum* was divided into 4 *risalahs* (squadrons) ; each *risalah* was further divided into *yaz* or *yazak* (troops) each having a *Yazakdar* (captain) at its head.

Yasawal, a state messenger.

Zakat means purification, and from this it is also used to express a portion of property given in alms. To pay *zakat* is a religious duty incumbent upon Muslims. On articles of merchandize a *zakat* of 2½% was realized on their value (Here it has been used in this sense). (see Hughes, *Dictionary of Islam,* s.v.).

Zakuti here, probably, means one who collects Zakat or customs duties. I have not been able to trace the origin of this word. In the Ottoman Empire the customs officer was called *Gumruk emini.* According to the diary (p. 231) it was Ismail Agha who was at this time the customs officer. This is corroborated by *Factory Records* (I.O.), No. 18, *f.* 356*a.*

Zar-i Mahbubi : This is from Persian *zar* (gold) and Arabic *mahbub* (favourite) It was a new coin struck in Turkey early in the 18th century and weighed 40 grains (2·5—2·6 grammes). (Gibb, *Islamic Society and the West,* vol. i, part ii, p. 55 and n. 7).

APPENDIX D

A SELECT BIBLIOGRAPHY

UNPUBLISHED MATERIALS

Abu Hakima (Ahmad Mustafa). *The Utbi States in Eastern Arabia in the Second Half of the 18th Century.* Unpublished Thesis. London University, 1960.

Affaires Étrangères, B Nos. 176, 177, 197 (*Correspondance Consulaire*)—*Bassorah* (*Golfe Persique*), 1743-91. Archives Nationales, Paris.

Affaires Étrangères, B 448 (*Correspondance Consulaire*)—*Constantinople.* 1787-90. Archives Nationales, Paris.

British Foreign Office Records: 78/71786, 78/8-1787, 78/9-1788. Public Record Office, London.

Factory Records : *Persia and the Persian Gulf* (India Office No. 18).

Hukm-namah, Asiatic Society, Calcutta, MS. No. 1677.

Miscellaneous Information Regarding Turkish Arabia, Vol. 5 ; *Foreign Department Miscellaneous Vol. 5.* National Archives of India, New Delhi.

Secret Proceedings, 24 April, 1786; Jauuary, 1787. National Archives of India, New Delhi.

PUBLISHED MATERIALS

Abbas al-Azzawi. *Tarikh al-Iraq bayna Ihtilalayn.* Baghdad, 1935-58. 8 vols.

Adamiyat, Fireydoun. *Bahrain Islands—A Legal and Diplomatic Study of the British-Iranian Controversy.* New York, 1955.

Bashayan al-Abbasi, Sheikh Abdul Qadir. *Al-Basra fi Adwariha al-Tarikhia.* Baghdad, 1961.

Bradley, F. B. *Through Persia.* London, 1909.

Burnell, A. C. *Hobson-Jobson.* London, 1886.

Constable, C. G. *Account of the Physical Geography of the Persian Gulf.* Transactions of the Bombay Geographical Society, Vol. XV.

—— and Stiffe, A. W. *The Persian Gulf Pilot.* London, 1898.

Forster, C. *Historical Geography of Arabia.* London, 1844. 2 vols.

Franklin, W. *Observations Made on a Tour from Bengal to Persia in* 1786-87. London, 1790.

Gazetteer No. 37, *Iraq*. U.S. Board of Geographical names. April 1957.

Geographical Handbook Series—*Persia*, September, 1945, Naval Intelligence Department.

Gibb, H. A. R. *The Travels of Ibn Battuta.* Cambridge, 1958-62. 2 vols.

—*Islamic Society and the West.* Oxford, 1950-57. Vol. 1 part I and II.

Hay, R. *The Persian Gulf States.* Washington D.C., 1959.

Heude, W. *Voyage up the Persian Gulf.* London, 1819.

Hikmet Bayur : *Maysor Sultani Tipu Ile Osmanli Padisah Larindan I. Abdulhamid VE III. Selim Arasindaki Mektuplasma.* Ankara, 1948.

Hourani, G. E. *Arab Seafaring in the Indian Ocean in Ancient and Early Medieval Times. Princeton,* 1951.

Huart, M. C. — *Histoire de Bagdad dans le Temps Modernes.* Paris, 1901.

Husain Ali Khan Kirmani. — *Nishan-i Haidari.* Bombay, 1307/1890.

Iraq Government. — *Survey Directorate's Index Gazetteer.* 1943.

Ives, E. — *A Voyage from England to India in 1754.. Also a Journey from Persia to England in 1758 and 1759 by way of Bassora, Baghdad etc.* London, 1773.

Journal of the Royal Society of Arts, 1915, vol. 63 pp. 505-19.

Kasravi, S. A. — *Tarikh-i Pan-sad Saleh Khuzistan.* Tehran, 1954.

Kelly, J. B. — *Sultanate and Imamate in Oman.* Oxford, 1959.

Kemball, A. B. — *Bombay Selections.* No. XXIV. *Extracts from Records of Bushire.* Calcutta, 1856.

Keppel, G. — *Personnal Narrative of a Journey from India to England by Bussorah*..in *1824.* London, 1827. 2 vols.

Kinneir, J. M. — *A Geographical Memoir of the Persian Empire.* London, 1813.

Krikpatrick, W. — *Select Letters of Tippoo Sultan.* London, 1811.

Laudon, P. — *Basra and the Shatt-ul-Arab.* Journal of Royal Society. 1591, Vol. 63.

Layard, A. H. — *A Description of the Province of Khuzistan,* Journal of the Royal Geographical Society, 1846, vol. XVI.

Le Strange, G. *The Lands of the Eastern Caliphate.* Cambridge, 1905.

Longrigg, S. H. *Four Centuries of Modern Iraq.* Oxford, 1925.

Lorimer, J. G. *Gazetteer of the Persian Gulf, Oman and Central Arabia.* Calcutta, 1908-15. 2 vols.

Mignan, R. *Travels in Chaldaea..Hillah and Babylon.* London, 1829.

Miles, S. B. *The Countries and Tribes of the Persian Gulf.* London, 1919. 2 vols.

Mirza Abu Talib, see Stewart, C.

Morier, J. A. *A Journey through Persia, Armenia, and Asia Minor to Constantinople in the years* 1808 *and* 1809. London, 1812.

Niebuhr, C. *Description de L'Arabie.* Amsterdam, 1774.

—— *Voyage en Arabie et d'autres Pays Circonvoisin.* Trans. from German. Amsterdam, 1776-80, 2 vols.

Olivier, C. A. *Voyage dans l'Empire Othman, l'Egypt et la Perse.* Paris, 1807. 6 vols.

Ousley, W. *Travels in Various countries of the East etc.*, 3 vols. London, 1819-23.

Ovington, F. *A Voyage to Suratt in the year 1699.* London, 1696.

Parsons, A. *Travels in Asia and Africa.* London, 1808.

Pelly, L. *Remarks on the Port of Lingah, the Island of Kishm* etc.

—— *Remarks on the Tribes, Trade, and Resources around the Shore Line of the Persian Gulf.*

—— *Recent Tour around the Northern Portion of the Persian Gulf.* Transactions of the Bombay Geographical Society. Vol. XVII

Pengelly, W. G. *Remarks on the Eastern Coast of Arabia between Muscat and Sohar.* Transactions of the Bombay Geographical Society Vol. XVI.

Philips, C. H. *Handbook of Oriental History,* London, 1951.

Plaisted, B. *A Journey from Calcutta to Busserah.* London. 1758.

Rawlinson, H. C. *Notes on Mohamareh and the Chaab Arabs.* Proceedings of the Royal Geographical Society, 1855-57, Vol. I.

Razmara, *Farhang Jughrafiya-i Iran.* Tehran, 1328-32 H.A. 10 vols.

Rousseau, J.-B.J.J. *Description du Pachalik de Baghdad.* Paris. 1809.

Sailing Directions, Red Sea and Gulf of Aden, Hydrographic Office, U.S. Navy, H.O. Pub. No. 157, p. 279.

Saldanha, *Precis of Turkish Affairs.* Simla, 1906.

— *Selections from State Papers, Bombay, Regarding the East India's Connections with the Persian Gulf* (1600-1800). Calcutta, 1908.

Salil-ibn-Razik. *History of the Imams and Seyyids of Oman from* 661-1856 A.D. Trans. by G. P. Badger. London, M.

Selections from the Records of the Bombay Government. New Series. Bombay, 1856, No. XXIV.

Sestini, *Voyage de Constantinople a Bassore en* 1781. Paris, 1797.

Stewart, C. *The Travels of Mirza Abu Talib Khan in Asia, Africa and Europe during the Years* 1799-1803. Trans. C. Stewart. London, 1810. 2 vols.

Thomas, B. *Arab Rule under the Abu Said Dynasty of Oman.* 1741-1937.
The Raleigh Lectures. British Academy, 1938.

Tweedy, M. *Bahrain and the Persian Gulf.* Ipswich, England.

Ussher, J. *A Journey from London to Persepolis.. Persia.* London, 1865.

Wellsted, J. R. *Travels to the city of the Caliphs along the Shores of the Persian Gulf.* London, 1840. 2 vols.

Wellsted, J. R. *Travels in Arabia, London,* 1838. 2 vols.

Whitelock, Lt. *Descriptive sketch of the Islands and Coast situated at the Entrance of the Persian Gulf.* Transactions of the Bombay Geographical Society (1836-38), Vol. 1, pp. 113-27.

Wilson, A. T. *The Persian Gulf.* London, 1928.

Wilson, H. H. *A Glossary of Judicial and Revenue Terms and of useful words occuring in Official Documents Relating to the Administration of the Government of India.* London, 1855.

Yaqut, Mujam al-Buldan. Ed. F. Wustenfeld. Leipzig, 1866-73. 6 vols.

ERRATA and ADDENDA

Rum in Muslim usage signified Eastern Roman or Byzantine Empire. Rum means the land of the Rhomaeans or Byzantines. Rum also sometimes meant Turkey in general. It is in this sense that the word has been used in the diary. For details about Rum see Encyclopaedia of Islam, s. v.

Page 22, line 14, *for* e *read* be
Page 25, line 3, for *Fakhurul-Marakib* read *Fakhr ul-Marakib* and thus elsewhere.
Page 27, line 7, *for* Jurra-i-klan *read* Jurra-i-Kalan
Page 27, line 8 from bottom, *for* plam *read* palm.
Page 27, last line, *for* consits *read* consists.
Page 32, line 19 from bottom, for I *mahmudis* read *mahmudi.*
Page 38, line 2, *for* Moniseur *read* monsieur.
Page 40, last line, *for* respctivee *read* respective.
Page 42, line 22, *for* care much *read* care (omit much)
Page 46, line 7 from bottom, *for* spend *read* spent.
Page 61, line 9, for *Qapji bashj* read *Qapiji bashi.*
Page 62, line 17, *for* 68 *read* 10.
Page 63, line 11, *for* complaisance *read* complacence.
Page 65, line 1, *for* Musa Raza the was *read* Musa Raza was the.
Page 74, line 12, *for* the which *read* which (omit the).
Page 87, line 12, *for* purveynor *read* purveyor.

وقائع منازل روم

وقائع منازل روم

تالیف

خواجه عبدالقادر

بسعی و اهتمام

محب الحسن

استاد تاریخ و تمدن هند

جامعه ملیه اسلامیه - دهلی نو

تقدیم بروان پاک مادر عزیزم

بسم الله الرحمن الرحیم

الحمدلله رب العالمین والصلواة والسلام علی خیر خلقه محمد و آله و صحبه اجمعین ـ اما بعد بدانکه این رسالهٔ ایست مسمی به وقایع منازل الروم حسب الارشاد کرامت بنیاد حضرت خداوند نعمت خلدالله ملکه به تسوید در آورده شد تا که بعد حصول شرف ملازمت عالی بکار آید ـ والله الموفق والمعین ـ

سابق از رسیدن جوانان اسداللهی و سزاول و صندوق جواهر وغیره ، غلام علی خان و شاه نورالله خان و لطف علی خان وغیره از حضور پرنور بتاریخ پانزدهم ماه حیدری سال جلو سنه ۱۱۹۹ هجری(۱) مرخص شده به موضع تدری به کنارهٔ دریا رسیده به تهیه اسباب و سر انجام جهازات پرداخته چهار زنجیر افیال وغیره اسباب ضروری برجهازات سرکار سوار نموده بودند که بتاریخ بست و هشتم ماه ایزدی
سال مذکور سنه الیه مطابق بست و هفتم ماه ربیع الثانی سنه ۱۱۹۹ هجری(۲) ۹
عبدالقادر منشی و سید جعفر مصدی و محمد علی بهاتو و جوانان اسداللهی و سزاول و رسالهٔ فقیر محمد وغیره داخل موضع تدری گردیدند ـ و در عرصهٔ دو سه روز به موجب ارشاد حضور پرنور غلام علیخان موجودات همه مردم مسطور دیده جوانان سزاول وغیره وجه طلبی یکماهه دست بدست تقسیم نموده بهمه ها تاکید نمودند که زود سرانجام ضروری خودها فراغت حاصل کنند که بتاریخ هفتم ماه بیاضی سال مذکور سنه الیه(۳) به جهازات سوار نموده خواهد شد ـ

۱ـ 14 Muharram 1200/17 November, 1785

۲ـ 27 February, 1786

۳ـ 6 Jumada I, 1200/7 March, 1786

و بتاریخ هفتم ماه مذکور روز سه شنبه غلام علی خان و شاه
نورالله خان و شکرالله خان و محمد حنیف سوداگر و مراد خان و محمد شفیع
داروغه ارماد و محمدعلی بهاتو و عبدالقادر و شیخ احمد علی منشی و سید جعفر
مصدی و جوانان اسداللهی و سزاول وغیره و بهرام وغیره اجناس سرکار بابت
بهته و اجناس تحایف معه(۱) دو زنجیر افیال که پیشتر سوار نموده بودند ،
برجهاز فخرالمراکب سوار شدند و پیش از دو سه روز لطف علی خان و
شمس‌الدین داروغه و یک جوقدار تعلقهٔ فقیر محمد معه جوانان یک جوق
۱ و دیگر سرانجام سرکار بر جهاز فتح شاهی معزی و یک زنجیر فیل سوار
شده بودند و ضیاء الدین(۲) و فقیر محمد خود معه جوانان یکجوق
و یک زنجیر فیل و دیگر سر انجام سوار نموده بودند و جعفر خان و
یکجوقدار تعلقهٔ فقیر محمد معه جوانان و دیگر سرانجام بر جهاز نبی بخش و
غراب سورتی سوارشدند ـ و بتاریخ نهم ماه مذکور سنه الیه بشب پنجشنبه
درطاس هفتم لنگر برداشته پیشتر بصوب بندر مسقط راهی گردیدند ـ

و بتاریخ پانزدهم از تلاطم امواج و شدت باد مخالف کمت بر جهاز
فخرالمراکب زیاده تر شده از حد گذشت و قریب غرق بود بدستور جهاز
فتح شاهی معزی وغیره ـ ازین جهت جوانان اسداللهی و سزاول و شاگرد
پیشه غلبانگ و هنگامه آرائی بسیار نمودند ـ غلام علی خان و شاه
نورالله خان به آنها تسلی داده ، از نجار و محمد شفیع وغیره تعلقه‌دار جهاز
مذکور به مرمت پرداختند ـ بعد دو سه روز بقدر سابق کمت باقی ماند ـ
و بتاریخ نوزدهم یک زنجیر فیل بابت جهاز فتح شاهی معزی که قریب
قریب جهاز فخرالمراکب بود تصدق فرق مبارک گردید ـ

و بتاریخ غره ماه احمدی سال مذبور سنه ۱۲۰۰ هجری (۳) روز

۱ـ معه Throughout the MS.

۲ـ ضیاوالدین Throughout the MS.

۳ـ 30 Jumada I, 1200/31 March, 1786

جمعه یک منزل جهاز انگریز از دور بجانب دست راست نمودار شده قریب
جهاز سرکار رسیده، کلاه پوش سردار آواز داد که سردار این جهاز کدام ١١
سردار است ـ از جهاز سرکار بجواب پرداخته از جهاز سرکار ندا کردند
که تو کدامی و از کجا می آی ـ اولاً گفت که از ولایت انگریز
برآمده قریب شش ماه شده حیران و سرگردانیم(١) و از عدم آب
بسیار عاجزیم و تاحال کنارهٔ هیچ بندر بنظر نمی آید، اگر قدری
آب داده آگاهی به رسیدن کنارهٔ بندری دهند مرهون منت خواهد شد ـ
بعد ازان از جانب سرکار به جواب پرداختند که آب هر قدر که ترا
درخواست آب باشد از مایان بگیر و کنارهٔ بندر مسقط هم قریب است
انشاء الله تعالیٰ عنقریب خواهند دید ـ باز کلاه پوش از جهاز خود ندا
کرد که خود از ملک بنگاله برآمده‌ام و در عرصه دوسه روز به بندر
مسقط رسیده به بندر بصره راهی خواهم گردید ـ و آب دوسه روز هم
باقی است و پیشتر از جهاز فخرالمراکب به صوب بندر مسطور راهی
گردید ـ

و به تاریخ مذبور یک زنجیر فیل بابت جهاز نبی بخش تصدق
شد و بتاریخ سیوم دو زنجیر فیل پرشاد گج و کشن پرشاد نام بابت
جهاز فخرالمراکب به شدت حرارت فلفل گرد تصدق گردیدند ـ و بتاریخ
هفتم بروز پنجشنبه به وقت نماز صبح پشته مچیره(٢) که عرض دریائی
بست درجه بود به‌نظر در آمد ـ و مسافت از جهاز تاکوه مذکور دو
جام بود ـ و به تاریخ نهم ماه مسطور به سرحد راس‌الحد رسیدند ـ ١٢

و بتاریخ دوازدهم به کنارهٔ بندر مسقط لنگر داده شاه نورالله‌خان
داخل شهر مسقط گردیدند ـ

و بتاریخ سیزدهم روز پنجشنبه غلام علی خان و لطف علی خان

١ـ گردانم .MS ٢ـ مصیره

یک یک حویلی علحده در بندر مسطور به کرایه گرفته داخل حویلی شدند ـ و وقت رفتن به بندر از شاه نورالله خان خلفان معه هر دو فرزند ملاقات نمود خیرعافیت پرسید ـ و به تاریخ چهاردهم جهاز نبی‌بخش معه ضیاء الدین داروغه و جوانان رساله فقیرمحمد وغیره سر انجام سرکار و بتاریخ پانزدهم غراب سورتی معه جعفر خان و جوانان بارگیر سرکار وغیره بخیریت به کنارهٔ بندر مسطور لنگر قایم نموده روز دوم فرود آمدند ـ

و به تاریخ شانزدهم شاه نورالله خان به اتفاق غلام علی خان وغیره نظر به امورات سرکار وجه خوراکی خودها وغیره جوانان متفرقات، سوای جوانان سزاول و بهرام وغیره، در سرکار وضع نموده، فی بهته یکماهه جوانان متفرقات یعنی هر دو منشی و هر دو چیلهٔ سرکار متعینه و محمد عمر چوبدار و شیخ مرتضی‌ا خدمتگار و محمد فاضل چوبدار بقدر یازده و نیم فلم کنتی رای در سرکار وضع نموده گفتند که در حضور معلی‌ا درین ماه معروض داشته خواهد شد ـ و خودها یک دام وضع نه نمودند جمله از یک آسامی مذکوره بست و سه فلم کنتی رای وضع ۱۲
نمودند ـ

و شاه نورالله خان معه عبدالقادر منشی و محمد کمال چیلهٔ سرکار و محمد شفیع کرانی و جوانان دو سه پهره سزاول جهاز نزد خلفان رفته هر دو منشور فیض گنجور موسوم امام و خلفان به خلفان دادند ـ نامبرده استفسار نوید فرحت جاوید خیروعافیت ملازمان عالی نموده اندازه ممالک و عساکر فیروزی مآثر حضرت ظل سبحانی خلدالله ملکه نمود ـ خان مسطور بپاسخ پرداختند که ممالک اطراف دارالسلطنت پتن سه ماهه راه است و سوار شصت هزار و مردم علاقهٔ جیش یک لک و پنجاه هزار و پیاده سه لک حاضر سواری خاص و باقی با مردم تعیناتی هر اطراف علحده است و منشور فیض گنجور موسومه خود بر سر و چشم

نهاده از عبدالقادر منشی خوانیده به دریافت مضمون فیض مشحون مسرور و خورسند گشته گفت اگرچه خود از اوایل منسلک به سلک ملازمان عالی بوده به انصرام هر امورات مامورهٔ سرکار ساعی و جاهد گشته سرفراز بود لاکن از صدور تازه فرمان عالی سرفرازی دوبالا بر خود افزوده به تقدیم امر جلیل‌القدر سعادت ابدی می اندوزد ـ و امام درشهر رسطاخ(۱) که از مسقط چهار منزل بالا از راه خشکی هست حاضر بود، فرمان معلیٰ خلفان نزد امام فرستاد ـ و شاه‌نورالله خان را خلفان ضیافت نمود ـ

و بتاریخ هفدهم جوانان اسداللهی و سزاول و بهرام و هرکاره
وغیره را به دفع ماندگی جهاز در باغیچهٔ خورد بیرون شهر خیمه‌ها ٣
دهانیده فرود آورانیدند ـ و به تاریخ بست و دوم ماه مذکور به جوانان اسداللهی وسزاول وبهرام و شاگرد پیشه وغیره را از ماوجی سیتهه دلال بندر مسقط قرض بطریق دستگردان گرفته وجه طلب یکماهه دست بدست بروبروی هر چهار سردار به اتفاق تقسیم نمودند ـ و چند کسان را یعنی شاه نورالله خان و لطف‌علی‌خان و جعفرخان وغیره را علی‌الحساب قدری قدری دهانیدند ـ و بعد دو سه روز محمدبیگ جوان علاقه بهرام گم گردید ـ

و غلام‌علی‌خان به خلفان دعوت ضیافت نمودند ـ خلفان معه دو پسر خود و پنجاه نفر ملازم خود به خانهٔ خان مسطور آمده طعام خورده رفت ـ به مجرا دادن زریکه به خرچ ضیافت در آمده شاه نورالله خان بچند امور تکرار نمودند ـ غلام‌علی‌خان از سرکار مجرا نه گرفته به طرف خود خرچ مسطور محسوب نمودند ـ و به تاریخ بست و هفتم امام مسقط سعید نام از شهر رسطاخ به بندر مسقط آمده بود ـ شاه نورالله خان به

۱ــ رستاق

مجرد استماع روز دوم معه عبدالقادر منشی و محمدعمر چوبدار و شیخ مرتضی خدمتگار نزد امام رفته ملاقات نمودند ـ امام استفسار نوید عافیت و تندرستی ذات والا صفات ملازمان عالی نموده کیفیت صلح و مصالح اهل فرنگ وغیره پرسید ـ خان معزی الیه به آئین بهین به جواب پرداختند ـ و باز امام به خلفان و پسرش تاکید نمود که بهر اموریکه درخواست خان موصوف به امورات سرکار باشد به وجه اتم و درستی تمام حسن انصرام دهند ـ من بعد شاه نوراللہ خان به فرود گاه خود آمده دو عدد پچهوری ریشمی گلدار تار پتری خورد و کلان و یک دوپته به انک پنج هزار و نهصد و هفتاد و پنج و دو تهان شیله یکی به انک ششصد و دیگر به انک یک هزار از صحابت محمدعمر چوبدار و شیخ مرتضی خدمت گار به اتفاق غلام‌علی‌خان وغیره بطریق سوغات و خلعت نزد امام فرستادند ـ امام قبول نمود ـ

و بتاریخ غره ماه بهاری سال جلو ۱۲۰۰ هجری(۱) عبدالرحمان خدمتگار به‌سبب عارضه اسهال کبدی بیمار بود به قضای الهی فوت کرد ـ و به‌تاریخ هشتم ماه مسطور به دلال یک دوپته به انک سه هزار و پنج صد و شصت و دو و نیم و یک شیله بچشم هفت صد و به برادر دلال یک دوپته به انک دو هزار و چهار صد و بست و پنج و یک شال عودی به قیمت بست روپیه غلام‌علی‌خان و شاه نوراللہ‌خان وغیره از سرکار دادند و این همه پارچه های سفید از نزد محمدحنیف گرفته بودند ـ و به تاریخ نهم ماه مذبور صندل تمام و کمال به نرخ فی کهندی پنجاه و هفت و نیم هون حیدری به معرفت ماوجی سیهته دلال مسقط محمد حنیف وغیره فروخت نمودند و نیز چهار و نیم کهندی الایچی به نرخ فی رطل پانزده هون حیدری به فروخت رسید ـ به تاریخ چهار دهم

۱ــ 29 Jumada II, 1200/29 April, 1786.

غلام‌علی خان و شاه نورالله‌خان کوایف روداد مفصل بذریعه عرایض به صحایت یک جوان هر کارهٔ سرکار از راه بندر بونبعی(۱) معه فیل بانان وغیره روانه نموده معروض داشتند۔

و به تاریخ پانزدهم روز شنبه به وقت ظهر شیخ اسماعیل دفعه‌دار علاقهٔ جوق سزاول و یک جوان دفعه ناموردہ حیات‌خان نام از یزک که بر دروازهٔ شاه نورالله‌خان بود معه پیک سرکار بر دنگی بندر بونبعی سوار شده به صوب بندر مسطور فراری گردیدند ۔ روز دوم به تقید و حفاظت جوانان دو یزک، یکی از علاقهٔ بهرام و دیگر از رسالهٔ فقیرمحمد به کناره دریای بندر مسطور نگاه داشتند۔ و بعد دوسه روز دفعه شیخ سلطان سقه علاقهٔ جوق سزاول گم گردید۔ و در باب موقوف ساختن و نگاه داشتن جهاز فخرالمراکب به بندر مسقط از قلت آب در نعل بصره، و همراه گرفتن سه منزل جهاز سرکار معه دو منزل داو کرایه‌دار بصوب بندر بصره، از غلام علی خان و شاه نورالله خان و لطف‌علی‌خان و جعفرخان و محمد حنیف وضیاء الدین و مرادخان نوشت و خواند به عمل آوردند و مهر و دستخط کسی بظهور نه انجامید۔

و به تاریخ بست و چهارم وجه طلب به جوانان سزاول دادند و بتاریخ بست و پنجم وجه طلب یکماهه و چهارده روزه دیگر برای مطابق شدن روز پیشی سزاول وغیره تا لغایت بست و چهارم شهر
مذکور به اتفاق هر چهار سردار بروبروی غلام علی خان دست بدست ۱۷
به جوانان اسداللهی تقسیم نمودند و به وضع وجه رسد پنج نفر فراری از جوق سزاول در وجه طلب جوقدار و سه سرخیلان به موجب حکم نامهٔ عنایتی خاص غلام علی خان و شاه نورالله خان وغیره به مصدی سرکار تاکید نمودند۔ جو قدار و سر خیلان مسطور وجه طلب خودها

۱— بمبئی

نه گرفته ، از غلام علی خان و شاه نوراللہ خان وغیره سوال و جواب نمودند که مایان به حضور پرنور معروض نموده‌ایم و مواجب خودها به مثل دیگر جوقداران و سرخیلان جیش حضور رسدی نیست بلکه ذاتیست ، چنانچه درین ماده به حضور معروض کرده‌ایم اگر شمارا درین ماده نوشتهٔ ضروریست به این مضمون نوشته می دهم که اگر حضرت خداوندنعمت مدظلهم‌العالی مجرا دهند خوب است والا در وجه طلب خودها مجرا خواهیم داد ۔ آخرالامر بنوشت و خواند مسطور از جوقدار و سه نفر سرخیل وجه طلب یکماهه آنها بلا وضع وجه رسدی به آنها رسانیدند ۔ و بتاریخ بست و ششم وجه طلب به جوانان علاقهٔ بهرام و شاگرد پیشه دست بدست تقسیم نمودند ۔

و بتاریخ دوم ماه جعفری سال دلو سنه الیه(۱) مبارک خان جوقدار اسداللهی به عارضه پیچش و تپ و لرزه بیمار بود به قضای الهی فوت شد ۔ و په تاریخ پانزدهم محمد ملک یک جوان سزاول از
۱ عارضه تپ و حرارت مریض بود به قضای الهی فوت گردید ۔ و به تاریخ هفدهم به جوانان سزاول و اسداللهی وغیره قدری قدری علی‌الحساب برای خرچ ضروری و سوار شدن بجهازات دهانیدند ۔ من بعد تقرر سوار شدن بر جهازات به تاریخ بست و هشتم به ظهور رسید ۔ و به تاریخ مسطور به چند امورات ضروری داو کرایه‌دار از موضع گودی بیرون نیاوردند متوقف ده دوازده روز شدند ۔ و بتاریخ بست و چهار ماه جعفری به جوانان اسداللهی و سزاول و بهرام و شاگرد پیشه و مصدی و منشی احمد علی وغیره وجه طلب مابقی تمام و کمال به موجب حکم حضور هر چهار سردار دست بدست برو بروی غلام علی خان تقسیم نمودند ۔ و به تاریخ بست و پنجم یک جوان سزاول جیونخان نام

---

۱ — 1st Sha'ban, 1200/30 May, 1786.

فراری گردید ـ و به تاریخ بست و ششم جوانان سزاول را بر جهاز فتح شاهی معزی سوار نمودند ـ و به تاریخ بست و هفتم نظر علی بیگ دفعه‌دار، که ضامن جوان فراری شده مذکوره بود، بحیله تفحص نامبرده در بندر مسقط رفته خود هم فراری گردید ـ

و خلفان معه دو پسر خود نزد غلام علی خان و شاه نوراللہ خان و لطف علی خان آمده ملاقات رخصتی نموده رفت ـ

و به تاریخ بست و هشتم ماوجی دلال بندر مسقط روز شنبه به‌وقت
رخصت یک دوشاله به غلام علی خان و یک دوشاله به شاه ۹
نوراللہ خان و یک شال به لطف علی خان و یک شال به جعفر خان و یک تهان تافته به شکر اللہ خان داده بر داو کرایه‌دار آمده از قریب موضع مطرح مرخص شده رفت ـ و بست هزار هون، منجمله شصت و پنج هزار هون حیدری، بابت تنخواه حضور که بر محمدحنیف وغیره شده بود، از معرفت محمدحنیف و ضیاءالدین نقد به وصول در آمده، و رسید برنج و دال تور و روغن زرد وغیره سرانجام بهته مردمان روانگی روم، محمد کمال‌الدین ماستر از غلام‌علیخان نویسانیده گرفت ـ

بتاریخ مسطور روز شنبه در ساعت مشتری غلام‌علیخان و شاه‌نوراللہ خان معه هر دو منشی و چیله واسداللهی وغیره بریک منزل داو کرایه‌دار بابت سیف داماد خلفان به کرایه گرفته سوار شدند ـ و لطف علیخان و جوانان سزاول و شمس‌الدین داروغه و سید جعفر مصدی بر جهاز فتح شاهی معزی، و ضیاءالدین و بهرام و چند شاگرد پیشهٔ سرکار و محمدعلی بهاتو بر جهاز نبی‌بخش، و جعفرخان و جوانان بارگیر و چند خدمتگار سرکار بر غراب سورتی، و بر یک منزل داو دیگر کرایه‌دار محمدحنیف و مرادخان و محمدشفیع وغیره، بهر دو داو مسطور به پنج
هزار و یک صد روپیه به کرایه گرفته بودند، سوار شده بوقت نماز ظهر ۲۰

لنگر برداشته به موضع مطرح که قریب بندر مسطور واقع است لنگر
قایم نمودند ـ و دلال به تکرار و خواهش تمام پانصد بورهٔ مرچ سیاه
به‌طریق امانت از محمدحنیف گرفت، اگرچه‌دلال مسطور همه بور های مرچ‌سیاه
وغیره سرانجام به نرخ بصره انچیکه مقرر خواهد شد از محمدحنیف وغیره
درخواست نمود، اصلا ندادند، و مرچ‌سیاه را تا چهل و چهار هون
درخواست نمود ندادند ـ باز روز دوم و صبحی لنگر برداشته پیشتر به‌صوب
بندر بصره راهی گردیدند و یک جوان اسداللهی مفرور شد ـ

و روبروی بندر مسقط چهار قلعه برکوه واقع است، منجمله آن
دو قلعه بطرف دست راست و دو بطرف چپ ـ و نامهای هر قلعه علحده
علحده است ـ منجمله دو قلعه که بطرف راست بوقت در آمد به بندر
مسقط واقع است، اولی را جرهٔ کلان و اخری را که متصل آبادی
است جلالی می نامند ـ و نام دو قلعه دیگر که بطرف چپ واقع است
اولی راجرهٔ خورد و نام اخری که متصل آبادی است کپتانی می نامند ـ
و جمله وسعت ملک محروسهٔ امام سی و یک روزه راه است، منجمله آن
وسعت ملک بالا گهات علحدهٔ که از بندر مسقط قلعه نجوه(۱) پانزده روز ۲۱
راه است ـ و وسعت ملک پائین گهات از راس‌الحد تا موضع صحار و
خور فقان(۲) شانزده روز راه است ـ و فاصله عرض دریائی از قلعه کپتانی
تا قلعه جلالی سه صد و هفتاد گز و فاصله عرض از قلعه جرهٔ کلان تا قلعه
جرهٔ خورد سه صد و یک گز ـ و افراط و تفریط آب کناره دریائی که
متصل آبادی است در ایام زایدالنور موازی هفده و نیم دست بالای
می گیرد و در ایام ناقص‌النور هفت دست کمتری پزیرد ـ و بندر مذکور
به اعتبار دارالسلطنت پتن بطرف بایب واقع است، و به وقت دخول به
بندر قبله بدست راست، و مشرق بطرف چپ، و جنوب بطرف روبرو،

۱ــ نزوی ۲ــ خورفکان

و شمال بر پشت ، و بطرف شمال دریا ، و به سه اطراف دیگر کوهستان،
و درمیان کوهستان و حصار بندر دو سه باغیچه و چند خانهای ادانی
که در آن گاذران و سقهای و چندی از افغان می باشند ـ و به دست
راست بوقت درآمد به بندر مسقط مطرح نام موضعی است به کنارهٔ
دریا بحجاب دو سه کوه از بندر مسطور و چند باغیچه واقع است و
بطرف جنوب شتاب (۱) نام موضعی است درمیان کوهستان و کنارهٔ دریا
بهحجاب یک کوه از بندر مذکور واقع است ـ و شهر رسطاخ که امام ۲
در آنجا سکونت دارد به طرف قبله واقع است و مسافت از راه خشکی از
بندر شش روزه راه است ـ و کوتهی سرکار بهطرف مشرق به اعتبار
وسط بندر واقع است ـ و دروازهای مسقط چهار است: دو بهطرف دریا
و شمال و درمیان آن یک حویلی خرید و فروخت اجناس و کچهری خلفان
که نامش فرده است و دو بطرف کوهستان بطرف جنوب واقع است ـ
و سه دروازه دیگر بر کوهستان: نام یکی شتاب و دویمی ریمام(۲)
وسیومی کلبو(۳) ـ اول بطرف لکن و دویمی بطرف قبله و مغرب وسیومی
بطرف بایب واقع است ـ و یک موضع گودی برای تیاری منازل داو
و دنگیها بوسعت مرمت یابی دو منزل جهاز در بندر مسقط متصل آبادی
بزیر پایهٔ قلعهٔ جلالی تیار نموده شده است ـ و داو و دنگیها مرمت
پذیر می شوند و جهازات تا حال مرمت پذیر نه شدهاند از عدم درستگی
موضع مذکور ـ و آبادی بندر مطرح و تمیز است، نه راستهای بازار
درست نه وسیع و نه کوچها بلکه از قیدخانه و زندان بدتر است ـ و
ترکیب خانهای عمده آنکه بر چهاردیواری تخت پوشی می نمایند و بالای آن
از گل و چونه پرسازند ـ اگر بالاخانه ضرور باشد، بدستور بالای آن عمارت
تازه می سازند ـ چنانچه حویلی امام و خلفان و چند حویلی های سوداگر و عرب ۳

۱ــ ستاب ۲ــ رنام ۳ــ کلبوه

هست، و طریق خانهای غیر عمده چنانچه بقال و بانی وغیره چوبهای خورد و برگ خرما بر چهاردیواری عرضاً و طولاً بلا فاصله بر چوبهای بزرگ که دوسه و چهار اول بر چهاردیواری بفاصله می نهندو ان را از گل و لا پر سازند - و طریق خانهای ادانی که بیرون شهر واقع است همه کلبه های برگ خرمائی هست - و در بندر نام چهار فصل باقی است لاکن همیشه سلسلهٔ تابستان جاریست و شدت تابستان تا سه ماه باشد، از ابتدای ماه جعفری تا آخر ماه هاشمی، که در اینجا ایام ربیع می گویند - و درین ایام خرما و انگور و انبه و انجیر و خربوزه و تربوز و شفتالو پخته می‌شوند - و سه ماه دیگر ایام خریف می نامند که بنای سرما از او هست، و درین روزها انار و نارنج و لیمون شیرین و ترنج و ترکنکری تیار می شوند - و سه ماه شتا یعنی ایام سرمای سخت، و درین ایام نیشکر تیار می شود - و سه ماه دیگر صیف، و درین ایام گل گلاب و میوه‌ها و سیب و دیگر غله‌جات بسیار پیدا و تیار می شوند - جمله حویلی عمده جات چهل و پنجاه و خانهای بقال و بانی نود و هفت که از ایشان محصول می گیرند - باقی چند خانهای عرب وغیره یک هزار و پنج صد
۲۳ هفت صد خواهد بود - و سوای این بیرون شهر دو هزار کلبهٔ برگ خرما خواهد بود - و لباس سردار عرب یک شال بسر و یایک لنگی بسر می بندند، و یک جبه در بر، و بالای آن یک ماشو، و یک پائجامه بزیر - و لباس سپاهی وغیره از عرب یک لنگی به سر، و یک لنگی بزیر، و یک جبه در بر، و لباس زنان اینها یک ازار یک جبه و یک چادر برقعه‌دار سیاه، اکثر لباس زنان اینها سیاه می باشد - و برادران امام معه خود پنج نفر، یکی خود سعید نام مالک جمیع ممالک محروسه خود دوم قیس مالک قلعه صحار و متعلقه قلعه مسطور و سیوم و چهارم سلطان و سیف مالک سمائیل و قلعه نعمان و پنجم طالب مالک قلعه ثور(۱) که متصل راس‌الحد

---

۱ — صور or سور

هست۔ این همه قلعه‌جات به ایشان از طرف امام سعید جاگیر هست۔ و پسران امام دو نفر، یکی احمد مالک قلعه برکه دوم حمید مالک قلعه سویق۔ و پسر خلفان پنج نفر، یکی سلیمان دوم محمد همشیر زاده امام سیوم علی و اسم چهارم و پنجم غیرمعلوم۔

و جهازات خاص امام سه منزل: یکی رحمانی و دو یمی کعبه رس و سیومی ناصری، و یک منزل غراب باز نام، جمله چهار منزل، و سوار
جنگی هشت منزل و داو هشت منزل و دنگی‌های دلال چهارده منزل و ۵
دنگی‌های گماشته‌ها و برادرش بست و پنج منزل۔ و محصول و آمد سالیانه امام چهارلک روپیه، منجمله آن دولک روپیه بابت محصول جهازات که از بنادر دیگر در بندر مسطور آمد و رفت می دارند و دو لک روپیه محصول و تحصیل ملک یعنی محصول درخت خرما وغیره و غله‌جات۔ و درماهه امام پنجاه روپیه و در ماهه خلفان بست روپیه و در ماهه دلال هفت و نیم روپیه و در ماهه محمدپسررزاق مصدی هفت و نیم روپیه و در ماهه سپاهی سه روپیه و به وقت جنگ به صبح پنج قیاس خرما و دو غاز و به شام پاو آثار برنج و گماشته های دلال دوازده نفر فی نفر پنجاه روپیه در ماهه و باقی داخل در بیت المال۔ و گذران اوقات بر پنجاه روپیه ماهواری و منافع جهازات و دنگی‌های خاص خودها است و وجه زکواة تنباکو به مرمت قلعه‌جات و حویلی‌های سرکار خرچ می نمایند۔ و به‌وقت آمد جهازات به بندر مسطور محصول می‌گیرند و به‌وقت روانگی اگر جنس لکوکها برند هیچ نمی‌گیرند معاف دارند۔ و محصول از جهازات وغیره کلاه پوشان انگریزی و فراسیسی و پرتگیشی فی جنس صدروپیه پنج روپیه می گیرند۔ و از عرب و از عجم فی صدروپیه شش و نیم روپیه،
و از هندو و بقال و بانی فی صدروپیه هشت روپیه، و از سرکار فیض آثار ۶
فی صدروپیه چهار روپیه می گیرند، و از هر بانی و بقال ساکن بندر پانزده غاز ماهواری گرفته به معذوران و فقرا می دهند۔ و جمله

بندوبست و انتظام ممالک محروسه وغیره و ترسیل رسل و رسائل بهر کس و انچه که به عمل می آید متعلق از خلفان است، سوای نام امام و مهر امام نیز به دست اوست ـ و غذای ادانی خرما و ماهی خشک و تر و قدری طعام و غذای عمده نان گندم و خرما و طعام و ماهی بریان، لاکن استعمال خرما و ماهی بسیار است ـ و امام همیشه در شهر رسطاخ ایام عمر خودبه عیش و عشرت می گذارد و گاه گاهی به طریق سیر به طرف بندر و یا ملک دیگر از املاک خود می رود و می آید ـ

و پیدائس میوه‌جات در بندر مسقط : خرما ، انگور، انجیر، انار، لیمون ، تربوز، خربوزه، انبه ، نیشکر، ترکنکری ، رتالو، زردآلو، شغتالو، مویز، مولی ، پیاز، شیرخشک ، کشنیزسبز ، کدوسفید ، کدوسرخ ، بادانجان ، ساگ‌چولائی ، ساگ‌میتهی ، ساگ‌خرفه ، شالی ، راگی ، باجرا ، جوار، مونگ ، برگ‌تنبول ، گندم ، عدس، نارجیل ،

و موسم آمد و رفت جهازات از بندر کوریال به بندر مسقط بعد
انقضای چهل روز از نه روز که ایام جشن است شروع و تا انقضای ۲۷
یک صد ونود روز آمد و رفت جهازات باقی ، و آمد و رفت داو و
دنگی‌ها از روز مسطور تا انقضای دو صد و دوازده روز بصوب مذکور
جاری ، و موسم آمد و رفت جهازات از بندر مسقط بصوب بندر بصره
بعد انقضای دو صد و هشتاد روز از نه روز مذکور شروع و تا سه صد
و چهل روز باقی ، و باد مراد حاصل اگرچه دوازده ماه موسم
آمد و رفت جهازات وغیره باقی است لاکن به شدت و خرابی و حصول باد
مخالف و موسم آمد و رفت جهازات از بندر کوریال بصوب جده بعد
انقضای هفتاد روز از نه روز مذکور شروع و تا یک صد و شصت روز
باقی ، و سلسلهٔ آمد و شد جهازات وغیره از هر بنادر به بندر مسقط
همیشه باقیست ـ

و نرخ اجناس بازار و نقدیات مرقوم تاریخ نوزدهم شهر احمدی

سال دلو سنه ۱۲۰۰ هجری(۱):

عطر صندل فی اثارخام ۱۰ روپیه - صندل فی کهندی ۸۷۰ هن حیدری - الائچی فی من ۱۵ هن حیدری - قرنفل فی من ۱۱۰ روپیه - جوتری فی من ۲۲۰ روپیه - جوز بویه فی من ۱۱۵ روپیه -
قند فی من ۹ روپیه - زعفران فی اثار خام ۱۰ روپیه - مشک فی مثقال ۸
۳ محمودی - کشمش فی من ۴ روپیه - دارچینی فی من ۴ روپیه - خشخاش فی من ۶ روپیه - شکر سفید فی کهندی ۸۰ روپیه - نابات فی کهندی ۱۶۰ روپیه - بادام فی کهندی ۵۲ روپیه - پسته فی کهندی ۱۲۰ روپیه - فندق فی کهندی ۲۰۰ روپیه - چهار مغز فی هزار عدد ۱ روپیه اٹهه‌آنه - خرمای تر فی من ۱۲ آنه - خرمای خشک فی کهندی ۱۵ روپیه - روغن زرد فی من ۷ روپیه - برنج اول فی بوره ۲۲ محمودی - برنج دوم فی بوره ۲۰ محمودی - برنج سیوم فی بوره ۱۸ محمودی ..... (؟) دال تور فی من ۱ روپیه - روغن کنجد فی من ۴ روپیه ۸آنه - پنبه فی من ۵ روپیه - ابریشم فی من ۱۳۲ روپیه - سونف فی من ۲ روپیه - تنبول فی من ۲ روپیه - صابن فی من ۲ روپیه - نمک طعام فی کهندی ۲ روپیه - هیزم فی من مسقطی ۲۰۲ غاز - رنگ قرمزی فی من مسقطی ۸۶ روپیه ۱۲ آنه - گندهک فی کهندی ۳۲ روپیه - شوره فی کهندی ۴۰ روپیه - سرب فی کهندی ۱۰۰ روپیه - سونت فی کهندی ۱۸ روپیه - آهن فی کهندی ۱۸ روپیه -
مس فی کهندی ۲۴۰ روپیه - وابر ملاکی فی من ۴ روپیه - ۹
برنجی فی من مسقطی ۱۱ روپیه - هینگ فی من ۳۰ روپیه - فلفل گرد فی کهندی ۳۴ روپیه - گندم فی من مسقطی ۴ محمودی -

---

۱— 18 Jumada 11, 1200/18 April, 1786.

املی مسقطی فی من ١٠٨ محمودی - جوار فی من مسقطی ١٢ غاز - باجره فی من ایضاً - مونگ فی من دهلی ٢ روپیه - جغرات فی قیاس ٢ غاز - گوشت فی قیاس ٣ محمودی - پیاز فی من مسقطی ٣ محمودی - شیر خشک فی من مسقطی ١٠٤ محمودی کشنیز خشک فی من مسقطی ٤ محمودی - زرد چوب فی من مسقطی ٤ محمودی - بوند قهوه فی من مسقطی ١٢ محمودی - قلعی فی من مسقطی ٢٤ محمودی - دندان فیل اول و بهتر فی کهندی هشت صد روپیه - دوم فی کهندی هفتصد - سیوم فی کهندی ٦٠٠ روپیه - بدستور پنج صد روپیه چهار صد روپیه -

فی هون بهادری بست محمودی نقره و فی روپیه پنج محمودی و فی ریال یازدهم و نیم محمودی و دوازده محمودی و فی محمودی بست
٣ غاز مسی و فی من مسقطی بست و چهار قیاس و فی قیاس چهارده روپیه وزن و فی کهندی بست من مسقطی -

و از کنارهٔ موضع مطرح بتاریخ بست ماه جعفری سال مذکور سنه الیه(١) مطابق سلخ ماه شعبان بوقت نماز صبح همه لنگر جهازات و داوها برداشته پیشتر بصوب بندر بصره راهی گردیده، داو کرایه دار که بر آن غلام علی خان و شاه نورالله خان وغیره سوار بودند و غراب سورتی بوقت سه پهر روز به کنارهٔ موضع رمیس که از ممالک محروسه امام متصل بندر به فاصله سه چهار کروه واقع است رسیده، بجهت انتظاری جهازات سرکار و داو کرایه دار محمد حنیف وغیره و هیمه آوری از کناره موضع مسطور برد او مرقوم تا یک و نیم پاس روز دیگر که سلخ ماه مذکور بود قایم نموده منتظر رسیدن جهازات سرکار بودند - درین اثنا به شدت باد صرصر مخالف وزیدن گرفت باز لنگر برداشته پیشتر

---

١ — 20 Ja'fari falls on 19 Sha'ban and not on 29 Sha'ban as mentioned in the Waqa'i.

به صوب بصره راهی گردیدند ـ

و به تاریخ غره ماه دارای سال سنه الیه(۱) روز سه شنبه بعد نماز مغرب داو کرایه دار بابت غلام علی خان به قطع چهل کروه به‌کنارهٔ بندر صحار که خوش موضعی است و آب و هوا و جایش
بسیار معتدل و بهتر و خورم و باغ و باغیچه و درختانش بسیار مقطع ۱
خوش اسلوب و دلکش و در هم و سواد باغهایش از آبادی بهتر چون سواد مینو برتر که برگذیده ممالک محروسه امام بندر مسقط است رسید ـ خوانین برای انتظاری جهازات سرکار و پر کردن آب لنگر به‌کنارهٔ که آب چهل و چهار گز بود قایم کنانیده به آوردن آب تاکید نمودند ـ

و روز چهار شنبه تاریخ دوم به وقت سه پاس غراب سورتی به موضع مذکور رسیده لنگر قایم نمود ـ و شاه نورالله خان وغیره به موضع مسطور رفته آبادی و باغها دیده باز به‌وقت سه پهر معه چند هزار دانه های انبه که موسم درپیش بود بخریدن گرفته برداو خودها سوار شدند ـ

و بتاریخ سیوم روز پنجشنبه جهاز فتح شاهی معزی و نبی بخش و داو کرایه‌دار محمد حنیف به تفاوت یک دو گهری پس و پیش به وقت دو پاس روز به موضع مذکور رسیده لنگرها قایم نمودند و همه‌ها را از آب و هیمه وغیره سر انجام ضروری هرچیکه درخواست بود تا آخر روز جمعه تاریخ چهارم از موضع مذبور گرفته بعد انقضای یک و نیم
پاس از شب شنبه تاریخ پنجم همه‌ها لنگر برداشته پیشتر بصوب(۲) ۳۲
بصره راهی شدند ـ

و به تاریخ هشتم روز سه شنبه داو کرایه‌دار بابت سواری غلام علی خان و شاه نورالله خان به وقت دو پهر قطع مسافت شصت

۱ــ Ist Ramzan, 1200/28 June, 1786.

۲ــ MS. بصوب بصوب

و هفت کروه نموده به موضع ماماسلامه که دو سه کوهست خورد خورد به آخر کوهستان که به جانب چپ به وقت رفتن به صوب بصره واقع می شود و در آن موضع همیشه شدت باد صرصر مخالف بسیار می باشد رسیده به صد چرخ و گرفتاری طی مسافت هشت کروه نموده به وقت نماز عشاء به کنارهٔ جزیرهٔ لارک که کوه گیرد و نمک در آنجا بسیار است و مقابله جزیرهٔ طویل و بندر قسم(۱) که مسکن عبدالله معینی است و به طرف پشت جزیرهٔ هرمز که مسکن پسر ناموروده است واقع و به طرف راست بندر عباس و بندر خمیر که معدن گوگرد در آنجا بسیار است از هفت هشت کروه نمودار بود و به طرف چپ کف دریا و آب چهل گز بود رسیده به سبب وفور شدت باد مخالف لنگر قایم نمودند ـ

۳۲ و به تاریخ نهم چند خلاصی و دو سه سپاهی و دو جوان اسداللهی و محمد شکرالله چیلهٔ سرکار برای آوردن آب و گوسفندان برای خوراک اسداللهی به آبادی جزیرهٔ لارک فرستاده بودند، آب شیرین و گوسفندان همدست نه گردید هلاک و سرگردان شده به وقت نماز عصر برداو رسیدند ـ و جهازات سرکار و داو محمد حنیف پستر ماندند ـ

و به تاریخ دهم روزپنجشنبه درساعت دوم لنگر برداشته بصوب منزل مقصود راهی شدند ـ و به‌وقت صبح شیخ اسماعیل یزک‌دار دفعه نتهوخان جماعدار اسد اللهی ، که به شب به اندیشه و توهم قطاع الطریق بندوق بارکرده بر یزک که متصل غلام‌علی‌خان و شاه نوراللہ‌خان وغیره بود ، از غفلت و جاهلی و جوانی دست به طریق مالش برسنگ چقماق بندوق نهاد فی‌الفور بندوق سرشده گولی سرب بر بازوی راست عبدالنبی خدمتگار غلام‌علی‌خان که از آنطرف می آمد ضرب بسیار رسانیده از بالای

۱ــ قشم

سینهٔ او بخیریت گذشت ، به فضل ایزد متعال و یمن توجه و اقبال
آنخداوند امانی خوانین وغیره بخریت مقرون شدند ، و به جوان مذکور
غلام‌علی خان و شاه‌نورالله خان تنبیه رسانیدند ـ و به وقت نماز عصر از ۴
ممر کثرت شدت بادمخالف شمالی به کنارهٔ متصل بندر قسم بعد قطع مسافت
یک و نیم کروه بصد چرخ و خرابی لنگر به جائی که آب دوازده گز
بود قایم نمودند ـ

و به تاریخ یازدهم روز جمعه بوقت نماز فجر لنگر یزداشته به قطع مسافت سه‌چهار کروه راه بصد چرخ و خرابی از وقوع شدت باد شمالی به وقت غروب آفتاب به کنارهٔ جزیزهٔ طویل که آب سی گز بود لنگر قایم نمودند ـ

و به تاریخ دوازدهم روز شنبه در طاس پنجم لنگر برداشته بصد چرخ و محنت بعد طی مسافت چهار پنج کروه بالا به کنارهٔ همون جزیرهٔ طویل که آب چهل و پنج گز بود متصل قریه شوذا(۱) به وقت نماز عصر لنگر قایم نمودند ـ

و به تاریخ سیزدهم روز یکشنبه از وقوع شدت باد شمالی لنگر برداشته آدمیان(۲) به قریه مذکور فرستاده قدری آب و شش راس گوسفند به قیمت پنج ریال برای جوانان اسداللهی اوردند ـ

و به تاریخ چهاردهم روز دوشنبه در طاس پنجم لنگر برداشته ۵ـ
قطع مسافت پنج شش کروه بالا به کنارهٔ جزیرهٔ مسطور در طاس دوم
شب پانزدهم لنگر قایم نمودند ـ

و به تاریخ پانزدهم روز سه شنبه در طاس سیوم لنگر برداشته به قطع مسافت دو سه کروه در طاس هشتم به کنارهٔ جزیرهٔ هنجام که ویران است و آب به مقدار یازده گز بود برای آب آوری از جزیرهٔ مذکور

۱ـ سوزا ۲ـ MS. ادمان

لنگر قایم نموده شاه‌نوراللّه خان و هر دو منشی و محمد کمال چیلهٔ سرکار و محمدعمر چوبدار و شیخ مرتضی و شیخ بدهن خدمتگار وغیره به زیارت روضهٔ حضرت سیدمحمد قدس سره که از اولاد حضرت‌امام‌علی موسی رضاعلیه السلام اند و به کنارهٔ جزیرهٔ مذکور واقع است رفته بشرف زیارت مشرف گردیده فاتحه و تلاوت قرآن نموده باز بر داو رسیدند ـ و قدری ریگ سیاه که به کنارهٔ جزیرهٔ مذکور بسیار بود بقدر ضرورت آوردند ـ و خلاصی‌ها تا به شام قدری آب آوردند ـ و داو کرایه دار محمدحنیف و مرادخان و محمد شفیع وغیره به وقت غروب آفتاب از ممر کثرت باد مخالف جهازات سرکار متعاقب گذاشته بخریت به کنارهٔ همون جزیره رسیده لنگر قایم نموده قدری آب از جزیره آوردند ـ

و به تاریخ شانزدهم روز چهار شنبه در طاس سیوم لنگر هر دو داو برداشته پیشتر راهی گردیده بعد قطع مسافت دو سه کروه به کنارهٔ جزیرهٔ طویل که آب بست و یک گز بود به وقت نماز شام رسیده لنگر هر دو داو قایم نمودند ـ

و به تاریخ هفدهم روز پنجشنبه در طاس سیوم هر دو لنگر برداشته پیشتر راهی گردیده بعد قطع مسافت شش کروه به آخر جزیرهٔ طویل و مقابل جزیرهٔ طم(۱) که گله‌های آهو بسیار و ویران افتاده است مگر یک روضه بزرگیست به کنارهٔ که آب شش گز بود هر دو داو پس و پیش قریب به وقت نماز شام لنگر قایم نمود ـ

و بتاریخ هجدهم روز جمعه در طاس پنجم لنگر هر دو داو برداشته قطع مسافت هشت کروه نموده در طاس اول شب نوزدهم به مقابله جزیرهٔ کنگ و لنگا(۲) که بجانب دست راست و جزیزهٔ نابیوه(۳)

۱– طنب　　۲– لنگه

۳– This is Nabiyu Tunb.

به طرف چپ واقع و آب ده گز بود لنگر هر دو داو قایم نموده در
طاس نهم شب مذکور به سبب شروع باد موافق قوسی هر دو لنگر ۷
برداشته پیشتر راهی شدند ـ

و داو محمد حنیف از اثنای راه در طاس سیوم روز شنبه تاریخ نوزدهم به‌طرف کنارهٔ جزیرهٔ بستانه که به جانب دست راست واقع و علاقهٔ سرحد ممالک ایران بود برای هیمه وغیره رفت ـ

و در طاس ششم داو بابت غلام علی خان از مقابل و متصل جزیرهٔ فرور که ویران است و در آنجا گله های گوسفند بسیار و بیشتر است پیشتر تجاوز نمود ـ و در طاس سیوم شب به کنارهٔ کوهستان سرحد ملک پارس(۱) متصل جزیرهٔ قیس که آب سی گز بود به قطع مسافت سی و پنج کروه لنگر قایم نمودند ـ و به تاریخ هشتم در طاس اول روز یکشنبه بوقت صبح لنگر برداشته به قطع مسافت دو سه کروه به کنارهٔ جزیرهٔ قیس که آب سی گز بود در طاس ششم رسیده برای خریدن چند اجناس ضروری و آب آوری لنگر قایم نموده آدمیان فرستاده روغن و گوسفندان وغیره برای جوانان اسداللهی بخریدی گرفتند ـ
و شاه نورالله خان وغیره چند کس برای دیدن جزیره و سر انجام ضروری ۰۸
خود رفته باز آمدند ـ و خلاصیان تا اول طاس شب دوشنبه آب آوری مشغول بودند، و بعد فراغت در طاس چهارم لنگر برداشته پیشتر راهی شدند ـ

و پیش از نمود صبح صادق باد مراد به شکل طوفان به شدت تا یک طاس وزیدن گرفت که یک اوزار چاک و ضائع گردید ـ بعد یک طاس کم گردید، همه روز دوشنبه تاریخ بست و یکم و شب سه شنبه تا اول طاس پنجم مسافت راه صد و بست کروه از قیس تا

۱ــ پارس or فارس

بندر کنگون که مقرر است طی نمود، و از آنجا تا جزیرهٔ اُم نخیله(۱) بست کروه راه تا طاس سیوم روز سه شنبه تاریخ بست و دوم طی نموده پیشتر نه کروه بالای جزیرهٔ مذکور تا طاس پنجم رسیده بود که باد ۱
مراد قوسی تمام و کمال منهدم گردید، تا آخر وقت نماز شام انتظاری باد مراد نمود ـ آخر الامر بجای که آب بست و چهار گز بود لنگر قایم نمودند ـ و در طاس دوم اثری از باد به وقوع رسید لنگر برداشتند فی‌الفور شدت باد مخالف شمالی چندان به ظهور انجامید که باز در همون طاس لنگر قایم نمودند ـ

۳ و به‌تاریخ بست و سیوم روز چهار شنبه در طاس دوم ضرورتاً لنگر برداشته به صد چرخ و خرابی پیشتر راهی گردیده مسافت هشت نه کروه طی نموده بعد نماز مغرب مقابل جزیرهٔ خان که بسرحد ملک فارس واقع است لنگر بجای که آب بست و چهارگز بود قایم نمودند ـ

و در طاس نهم شب پنجشنبه تاریخ بست و چهارم لنگر برداشته پشتر راهی شدند ـ و داو محمد حنیف علی‌الصباح نمودار شده در طاس دوم مقابل گردید ـ و به وقت سه پهر یک منزل جهاز انگریز که در راه بندر مسقط مقابل گردیده بود از صوب بندر بصره از فاصلهٔ یک کروه مقابل شده پیشتر بصوب بندر مسقط راهی گردید ـ و به وقت نماز عصر بعد قطع مسافت دو سه کروه بصد چرخ و خرابی لنگر هر دو داو بجای که آب چهل گز بود، به عدم باد مراد و مخالف قایم کردند ـ

و در طاس پنجم شب جمعه باز لنگر برداشته بعد قطع مسافت دو سه کروه در طاس سیوم روز جمعه تاریخ بست و پنجم از عدم باد لنگر هر دو منزل در آب سی و شش گز به کنارهٔ کوهستان بنادر سروج علاقهٔ ملک پارس قایم نمودند ـ و در طاس هفتم غلام علی خان

۱ــ نخیلو

و شاه نورالله خان محمد عمر چوبدار را نزد محمد حنیف فرستاد محمد شفیع را طلب داشتند ـ مراد خان و محمد شفیع نزد غلام علی خان و شاه نور الله خان رسیده سوال و جواب فروخت نمودن اجناس سرکار در بندر
ابوشهر نموده باز رفتند ـ و در طاس هشتم روز لنگر هر دو منزل برداشته ۰
پیشتر راهی شده به سبب وقوع باد مخالف قوسی از وقت شام تاشش طاس شب شنبه قطع مسافت ده کروه نموده متصل بندر ابوشهر به فاصله دو سه کروه به جای که آب دوازده گز بود لنگر هر دو داو قایم ساختند ـ

و بتاریخ بست و ششم روز شنبه در طاس هفتم بعد شروع باد قوسی لنگر هر دو داو برداشته پیشتر بقطع مسافت دو کروه به کنارهٔ بندر ابوشهر که درآن کوتهی خلفان و دلال بندر مسقط و کوتهی انگریز واقع است و آبادی خورد و خوب و بازار آباد و پر، هر چیز میسر و حاصل لاکن آب شیرین از یک کروه می آرند لنگر قایم نمودند ـ و محمود ناخدا و عبدالله کرانی وغیره چند مردم علاقهٔ داو فرود آمده به بندر ابوشهر رفتند ـ غلام‌علی‌خان و شاه‌نورالله‌خان به زبانی ناخدا و کرانی به شیخ ناصر (۱) حاکم بندر مذکور سلام و تحنیت گفتند ـ کرانی و ناخدا از شیخ ناصر ملاقات نموده سلام رسانیده، کرانی وغیره باز در طاس چهارم شب یکشنبه به داو رسیده اظهار نمود که سلام شماها به شیخ ناصر حاکم بندر مذکور رسانیدم ـ شیخ مسطور حقیقت رسیدن شماها وغیره درین صوب پرسید همه حقیقت ظاهر ساختم باز گفت که فردا من هم آدم برای فرود آوردن شاه‌نورالله‌خان می فریسم ـ

روز دوم تاریخ بست و هفتم غلام علی خان دوسه مردم را برای
خریدن چنداجناس ضروری بهته به جوانان اسداللهی به بندر فرستاده ۱
طلبیدند ـ آدمیان (۲) مذکور به وقت نماز مغرب معه اجناس مطلو به بر داو

۱ـ MS. شیخ ناصر بن مذکور

۲ـ MS. ادمان

رسیدند - و در همون روز مالک داو چند بسته‌های سرانجام علاقهٔ مالک داو بابت خرید و فروخت بندر ابوشهر از داو برآورده به بندر فرستادند - و به وقت سه طاس روز برآمده گماشته های ماوجی سیتهه و خلفان که در ابوشهر به کوتهی خودها سکونت دارند بنابر ملاقات غلام علی خان و شاه نوراالله خان آمده ملاقات کردند - شاه نور الله خان نرخ بعضی اجناس مطلوبه از اوشان پرسیده گفتند که نزد مایان این اجناس است درین بندر به کفایت به فروخت خواهند رسید - گفتند که نمونه از اجناس مذکور بدست مایان بدهند، البته به ساهوکاران و تجاران بندر نمایش نموده، اگر اتفاق افتد بهتر و الا باز پس آورده جواب داده خواهد شد - شاه‌نوراالله‌خان خود معه سیتهه های مذکور بر داو محمدحنیف رفته به اتفاق محمدحنیف که مریض وقت بودند و مرادخان وغیره نمونه اجناس سپرد گماشته‌های مسطور نمودند -

و بتاریخ بست و هشتم شیخ ناصر پسر و ابوالحسن اهلکار خودرا معه نود وسه عدد حجب یعنی هندوانه و سه سبد پر از خوشه های انگور و یک سبد پر از شفتالوی خام ونه راس گوسفند بطریق لازمه
مهانداری نزد غلام‌علی خان و شاه نوراالله خان فرستاده به زبانی پیام نمود ۴۲
که از آمدن شماها بسیار خوشی و خورمی عاید وقت خویش گردید، و فیمابین خود و آقای شماها از مدت ممتد شیوه یگانگی و یکجهتی مرعی است، و این بندر و خود همه از ملک و آن سرکار است و دوسه حویلی معتبر و هوادار برای شماها در بندر خالی نموده شده است بلا تکلف فرودآمده دفع ماندگی جهازات نمایند، و انچناکه به امورات سرکار درخواست باشد ایما نمایند، البته بسر و چشم به تقدیم رسانیده خواهد شد - خوانین پسر شیخ ناصر را به عزت و حرمت نشانیده به جواب پرداختند که فی الحقیقت مابین شما و آقای مایان رابطه اتحاد و مودت مربوط لاکن مایان به سبب تعقیب جهازات سرکار که امروز فردا خواهند رسید

دو سه روز درین جا خواهند ماند و زود پیشتر راهی شدن و به منزل
مقصود رسیدن ضرور، درین صورت فرود آمدن مایان محال ـ ابوالحسن
اهلکار مذکور گفت که شیخ ناصر اراده مستقیم دارد که چند اشخاص
باهوش را با تحایف و سوغات ایندیار و بندر خود برای درخواست یک
مکان کوتهی در بندر کوریال و تقرر مکان کوتهی سرکار در بندر خود
نزد آقای شماها بفربسد، اگر درین ماده عرضداشت بنویسند اولی و انسب ـ
خوانین استدعا را به درجه اجابت مقرون ساخته یک عدد پچهوری خورد ۲۳
کلدار ابریشمی تار پتری و دوتهان خورد چهینت برهانپوری که به قیمت
سی روپیه در بندر مسقط بخریدن آورده بودند خلعت داده روانه نمودند ـ
و میوهٔ مذکور را بخود و جوانان اسداللهی وغیره تقسیم نمودند و نیز یک
راس گوسفند به غلام علی خان و یک راس بهر دو منشی وچیلهٔ سرکار و
چوبدار و خدمتگار و چهار راس به جوانان اسداللهی تقسیم نمودند ـ و
به تاریخ غره ماه هاشمی سال دلو ۱۲۰۰ هجری(۱) روز پنجشنبه ابوالحسن
اهلکار را غلام علی خان و شاه نورالله خان نزد خود طلبیده یک یک
عرضداشت علحده از طرف خودها به حضور پرنور دربارهٔ سفارش شیخ مذکور
نوشته بصحابت اهلکار مسطور نزد شیخ که بکار خود از بندر قطع مسافت
چهار کروه نموده بجای دیگر برای جنگ با سواران فرستادهٔ جعفر خان
برادر زاده کریم خان رفته بود فرستادند ـ

و به تاریخ دوم ماه مذکور روز جمعه که روز عید سعید فطره
بود از کنارهٔ بندر مسطور لنگر هردو داو بر داشته بصد چرخ و خرابی
بعد قطع مسافت دوسه کروه به کنارهٔ شط بنوتمیم انصاری که موضعی
است بسیار خوب و رودی است عظیم و آبادی بنا کردهٔ بنوتمیم انصاری
است و گندم و بسیار چیزها در آنجا می شوند به ابوشهر و بصره می برند، ۲۴

۱ـ 30 Ramazan, 1200/27 July, 1786.

درآب نه گز لنگر قایم نمودند - و جهاز نبی‌بخش از دو روز نمودار بود بتاریخ مسطور در طاس نهم متصل داو محمدحنیف بخریت رسیده لنگر قایم نمود - و محمدحنیف از دوسه روز در سکرات‌الموت هلاک بود -

و بتاریخ سیوم روز شنبه بعد نماز مغرب لنگر هر دو داو برداشته بعد نیم ساعت به سبب کثرت باد صرصر مخالف لنگر داو بابت سواری غلام‌علی خان قایم نمودند و داو محمدحنیف پیشتر راهی گردید -

و به تاریخ چهارم روز یکشنبه علی‌الصباح لنگر داو کرایه‌دار برداشتند - و در طاس دوم جهاز نبی بخش متصل داو رسید و غلام علی خان و شاه نورالله خان عبدالرحمان چیله و محمد فاضل چوبدار سرکار را به جهاز مذکور فرستاده خبر جهاز فتح شاهی و غراب سورتی استفسار کنانیدند - ضیاءالدین که بر جهاز مذکور بود گفته فرستاد که از نه روز اثر جهاز و غراب پدیدار نه گردیده و پیشتر ازین نزد جزیرهٔ هنجام و هرمز لنگر قایم نموده بودند - بعد قطع مسافت دو سه کروه در طاس دوم شب دو شنبه لنگر جهاز و داو پس و پیش به‌کنارهٔ جزیرهٔ
مبارک خارج در آب بست و هشت گز قایم نمودند - و جزیرهٔ ۳۵
خوارج(۱) که در آن بست و پنج درخت خرما و چند چاى‌هاى آب شیرین است بجانب دست راست واقع بود - و داو محمد حنیف پیشتر از یک ساعت لنگر قایم نموده بودند -

یادداشت نرخ اجناس بازار بندر ابوشهر مرقوم تاریخ بست و نهم ماه دارائی سال دلو سنه ۱۲۰۰ هجری(۲)انکه

شکر فی من تبریز ۸-۷ محمودی - نبات(۳) فی من مذکور ۷ ۱ محمودی - صندل فی من ۲۵ محمودی - مرچ سیاه فی من ۹۰ (محمودی) قلعي فی من

۱— Khargu

۲— 29 Ramazan, 1200/26 July, 1786.

۳— MS. نابات

٢٣ (محمودی) - سرب فی من ٨ (محمودی) - آهن فی من ٦ (محمودی) -
پولاد فی من ١٢ (محمودی) - مس فی من ١٩ (محمودی) - زرد چوب فی من
۴ (محمودی)- زنجبیل فی من ٦ (محمودی)- دار چینی کوریالی فی من ٨ (محمودی)-
دارچینی سیلانی فی من ۴٠ (محمودی) - سنگ بصری فی من ١٢ (محمودی) -
برنج اول فی بوره ٣٠ (محمودی) - برنج دوم فی بوره ٢٥ (محمودی) - گندم فی
من ١ (محمودی) - مونگ فی من ٣ (محمودی) - هینگ فی من ٣٢ (محمودی) -
نخود فی من ٢ (محمودی)- روغن زرد فی من ١٣ (محمودی)- روغن کنجد فی من
٨ (محمودی)- قرنفل فی من ١٩٠ (محمودی)- جای پهل فی من ٢٢٠ (محمودی) -
جوتری فی من ٦٠ (محمودی) - پنبه فی من ١٠ (محمودی) - پیاز فی من
٨٠ (محمودی)- شیرخشک فی من ۴ (محمودی) - کشنیزخشک فی من ۴ (محمودی) -
زیره میتهی فی من ٣ (محمودی) - نمک فی من ۴ (محمودی) - بادام فی من ٢٦
٣ (محمودی) - پسته فی من ٨ (محمودی) - اکروٹ فی من ٦ (محمودی) -
آلوی خشک فی من ۴ (محمودی)- انجیرخشک فی من ٣ (محمودی) - انجیرتر فی من
١ (محمودی) - کشمش فی من ٧ (محمودی) - خرما فی من ١ (محمودی) -
خشخاش فی من ٥ (محمودی) - گل گلاب خشک فی من ٥ (محمودی) -
گلاب شیرازی فی من ٩ محمودی - سرکه انگوری فی من ۴ (محمودی) -
خربوزه فی من ٨٠ (محمودی) - هندوانه فی من ٨٠ (محمودی) - انگور فی من
١٢٠ (محمودی) - گوسفند دنبه فی عدد ١٥ - بادانجان فی من ٨٠ (محمودی) -
تنباکوی اول فی من ٦ (محمودی) - تنباکو دوم فی من ۴ (محمودی) -

این همه رقوم که مرقوم شد محمودی‌ها است، و همه من‌ها من تبریز است، فی من کوریالی سه و نیم من تبریزی و یک من تبریزی را شانزده قیاس بندر مسقط است -

و بتاریخ پنجم ماه هاشمی سال دلو سنه ١٢٠٠ هجری(١) روز دوشنبه

١- 4 Shawwal, 1200/31 July, 1786.

صبحی مراد خان و محمه شفیع وغیره محمد حنیف را که در سکرات الموت
از هفت هشت روز گرفتار بود فرود آورده بر روضهٔ مبارک مقدسه
حضرت حنیف شاه صاحب کد بر دروازهٔ گنبد مبارک نوشته است که
السلام علیٰ ساکن هذا المشهد امیرالمومنین محمد بن امیرالمومنین علی علیه السلام
بیرون بر پشته واقع است، بردند ـ و در طاس دوم شاه نورالله خان و هر دو ۴۷
منشی و چیله های سرکار و چوبدار و خدمتگار وغیره فرود آمده در
قلعهٔ جوزا ویران از ده سال، که در طول شش صد و پنجاه گز و در
عرض پنج صد و نود گز، و چهار برج به‌چهار گوشهٔ قلعه و دو
برج بر دو دروازه کنارهٔ دریا، یکی بسته و مسدود است بدست راست
واقع، و دو دروازهٔ دیگر، یکی بطرف دریا دوم به طرف آبادی، و روضهٔ
مقدسه حضرت محمد حنیف بن امیرالمومنین علی کرم‌الله وجهه و روضهٔ
محمد بن امیرالمومنین ابی بکر رضی‌الله‌عنه بدست چپ، و بطرف راست روضهٔ
عبدالله بن امیرالمنین عمر رضی‌الله‌عنه و روضهٔ عبدالله انصاری، و روضهٔ میر
عبدالله علم بردار بطرف چپ بر پشت، و روضهٔ خادم دیدبان بر پشته
و کوه واقع است و جای چله کشی خضَر علیه السلام در راه بدست راست
واقع است ـ و در جزیره چند خانه آباد و ویران است و چند باغیچه
واقع است ـ و اندرون قلعه چند سرا و حویلی و بازار و دکاکین سقفی
و یک مسجد و یک مکان کوتهی خاص ولندیز بطریق قلعه بالا متصل
برج کوثر و چاه های آب شیرین و یک حویلی چهارده دری بر دروازهٔ
برجی کنارهٔ دریا ویران و افتاده است داخل شده در حویلی چهارده دری ۴۸
سکونت ورزیدند و نیز ضیاءالدین و محمد علی بهاتو و جوانان علاقهٔ
بهرام و چند نفر شاگرد پیشه که بر جهاز نبی بخش بودند فرود آمدند ـ
و در طاس ششم غلام علی خان و جوانان اسدالله اللهی فرود آمده داخل
حویلی مذکور شدند ـ و در طاس دهم محمد حنیف که از شش هفت
روز در سکرات الموَت بودند به قضای الهی فوت کردند ـ محمد شفیع

و مراد خان پیش دروازهٔ گنبد مقدس موصوف بدست چپ در طاس چهارم شب سه شنبه مدفون ساختند ـ

و به تاریخ ششم روز سه شنبه در طاس سیوم شاه نورالله خان به‌زیارت روضهٔ مقدسه مسطور که بیرون قلعه بر پشته واقع است و یک مینار خشت بندی چینی نموده مضموم گنبد مبارک است کهنه، رفته بشرف زیارت مشرف شده، باز در یک ساعت بیامدند ـ و بجوانان اسداللهی وغیره چند قرص رومی علی‌الحساب داده ـ و بر غار مبارک که در آن حضرت تشریف برده اند، یک صندوق چوبی در طول هفت گز و در عرض چهار گز و در بلندی یک و نیم گز قدرے کم بود، واقع است، و بر صندوق آیات کلام مجید کندیده است ـ تاریخ ترتیب(؟) و مرمت گنبد و مینار هفت صد و سی و دو سال از سنه هجری نبوی علیه السلام و پیشتر از آن صرف گنبد مبارک خورد بود، من بعد یکی از اهل ایران مینار دوازده دری مضموم گنبد مبارک ساخته مشرف گردید ـ و بنا کننده و معمار گنبد مبارک سید علی بن حسین‌البخاری ـ و در گنبد مبارک یک قبر اخون حضرت صاحب روضه موصوف است که بر آن چند اجزای کلام‌الله نهاده اند، هر که به زیارت می آید کلام‌الله می خواند ـ و قبر سازندهٔ گنبد ۲۹
یعنی سید علی بن حسین بدست چپ بطرف سر بیرون گنبد واقع است و هفت قبور بر پشت گنبد یعنی بدست راست و پائین، و سوای ایں در چهار دیواری دیگر سه قبور معه یک قبر طفلک بطرف چپ پائین واقع است ـ و یک پنجهٔ آهنی بر گنبد و مینار مبارک نهاده اند و هزاران قبور گردا گرد گنبد مبارک است و نیز گنبد مبارک محمد بن امیرالمومنین ابی بکر رضی‌الله‌تعلیٰ‌عنه و گنبد عبدالله بن امیرالمومنین عمر رضی‌الله‌تعلیٰ‌عنه و گنبد علم بردار و چهار دیواری روضهٔ عبدالله انصاری و چهار دیواری چله کشی حضرت خواجه خضر علیه السلام، و یک گنبد

خورد خادم دیدبان بر پشته واقع است، بر گردا گرد روضهٔ مبارک است، و چند قبور بزرگ دیگر است که نام آنها معلوم نیست ـ

و نیز کیفیت دیگر به تحقیقات رسیده که حضرت موصوف معه افواج قاهره که همه بزرگان مسطور سردار فوج بودند در جزیرهٔ مبارک رسیدند و بسیار کفار بجنگ حضرت در آمده بودند، همه را کشتند و همه افواج و سرداران حضرت علیه السلام به شهادت رسیدند ـ من بعد حضرت در گوشه نشسته بودند که هفت منازل جهازات بافوج و سلاح مشحون معه یک پیر زن قوی هیکل و بلند بالا فاحشه و مکاره و ساحره به کنارهٔ جزیرهٔ مبارک رسیدند ـ همه سرداران فوج وغیره بزن مکاره گفتند که مایان بروبروی حضرت رفتن نمی توانند ـ زن ساحره گفت: شما بلاخوف پس پشت من بیائید، اگر حضرت ولی صفت هستند هرگز بر من زن عریان دست انداز نخواهند شد، اگر ساحر باشند البته سحر خواهند نمود، بدلهٔ سحر بعمل آورده خواهد شد، شما خاطر جمع باشند ـ من بعد همه افواج کفار پس پشت زن مکاره برهنه شده روبروی حضرت آمدند ـ حضرت از گوشه بیرون آمدند دیدند که یک پیر زن مکاره برهنه مع فوج مقهوره می آید، بجناب کبریا دعا نمودند که اینها را همه سنگ سازد، به برکت دعای حضرت همه افواج و جهازات و پیر زن مسطور سنگ گردیدند و حضرت سنان خود بر زمین زدند، غاری عظیم پیدا گردید در غار تشریف فرمودند ـ حالا برهمون غار یک صندوقِ بزرگ چوبین مانند تربت ساخته برغار نهاده اند و بر آن بنای گنبد مبارک ساخته اند ـ و تا حال از علامات جهازات و افواج کفار که سنگ شده اند علامتی پیدا است و دو جای قدم مبارک حضرت و سم اسپ مبارک بر سنگ برخاسته اند و بر یک جای به کنارهٔ دریا بطرف سر بر بازو بتفاوت بسیار سه نیزه بدست مبارک زده اند، سه چاه‌های(۱)

۱ــ .MS چاه

آب شیرین و خنک پیدا است، سوای این چاههای آب شیرین بسیار است ـ
و تاریخ عرس حضرت معلوم نیست، مگر از حکم حضرت در روز عیدین
طعام می پزند و به فقراء و مساکین وغیره می خورانند ـ و چهار مینار خورد
طلائی بر چهار گوشهٔ صندوق مبارک حضرت میر مهنا که بعد ولندیز
حاکم جزیرهٔ مذکور بود بطریق قبه نهاده است و نام حضرت و نام خود
بر مینار مذکور نوشته است و چهار عدد آئینهٔ بزرگ در مینار باندرون
بر فوق نهاده است ، دو بطرف گنبد و دو برو برو ، سوای این دو سه
آئینه خورد و بر دیوار گنبد نشانیده است ـ

و سبب ویرانی جزیرهٔ مذکور می گویند که اول ولندیز قلعه
برپا کرده محصول از جهازات گرفته تجاران و ساهوکاران را طلب داشته
بقول و قرار راست و درست جزیره را آباد کرده بود که روزی ولندیز
خوک‌ها را پرورش می نموده بود که یک خنزیر از آن میان نزد روضهٔ
مبارک رفت ـ حضرت بر ولندیز برهم و غضبناک شده میر مهنا را که
از قوم چعب است ارشاد شد که ولندیز را دور کن ـ میرمهنا اگرچه فوج ٢
کم داشت بر حکم‌عالی متعالی آگاه شده با فوج قلیل خود بر جزیره آمده
با کلاه پوش ولندیز جنگ نمود ـ آخر الامر فتح نصیب شده چند مدت
حکومت کرد ـ من بعد میرمهنا آمد و شدگان را ایذا دادن شروع نمود ـ
حکم عالی بر باشندگان جزیره و بندر بصره صادر گردید که میرمهنا را
بکشند ـ این خبر بمیرمهنا رسید هولناک شده به بندر بصره گریخت ، در راه
بصره از دست بصریان مقتول گردید ـ از آن مدت جزیرهٔ مسطور ویران است ـ

و غراب سورتی از صبح نمودار شده به شدت تمام در طاس چهارم‌شب
چهار شنبه به کنارهٔ جزیرهٔ مبارک لنگر قایم نمودند ـ و چهار راس
گوسفند و چند عدد هندوانه بطریق مهمانداری از طرف میرعلی حاکم
جزیره که بکار خود بجنگ همراه شیخ ناصر رفته بود متولی روضه شیخ
سلمان نام نزد غلام علی خان و شاه نور الله خان آورد و داد یک راس

گوسفند به غلام علی خان و یک راس به شاه نورالله خان و یک راس به ۵۲
فراشان و جوانان بهرام و مشعلچی و هرکاره و یک راس بهر دو منشی و چوبدار و خدمتگار وغیره تقسیم نمودند۔

و بتاریخ هفتم جعفر خان و چند بارگیر معه لاش محمد قاسم بارگیر سرکار علاقه مراد خان که از دو ماه بیمار بود به قضای الهی فوت شد، نزد روضهٔ مبارک رسیده محمد قاسم تجهیز و تکفین نموده بشرف زیارت همون جا ماندند۔

و بتاریخ هشتم در طاس چهارم روز پنجشنبه غلام علی خان و شاه نورالله‌خان هر دو به زیارت روضه مبارک رفته، زیارت امام حسین‌علیه‌الصلوة و السلام خوانیده، بست قرص رومی نقد نذر روضهٔ مبارک به مجاور شیخ سلمان و ناصر که برادر زادهٔ اوست دادند و محمودیهاے شا نزده قرص و گندم بست قرص یک صد و دوازده من تبریزی به فقرا خیرات نمود۔ بعد زیارت در طاس هفتم مراجعت به فرودگاه نمودند۔

و به شب یازدهم هنگامه غیر واقع برپا گردید که چهارصد نفر از عرب و عجم به قتل و غارت می آیند۔ به استماع این خبر سوای غلام علی خان و جعفر خان وهر دو منشی همه کسان و شاه نورالله خان
بسیار هولناک شده، کنیزک خودرا معه حرم شکرالله خان و زوجهٔ ۵۳
محمدعمر چوبدار و محمد فاضل چوبدار و شیخ بدهن خدمتگار سرکار و شیخ نهنی خدمتگار غلام علی خان معه سرانجام و اسباب بر داو شباشب سوار نمودند و خود هم شاه نورالله خان عازم سواری بودند که درین ضمن غلام‌علی خان گفتند که هرچیکه شدنی باشد می شود خود در شب بر داو سوار نخواهم شد و بحفاظت شب خواهم پرداخت رفتن خود موقوف ساختند۔

و به تاریخ یازدهم روز یکشنبه بوقت سه پهر گماشته سیهته دلال بندر مسقط که در بندر ابوشهر است برای خریدن پنج کهندی الائچی

و بورهای مرچ سیاه نزد شاه نورالله خان رسیده خبر داد که جهاز فتح شاهی معزی عنقریب برسد ـ و در طاس یازدهم جهاز مذکور نمودار شده درطاس نهم شب دوشنبه به کنارهٔ جزیرهٔ مبارک رسیده لنگر قایم نمود ـ

و به تاریخ دوازدهم روز دوشنبه صبحی غلام علی خان و شاه نورالله خان محمد فاضل چوبدار و شیخ مرتضی خدمتگار سرکار را به جهاز مذکور فرستاده، باعث دیرکشی و خیرعافیت استفسار کنانیده به لطف علی خان و جوقدار سزاول و سید جعفر مصدی را گفته فرستادند که زود امروز فرود آمده زیارت روضهٔ مبارک نموده هرچیکه از سرانجام ضروری ضرور باشد تهیه کرده باز سوار شوند که امشب لنگر جهازات برداشته خواهد شد ـ آنها باعث دیر کشی وقوع شدت باد صرصر مخالف وغیره اظهارکرده قبول نمودند ـ و درطاس چهارم لطف علی خان و جوقدار وغیره فرود آمده زیارت شریف حاصل نموده نزد غلام علی خان و شاه نورالله خان در حویلی و بام چهارده دری آمده احوال خود بایکدگر ظاهر ساخته به ٥
جوانان سزاول سر نفر چهار قرص رومی و به لطف علیخان صد قرص علی‌الحساب دهانیدند ـ و شاه نورالله خان یک قطعه خط از جانب خود به محمد شفیع دربارهٔ دادن الائچی پنج کهندی به نرخ فی رطل شانزده هون حیدری پاو بالا و سه صد بورهٔ مرچ سیاه بطریق امانت، انچیکه قیمت و نرخ در بندر بصره مقرر خواهد شد، ادا نموده آید، به گماشته سیهته دلال که از بندر ابوشهر رسیده بود نوشتند که شماها نمی دهند خوب نمی کنند، اگر به این قیمت در بصره بفروخت نرسد ندامت کشیدن مناسب نیست، هرچیکه بفروخت می رسد بهتر است ـ من بعد آنها پنج کهندی الائچی به دشواری دادند و در دادن بورهای مرچ سیاه ضیاءالدین حرکت بیجا نمود ـ

و بتاریخ سیزدهم روز سه شنبه چند جوان سزاول فرود آمده زیارت نموده سر انجام ضروری خریده بر جهاز سوار شدند ـ و به لطف علی خان

و شاه نوراللّه خان وجه طلب دو ماهه اوشان از روی حساب واجبی دادند ـ و در طاس نهم شاه نوراللّه خان وغیره از جزیره برآمده بر داو کرایه‌دار سوار شدند، و در طاس دهم همه‌ها بر جهازات خودها سوار شدند ـ و در طاس دوازدهم غلام علی خان معه جوانان اسداللهی بر داو سوار شدند ـ و غلام علیخان و شاه نوراللّه خان یک عدد شال به قیمت بست روپیه و ده قرص رومی بنام میرعلی حاکم جزیره به شیخ سلمان متولی مجاور روضهٔ مبارک دادند که شال بمیر علی برساند و ده قرص خیرات به فقراء نماید ـ

٥٦ و در طاس اول شب چهار شنبه لنگر جهازات سرکار و داو کرایه دار معه شانزده و هفده منزل اغیار برائے خطر در راه بصره از قوم چعب واقع است منتظر بودند برداشتند، به مجرد برداشتنن لنگر باد مخالف شمالی شدت نمود، باز لنگر بد کنارهٔ جزیرهٔ خوارج در آب پانزده گز قایم نمودند و بتاریخ چهاردهم روز چهار شنبه در طاس دوم لنگر همه‌ها برداشتند، بصد چرخ و خرابی یک قدم پیشتر نرفته باز در طاس ششم درمیان دریا که آب سی گز بود لنگر قایم نمودند و باز در طاس نهم لنگر برداشته به کنارهٔ جزیرهٔ خوارج لنگر قایم نمودند ـ

نرخ اجناس بازار و خانهای ویران جزیرهٔ خارج مرقوم یازدهم ماه هاشمی سال دلو سنه ۱۲۰۰ هجری(۱) آنکه

برنج فی‌من تبریزی ۳ محمودی ـ گندم فی من ۱۰۸ (محمودی) ـ آرد گندم فی من ۲۰۸ (محمودی) ـ روغن زرد فی من ۱۶ (محمودی) ـ عدس فی‌من ۳۰۸ (محمودی) ـ خرما ۳ (محمودی) ـ رطب فی من ۲۰۸ (محمودی) ـ هندوانه فی من ۲ (محمودی) ـ بادانجان فی‌من ۱۰۸ (محمودی) ـ گوسفند فی‌عدده ۱ (محمودی) ـ مرغ فی عدد ۱ (محمودی) ـ هیزم فی من ۸ غاز ـ سوای برنج و هیمه همه

۱ــ 10 Shawwal, 1200/ 6 August, 1786.

اشیاء و اجناس مسطوره در جزیرهٔ مذکور پیدا می شوند ـ

و به تاریخ شانزدهم ماه مذکور لنگر همه جهازات سرکار وغیره
بروز جمعه در ساعت یازدهم از جزیرهٔ خوارج برداشته روز دوم که تاریخ ۷
هفدهم است در طاس دهم بعد قطع مسافت دوازده کروه به کنارهٔ بندر
دیلم و بنک و بحرگان در آب بست و شش گز قایم نمودند ـ و در طاس
یازدهم روز مذکور باز لنگر برداشته بعد قطع مسافت هجده کروه در
طاس هشتم روز یکشنبه تاریخ هجدهم در سرحد خرابات در آب سیزده گز
لنگر همه جهازات سرکار وغیره قایم نموده دو خط که غلام علی خان
و شاه نورالله خان از جانب خودها علحده علحده در جزیرهٔ خارج
موسومه ابراهیم آغا حاکم بصره بنابر اطلاع ناموده و چند امورات
سرکار نویسانیده مقرر نموده بودند که محمد شفیع را معه چوبدار سرکار
و دهلیت پیشتر به بصره روانه نماید ـ محمد شفیع از نرم‌دلی به اقبال این
معنی نه پرداخت، ازین جهت امر مذکور ملتوی مانده بود ـ بصحابت
محمد فاضل چوبدار سرکار و عبدالله خان خدمتگار شاه نورالله خان بر بتیل
میر حیدر ساکن جزیرهٔ جناوه و خارج به اجوره شانزده قرص رومی سوار
نموده پیشتر روانه کردند ـ و به وقت نماز مغرب باز لنگر همه جهازات
سرکار وغیره برداشته بعد طی مسافت هفت هشت کروه در طاس ششم ۱۸
شب دو شنبه بعدم باد در سرحد خراب یعنی هفت موضع آبادئی عظیم
کفار بود که حضرت امیر المومنین علی کرم‌الله وجهه به قتل رسانیده در
آب دریا غرق فرمودند، چنانچه اثری از آبادئی مسطور قدری قدری
به وقت جذر آب بنظر می آید، و نیز چند علامات دیگر است، یعنی
در جای پانزده گز آب است و در جای ده گز و در جای صد
گز وعلی هذالقیاس در آب سیزده گز، لنگر همه جهازات وغیره قایم
نمودند ـ

و در طاس چهارم روز دوشنبه تاریخ نوزدهم باز لنگر همه جهازات

وغیره برداشته در طاس نهم بعد طی مسافت ده دوازده کروه و قطع عرصه خور موسی علیه‌السلام در میدان حضرت امیرالمومنین علی مرتضی علیه‌السلام که آب دوسه گز بود لنگرها قایم نمودند ـ

و در طاس چهارم شب سه شنبه باز لنگر همه جهازات سرکار وغیره برداشته طی مسافت هشت نه کروه نموده در سرحد مهدا یعنی خرابه که در آنجا آب یک دو گز شاهی باشد مقابل و روبروی خور عبدالله و خور بهم‌شیر و خور بصره در طاس هشتم لنگرها درآب چهار پنج گز قایم نمودند ـ

و به تاریخ بیستم روز سه شنبه در طاس پنجم لنگر همه جهازات سرکار وغیره برداشته بصد چرخ و خرابی قدری پیشتر رفتند که دو اوزار داو کرایه‌دار سیف داماد خلفان وکیل امام بندر مسقط که برآن غلام علی خان و شاه نورالله خان و هر دو منشی و چیله و جوانان اسداللهی وغیره سوار بودند از شدت باد شمالی چاک و ضایع گردید ـ و در طاس دهم لنگر درآب چهار گز همونجا قایم نمودند و به دستور لنگر همه جهازات سرکار وغیره پیشتر بتفاوت قریب قایم نمودند ـ

و در طاس ششم شب چهار شنبه باز لنگر هر سه جهازات سرکار وغیره برداشته به قطع مسافت چهار پنج کروه در طاس نهم در خور بهم شیر که آب دوسه گز بود پس و پیش بتفاوت و فاصله قرب و بعد لنگرها قایم نمودند ـ

و به تاریخ بست و یکم روز چهار شنبه در طاس چهارم لنگر همه جهازات وغیره برداشته پیشتر راهی گردیدند ـ و در طاس هشتم دومرتبه داو سیف از قلت آب بر زمین نشست ، بصد چرخ و محنت از زمین بر آورده بعد قطع مسافت سه چهار کروه نزدیک روی خور بصره به سبب شدت باد شمالی و کشش آب به طرف بندر مسقط و قلت آب که دو سه گز بود در طاس نهم لنگر داو سیف و داو کرایه‌دار عبدالله بن ابوالشیخ

که برآن محمدحنیف متوفی و مراد خان و محمدشفیع وغیره سوار بودند پس و پیش بتفاوت و فاصله قایم نمودند۔ و هر سه جهازات سرکار بتفاوت و فاصله دو سه کروه عقب ماندند۔

و در طاس هشتم شب پنجشنبه باز لنگر هر دو داو برداشته ، بوقت نماز صبح داو سیف در خور بصره یعنی رود فرات و شطعرب باهم که از بالای بندر بصره می آید و به عرض هفت صد گز شاهی و به طرف دست راست ریگستان علاقهٔ ملک چعب که پیش از این قطاع الطریقی می نمودند از تنبیه و صلح حاکم بصره دست اذیت باز داشتند۔ و به طرف دست چپ نیستان علاقهٔ ملک بصره واقع است داخل گردید۔

و در طاس دوم روز پنجشنبه تاریخ بست و دوم بسرحد مینوحی(۱) که درآنجا نخلستان و آبادی علاقه چعب بطرف راست واقع ، بعه قطع مسافت یک کروه رسیده ، در آب ده گز لنگر داو سیف به سبب شدت باد شمالی و جذرآب بصوب مسقط قایم نموده ، شاه نورالله خان به آوردن سرانجام ضروری آدم خود را به کنارهٔ چعب فرستادند۔ و داو عبدالله به فاصله دو سه کروه عقب ماند و در طاس نهم لنگر برداشته بغیر اوزار از اعانت مد آب رود فرات به طرف منزل مقصود و کشش مجهوه تایک دوکروه ۶۱
پیشتر راهی شده در طاس دوازدهم در آب دوازده گز لنگر قایم نمودند۔

و در طاس دهم شب جمعه باز لنگر برداشته به کشش آب و مجهوه قطع مسافت دو سه کروه نموده به کنارهٔ سرحد چبده علاقهٔ ملک بصره که آبادی و نخلستان بسیار و چند جزایر خورد و یک مکان چله کشی خضر علیه‌السلام و یک گنبد شیخ آبادان ولی کامل در آنجا است و

۱ــ منجوحی or منوحی

دو جزیرهٔ بزرگ یکی به اول سرحد دوم به آخر چبده واقع است لنگر قایم کردند و خواستند که از آبادی چبده سرانجام ضروری بخرید آرند۔ درین ضمن باد قوسی که از ده روز بالکل کم بود پیدا گردید، باز لنگر برداشتند اوزار بلند کردند، باز در یک آن باد قوسی کم گردید آثار باد شمالی هویدا شد، باز اوزار فرود آوردند و از مچهوه کشش نموده به کنارهٔ قریهٔ شطیط و بویرده سرحد ملک چعب در طاس چهارم روز جمعه تاریخ بست و دوم در آب چهارده گز قایم نمودند۔ و چند مردم سرکار به آوردن روغن زرد وغیره به قریهای مسطور رفته قدری روغن زرد وغیره به خرید آوردند ۔ و شیخ سالم تعلقه دار قریهٔ مذکور هشت نه عدد طبق پر از خرمای تر و سه مرغ نزد غلام علی خان و شاه نورالله خان به طریق مهمانداری آورد، پنج قرص رومی به
شیخ مذکور دادند و خرما بخود و همه کسان تقسیم نمودند۔ و قریه ٦٢
شبانه و خست در سرحد بصره واقع بود ۔ و در طاس دهم لنگر برداشته به کشش مچهوه و آب رود پیشتر راهی شدند و داو عبدالله هم متصل نمودار شد ۔

و در طاس چهارم شب شنبه از سرحد قریهٔ صحیان(۱) علاقهٔ بصره و قریهٔ بریم و نهر شیخ(۲) علاقهٔ چعب بقطع مسافت چهار پنج کروه در آب ده گز لنگر قایم نمودند ۔ و به وقت طلوع صبح صادق باز لنگر برداشته اوزار بالا کردند و پیشتر راهی شده بعد طی مسافت سه چهار کروه از سرحد مطوعه(۳) و زین علاقهٔ ملک بصره و قریهٔ محله و حده و محمره و در بند علاقهٔ ملک چعب گزشته بودند، که به اطلاع محمد فاضل چوبدار سرکار و عبدالله خان خدمتگار شاه نورالله خان که

۱—سیحان ۲—نهرالشیخ

۳—مطوعیه or مطاوع ۴—حد

بیشتر از هفت هشت روز نزد ابراهیم آغا حاکم بصره رفته بودند۔ حاکم
مذکور حاجی محمد آفندی دفتردار وکیل دولت سلطانی و حاجی جواد
داروغهٔ جهازات و غرابات ارماد بصره معه هشت منزل جهاز و غراب
ارمادی به استقبال و حفاظت تطاوری قطاع الطریق چعب فرستاده بود ،
در طاس چهارم رسیده متصل داو کرایه‌دار سیف لنگر قایم نموده نزد
غلام‌علی خان و شاه نورالله خان حاجی محمد و حاجی جواد معه دو سه مردم ٦٣
دیگر رسیده خطوط در جوابی از نزد حاکم بصره موسومه خوانین متضمن
بذل الطاف اتحادانه آورده بودند ، دادند۔ خوانین استفسار کفیت بصره
و حاکمش و عثمان خان که نزد سلطان روم رفته‌اند نمودند ۔ حاجی
مذکور مفصل اظهار نمود ، خوانین مدارای قحوه نموده مرخص نمودند۔
و در طاس پنچم یک عدد شال طوسی به قیمت پنجاه روپیه که در
بندر مسقط بخرید آورده بودند و یک عدد پچهوری اول ابریشمی
تارپتری کلدار بحاجی محمد ویک پچهوری دوم بحاجی جواد بصحابت
محمد عمر چوبدار و شیخ بدهن خدمتگار بر جهاز استقبالی بطریق
خلعت و سوغات ممالک سرکار از طرف سرکار فرستادند۔ هر دو حاجی
هر دو جنس مرسوله(١) گرفته سه زر محبوبی به محمد عمر و دو قرص به شیخ
بدهن بطریق انعام دادند۔ و داو عبدالله هم در آن وقت متصل لنگر
قایم نموده بود ۔ بحسب اطلاع و طلب خوانین مراد خان و محمد شفیع
و بارگیران سرکار وغیره بخدمت غلام‌علی خان رسیده از هر دو حاجی
مذکور ملاقات نموده باز رفتند ۔ و در طاس ششم هردو حاجی دو غراب
به حفاظت نزد داو کرایه‌دار وا گذاشته خود معه شش منزل جهاز و
غراب پیشتر نزد جهازات سرکار که عقب ماندند به حفاظت قطاع الطریق ۴
رفتند ۔ و در طاس هفتم یکی سردار علاقهٔ دو غراب وامانده نزد غلام‌علی

١— مرسله

خان و شاه نورالله خان آمده ملاقات نمود ، بمدارات قحوه مروت یافته رفت۔ و در طاس دهم یکی خدمتگار علاقهٔ غراب مذکور دوطبق پر از خرمائی تر نزد خوانین آورده یک قرص رومی بطریق انعام دادند۔ و یک شخص حمده نام ساکن قریهٔ زین چهار طبق پر از خرما نزد خوانین آورد ، یک لنگ یه قیمت هفت محمودی خریده بطریق انعام دادند و خرما بخود و همه کسان تقسیم نمودند۔

و در طاس اول شب یکشنبه تاریخ بست و پنجم باز لنگر هردو داو کرایه‌دار معه دو منزل غراب استقبالی بصره به قطع مسافت دوسه کروه از سرحد قریه شمارطه(۱)و موفلی(؟)و قریه سالم‌علی و کلیسیان(۲) و کاوس(۳)و بلجان(۴)و عامیه بسرحد بصره و قریهٔ خیں(۵)و بوچبده و نهر یوسف و طمار بطرف چعب واقع بود گذشته در طاس پنجم روز یکشنبه تاریخ بست و پنجم به آب ده گز لنگر قایم نمودند۔ و در طاس هشتم
٦١ شب مذکور رستم آدم محمدعمر چوبدار به کنارهٔ داو کرایه‌دار درخواب غفلت بود از گردش پهلو به پهلوی دیگر در آب اُفتاد و مرد ، وسیل رود فرات (٦) به زودی تمام برد که اثری ازان پدیدار نه گردید۔

و بتاریخ بست و پنجم در طاس اول باز لنگر چهار منزل داو و غراب برداشته به طی مسافت دو سه کروه از سرحد قریهٔ فیاضی و بگیح(۷) و بوالخسیب(۸)سرحد بصره و قریهٔ خمیسه و دعیجی و نهر امیر گذشته در آب دوازده گز در طاس چهارم لنگر هر چهار منزل قایم نموده منتظر جهازات سرکار وغیره که پستر ماندند شدند۔ و در طاس پنجم از یک بتیل روندهٔ بصره خبر رسید که جهاز بنی بخش بشب شنبه تاریخ بست

۱— شمرته Niebuhr, *Voyage in Arabie*, P. 168 has

۲— کلیسا Ibid.,

۳— or قاوس

۴— بلجانیه

۵— خیین

٦— شط العرب

۷— ابوابکیح

۸— or ابوالخسیب

و سیوم سوخته و مغروق شد و پنجاه مردم معه‌ضیاءالدین و فقیرمحمد سوخته مغروق گردید و باقی همه خلاصی و چند کسان ملازم سرکار از دستیگری جعفرخان جان بسلامت بردند ـ و در طاس ششم حاجی محمد دفتردار بر یک غراب سوار شده متصل داو سیف رسیده لنگر قایم نموده دو غراب
بادشاهی همراهی داو سیف را باز نزد جهاز مغروق پس و پیش روانه نمود ـ ٦٦

و در طاس هفتم آفندی معه خط شمس‌الدین داروغه جهاز فتح شاهی معزی متضمن کیفیت جهاز مغروق نزد غلام‌علی خان و شاه نوراللهخان رسیده همه کیفیت جهاز مغروق و بندوبست خود به برآوردن اموال و اجناس جهاز مغروق و نگاهداشت جهازات بادشاهی و تاکید نمودن به تعلقه‌دار آنها ظاهر نمود ـ خطی به مراد خان درماده تاکید موسومهٔ حاجی جواد، متضمن اینکه همه اسباب و سرانجام جهاز مغروق انچیکه همدسیت خواهد شد برآرند و قصور نه نمایند، بحسب درخواست شاه نورالله نوشته داد و رفت ـ و درطاس نهم مراد خان و محمد شفیع معه خط تاکید مذکور در غراب دوم ارماد بصره سوار شده نزد جهاز مغروق رفتند ـ

و در طاس یازدهم جهاز فتح شاهی و غراب سورتی نمودار شدند ـ و در طاس هشتم سیدعلی بن صالح شیخ قریهٔ بوالخسیب معه دو راس گوسفند و چهار دست کبوتر و یک سبد و دو طبق پر از خرمای تر
و پنجاه عدد انار و شش عدد ترکنکری و یک عدد هندوانه بطریق ٦٧
مهمانداری نزد غلام‌علی خان و شاه نورالله خان آورده ملاقات نمود ـ هر دو خان موصوف یک فرد پچهوری گلدار ابریشمی تارپتری به سیدعلی مذبور داده مرخص نمودند ـ و یک راس گوسفند به شاه نورالله خان و غلام‌علیخان یک راس به جوانان اسداللهی و خرما وغیره به خود و جوانان متفرقات و چهار دست کبوتر و یک خوشهٔ خرما به مراد خان و محمدشفیع تقسیم نمودند و فرستادند ـ و از مراد خان و محمدشفیع پا نزده عدد مهتاب و بست عدد شمع مومی شاه نورالله خان از جانب خود خطی نویسانیده

طلب داشته بودند ، نامبرده‌ها دوازده عدد مهتاب و پانزده عدد شمع مومی فرستادند ـ

و در طاس چهارم شب سه شنبه جهاز فتح شاهی معزی و غراب سورتی و غراب حاجی محمد دفتردار برداشته بعد طی مسافت پنج کروه از قریه های لبانی و نهر خوز(۱) و ابومغیره و سبلیات(۲) و یهودی و حمدان و یوسفان و مهجران(۳) و فحه(۴) و ابوسلال و شریعت صحر(؟) و سراجی و براضیعه و(۵) مناوی بسرحد بصره و نهر قاسم و کوت الجوع و گردلان بسرحد چعب بود گذشته به کنارهٔ بندر بصره لنگر هر دو منزل داو و غراب سورتی و غراب آفندی در طاس دهم در آب پانزده گز قایم نمودند و جهاز فتح شاهی ٦٠
معزی پیشتر بفاصله دو کروه ماند ـ

و به تاریخ بست و هفتم روز سه شنبه جهاز فتح شاهی معزی معه غرابات سلطان به کنارهٔ بصره رسیده لنگر قرار نمودند ـ و در طاس هشتم حاجی محمد آفندی وغیره از طرف ابراهیم آغا نزد غلام‌علی خان و شاه نورالله خان آمده بسیار تشفی و تسلی نمود که تقدیر از تدبیر مبدل نمی شود ، هرچه که خواهش ایزدی بود به ظهور انجامید که به مقتضای تلف المال خلف العمر زیادتی عمر و دولت آقای شما است ، خاطر جمع دارند هرچه که در جهاز مغروق سوای اجناس سیل بوده در ته آب باشد از دست غواصان بر آورده خواهد شد ، و جهاز از مال شما نبود بلکه از مال سلطان روم بود ـ غلام‌علی خان و شاه نورالله خان به جواب پرداختند که اگرچه جواهر و اجناس خوب و بهتر وغیره و چند اشخاص معتبر بر جهاز سوار بودند مستغرق شدند لاکن به اعتبار علو همت و سمو نهمت حضرت خداوند نعمت خلدالله ملکه هیچ بضاعتی و قدری ندارد ،

۱ــ or نهرخوس ۲ــ سبیلیات ۳ــ میهجران

۴ــ Perhaps فاد ۵ــ or براذعیه

هرچه که قضای الهی بود به وقوع رسید و تصدق فرق مبارک آقای ما و سلطان روم گردید۔ و در طاس نهم باز یهودی دیوان حاکم بصره آمده بسیار بسیار ازین قبیل به تشفی و دلاسا پرداخت و رفت۔ درین ضمن معاً چوبداری معه دو سبد پر از هندوآنه و دو سبد پر از ترکنکری
و دو سبد پراز انار و یک پر از بهی از جانب متسلم حاکم بصره ۶۹
رسید۔ غلام‌علی خان و شاه نورالله خان یک فرد پچهوری تارپتری بچوبدار مذکور به طریق انعام داده روانه نمودند۔ و لطف‌علی خان فرود آمده در حویلی خوب و بهتر از حویلی‌هاے حصار کوتهی ولندیز ویران افتاده داخل شدند۔ متسلم طعام ضیافت نزد خان مسطور فرستاد، غلام علی‌خان و شاه نورالله خان میوه مسطور بجوانان اسداللهی و سزاول و بهرام وغیره تقسیم نمودند۔

و به تاریخ بست و هشتم ماه هاشمی روز چهارشنبه سال دلو ۱۲۰۰ھ (۱) مطابق بست و هفتم ماه شوال المکرم سنه‌الیه(۱)در طاس دوم آفندی معه محمد فاضل چوبدار سرکار بست و پنج راس اسپ و جوانان و سواران جلو خودها تیار کرده بر کنارهٔ رود فرات نگاه داشته بر داوسیف نزد غلام‌علی خان و شاه نورالله خان آمده گفت که فرود آیند۔ من بعد در طاس چهارم غلام‌علی خان و شاه نورالله خان و جعفر خان معه جوانان اسداللهی و سزاول و بهرام معه بیرق وغیره جوانان متفرقات کنارهٔ رود مذکور فرود آمده غلام‌علی‌خان بر پالکی خود معه چهتری و تکیه پالکی سرکار و شاه نوراللہ‌خان بر پالکی‌سرکار کهنه معه سرانجام آن سوار شده مع جوانان مذکور
و جلو از مابین آبادی بصره در حویلی علاقهٔ کوتهی کاه پوش و لندیزی ۷۰
ویران افتاده داخل شدند۔ به وقت دخول درآبادی همه زنان خانهای راسته بازار به لولوی شادکنان بودند۔ غلام‌علی خان و شاه نورالله خان

۱۔ 27 Shawwal, 1200/23 August, 1786.

و لطف‌علی خان مع جوانان اسداللهی وغیره در حویلی مذکور ماندند و جعفر خان. و جوانان سزاول و بهرام و چند شاگرد پیشه در حویلی های متعدد خارج از علاقهٔ کوتهی مذکور فرود آمدند۔ و در طاس ششم متسلم حاکم بصره چند خوان طعام و خورش بطریق مهمانداری فرستاد۔ غلام‌علی خان و شاه نورالله خان و جعفر خان به همه کسان یعنی به لطف‌علیخان و جوانان اسداللهی و سزاول و بهرام وغیره تقسیم نموده معه عبدالقادر منشی و سید جعفر مصدی و محمدامام جوقدار سزاول و یک بارگیر سرکار طعام مذکور تناول نمودند۔

یاد داشت اسمهای بنادر و جزایر که درو جواهر بسیار پیدا
می‌شود و اسمهای حاکم آنجا۔ مرقوم تاریخ بست و هشتم ماه هاشمی
سال دلو ۱۲۰۰ هجری بندر ذوالفار، بندر شارجه، بندر ام‌القیوین، جزیرهٔ
حمره حاکمش شیخ راشد بن مطر بن رحمان عرب قوم قاسمی اهل تسنن،
و بندر زباره و جزیرهٔ بحرین علاقهٔ شیخ خلیفه عرب قوم عبتی اهل
۷۱ تسنن، و نقرین(۱) و جزیرهٔ فیلکه علاقهٔ شیخ عبدالله بن صباح عرب قوم
عتبی، و بندر لعجیر(۲) و بندر قطیف از ولایت لحسه علاقهٔ شیخ بطاین
ابن عرعر بن خالد عرب اهل تسنن۔

بیان عرض طول دریائی از خط استوا تا بندر مسقط و بندر بصره وغیره آنکه طول از خط استوا تا بندر مسقط هشتاد و دو درجه سه دقیقه و عرض بست و سه درجه و چهل و پنج دقیقه و تا جزیرهٔ لیما طولاً ۷۹ درجه ۳۹ دقیقه عرضاً ۲۵ درجه ۴۹ دقیقه، بندر ذوالفار طولاً ۷۸ درجه عرضاً ۲۵ درجه ۲۸ دقیقه، جزیرهٔ قیس طولاً ۷۰ درجه عرضاً ۳۰ درجه ۱۵ دقیقه، بندر بصره طولاً ۷۰ درجه عرضاً ۳۰ درجد ۵۰ دقیقه، بندر سورت طولاً ۳۶ درجه عرضاً ۲۱ درجه ۱۵ دقیقه، بندر هرونچه (؟)

۱— القرین ۲— العقیر or الحجیر

طولاً ۹۶ درجه عرضاً ۲۱ درجه ۴۵ دقیقه، بندر جگت (؟) طولاً ۹۲، درجه ۲۰ دقیقه عرضاً ۲۲ درجه ۲۸ دقیقه، بندر لاری طولاً ۹۰ درجه ۴۰ دقیقه عرضاً ۲۴ درجه ۳۰ دقیقه، بندر جاسک (۱) طولاً ۸۱ درجه عرضاً ۲۵ درجه ۱۷ دقیقه، جزیره هرمز طولاً ۷۹ درجه ۳۵ دقیقه عرضاً ۲۷ درجه ۲۷
دقیقه، بندر ابوشهر طولاً ۷۳ درجه ۵۲ دقیقه عرضاً ۲۵ درجه ۱۵ دقیقه، ۷۲
خور موسی طولاً ۵۲ درجه ۳۹ دقیقه عرضاً ۲۹ درجه ۵۵ دقیقه، خور بصره طولاً ۷۱ درجه ۳۵ دقیقه عرضاً ۳۰ درجه - و فی درجه ۶۰ دقیقه و فی دقیقه دو ثلث فرسخ یعنی یک کروه (؟)

و بتاریخ بست و نهم ماه هاشمی سال دلو سنه ۱۲۰۰ هجری(۲) روز پنجشنبه درطاس سیوم ابراهیم آغا حاکم بصره عرف متسلم معه حاجی محمد دفتردار آفندی و آغا علی سلاح بردار سلیمان پاشا حاکم بغداد وزیراعظم سلطان روم نزد غلام علی خان و شاه نورالله خان وغیره که در یکجا بودند فرش و فروش نموده مجلس آراسته بودند آمده، بعد ملاقات از سوخته شدن جهاز نبی بخش بسیار بسیار به لوازمَ تسلی پرداخته گفت که بر اجناس تحایف سلطان روم هر قدر که همراه شما هست و می برند و انچیکه سوخته شد اطلاع دهند و یک قطعه خط از جانب خودها بنام سلیمان پاشا حاکم بغداد بنویسند البته به صحابت قاصدی با خط متضمن کوایف روداد شماها روانه نموده خواهد شد - این معنی را هر چهار سردار قبول نموده به مدارای قهوه و مربه و شربت و تنبول و قرنفل و الایچی پرداخته بعد نیم ساعت مرخص نمودند - و آن وقت
شکرالله خان و احمد علی و عبدالقادر منشی و سید جعفر مصدی و ۷۳
محمد علی بهاتو و محمد امام جوقدار سزاول و محمد نتهو سرخیل و جوقدار

۱- جاشک

۲- 28 Shawwal 1200/24 August, 1786.

اسداللهی و جمیع چیلهٔ سرکار و چوبدار و خدمتگار وغیره حاضر خدمت بودند - و در طاس چهارم متسلم ده راس گوسفند به صحابت چوبدار خود بطریق مهمانداری نزد غلام علی خان و شاه نورالله خان فرستاد و شیخ سوینی عسکردار یک لک نفر بدوی نیز ده راس گوسفند و ده سبد پر از خرما و چهار سبد پر از انگور بطریق مهمانداری فرستاد - غلام علی خان وغیره سرداران دو دو راس گوسفند به خودها و دو راس به جوانان سزاول و شش راس به اسداللهی و یک راس به شکرالله خان و یک راس به بهرام و یک راس به شاگرد پیشه و یک راس بهر دو منشی و کنک پله و هر سه چیله و مصدی توشک خانه تقسیم نمودند -

و در طاس پنجم به دفتری آفندی همه اشیای بابت نذر سلطان روم شاه نورالله خان برو بروی غلام علی خان وغیره به این مضمون نویسانیدند که آقای مایان خلدالله ملکه یازده رقم جواهر منجمله آن سه رقم فلکی
۷۴ یکی زمردی دویمی یاقوتی سیومی الماسی و بدستور سه رقم پدک و سه رقم
سر پیچ و دو رقم بازوبند و دو زنجیر افیال معه عماری نقره و یک منزل پالکی لاجوردی معه سرانجام زری وغیره آن و یک چارپایه صندلی و عطر صندل پنجاه من و خلعت سی و سه عدد جمله دو صد و دو فرد و اشرفی سلطانی صد عدد و حیدری هون دو صد عدد و حیدری نقرهٔ کلان پانصد عدد وغیره اشیای دیگر و به چهار وزیران سی و شش عدد خلعت همراه مایان داده بودند، یازده رقم جواهر تمام و کمال در جهاز نبی بخش به حرق و غرق درآمد و دو زنجیر فیل معه دو زنجیر دیگر در اثنای راه بندر مسقط از شدت حرارت مردند و باقی اشیای مسطور حاضر هستند و نه رقم جواهر مرسلهٔ حضور لامع‌النور را شاه نورالله خان برو بروی خوانین مسطور به آفندی نمایش کرده گفتند که این جواهر از ملک غلام علی خان و شاه نورالله خان و لطف علیخان هست اگر پسند شماها باشد البته قدری از ان نذر سلطان روم نموده خواهد شد - و نیز

مقدار و اندازهٔ مرچ سیاه و پارچهٔ سفید و سیاه وغیره اجناس را به این ۷۵
تفصیل به حاجی محمد آفندی نویسانیدند ۔

مرچ سیاه ۱۰۳۰ کهندی ۔ صندل ۸۷۰ کهندی ۔ الایچی ۲۶ کهندی ۔ پارچهٔ سفید و سیاه وغیره دو لک و نود هزار روپیه ۔ روغن صندل ۱۰ من ۔ زنجبیل ۲۹ کهندی ۔ زرد چوب ۱۰ کهندی ۔

در پارچهٔ سفید و سیاه وغیره بابت سرکار دو لک و چهل هزار روپیه، و پارچهٔ سیاه وغیره بابت ساهوکار پنجاه هزار روپیه، و بابت خوانین چهل هزار روپیه ، و بجهت دادن مردمان به‌طریق انعام و سوغات پانصد تهان سفید یازده هزار روپیه، منجمله پارچهٔ سفید و سیاه وغیره دو لک و نود هزار روپیه و زنجبیل و زرد چوب بابت ساهوکار و مرچ و صندل و الایچی و روغن صندل مال سرکار ۔

و بتاریخ غره ماه واسع سال دلو سنه ۱۲۰۰ هجری(۱) روز جمعه در طاس اول غلام علی خان، احمد علی منشی و محمد کمال و عبدالرحمان
و شکرالله چیلهٔ سرکار و محمد عمر چوبدار را بر داو سیف و عبدالله ۷۶
فرستاده اسباب بابت نذر سلطان روم وغیره و یک پتارهٔ خلعت جده و مکه معظمه، که محمد حنیف در حین حیات نزد خود بر داو عبدالله به این اراده داشته بودند که بعد فراغت امورات سرکار به جده و مکه رفته خلعت مذکور به حکام مکان مسطور داده زیارت کعبهٔ معظمه نموده خواهد شد، فرود آورده، در یک مکان علاقهٔ حصار کوتهی ولندیز نزد خود داخل توشکخانه کرده به حفاظت و احتیاط آن یک یزک از جوانان علاقهٔ سزاول نگاه داشتند و محمد کمال و عبدالرحمان چیلهٔ سرکار را تاکید اکید نمودند که بسیار حفاظت و احتیاط به‌عمل آرند ۔

و در طاس یازدهم غلام علی خان و شاه نورالله خان دو قطعه

---

۱ ـ 29 Shawwal, 1200/25 August, 1786.

خطوط از جانب خودها به جعفر خان برادر زادهٔ کریم خان والی و حاکم ایران و اصفهان به مضمون اینکه حضرت خداوند نعمت خلدالله ملکه می خواسته بودند که به ترسیل و تبلیغ رسل و رسایل و نزول تجار ذوی‌الاعتبار به بنادر ممالک محروسهٔ آن شوکت و حشمت دستگاه بنیان اتحاد و اخلاص قدیمی را مستحکم سازد، درین ضمن حقیقت بغی و فساد
۷۷ بعضی حکام بنادر مذکور ظاهر گردید، این معنی در پردهٔ التوا ماند و مایان را از بابت نذورات عتبات عالیات رضی‌الله تعالیٰ‌عنهم و سلطان روم خادم‌الحرمین الشریفین به ولایت روم فرستادند و حکم اشرف به نهر آوری در نجف اشرف صدور یافته است، از منشی عبدالقادر نویسانیده به صحابت عبدالتواب یساول ملازم جعفرخان بادشاه ایران به مقتضای قضیه اتفاقیه نزد غلام علی خان و شاه نورالله خان‌رسیده بود فرستادند ـ

و بتاریخ دوم ماه مذکور روز سه شنبه در طاس سیوم شیخ سوینی عسکردار یک لک سوار بدوی و شیخ مسعود وغیره چند نفر نزد غلام علی خان وغیره آمده به حصول ملاقات مراجعت بخانهٔ خود نمود ـ و در طاس چهارم غلام علی خان و شاه نورالله خان و لطف علی خان سه قطعه خطوط از جانب خودها موسومهٔ سلیمان پاشا متضمن کوایف رسیدن خودها از حضور پرنور به بندر بصره و راهی شدن از راه نجف اشرف و کربلای معلیٰ به بغداد شریف بعد رسیدن در جواب این خطوط از نزد حاکم مذکور نویسانیده بدست دفتردار آفندی دادند که به صحابت هرکاره و قاصد متسلم حاکم بصره روانه بغداد شریف نمایند ـ

۷۸ و در طاس دوم شب یکشنبه غلام علی خان وغیره از دو خلعت جده و مکه یک تهان کارچوبی بوته دار و یک دستار و یک کمربند کارچوبی و یک تهان مشروع و یک خلعت سفید دستار زری پلو یک و یک دوپته زری پلو یک عدد و دو شیلهٔ نادر پاکی و یک سنجرخانی، سوای این دو تهان چهینت مچهلی بندری از خلعت بابت مکهٔ شریف

برآورده پنج عدد شیشهٔ عطر صندل وزن چهار آثار خام و طبلے صندلی سه عدد و بادسنج صندلی سه عدد معه منشور فیض گنجور از منشوره‌های متعدد بصحابت محمد کمال و عبدالرحمان چیلهٔ سرکار و محمد عمر و فاضل چوبدار و شیخ بدهن محمد حسین خدمتگار سرکار نزد متسلم فرستادند ـ متسلم از راه خوف حاکم بغداد و آفندی دفتردار مخفی و پوشیده گرفت و ما بقی زر خلعت جده و مکه باز به حسب طلب مراد خان وغیره باز واپس نمودند ـ

و بتاریخ سیوم روز یکشنبه در طاس اول شیخ عبدالله شیخ‌الاسلام بصره نزد غلام علی خان وغیره آمده ملاقات کرد و رفت ـ و در طاس سیوم پنج کس وکیل انگریز از کوتهی بصره منجمله ان نام سه کس ۷۹
پیت روس(۱) و نام چهارم انتونی استنبول و نام پنجم کیول(۲) نزد غلام علی خان وغیره آمده ملاقات کرد و گفت که پیشتر از دو سه سال فیمابین آقای ما و شما خلشی درپیش بود، حالا به سبب صلح در بندر کوریال شیوهٔ اتحاد و اخلاص فیمابین باقی و جاریست، ازین طرف نیز غلام علیخان بدستور بجواب پرداختند، به خوشی تمام مراجعت بخانهٔ خود نمود ـ

و در طاس چهارم غلام علی خان و شاه نورالله خان و لطف علی‌خان و شکرالله خان و محمد علی بهاتو و احمد علی و عبدالقادر منشی و سید جعفر مصدی و محمد امام جوقدار سزاول و محمد نتهو سرخیل اسداللهی و چوبدار و خدمتگار سرکار فیض آثار برای ضیافت خوری به خانهٔ متسلم حاکم بصره رفته، بعد فراغت از طعام و خورش ده یازده قسم و شربت و قهوه مراجعت بخانهٔ خود در عرصهٔ دو ساعت نمودند ـ و جعفر خان به سبب تکسل مزاج به ضیافت نه رفتند ـ

۱ــ پطرس　　　۲ــ کیمبل

و به وقت نماز مغرب موسی موستی(۱) و موسی ادوار(۲) گماشتهٔ
فراسیس بهمراه دو کس دیگر پادری و دو کس تجار از قوم کلاه پوش
۸۰ فراسیس علاقهٔ کوتهی بندر بصره و یک قطعه خط موسی روسو(۳) فراسیس
گماشتهٔ کوتهی بغداد موسومهٔ غلام علیخان وغیره مبهم متضمن اینکه
از قدیم‌الایام فیمابین نواب مغفرت نشان و بادشاه فرنکسیسیه شیوهٔ اتحاد
و یکجهتی مربوط و نموط است و از نزول شماها درین ضلاع و نواح
خوشی و خورمی به وفور عاید، حال خود گردید و به ازدیاد مواد مودت
و مواخات تاکید اکید در بارهٔ اطاعت و انقیاد در امورات سرکار دولت
بنیاد به گماشته‌های کوتهی بصره نوشته شد، لازمهٔ تودد و اتحاد
آنست که انچیکه در ماده سرکار دولت مدار به مقتضای قضیهٔ اتفاقیه
اگر اتفاق و مطلوب افتد بلا تکلف از کوتهی بصره بگیرند، نزد غلام‌علی
خان وغیره آمده بملاقات و تکلم کلام اتحاد و اخلاص آمیز و مدارات
شربت و قهوه مسرور و خورسند شده به درخواست خط مذکور مراجعت
به خانهٔ خود نمود - خوانین گفتند که فی‌الحقیقت فیمابین حضرت خداوند
نعمت خلدالله ملکه و راجهٔ شما از ابتدا رابطه اتحاد و یگانگی مربوط
۸۱ است و به هیچ وجه جدائی فیمابین متصور نیست، و مایان به همین
باعث از حضور پرنور بهمه اسباب و سرانجام بیفکر و آماده شده مامور
رفتن نزد راجهٔ شما هستیم، انشاءالله‌تعالی بعد طی منازل ولایت روم و
وصول مقاصد به ولایت شما خواهیم رفت و در جواب خط موسی روسو فردا
خواهیم داد به صحابت آدم شما روانه بغداد نمایند - و بتاریخ چهارم
روز دوشنبه غلام علی خان یک قطعه خط و شاه نورالله خان یک قطعه
خط بدر جواب خط موسی روسو که از بغداد رسیده بود نویسانیده
بصحابت محمد علی بهاتو و محمد عمر چوبدار سرکار نزد موسی موستی

۱— مسیو سیر موستیر ۲— مسیو ایڈورڈ ۳— مسیو روسو

فراسیس تعلقدار کوتهی بصره فرستادند که پیشتر به‌بغداد روانه سازد ـ

و بتاریخ پنجم روز سه‌شنبه غلام علی خان و شاه نورالله خان وغیره از لطف علی خان در ماده بر آورد خرج نذر و غلاف روضهٔ مقدسه شاه نجف اشرف و کربلای معلی و بغداد شریف وغیره مشورت نمودند ـ خان مسطور بجواب پرداختند که در شصت و پنج هزار هون حیدری عنایتی خاص مهم سه ساله گذرانیدن امر دشوار بنظر می آید، به کدام نوع نذر و غلاف بجا آورده خواهد شد، اگر غلاف بردن به نجف اشرف
۸۲ ضرور بر ضرور است یک تهان شیله صندلی نموده غلاف ساختن کافی است، غلام علی خان وغیره ازین سخن بذله محظوظ گشته خاموش شدند و پیشترهم دو سه دفعه بدستور گفته بودند ـ

و بتاریخ ششم روز چهار شنبه صندوق جواهر و پیالهٔ نقروی و چینی بابت قهوه خوری و یک قهوه دان نقروی که در بندر مسقط به سبب ضرورت تیار ساخته بودند و یک صندوق اشرفی سلطانی وغیره و دو صندوق بنادیق وغیره بابت نذر سلطان روم که غلام علی خان نزد خود به حفاظت تمام نگاه داشته بودند داخل توشکخانهٔ سرکار نموده بهر دو چیله متعینه توشکخانهٔ سرکار تاکید اکید نمودند که به حفاظت اجناس توشک خانه پردازند ـ

و بتاریخ هفتم روز پنجشنبه غلام علیخان وغیره به اتفاق دوازده هزار روپیه بابت نذر و غلاف کیمخابی و باناتی در نجف اشرف و کربلای معلی و بغداد شریف و سامره و کاظمین وغیره موضعات مقدسات منجمله آن چهار هزار روپیه نقد بابت نذر وغیره و هشت هزار روپیه بابت غلاف
۸۳ کیمخابی و باناتی وغیره تخمیناً مقرر نموده نظر به امر جلیل‌القدر و نام آوری سرکار فیض آثار بر آورد ساختند ـ لطف علی خان طوعاً و کرهاً به اقبال این معنی پرداختند ـ

و بتاریخ نهم روز شنبه غلام علی خان وغیره دوازده طاقه‌های باناتی

از کوتهی بصره علاقهٔ فراسیس به نرخ فی گز بصری که یک و نیم دست میشود سه قرص رومی به معرفت محمد علی بهاتو به خرید آورده باز در طاس یازدهم از معرفت عیسیٰ یهودی دلال باشی بصره از جای دیگر دوازده طاقه‌های باناتی کنده برای غلاف چند روضات مقدسات سوای نجف اشرف و کربلای معلیٰ و بغداد شریف به نرخ فی گز بصری دو روپیه ده آنه خرید نموده طاقه‌های بابت کوتهی فراسیس واپس نمودند ـ کلاه پوش علاقهٔ کوتهی مذکور بدل آزرده شده در خانهٔ خود گفت که این چهار سردار چه نوع بود و باش و سوال و جواب می نمایند، از زبانی محمد علی بهاتو ظاهر گردید ـ

و بتاریخ دهم روز یکشنبه شاه نوراللہ خان به اتفاق و ملاحظه لطف علی خان، که پیشتر ازین در جهاز فتح شاهی معزی از محمد امام جوقدار سزاول در بعضی امورات خود مناقشه داشته بودند، برای وضعیات

۸۴ وجه طلب نظر علی دفعه‌دار و جیون خان یزکدار که پیش از سه چهار روز از روز مقرری سرکار طلب گرفته بوقت سوار شدن بر جهازات سرکار از بندر مسقط فراری شدند، در طلب جوقدار مذکور از جوقدار روبروی غلام علی خان وغیره تکرار بیجا و بی موقع فیمابین تا یک طاس کامل به ظهور رسید، آخرالامر جوقدار به فرودگاه خود رفت و غصهٔ ایشان فرو نشست و به وقت تقسیم وجه طلب از راه مهربانی و سرداری مهربان شده بعد دریافت تمام زر مذکور موقوف ساختند ـ

و بتاریخ یازدهم روز دوشنبه هر دو منشی بدریافت وسعت آبادی بصره بر حصار بندر بصره از طرف گوشهٔ مغرب و جنوب سوار شده تا برج و دروازهٔ بغدادی رفته چند ضرب اتواب درمیان آن بروج دیده باز بخانهٔ خود مراجعت نمودند ـ منجمله آن دو ضرب توپ دوازده رطل بیتری بشکست و ریخت درآمده بر یک برج گوشهٔ نیرتی، و یکضرب به دستور مذکور بر برج گوشهٔ مغربی ، و دو ضرب هژده رطل بیتری

بروبروی دروازهٔ بغداد که فوج برادر کریم خان والی ایران مقابل آن فرود آمده مور چال نموده بودند، اندرون آبادی، و یک ضرب هفت ۸۵
جوشی و یک ضرب بیتری دوازده رطل بر برج دروازهٔ مسطور واقع است ـ و بروج سی و نه برج از گوشهٔ مذکور تا دروازهٔ بغداد واقع، و بیرون حصار مذکور ویرانی لاکن شارع بغداد است و به فاصلهٔ یک کروه یک قطعهٔ باغ و حویلی خوش فضا بنظر می آید و در آنجا کلاه پوش انگریز یک قطعهٔ باغ و حویلی تیار نموده است و جوانان بست نفر به حفاظت دروازهٔ مذکور متعین اند ـ

و حاکم بصره به شاه نورالله خان گفته فرستاد که جهازات ارماد بصره برای جنگ و تنبیه از قوم چعب که طغیانی می نمایند می روند، به حفاظت اموال و اجناس و مردم شماها که نزد جهاز مغروق و محروق اند جهازات شماها را بفریسیند و به احتیاط پردازند ـ شاه نورالله خان به اقبال این معنی پرداخته به شمس‌الدین داروغهٔ جهاز فتح شاهی معزی گفته فرستادند که همه اموال و اجناس تجارتی فرود آورده جهاز مذکور را نزد مراد خان و محمد شفیع که برای بر آوردن اموال جهاز مغروق رفتند بحفاظت آنها بفریسند ـ شمس‌الدین به استماع این کیفیت به اقبال این معنی پرداخت ـ

و بتاریخ سیزدهم نه قرص رومی بخریدن یک تهان تافته سرخ حلبی ۸۶
برای بیرق‌ها شاه نورالله خان از سرکار گرفته بیرقها ساختند ـ و غلام علی خان وغیره می خواستند که وجه طلب جوانان اسداللهی و سزاول و بهرام وغیره به نرخ فی هون حیدری بست محمودی مسقطی که سه قرص رومی و سه و نیم محمودی در بندر مسقط تا جزیرهٔ خارج بود تقسیم نمایند، چنانچه محمد امام جوقدار سزاول و محمد نتهو سرخیل اسداللهی قبول نمودند ـ درین ضمن لطف علیخان تکرار این معنی نمودند که درین جا قرص رومی به پنج محمودی مسقطی می ارزد، ـ باید که تتمهٔ قرصهای وجه طلب

دو ماهه‌ٔ خود که ذر جزیرهٔ مذکور بهتی مقرر نموده تمام و کمال
باید داد - ازین مر همه کسان یعنی محمد امام جوقدار و محمد نتهو سرخیل
وغیره متوهم شده از بازار بندر بصره خبر گرفتند و بروبروی هر چهار سردار
اظهار نمودند که فی هون حیدری چهار قرص رومی، بلکه مع شه زاید،
و فی رومی پنج محمودی مسقطی در بازار بصره می ارزد، مایان را بحساب
۸۷ فی هون حیدری که چهار قرص رومی می شود وجه طلب تقسیم نمایند -
غلام علی خان وغیره از استماع آن کیفیت بعد تامل و تفکر و دریافت
تمام یک نوشته به مضمون اینکه آینده در بغداد یا جای دیگر که
پیش نهاد مایانست به نرخ همون حیدری بنوعیکه خواهد ارزید وجه
طلب شماها بگیرند و تکرار ننمایند، از محمد نتهو سرخیل اسداللهی
گرفتند و بدستور وجه طلب مردم اسداللهی بروبروی هرچهار سردار تقسیم
نمودند و نیز به سید جعفر مصدی تاکید نمودند که از محمد امام جوقدار
سزاول نیز نوشته‌ٔ بدستور نویسانیده به دفتر نگاه دارند - و باز لطف علی
خان شقه‌ٔ بنام شاه نورالله خان نوشتند که جزیرهٔ خارج وجه طلب دو ماهه
خود بحساب فی قرص رومی پنج و نیم محمودی و مسقطی و فی هون
حیدری بست محمودی در جزیرهٔ مسطور داده بودند، حالا نیم محمودی
تتمه‌ٔ آنها بحساب اینجا که باقی می ماند بدهند - شاه نورالله خان به
جواب نپرداخته بشب بعد نماز مغرب نزد غلام علی خان رفته از لطف علی
خان که در آنجا حاضر بودند گفتند که شما در جزیرهٔ مسطور وجه طلب
دو ماهه شما بحساب پنج و نیم محمودی در قرص رومی به نرخ بازار
ویران افتاده جزیرهٔ مذکور تمام و کمال از سرکار گرفتند، چنانچه یک
۸۸ و نیم محمودی منجمله آن باقی مانده بود، بارها از سید جعفر مصدی و
کنک پله درخواست نمودند آخرالامر لاچار شده از زر روزینه‌ٔ جوانان
اسداللهی که از توشکخانه‌ٔ سرکار بر آورده بودند ازان یک محمودی بدست
خود گرفته گفتند که بر این محمودی ضرب علی کرم‌الله وجه نوشته

است و مضروب به کلمهٔ طیب لااله‌الاالله محمدرسول‌الله علی ولی‌الله وهی
رسول‌الله است و حال انکه بطریق نوشتهٔ صدر نبود، غرض بآئینی گرفتند
و عوض یک و نیم محمودی نمودند که همه کسان مجلس تمسخر نمودند،
حالا چرانیم محمودی تتمهٔ قرصهای وجه طلب دو ماههٔ شما درخواست
می نمایند و علی‌الحساب هم بگرفته بودند که حالا تتمهٔ مذکور داده آید،
ازین تکرار معلوم می شود که شما را نقصان سرکار منظور است۔ ازین
قبیل بسیار تکرار به عمل آوردند و لطف علیخان قسم و سوگند کردند
که از شما آینده وجه طلب خود تا وقت شرف ملازمت عالی نخواهم
گرفت و بهر عنوان گذران خود خواهم نمود ۔

و شمس‌الدین بورهای مرچ سیاه وغیره بر مچهوهٔ سرکار و کریه‌دار
از جهاز فتح شاهی معزی وغیره فرود آورده در یک مکان کرایه دار
کوتهی فراسیس گرفته بحفاظت نگاه داشتند ۔ و به وقت دو پهر هر دو ۸۹
منشی بر حصار بندر بصره از دروازهٔ زبیر سوار شده تا نهر متصل مقام
علی مشکل کشا، مشکلم بکشا که کشاینده توئی، همه برجها و نخلستان
و آبادی و ویرانی همه بنظر درآورده بوقت شام از مقام موصوف مراجعت
بخانهٔ خود نموده بعرصهٔ چهارگهری شب داخل فرودگاه گردید ۔ بر
دروازهٔ مذکور یک ضرب توپ هجده رطل هفت جوش و یک ضرب
بیتری شکسته افتاده ، و یک ضرب بیتری نصف شکسته به برج آخر
حصار متصل رود فرات که در آنجا جهازات وغیره لنگرها قایم می سازند
واقع است ۔ و از دروازهٔ مذکور تا آخر حصار متصل رود مذکور دو
دروازهٔ دیگر، یکی سراجی نام دارد و دویمی مجموعه و بر هر دروازه بست
بست جوان از عرب به حفاظت چوکی و پهره متعین اند ۔ و بیرون حصار
نهری عظیم بطرف نیرت و مغرب می رود که ازو چند نهرها اندرون
حصار جاری است و به طرف رود مذکور که لنگرها قایم می نمایند
حصار ندارد و قلعهٔ مینوحی هم در آنجا است لاکن تداخل قلعهٔ بصره

٩٠ است ـ و دو ضرب هفده جوشی و یک ضرب بیتری هر سه نه رطلی بروبرو
فردهٔ بری بصره به کنارهٔ نهری عظیم که اندرون شهر می رود واقع است ـ
و در بصره دو فرده، یکی بحری که متصل کنارهٔ رود مذکور است و
دیگر بری بفاصله در آبادی، واقع است ـ و از دروازهٔ سراجی نخلستان
بیرون شهر واقع تا دروازهٔ مجموعه، و از مجموعه نخلستان اندرون و بیرون
بکثرت و وفور واقع است ـ و از دروازهٔ زبیر تا آخر حصار متصل رود
مسطور هشت هفت بروج گلی است و از ابتدا به اطراف آبادی بفاصله
دو سه تیر پرتاپ فضا و میدان وسیع که در آنجا درخت‌های خرما است و
تره‌کاری پیدا می شود، چنانچه از دروازهٔ زبیر تا نهر متصل مقام علی
مشکل کشا رضی‌الله تعالی‌عنه بسیار خانها ویران، و نخلستان به وفور،
و گلبن گل گلاب و تره‌کاری وغیره بسیار است و یک مسجد و گنبد
سلیمان پاشا حاکمی از حکام بصره بود به آخر حصار متصل رود مذکور
واقع است و بطرف رود بسیار نخلستان است ـ

و بتاریخ چهاردهم روزِ چهارشنبه بعد دریافت نمودن لطف علی خان
حساب و کتاب سه چهار بهتی جوانان سزاول وغیره از سید جعفر
٩١ مصدی پیشتر از دو سه روز بسبب آنکه بارها خان مسطور شکایت
لا یعنی خورد و برد سید جعفر مصدی و محمد امام جوقدار سزاول از
غلام علی خان وغیره اظهار نمودند، چنانچه در جزیرهٔ خارج تا دو سه
ساعت از غلام علی خان و شاه نورالله خان شکوه گذاری به این طریق
نمودند که متصدی و جوقدار مذکور باهم به اتفاق تمام متفق شده در
تقسیم وجه طلب مردم سزاول بسیار خورد و برد نمودند، شما را معلوم
نیست و منکه از ضوابط و قواعد سرکار آگاه هستم مرا همه تغلب و
تصرف ایشان معلوم است، باید که بعد نزول در بندر بصره تغلب ایشان
بجزرسی تمام بدریافت آرند ـ غلام علی خان و شاه نورالله خان به جواب
پرداختند که مایان به سبب تکسل مزاج شما به شما تکلیف قدم رنجگی نداده

بدریافت حساب و کتاب به آئین بهین از دست مصدی مذکور و کنک پله
و شکرالله چیلهٔ سرکار پرداخته وجه طلب مردم سزاول وغیره را برو بروی
مایان دست بدست تقسیم نموده بودیم، اگر درین ماده به خاطر شما
توهم و خلشی و ترددی راه یابست خوب، بعد نزول مایان به بندر
بصره سید جعفر مصدی وغیره را معه حساب و کتاب نزد شما فرستاده
خواهد شد، بجزرسی تمام خوب بدریافت آورده انچیکه بازیافت از ایشان
کردنی باشد بازیافت از ایشان نمایند ـ من بعد بعد نزول به بندر مذکور
برو بروی هر چهار سردار موجودات مردم سزاول وغیره دیدند و بدریافت ٩٢
حساب سه بهتی سابق بجزرسی تمام پرداختند، اصلا. اثری ازان تغلب و تصرف
اینها به ظهور و وقوع نه انجامید ـ آخرالامر منفعل شده گفتند که در بندر
مسقط بوقت سوار شدن به جهازات سرکار مردم سزاول وغیره را پیش از سه
چهار روز از اتمام سی و شش روز مقرری سرکار تقسیم وجه طلب چرا
نمودند، حالا زر وجه طلب نظر علی دفعه‌دار و جیونخان یزکدار که وجه
طلب خودها پیش از درآمد روز مقرری از سرکار گرفته راه گریز
فرا گرفتند، بموجب ضابطه و قاعدهٔ سرکار که هرکس به این نوع می گریزد،
طلب جوان مفرور از وجه طلب جوقدار در سرکار وضع می نمایند، از
محمد امام جوقدار مفرور بگیرند ـ شاه نورالله خان به اتفاق و ملاحظهٔ
لطف علی خان اگرچه ضابطهٔ سرکار نبود عمداً از محمد امام جوقدار مذکور
برای وضعیات زر مسطور پیشتر از دو سه روز بسیار فیمابین کلمه و کلام
مناقشه آمیز بظهور(١) رسانیدند ـ آخرالامر هر چهار سردار به دریافت
و تامل تمام وضع زر مذکور موقوف ساخته به تقسیم وجه طلب مردم ٩٣
سزاول و بهرام وغیره به مصدی و کنک پله حکم نمودند ـ مصدی
مذکور وغیره بموجب امر وجه طلب مردم مذکور به حساب فی هون

(١) MS. بظهور بظهور

حیدری چهار قرص رومی دست بدست بروبروی هر چهار سردار تقسیم نمودند و به کمی جوانان یک پهرا و دو دفعه‌دار در جوقه سزاول جماعداری عبدالنبی اعظم پوری جماعدار را برای پهره بندی زایل ساخته به عبدالنبی یزکدار دفعهٔ رحیم خان جماعدار دفعه‌داری به موجب قاعده و ضابطه سرکار دادند و بدستور(۱) بجوانان علاقهٔ بهرام وجه طلب دو ماهه و به محمد علی بهاتو به سبب شرارت و نمک حرامی دو دو هون در وجه خوراکی وضع نموده باقی دادند و گفتند که آینده مابقی وجه خوراکی به موجب اقساط بندی گرفته خواهد شد ـ وقت صبح مراد خان و محمد شفیع وغیره چند کسان معتمد را نزد جهاز مغروق گذاشته خود برای فرود آوردن اجناس تجارتی و فروخت نمودن آن از جهازات سرکار به کنارهٔ بندر بصره رسیدند ـ و حاجی جواد معه داروغهٔ ارماد نیز رسیدند ـ

و به وقت صبح هر دو منشی از دروازهٔ بغداد بر حصار بصره سوار
۹۴ شده تا آخر حصار بصره متصل رود فرات رفته همه بنظر در آوردند ـ
یک ضرب توپ هفت جوشی هجده رطل در برج مقابل مورچال فوج برادر کریم خان بود ـ و یک ضرب توپ بیتری و یک ضرب توپ جوشی بست و چهار رطل بر برج آخر حصار متصل رود مذکور واقع بود ـ و یک دروازهٔ خورد باب‌الرباط نام بطرف مورچال واقع، و بروج از دروازهٔ بغداد تا آخر حصار متصل رود مذکور چهل و سه بروج است ـ و بیرون و اندرون حصار نهری عظیم واقع، و نخلستان و باغات و نهرها و خانهای خورد بسیار است ـ و به طرف دروازهٔ باب‌الرباط اندرون چند خانها آباد و یک مسجد و محله بزرگ است ـ و بمقام علی مشکل کشا، که به کنارهٔ رود فرات از آخر حصار مذکور بفاصلهٔ سه چهار تیر پرتاب است، و به دست چپ مقام موصوف نهری عظیم در آبادی شهر برود ـ و مقام علی میناریست

(۱) MS. دستور دستو

بلند - و یک نقش قدم مبارک بر سنگ‌مرمر منقش، درآن نهاده که حضرت موصوف رضی‌الله‌عنه در زمان خود مدتی در مقام موصوف استقامت فرموده بودند - به دروازهٔ مینار مذکور مسجد مضموم و متصل چنانست که بجای محراب دروازهٔ مینار مبارک است - و درآن مسجدیک منبر سقفی دو مینار دار خورد قایم است و بروبروی محراب بر بالای دروازهٔ مسجد اندرون
تخت پوشی نموده جای نشست واعظ مقرر نموده اند که در آنجا بروزجمعه ٩٥
واعظ نشسته وعظ می گوید و بدستور در همه مساجد دیگر منبر و جای نشست واعظ بنامی سازند - و سنه بنای مسجد بر دروازهٔ متصل مسجد نوشته است که یک هزار و شصت و هفت سال از هجرت نبوی صلی‌الله علیه‌وسلم -

بتاریخ چهاردهم روز پنجشنبه حاجی جواد داروغهٔ ارماد شاهی متعینه بصره و مراد خان و محمد شفیع و شمس‌الدین نزد غلام علی خان و شاه نورالله خان وغیره آمده اظهار کیفیت سوخت و غرق و بسیل رفتن جهاز نبی بخش معه مردم و سرانجام و اسباب آن نموده بخانهٔ خودها رفتند و گفتند که چهار ضرب توپ وغیره اجناس آهنی جزوی که در ته آب باقی مانده بود از دست غواصان دو حصه بسرکار گرفته و یک حصه به غواص داده و چهار ضرب اتواپ مذکور وغیره را قیمت یک حصه آن مقرر نموده قیمت نقد به غواصان داده شد - و در جهاز نبی بخش چهل و نه نفر ملازم سرکار وغیره محروق و مغروق شدند - منجمله آن ضیاءالدین معه حرم و بچه و غلام وغیره پنج نفر، و فقیر محمد رساله‌دار معه جوانان علاقهٔ خود یازده نفر، و بارگیر سرکار دو نفر، و معلم معه
پسر دو نفر، و علاقهٔ بهرام هفت نفر، و هرکاره چهار نفر، و آدم محمدعلی ٩٦
بهاتو و کنک پله و میران فراش سه نفر، و گوله انداز یک نفر، و

١ - The date should be 15th. The day does not tally with the date.

نجار سرکاری یک نفر، خلاصی سه نفر، و باقی یک صد و شصت و نه نفر ملازم سرکار وغیره از اعانت و مدد گیری جعفر خان جان به سلامت بردند - و شمس‌الدین داروغهٔ جهاز فتح شاهی معزی و لطف علیخان که برآن سوار بودند با وصف اتصال از جهاز مغروق اصلاً بخبر گیری نپرداختند -

و بتاریخ هفدهم روز شنبه سید علی صاحب نامی فقیر پیرزاده از اولاد حضرت خواجه بنده نواز قدس‌الله‌سره‌العزیز، که از خواهش و التجا و استدعای شاه نورالله خان نظر بحصول شرف زیارات مقدسات سفر این دیار قبول نموده، به بصره رسیدند، بتاریخ مسطور که روز صندل خواجه موصوف بود لوازم صندل معه چراغ افروزی بجا آوردند - مردم شهر بصره نظر به چراغ افروزی وغیره نموده بسیار متعجب شدند -

و بتاریخ هجدهم روز یکشنبه هر دو منشی بعد نماز ظهر از طرف
گوشهٔ نیرت بر حصار بندر بصره سوار شده تا دروازهٔ زبیر، که باقی ٩٧
مانده بود، بنظر در آوردند - بروج سی و یک عدد بود - و دو ضرب
بیتری بست و چهار رطل ضایع شده، بر دو برج مقابل مورچال فوج
برادر کریم خان واقع است - و مورچال هم دو طرف نموده بود: یکی
بطرف دروازهٔ بغداد تا مقابل مقام علی رضی‌الله‌عنه، و دوم از گوشهٔ
مغرب تا دروازهٔ زبیر - و جمله مسافت حصار گرداگرد بصره قیاساً
هفت کروه خواهد بود و به طول چهار و نیم کروه بادشاهی و به عرض
یک و نیم کروه - و جمله بروج یک صد و سی و یک عدد و جمله
اتواپ پانزده ضرب شکسته بر بروج افتاده، و سه ضرب برکنارهٔ نهر عظیم
متصل و روبروی فردهٔ بصره واقع است - و حصار و بروج قلعه بسیار
شکسته و ریخته و مرمت طلب است - و بیرون آبادی شهر از دروازهٔ
زبیر تا کنارهٔ رود فرات نخلستان است، لاکن از دروازهٔ سراجی،....(١)

١— MS. damaged

۹۸ بکثرت واقع است و به دستور از دروازهٔ بغداد تا کنارهٔ رود مذکور نخلستان قدری قدری واقع است و اندرون شهر از دروازهٔ سراجی تا آخر حصار و مقام علی رضی‌الله‌عنه تا کنارهٔ رود مذکور به وفور موفور - و حصار گرداگرد بصره از آبادی به فاصله دو سه تیر پرتاب واقع است - و درمیان آن نخلستان و باغات که در آن گل گلاب و انگور و انجیر و انار و تره‌کاری وغیره پیدا می شود -

و در طاس پنجم آفندی وغیره نزد غلام علی خان و شاه نورالله خان وغیره آمده از طرف خود و متسلم حاکم بصره اظهار نمود که دیروز لوازم صندل و چراغ افروزی بزرگی بجا آوردند و مایان را طلب نداشتند - غلام علیخان و شاه نورالله خان به در جواب پرداختند که سید علی صاحب پیرزاده مرشد مردم عسکر مایان دیروز صندل جد بزرگوار خود نمودند و امروز که روز عرس است البته روشنی چراغان بسیار خواهد شد، شما بیایند و به بینند - من بعد پیرزاده مذکور تا نصف شب بلکه
۹۹ زیاده ازآن چراغ افروزی به آئین بهین نمودند - آفندی وغیره اعیان بصره و بسیار مردم شهر به تماشا آمده بسیار متعجب شدند و به مداری قهوه وغیره به وفور مسرت و بهجت مراجعت بخانهٔ خودها نمودند -

و بتاریخ نوزدهم روز دوشنبه بوقت چهار طاس روز برآمده متسلم حاکم بصره مراد خان و محمد شفیع و شمس‌الدین را معه بارگیر و چیلهٔ سرکار به خانهٔ خود طلبیده ضیافت نمود - اینها بعد ضیافت خوری از حاکم بصره گفتند که مایان معه اموال و اجناس ازآن شما هستیم و فیمابین آقای مایان و شما به هیچ وجه جدائی متصور نیست، لازمه تودد و شفقت آنست که به انصرام امورات سرکار بزودی مایان را به وطن مالوف روانه نمایند - حاکم بصره به وفور مسرت به لسان حال به اجابت این معنی پرداخت -

بتاریخ بیستم روز سه شنبه وقت مغرب عبدالله یهودی دلال نایب

متسلم حاکم بصره و مراد خان و محمد شفیع و شمس‌الدین نزد غلام‌علی
خان و شاه نوراللہ خان و لطف علی خان وغیره آمده برای فروخت نمودن
اجناس تجارتی سرکار سوال و جواب نمودند و رفتند ـ

١٠٠ و بتاریخ بست و یکم ماه مذکور روز جمعه صبحی شاه نوراللہ خان
و لطف علی خان معه هر دو منشی و سید جعفر مصدی و معلم و محمدامام
و محمد امین جوقدار و سرخیل سزاول معه چند جمعدار و جوانان علاقهٔ خود
و محمد نتهو سرخیل و جوقدار اسداللهی معه چند جوانان علاقهٔ خود و
محمد کمال و عبدالرحمان و شکرالله چیلهٔ سرکار و محمد عمر و شیخ بدهن
وغیره چوبدار و خدمتگار سرکار و نیز چند جوانان علاقهٔ بهرام معه بیرق
و نیز مراد خان و محمد شفیع و شمس‌الدین و بارگیران سرکار وغیره برای
زیارت خواجه حسن بصری و طلحه و زبیر رضی‌اللہ‌عنهما از دروازهٔ زبیر
بیرون شهر عبور کرده در طاس پنجم به سرحد بنای مسجد مبارک
حضرت امیر المومنین علی ابن ابی طالب رضی‌اللہ‌عنه، که در زمان خود
مسجد مذکور را بنا فرموده بصوم و صلواة خود مزین و مشرف ساخته
بودند، و در آنجا آبادی عظیم‌الشان و بسیار آباد و نهری عظیم واقع بود
و جنگ جمل هم در آنجا به ظهور رسیده بود، حالا از بنای مسجد مذکور
دو ستون گوشه دیوار و مینار مسجد شکسته و ریخته شده باقی است و
١٠ نیز قبرستان به وفور است، رسیده دو رکعت نماز تحیهٔ المسجد همه
کسان گذاردند ـ به زیارت طلحه رضی‌اللہ‌عنه، که متصل مسجد مذکور
به دست چپ گنبد خورد و اندرون گنبد یک صندوق چوبین که طولش
چهار و نیم گز و عرضش دو گز و بلندی یک و نیم گز است، رفته
زیارت نمودند ـ و لطف علی خان بزیارت خوانی در مسجد مسطور مشغول
شدند و زیارت نه نمودند ـ من بعد به قریهٔ موسومهٔ زبیر، که از مسجد
مذکور فاصلهٔ نیم کروه دارد و آبادی مذکور به اطراف قریب یک
کروه خواهد بود لاکن همه ویران و چند خانها آباد است و بازار و

دکاکین قریپ یک صد عدد و دو سه عدد قهوه خانه آباد است، برای
زیارت زبیر، که اندرون قریهٔ زبیر مسجدیست و بطرف راست منبر مسجد
بر پشت دروازهٔ گنبد زبیر است و بر یمین مسجد مذکور پائین یک قبه
خورد که در آن یک قبر غریز زبیر است و بر یسار پنج و شش عدد
قبور از اهل قوم چلبی سوداگر بندر سورت در چاردیواری واقع است و
اندرون گنبد گرداگرد قبر به تفاوت یک و نیم دست جالی نقشی چوبی،(۱) ۰۲
در طول چهار و نیم گز و در عرض سه و نیم گز و در بلندی سه گز،
ساخته چلبی سوداگر از مدت شش سال است و اندرون جالی مذکور
قبر در طول سه گز و پاو بالا و در عرض یک و نیم گز و در بلندی
دو گره، همه مردم در گنبد مذکور رفته زیارت نمودند، الا لطف علی خان
که در مسجد مذکور به استراحت تمام به اکل و شرب مشغول شدند ـ
من بعد در یَک خانهٔ کلان خالی ساخته همه کسان سوای سزاول فرود
آمدند ـ و بعد اکل و شرب شاه نوراللّٰه خان و لطف علی خان به نذر و
خیرات فقرا قریب یک صد و هفتاد قرص رومی به اعتبار مایؤل خواهد
شد ـ و به اعتبار قریب یک صد و بیست و یک رومی سه محمودی از
سرکار بخرچ در آوردند و نیز یک غلاف باناتی برای قبر زبیر تیار ساخته
بر قبر انداختند ـ من بعد در طاس یازدهم بیرون قریهٔ زبیر بطرف جنوب
به فاصلهٔ دو سه تیر پرتاب روضهٔ مقدسهٔ حضرت خواجه حسن بصری
رضی‌اللّٰه‌عنه واقع بود، لطف علی و شاه نوراللّٰه خان وغیره رفته به شرف ۰۳
زیارت مشرف و لطف یک سبد خرمای تر به خرید آورده به فقرا و
مساکین خیرات نمودند و شاه نوراللّٰه خان دو سه من نابات مصری فاتحه
داده به فقرا دادند ـ و گنبد مبارک دو قبه دارد، و به اندرون یک قبه
قبر مبارک، و در قبهٔ دیگر به پائین قبر احمد استاد گنبد است، و

۱ــ .MS چوبیں

بطرف بالین گنبد مبارک در یک چهاردیواری علحده دو راسته قبور چهارده شهید است ـ و به اطراف گنبدهای خورد خورد حکام بصره وغیره و قبرستان بسیار است ـ و بالا تر ازان یک قبرستان دیگر و اثر بنای مسجد حضرت خواجه موصوف واقع است ـ و قبر مبارک در طول دو و نیم گز و دو گره و در عرض یک گز دو گره و در بلندی یک و نیم گز دو گره بود ـ و باز به فرودگاه در موضع قریهٔ موسومهٔ زبیر آمده بعد نصف شب برخاسته تا وقت صبح به فرودگاه خود در بندر بصره رسیدند، و به روضهٔ انس بن مالک رضی‌الله‌عنه، که از خواجه حسن بصری رضی‌الله‌عنه
به فاصلهٔ پنج شش کروه پیشتر در صحرا و ویرانی بود و آب نبود بسبب ۱۰۴
خطر و درماندگی از عدم آب، نرفتند ـ

تاریخ بست و سیوم روز شنبه در طاس چهارم به شاه نورالله خان چند اسهال و استفراغ(۱) شدند، من بعد از حکیم میر شفیع نامی و طبیب ارمنی و فرنگی رجوع آوردند، بعد دو سه روز مقرون به صحت شدند ـ

و بتاریخ بست و پنجم روز یکشنبه وقت مغرب مراد خان و محمد شفیع وغیره معه سیوا گماشته دلال بندر مسقط نزد شاه نورالله خان آمده گفتند که محمد حنیف در بندر مقسط مرچ سیاه و پارچهٔ سفید وغیره را با وصف خریدار به نرخ مقصود نه فروختند، اگرچه مایان و شما و دلال بسیار گفت و شنود و فهمایش به آئین بهین نمودند ـ و به دستور در جزیرهٔ خارج ضیاء الدین هم مرچ سیاه و پارچهٔ سفید را سوای دستار بدو خریدار و تاجر بهتر و خوب که موافق مقصود رسیده بودند نفروختند،
حالانکه بسیار بسیار به عنوانات به ضیاءالدین مایان و شما گفتند و نوشتند ۱۰
و خودها بردند و ملامت بر سر مایان گذاشتند، و حالا درینجا جنسی از اجناس سرکار به نرخ سابق و سرکاری نمی ارزد، به کدام نوع به انصرام

۱- .MS استقراق

امورات سرکار پرداخته شود - شاه نورالله خان و مراد خان وغیره بجای‌خود مقرر نموده که مرچ سیاه فی کهندی بحساب چهل و سه هون حیدری و پارچهٔ سیاه و سفید وغیره فی انگه یک روپیه دوازده آنه کم نه باید فروخت و زرد چوب و زنجبیل به نرخ بازار بصره - من بعد مراد خان وغیره از شاه نورالله خان گفتند که درین ماده محضری مفصل نویسانیده مرحمت فرمایند - خان مذکور به جواب پرداختند که نزد غلام علی خان و لطف علی خان این کیفیت ظاهر سازند اگر مزاج آنها درین ماده باشد البته من هم حاضرام - مراد خان از آنجا برخاسته نزد غلام علی خان رفته به اظهار کیفیت مسطور درین ماده بسیار عجز و التجا نمودند -
خان مسطور جواب دادند که خود در کار سوداگری و جهازات شماها ١٠٦
نیستم و به حضور همین کلمه اظهار نموده ام که در کارخانهٔ سوداگری و جهازات سرکار و منزل و مقام کاری و دخلی ندارم و بعد رسیدن به ولایت روم انچیکه جواب و سوال سرکار فیض آثار خواهد بود بجا آورده خواهد شد - درین صورت در امورات متعلقهٔ شماها دخلی نیست و نه‌دارم، شماها مختارند، بنوعیکه می خواهند به انصرام امورات سرکار پردازند - مراد خان وغیره باز عجز و الحاح بسیار نمودند، غلام علی خان نظر به وفور عجز و التجا قبول نموده گفتند که اگرچه تا این مدت در مادهٔ کارخانهٔ شما کلمهٔ نیک و بدی در عرض داشت حضور پرنور نه نویسانیدم و حالا نظر به عجز و حالات روداد شماها کیفیت گذشته از بندر مسقط تا اینجا در عرضداشت حضور نویسانیده بدست شماها خواهم داد، خاطر جمع دارند -

بتاریخ بست و هفتم روز سه شنبه در طاس پنجم شاه نورالله خان در توشکخانهٔ سرکار آمده یک پیتارهٔ خلاع وزیران انگریز بتوهم و اندیشه درهم و برهم و شکست و ریخت از صدمات آورد و برآورد در
جهازات سرکار وغیره واز کردند - نه بستهٔ خلعت چهینت بندری و ده ١٠٧

بستهٔ خلعت مومی بود، یک بستهٔ خلعت چهینت بندری و یک بسته خلعت مومی واز کرده دیدند، خوب و درست بود - باز به دستور سابق همه خلاع در پیتارهٔ مذکور نهاده از ریسمان سوتی بسته سرِبمهر نموده در توشکخانهٔ مذکور نهاد و باز دیگر پیتاره خورد بابت خلاع سفید راجهٔ انگریز که اندکی بشکست درآمده بود واز کردند - شش بستهٔ خلعت سفید و یک بستهٔ رومال نادرپاکی که درآن دو چهانپ بود، منجمله آن یک بستهٔ خلعت و یک بستهٔ چهانپ رومال مذکور، واز کرده بنظر در آورده باز به درستگی تمام داخل پیتارهٔ مذکور نموده از ریسمان سوتی بسته سر به مهر شاه نورالله خان نموده داخل توشکخانهٔ مذکور کردند و به خانهٔ خود رفتند -

و بتاریخ بست و هشتم روز چهار شنبه متسلم حاکم بصره معه حاجی محمد دفتردار آفندی و علی آغا سلاح بردار سلیمان پاشا حاکم بغداد به عیادت تکسل مزاج شاه نورالله خان، که از سه چهار روز به وقوع
۱۰۸ وفور اسهال و استفراغ(۱) بود، نزد غلام علی خان و شاه نورالله خان وغیره آمده بیمار پرسی نمود و گفت شماها به خانهٔ خود چرا نمی آیند و توجه نمی فرمایند - غلام علی خان عذر لنگی پای خود درپیش آوردند و شاه نورالله خان عذر امورات ضروریات و تکسل مزاج خود بیان نموده گفتند که بعد صحت به خانهٔ شما خواهم آمد - و به دستور لطف علیخان تعذر تکسل مزاج خود که از لغایت فرود آمدن به بندر مسقط واقع است ظاهر نمودند - من بعد متسلم خوانین را به ضیافت دوباره دعوت کرد - این‌ها به اجابت پرداخته گفتند که حالا پنج شش روز کار حاضری حضرت عباس رضی‌الله‌عنه درپیش است، بعد فراغت البته به اقبال این معنی خواهند پرداخت و شماهم ضیافت مایان چرا قبول نه کردند -

---

۱— MS. استفراق

متسلم گفت: ده دوازده روز تکسل مزاج بود، حالا که مقرون به صحت شدم به سر و چشم حاضرام - خوانین گفتند: بعد پنج و شش روز اول شما درین جا بیایند و به ضیافت خوری مایان مسرور سازند و روز دوم یا سیوم مایان را بخانهٔ خود بطلبند حاضرام - متسلم قبول کرد و به ٩٠
خانهٔ خود به وفور مسرت مراجعت نمود -

و در طاس سیوم گماشتهٔ فراسیس علاقه دار کوتهی بصره نزد غلام علی خان و شاه نورالله خان وغیره آمده بعد ملاقات رفت - و در طاس چهارم غلام علیخان و شاه نواالله خان و لطف علیخان یک جا شده و محمد علی بهاتو و محمد عمر چوبدار و دوبهانسی(۱) سرکار، را که به شب گذشته بوقت نیم شب هر سه کس در خانهٔ یهودی رفته شراب خوری نموده، دوبهانسی مذکور را نبرد و خورد آوردند، فریاد بر دروازهٔ غلام علی خان آوردند - خان مسطور دوباشی را خوب کفش کاری نموده همه‌ها را(۲) نظر شب نموده بخانهٔ آنها برآنیده بودند، طلب داشته هر سه سردار به آئین بهین هر سه شراب خوار را فضیحت و تنبیه نمودند -

بتاریخ بست و نهم روز جمعه(۳) در طاس چهارم آفندی در خدمت غلام علی خان و لطف علیخان آمده باز رفت، و به وقت مغرب مراد خان و شمس‌الدین نزد غلام علی خان آمدند و رفتند - غلام علی خان و شاه نورالله خان دو قطعه عرضداشت متضمن کیفیت گذشته از بندر مسقط تا الی الآن بتاریخ ماه زبرجدی سال مذکور سنه الیه(۱) روز جمعه در ١١٠
نصف شب نویسانیده، بر دنگی فرنگی انگریز علاقه دار کوتهی بصره که به بندر مسقط می رفت، نزد دلال مسقط روانه نمودند، تا که از آنجا به حضور پرنور فایز شود - و به وقت نماز مغرب یک نفر دوبهانسی

۱— دوباشی ۲— همه را

۳— 28 Zul-Qa'da, 1200/22 September, 1786.

زبان عربی و ترکی و انگریزی به ملازم سرکار داخل نموده، سی روپیه به جنس در ماهه مقرر نمودند و به سی و شش روز سی روپیه به جنس باید داد، غلام علی خان و شاه نورالله خان و لطف علی خان وغیره به اتفاق خودها مقرر نمودند ـ

و بتاریخ دوم ماه زبرجدی سال دلو سنه ۱۲۰۰ هجری روز یکشنبه (۲) غلام علی خان به نیاز حضرت عباس رضی‌الله‌عنه طعام خوب دو سه نوع معه لوازم پخت و پز نموده تورهای(۳) طعام به خانهٔ لطف علی خان و شاه نورالله خان و جعفر خان مع پنج نفر بارگیر سرکار و سید علی صاحب پیرزاده و عبدالقادر منشی و مراد خان و شمس‌الدین و محمد شفیع و بارگیران سرکار علاقهٔ ارماد و محمد کمال و عبدالرحمن و شکرالله چیلهٔ سرکار و محمد عمر و محمد فاضل و شیخ بدهن و عبدالنبی چوبدار سرکار و شیخ مرتضی و محمد حسین و شیخ بدهن و یعقوب خدمتگار سرکار
و چند مردم باشندهٔ بصره را فرستادند ـ و بتاریخ سیوم روز دوشنبه ۱۱۱
بدستور طعام پزانیده به جوانان اسداللهی و بهرام وغیره درویست وغیره خورانیدند ـ شاه نورالله خان عبدالله یهودی را از معرفت سیوا گماشتهٔ دلال بندر مسقط طلبیده به چند عنوانات بنام برده برای فروختن اجناس تجارتی سرکار گفتند ـ نام برده قبول نموده گفت که حالا به سبب خواهش و تودد شما کاغذ زر بقدر مطلوب شما بر ساهوکار بغداد نموده می دهم، شما پیشتر راهی شوند و اجناس تجارتی هم عنقریب کم و بیش بقدر مناسب بفروخت می رسانم، خاطر جمع دارند ـ و بتاریخ چهارم روز

۱ــ 30 Zu'l-Qa'da, 1200/24 September, 1786. The day should be Sunday. The day of the month in the *waqa'i'* is incorrectly given. 29 Wasai, falls on Friday; and since Wasai consists of 30 days, 1 Zabarjadi cannot fall on Friday, as mentioned in the Waqa'i', but on Sunday.

۲ــ This should be Monday

۳ــ MS. طورهای

سه شنبه به جوانان سزاول وغیره چند مردمان بصره طلبیده طعام نیاز پزانیده خورانیدند -

تاریخ پنجم روز چهار شنبه در طاس سیوم شاه نورالله خان به خانهٔ متسلم رفته بعد یک ساعت از آنجا به کوتهی فراسیس، که مکان کرایه دار مراد خان و محمد شفیع وغیره بود، رفته، برای چند تهان شیله و سنجرخانی و چهینت پامری به خان مسطور تاکید نمودند که از بسته‌های پارچهٔ سفید وغیره برآورده بدهند، البته در زر تنخواهی به نرخیکه بجای دیگر اجناس تجارتی سرکار بفروخت خواهد درآمد، مجرا و محسوب خواهد شد و به کنک پله و شکرالله و عبدالرحمان چیلهٔ سرکار رجوع و مقابله ۱۲
نمودند و مراد خان و محمد شفیع وغیره فلفل گرد را بحساب فی کهندی سی و نه هون تمام و کمال بفروخت رسانیدند - و بتاریخ ششم روز پنجشنبه دو غلاف باناتی یکی برای روضهٔ خواجه حسن بصری رضی‌الله‌عنه و دیگر برای روضهٔ طلحه رضی‌الله‌عنه به صحابت شیخ مرتضی‌ای خدمتگار و چند جوانان سزاول بروضهٔ موصوف فرستادند -

و بتاریخ هفتم روز جمعه غلام علی خان بستهٔ حاضری حضرت عباس رضی‌الله‌عنه کرده به سید علی صاحب پیرزاده و لطف علی خان و هر دو منشی و سید جعفر مصدی و شکرالله خان وغیره اسامی را خورانیدند و خودهم خوردند -

و بتاریخ هشتم هر چهار سردار برآورد ضیافت متسلم حاکم بصره نموده بدعوت دوازده آسامی معه حاکم مذکور و تهیه سرانجام ضیافت پرداختند - و چهل و پنج روپیه به اسلام آوردن سه نفر هنود علاقهٔ بهرام بدست غلام محی‌الدین سرخیل بهرام به اتفاق هر چهار سردار فی نفر پانزده روپیه مقرر کرده از سرکار دهانیدند -

و بتاریخ دهم روز دوشنبه دو قطعه خطوط بدر جواب خط غلام علی خان و شاه نورالله خان از طرف احمد دیوان سلیمان پاشا متضمن

وصول خطوط ایشان و حصول مسرت و بهجت از رسیدن ایشان به بصره،
و از نظر گذرانیدن خطوط ایشان به سلیمان پاشا حاکم بغداد، و صدور ۱۱۲
حکم عالی به حاکم بصره بر این معنی، که شما را با بدرقه و احتشام
تا موضع سمولت(۱) که از بصره هفت منزل است رساند، و در آنجا از بغداد
سوار وغیره بقدر کفاف و احتیاج روانه نموده خواهد شد، به فراغت و
حصول شرف زیارات مقدسات به دارالسلام بغداد آمده بعد دفع ماندگی
سفر عازم مکان پیش نهاد شوند، معه خط تاکید موسومه متسلم حاکم بصره نزد
متسلم رسیده بود - خط موسومهٔ خود گرفته دو قطعه موسومهٔ غلام علی خان
و شاه نورالله خان به صحابت چوبدار خود نزد ایشان فرستاد - ایشان مضمون
آن بدریافت آورده به چوبدار یک پچهوری تارپتری گلدار ابریشمی و یک دستار
سفید بطریق انعام دادند - و در جواب خط لطف علی خان، که بوقت روانگی
خطوط موسومهٔ حاکم بغداد ازین جا به غلام علی خان و شاه نورالله خان
گفتند که شما از طرف خودها به حواله یکدیگر خطوط نوشتند و از
جانب من نه نویسانیدند و نام من هم در خطوط نه نوشتند باعث چیست،
بسیار تکرار نموده، آخرالامر یک قطعهٔ خط از جانب خود موسومهٔ حاکم
بغداد و نیز در خط غلام علی خان نام خود نویسانیده، هر سه قطعه
خطوط بدست آفندی داده نزد متسلم روانه ساختند - و ازانجا متسلم ۱۱۱
نزد حاکم بغداد روانه کرد - چنانچه در جواب دو قطعه غلام علی خان و
شاه انورالله خان، سوای در جواب خط لطف علی خان، به وصول درآمد -
از عدم رسیدن در جواب خود لطف علی خان بسیار استفسار و تکرار
نموده ظن بد بر شاه نورالله خان داشتند، که مانع وصول در جواب
خط خود شاه نورالله خان است، و از متسلم که برای ضیافت خوری
آمده بود، باعث عدم رسیدن در جواب خود چیست - متسلم که صرف نام

۱ــ سماوه

حکومت بصره دارد باقی کارخانه جات وغیره آفندی و علی آغا و عبدالله
یهودی دلال می کنند هیچ معلوم نیست، می گفت که دو قطعه خطوط
از نزد شما رسیده بود نزد حاکم بغداد فرستاد ـ ازین سبب ایشانرا ظن بد
زیاده تر شد و از آفندی نیز این معنی استفسار کردند ـ آفندی گفت
که من سه قطعه خطوط شما معه خط خود نزد حاکم بغداد روانه نمودم
و حاکم بغداد در جواب نه نوشته است، این معنی را من چه کنم،
من در فرستادن خطوط شما قصور نه کردم، اگر قصور کرده باشم بعد
رسیدن به بغداد از حاکم آنجا به پرسند که چند خطوط رسیدند، اگر سه
قطعه بگویند ، بهتر است، و الا شکایت مرا بنوعیکه خواهند بکنند، فی‌الفور
مرا از خدمت دفترداری معزول خواهد کرد، و در دربار ما اصلا تغلب
و تصرف نیست و نمی شود ـ

و متسلم معه قاضی و مفتی و اعیان بصره جمله دوازده آسامی نزد ۱۵
غلام علی‌خان و شاه نورالله خان وغیره که مضیف بودند آمده ضیافت به آئین
بهین خورده مسرور و خورسند شده، گفت که ضیافت مایان هم یک روز
قبول کنید ـ غلام علی خان گفتند که مایان را زود به بغداد روانه سازند ـ
البته پیش از یک دو روز از روز روانگی بخانهٔ شما خواهیم آمد، شما اگر
ضیافت می کنند بهتر و قبول است بسیار خورسند گردید ـ و عماری معه
سرانجام تیار گردانیده به متسلم نمایش کردند، دیده بسیار متعجب شد و
باروت که در آب می سوزد برو‌بروی او قدری سوزانیدند بسیار پسند کرده
از شاه‌نورالله‌خان گفت که چند است، به جواب‌پرداختند که نزد آقای
مایان بسیار است، اگر شما را درخواست باشد بنویسند البته خواهند
فرستاد ـ و باقی یک صد نفر خدمتگار و چوبدار و چاوش وغیره ملازم
متسلم را طعام خورانیدند ـ و به وقت رفتن نزد سیدعلی‌صاحب پیرزاده
که زیر بام در توشکخانه استقامت دارند آمده ملاقات کرد و رفت ـ
و بتاریخ یازدهم روز سه شنبه به عبدالقادر منشی وجه طلب یک ماهه

بعد اتمام سی و شش روز مقرری از سرکار دادند ـ

و بتاریخ دوازدهم روز چهار شنبه غلام علی خان به خانهٔ لطف علی خان به تهنیت عید سعید عیدالضحیٰ رفتند و ازآنجا معه لطف علی خان به خانهٔ شاه نورالله خان آمدند واز آنجا هر سه سردار ۱۱۰
نزد سید علی صاحب پیرزاده در توشکخانهٔ سرکار فرود آمدند و بعد ادای لوازم تهنیت باز به خانهٔ خودها رفتند ـ

و بتاریخ سیزدهم روز پنجشنبه محمد امام و محمد امین جوقدار و سرخیل سزاول معه جوانان علاقهٔ خود طعام بتبرک بنام خواجه حسن بصری وغیره رضی‌اللّٰه‌عنه پخت و پز نموده، شاه نورالله خان و جعفر خان و هر دو منشی و شکرالله خان و محمد علی بهاتو و چیلهٔ سرکار و جوانان اسداللهی و مراد خان و محمد شفیع و شمس‌الدین و محمد رفیق علاقهٔ محمد حنیف و بارگیر سرکار و چیله‌ها را به فرودگاه خود طلبیده به مدارای طعام و خورش پرداختند، و شاگرد پیشهٔ سرکار و بهرام وغیره را روز جمعه تاریخ چهاردهم طعام خورانیدند، و به خانهٔ لطف علی خان طعام فرستادند ـ

و به تاریخ پانزدهم روز دوشنبه بدستور بخانهٔ غلام علی خان طعام پخت و پز نموده فرستادند و غلام علی خان و شاه نورالله خان یک قطعه خط به در جواب خط شیخ سوینی عسکردار یک لک سوار بدوی از جانب خودها متضمن خیر و عافیت نویسانیده بدست عبدالله یهودی دلال بصره داده نزد شیخ مذکور که ازینجا به فاصلهٔ چهارپنج کروه
در قربه و خانهٔ خود می ماند، روانه نمودند ـ ۱۱

و بتاریخ شانزدهم روز یکشنبه حسین آغا، میر منزل بصره تا بغداد، نزد غلام علی خان و شاه نورالله خان وغیره از طرف متسلم آمده گفت که شما از راه خشکی می‌روند یا از راه تری و راه امن راه تری است ـ ایشان گفتند آنچیکه متسلم مقرر نماید مایان را قبول است ـ و بتاریخ

هفدهم روز دو شنبه محمد مرتضی خدمتگار نزد متسلم فرستاده پیام نمودند که مایان را زود روانه بغداد سازند - به جواب پرداخت که عبدالله یهودی را تاکید کرده ام، البته در عرصهٔ قریب روانه خواهد نمود و آفندی را نزد شما می فریسم، شما را مفصل کیفیت روانگی ظاهر خواهد کرد - من بعد آفندی آمده گفت که یک دو منزل داو بسیار کلان و خوب است برآن سوار شده از راه تری بروند - شاه نورالله خان خوب بعد ملاحظهٔ آن معلوم خواهد شد - و بست و سه طاقه‌های کیمخاب غلاف روضات مقدسات به قیمت دو هزار و پنج صد و نود و هفت روپیه غلام علی خان و شاه نورالله خان و لطف علی خان به اتفاق خرید نمودند -

و بتاریخ هجدهم روز سه شنبه آفندی به خدمت غلام علی خان وغیره آمده بود - و بتاریخ نوزدهم روز چهار شنبه شاه نورالله خان و لطف علی ۱۱۸
خان برای دیدن سه منزل کشتی سرکار متسلم بصره، که می خواهد که برآن هر چهار سردار وغیره را سوار کرده روانه بغداد نماید، رفته، بعد ملاحظه باز آمدند و وجه طلب یکماهه جوانان اسداللهی و سزاول و بهرام بروبروی هر چهار سردار دست بدست تقسیم نمودند -

و بتاریخ بستم روز پنجشنبه عبدالله یهودی دلال نزد شاه نورالله خان آمده گفت که پارچه‌های سفید خصوص پارچهٔ سیاه بسیار خراب و گران است و به حساب فی انگه دوازده آنه درخواست نمی نماید - شاه نورالله‌خان و جعفر خان همراه دلال مسطور نزد مراد خان و محمد شفیع وغیره بدلال‌مسطور و تجار پارچه ها نظر گذرانیده، به عنوانات فهمایش نمودند، اصلا به قیمت مقصود قبول نه کردند و تجار به خانهٔ خودها رفتند - اخرالامر دلال مذکور از شاه نورالله خان گفت که اگر نقصان اموال و اجناس نمی خواهند همه اجناس به خانهٔ من واگذارند، من به عنوانیکه نقصان شما نه شود می فروشم - ایشان قبول کرده به خانهٔ خود مراجعت نمودند -

و بتاریخ بست و یکم روز جمعه عبدالله یهودی نزد شاه نورالله خان

۱۱۹ آمده بود - شاه نورالله خان گفتند که اگر تو پارچهٔ سفید وغیره
می گیری بنرخیکه مراد خان و محمد شفیع وغیره می گویند، بگیر و الا
جواب صاف بده که همه اسباب و سرانجام تجارتی بر جهاز سرکار سوار
کرده مراد خان وغیره را روانه حضور می سازم و خودهم بصوب مکان
مقصود راهی می شوم و پیش سلطان روم کیفیت اجناس تجارتی و
سلوک تو اظهار خواهم کرد - دلال مسطور به تفکر تمام طوعاً و کرهاً
قبول نموده نزد مراد خان وغیره رفته گفت که یک پارچه به کسی نه
دهند من همه پارچه وغیره می گیرم -

و به وقت شام محمد علی بهاتو، از عدم رسیدن وجه طلب خود
و وضع نمودن در خوراکی دو ماهه بابت جهازات و شدت کاوش قرضداران
از هر چهار سو و اعتراض غلام علیخان و شاه نورالله خان و لطف علی خان
وغیره ، نزد جعفر خان رفته فرود آمده، به آدم خود نزد غلام علی خان
گفته فرستاد که از شدت کاوش قرضداران نزد جعفر خان
فرود آمده ام - غلام علی خان گفتند که به شاه نورالله خان بگو - آدم
مسطور نزد شاه نورالله خان رفت و گفت - معاً آدم مسطور را بزد و خورد
آورده، محمد عمر چوبدار را نزد جعفر خان فرستاده گفتند که محمد علی بهاتو
را نزد خود طلب داشته فرود آوردن چه باعث بود - جعفر خان به
۱۲۰ جواب پرداختند که محمد علی خودبخود درین جا آمده فرود آمدند ،
هر چیکه شماها می خواهند بر این شخص بکنید، محمد عمر چوبدار باز
آمده گفت - شاه نورالله خان باز به زبانی شیخ بدی چوبدار به محمد علی
بهاتو گفته فرستادند که اگر خیریت خود می خواهند به جای سابق
فرود آیند و الا فی‌الفور طوق و زنجیر نموده به جهاز سوار کرده روانه
حضور می نمایم - محمد علی بجواب پرداخت : اگر فکر ادای قرض می
نمایند من همون جا می آیم، و الا چه طور آمده خواهد شد که قرضداران
کاوش سخت می نمایند و خواهان آبرو می شوند، به چه طور برداشت

نموده خواهد شد - من بعد جعفر خان گفتند : اگر درین وقت حرکات
بیجا و بجا به ظهور رسد مناسب نیست، تا شب تاخیر کرده صبحی
هر چیکه خواهند بندوبست نمایند - شیخ بدی نزد شاه نورالله خان
آمده من و عن اظهار نمود - صبحی شاه نورالله خان محمد علی بهاتو
را در یزک سزاول نگاهداشتند - من بعد بتاریخ بست و دوم روز شنبه
جعفر خان و محمد علی را شاه نورالله خان نزد غلام علی خان طلب داشته
بروبروی هر چهار سردار و مراد خان و محمد شفیع وغیره دربارهٔ روانگی ۲۱
محمد علی به حضور پر نور همراه بری مشورت نموده، آخر الامر مقرر
نمودند که روانه حضور مع عرضداشت مخلصی محمد علی بهاتو همراه
مراد خان وغیره نماید و زر وجه طلب نامبرده تنخواه بر مراد خان
سازد - و مراد خان و محمد شفیع و شمس‌الدین کاغذ محضری دربارهٔ
مخلصی خودها و حقیقت روداد از موضع تدری تاالی‌الان تیار نموده به
شاه نورالله خان مسموع گردانیدند - شاه نورالله خان گفتند که به
کاغذ دیگر صاف کرده به ملاحظه غلام علیخان و لطف علی خان وغیره
در آورند، البته ما همگان مهر کرده خواهم داد - باز کاغذ مسوده
گرفته شمس‌الدین به فرود گاه خود رفتند، و مراد خان و محمد شفیع نزد
غلام علی خان رفته بعد یک گهری به خانهٔ خودها رفتند -

و بعد دوپهر روز برآمده بعد چلبی نامی از اعیان بصره معه خط سلیمان
پاشا حاکم بغداد نزد غلام علی خان و شاه نورالله خان آمده، خط
مذکور متضمن مهمانداری ایلچیان حضرت خداوند نعمت خلدالله ملکه بود،
مسموع گردانیده، گفت که از کدام راه به کدام روز بروند بگویند - ایشانان
(۱) گفتند بروزیکه متسلم روانه خواهدکرد روانه خواهم شد - باز گفت
که باز از بغداد پیشتر حاکم بغداد خود را مهماندار شما خواهند کرد و ۲۲

۱— ایشایان .MS

به خانهٔ خود مراجعت نمود - و یک جوان دفعه‌دار سید محمد معه پیک سرکار و ولی محمد یزکدار علاقهٔ اسداللهی مفرور شدند -

و بتاریخ بست و سیوم روز سه‌شنبه حسین آغا داروغهٔ ارماد بصره و میر منزل نزد غلام علی خان وغیره آمده گفت که سه منازل کشتی سرکار حاضر است، کدام روز روانه می شوند بگویند - غلام علی خان بجواب پرداختند که فردا نزد متسلم بضیافت خوری خواهم رفت، از متسلم پرسیده جوابش داده خواهد شد - و به وقت شام چوبدار متسلم نزد غلام علیخأن و شاه نوراللهخان وغیره آمد، از جانب متسلم دعوت کرد که فردا وقت یک طاس روز برآمده هرچهار سردار و سید علی صاحب پیرزاده معه کسان همسفره بیایند - ایشان قبول نمودند و بتاریخ بست و پنجم روز سه شنبه غلام علی خان بر پالکی خود معه چهتری و تکیهٔ پالکی سرکار، و شاه نورالله خان بر پالکی کهنهٔ سرکار معه سرانجام کهنهٔ آن، و لطف علی خان بر پالکی خود معه سرانجام آن، و جعفر خان و سید مذکور بر دو راس اسپ متسلم، سوار شده به خانهٔ متسلم راهی شدند -

۱۲ و شکرالله خان و عبدالقادر منشی و سید جعفر مصدی و محمد علی بهاتو به حسب خواهش و گفتهٔ غلام علیخان اگرچه مرضی شاه نورالله خان نبود پای پیاده از راه قریب بخانهٔ متسلم رفتند - اول به مربه و قهوه خوری مائل شده، من بعد سفره طعام پنج نوع و پنج شش نوع خورش بطریق خود درپیش کشیدند و طعام خوردند - و شاه نورالله خان روانگی خود بصوب بغداد از متسلم پرسیدند که چند روز خواهند کشید - متسلم بجواب پرداخت: انشاءاللهتعالی تا دوم ماه محرم‌الحرام روانگی شمایان به ظهور خواهد انجامید - و غلام علی خان یک طبلهٔ خوردبدری که در آن الایچی و دانهٔ ریوند داشته بودند به متسلم دادند و باز به طریق محبت ویگانگی چند کلمه و کلام به میان آوردند و مرخص شدند و پالکی و تکیه وغیره سر انجام بابت سرکار باز امانت نگاهداشتند -

و بتاریخ بست و ششم روز چهار شنبه یک درویش سدی نزد غلام علی خان آمده گفت که خود به ولایت روم رفته بود، وزیراعظم چهار صد رومی بخرچ راه به طواف حج اکبر داد و عثمان خان ملازم سرکار به خانهٔ وزیراعظم منتظر رسیدن شماها است، و همه روز وزرا و ۲۴
امرا را گویند که آمدن شماها به این ضلاع غلط محض و امر محال است، من بعد خبر برآمد شماها از بندر کوریال رسید، سلطان روم به طلب داشتن شماها دو منزل جهاز در شهر مصر تیار نموده بود، چنانچه این همه کیفیت عثمان خان ظاهر کرد و گفت: وقتیکه تو به ولایت هند میروی، البته دراثنای راه غلام علی خان و شاه نورالله خان خواهند رسید بعد ابلاغ بندگی همه کیفیت ظاهر کرده بگوئی(۱) که زود به ولایت روم برسند که همه منتظر قدوم شماها هستند - و ولایت روم گذاشته هفت ماه شده بود -

و عبدالله یهودی دلال و حسین آغا داروغهٔ ارماد بصره آمده تفصیل خرچ یک منزل کشتی کلان باشترده نام معه دو منزل خورد دیگر که دو هزار و سی و پنج قرص رومی بروبروی غلام‌علی خان و شاه‌نورالله خان وغیره بیان نموده درخواست کرد - خوانین به دلال گفتند چه مضایقه دارد، نزد متسلم رفته دو هزار قرص بدست حسین آغا از طرف مایان ۱۲۵
بده - و نیز برای تقرر نرخ پارچهٔ سیاه محمدشفیق و شمس‌الدین همراه عبدالله یهودی مذکور آمده بودند - محمدشفیق باز به کوتهی فرودگاه خود بحسب گفتهٔ شاه نورالله خان رفته سه چهار طاقه پارچهٔ سیاه و سه چهار طاقهٔ کهادی محمودبندری و نیرملی آورده بتقرر نرخ از شاه نورالله خان گفتند - شاه نورالله خان از دلال مسطور بسیار به عنوانات گفتند - دلال به اتفاق حسین آغا گفت که پارچهٔ سیاه بحساب فی انگه

۱- MS. بگوید

دوازده آنه بدهند ـ ایشان قبول نه کرده گفتند: تایک روپیه و چهار آنه خواهم داد، و باز فی طاقه پارچهٔ سفید محمود بندری به تردد تمام نرخ مقرر نمودند که یازده روپیه بدهند ـ درآن غلام علی خان از دلال پنجاه طاقه گرفتن مقرر نموده درخواست نمودند ـ و چند برای خیمه سازی سرکار به عوض خیمه های عنایتی سرکار که در جهاز مغروق سوخته شد و شاه نورالله خان و لطف علی خان درخواست نمودند و باقی به تقرر نرخ پارچهٔ سفید نرملی و پارچهٔ سیاه به دلال گفتند که امروز تمام بکن قبول نموده به خانهٔ خود رفت ـ و پارچهٔ سفید تمام و کمال دو حصه بدلال و یک حصه سیوا گماشته دلال بندر مسقط، و شاه نورالله خان ۱۲۰
برای مردم متعینهٔ خود و دادن بر امورات سرکار به مردم موضعات پیش نهاد به طریق انعام و سوغات بحساب فی صد انگه یک و نیم رومی به فروخت رسانیدند ـ و وجه طلب یکماهه غلام‌علی خان و لطف‌علی خان و شاه نورالله خان و شکرالله خان و احمدعلی منشی و جمیع شاگرد پیشهٔ سرکار بروبردی غلام‌علی خان وغیره دست بدست تقسیم نمودند ـ و غلام علی خان سه عدد دستار خورد چهینت برهانپوری سه قسمی گلدار بصحابت محمد فاضل چوبدار سرکار برای پنجه بندی به متسلم فرستادند ـ و بتاریخ بست و هفتم روز پنجشنبه نیم آثار خام روغن صندل به قیمت شش رومی از سرکار بابت نذر، چهار سبو پر از روغن صندل بودند، برآورده گرفتند ـ

و بتاریخ بست و هشتم روز جمعه مراد خان و محمدشفیع و شمس‌الدین و عبدالله یهودی دلال بصره نزد شاه نورالله خان آمده نرخ پارچهٔ سیاه تمام و کمال فی صد انگه سیزده آنه روپیه بدشواری تمام مقرر نموده به فروخت رسانیدند ـ و غلام‌علی خان و شاه نورالله خان وغیره
وجه قیمت بست و سه طاقه های کیمخاب که پیشتر ازین بخریدن ۱۲
آورده بودند ادا ساختند ـ

و بتاریخ بست و نهم روز شنبه احمد چلبی مهاندار نزد غلام‌علی خان و شاه نورالله خان آمده بود ـ شاه نورالله خان پرسیدند که مایان کی بر کشتی سوار می کنی ، و مایان دوهزار رومی به معرفت دلال به خرچ سه منزل کشتی سرکار شما فرستاده ایم و همه امورات مایان به انصرام رسیدند ـ گفت که بتاریخ دوازدهم محرم‌الحرام برکشتی سوار خواهم کرد ـ و گفت که خیمه برازی فرودگاه خود ساخته اند یانه ، اگر ساخته‌اند خوب است ، و الا تیار سازند ، که در راه بغداد ضرور خواهد بود ـ ایشان به جواب پرداختند که ده دوازده عدد خیمه‌ها حاضر بود در جهاز مغروق به حرق و غرق درآمد، بالفعل یک دو خیمه تیار خواهند ساخت ـ

و بتاریخ سلخ روز یکشنبه مراد خان و محمد شفیع و شمس‌الدین و عبدالله یهودی دلال بصره نزد شاه نورالله خان آمده پارچهٔ سیاه را بحساب فی صد انگه سیزده آنه به شدت و محنت تمام مقرر ساختند ـ

و بتاریخ غره ماه حیدری سال دلو سنه ۱۲۰۰ هجری(۱) روز دو شنبه دو قطعهٔ خطوط موسومه به غلام علی و شاه نورالله خان بدر جواب دو قطعه خطوط دو خان مسطور، که سابق ازین بدر جواب خط موسی روسو فراسیس تعلقدار کوتهی بغداد به معرفت تعلقدار کوتهی بصره روانه بغداد ۱۲۸
نزد موسی روسو نموده بودند، متضمن این مضمون رسیدند که نظر به اتحاد و یگانگی نواب مستطاب غفران مآب و آن خداوند نعمت لا زال اقباله به تقدیم شیوه اخلاص و یک جهتی به علاقه‌دار کوتهی بصره خط تاکید به ترقیم در آورده به خدمت عالی متصدع گردیده با وصف ترقیم رقایم الوداد و وصول تاکید به علاقه‌دار کوتهی مذکور چیزی از کوتهی مسطور نه گرفتند ـ و در خط شاه نورالله خان و غلام علی خان

۱ـ 29 Zul-Hijjah, 1200/23 October, 1786.

یک شقهٔ دیگر متضمن اینکه طریقهٔ دولتمندی و نام آوری و کارپردازی به بسطید و انعام و اخراجات است، و از طریقهٔ اهل عرب اعلا واقف نیستند خوب، وقتیکه شماها در این جا خواهند رسید خود به عرض خواهد پرداخت، و به هر خوانین به القاب نوابی وغیره به بزرگی و تودد و اخلاص تمام نیازمندانه ترقیم نموده بود ـ

و شاه نورالله خان از دلال گفته صد تهان پارچهٔ سیاه محمود بندری به خرج خود و غلام علی خان وغیره گرفتند ـ و بتاریخ دوم ماه مذکور روز سه شنبه محمد علی بهاتو نزد شاه نورالله خان رفته به عفو تقصیرات
۱۲ خود پرداخت ـ خان مسطور اجابت نموده به نصائح سود مندانه در پیش آمدند و پنج روپیه از جانب خود دادند ـ

و بتاریخ چهارم روز پنجشنبه احمد چلبی و حسین آغا نزد غلام علی خان و شاه نورالله خان وغیره آمده بود ـ مراد خان و محمد شفیع و شمس‌الدین محضری متضمن کیفیت گذشته خود از موضع تدری تا الی‌الان تیار نموده نزد غلام علی خان وغیره آورده بودند ـ و روز جمعه احمد چلبی آمده بود ـ

و بتاریخ ششم روز شنبه عظمت خان یک جوان دفعهٔ محبت خان علاقهٔ سزاول به مرض پیچش از قضای الهی فوت شد و قوتیانه چهار روپیه از سرکار دهانیدند ـ و بوقت شب مراد خان و شمس‌الدین وغیره محضری متضمن کوایف روداد خودها و فروخت نمودن پارچه و اجناس تجارتی سرکار تیار نموده پیش غلام علی خان و شاه نورالله خان و لطف علی خان آوردند ـ خوانین مسطور مهر و دسخط نمودند ـ و جعفر علی خان روز دوم مهر نمودند ـ و شکرالله خان و احمد علی منشی و سید جعفر مصدی و محمد امام جوقدار سزاول و محمد نتهو سرخیل و جوقدار اسداللهی به اتفاق برای دیدن کشتی های بصره کرایه دار رفته خوب بملاحظه در آورده نز و خوانین آمده اظهار نمودند ـ خوانین

به هر یک کشتی چند جوان مقرر نمودند که بر آن سوار شوند، و یک ٣٠
کشتی دیگر بعدم موافقت و کفایت در سه منازل کشتی مذکور، یک
کشتی به معرفت اسحاق یهودی به اقرار آنکه هشت صد روپیه از
سرکار می دهند در محصول انتفاع آن، سی جوانان را بر آن سوار نماید،
و مبلغ مسطور بعد رسیدن ببغداد عاید سرکار نماید مقرر نمودند ـ

و بتاریخ هفتم روز یکشنبه شاه نورالله خان در کوتهی فراسیس نزد مراد خان وغیره رفته به شدت تمام از عبدالله یهودی مقدمه بیع و شرای همه اجناس سرکار به انصرام رسانیده باز آمدند ـ و دو قطعه خطوط موسومهٔ غلام علی خان و شاه نورالله خان از طرف دلال بندر مسقط متضمن خبر خیریت رسیدند ـ

و بتاریخ نهم روز سه شنبه چند اطفال بصره در دست خودها یک یک چوب گرفته و بر بازوی خود نشترها زده با ماتم و تعزیه حضرت امام حسین رضی‌الله‌عنه نزد غلام علی خان آمده بودند ـ خان مسطور چهار رومی دادند ـ و یک قطعه خط از جانب شاه نورالله خان بدر جواب خط دلال بندر مسقط نویسانیده مرسل بصوب بندر مذکور ساختند ـ

و بتاریخ دهم روز چهارشنبه به اسحاق یهودی دو هزار و دو صد ١٣١
رومی برای خریدن خرما و کرایه نمودن یک کشتی برای سوار گردانیدن
شصت نفر مردم سزاول به اقرار اینکه بعد رسیدن به بغداد مبلغ مذکور
بسرکار عاید نماید، و در انتفاع آن سواری شصت نفر مذکور به عمل
آید، شاه نورالله خان دادند ـ و پیش ازین نیز پنج صد رومی برای یک
کشتی خورد لایق سواری سی نفر به یهودی مسطور داده بودند، باز
بوقت شام به گفتهٔ حسین آغا داروغهٔ ارماد بصره و عبدالله یهودی دلال
بصره به فروخت رسانیده مبلغ مذکور واپس گرفتند ـ

و بتاریخ یازدهم روز پنجشنبه دلال بصره نزد شاه نورالله خان آمده

فریاد کرد که کارهای بهونگیری همه بوسیده و ریخته شده اند، و انک
زیاد دارند، مرا درکار نیست ، و بر پارچه بابت نمونه انک کم بود ـ
خان مسطور به خانهٔ دلال رفتند ، دلال چند طاقه های بهونگیری
نمایش کرده همه پارچه بابت بهونگیری واپس نمود ـ شاه نورالله خان
گفتند که اول بوقت بردن بخانهٔ خود همه بسته ها واز کرده ندیدی،
حالا در خانهٔ خود آورده واز کرده، می گوئی که خوب نیست ، چه
طور می شود، بسیار گفت و شنود به عنوانات درمیان آمد ـ آخرالامر
خان مسطور به جواب پرداختند که این مال مال سرکار است، اگر واپس
۱۳۲ می دهی خوب ، به سرکار باز گردانیده خواهد شد ، لاکن این مذکور و
طریقه پیش سلطان روم مذکور خواهد شد، الخیر فیما وقع ـ حالا مایان
را زود روانه بغداد بکن، قبول کرد، خان مسطور بخانهٔ خود باز آمدند ـ
و ترسنگ راو جوان دفعهٔ عبدالنبی فراری گردید، بسیار تفحص نمودند
نیافتند ـ و چند جماعدار و دفعه‌دار جوق سزاول فقیر محرم‌الحرام شده
نزد غلام علی خان و لطف علی خان و شاه نورالله خان و جعفر خان
رفتند ـ غلام علی‌خان پنجاه روپیه و لطف علی خان چهل روپیه بدشواری تمام
و شاه نورالله خان سی روپیه و جعفر خان ده روپیه و مراد خان که نزد
سید علی صاحب پیرزاده آمده بودند ده روپیه دادند ـ

و بتاریخ دوازدهم روز جمعه که روز عاشور بود همه زن و مرد
بصره از محبان اهل بیت رسول‌الله صلی‌الله‌علیه‌وسلم در مقام علی مشکل کشا
رضی‌الله‌عنه گرد آمده بودند و زیارت کردند و خواندند و به ماتم و تعزیه
حضرت امام حسین رضی‌الله‌عنه کردند ـ و چند مردم از اهل عرب شمشیر
و چوب به دست گرفته به تعزیه و ماتم می کردیدند و چند زنان از اهل
عرب و عجم بر یک گهواره چادر انداخته به تصور لاش حضرت علی اصغر
۱۳۳ رضی‌الله‌عنه به ماتم و تعزیه پرداختند و چند مردان اهل عجم بسیا
تعزیه و ماتم نمودند و چندی به مدح حضرت کرار رضی‌الله‌عنه پرداختند ـ

و در یک درخت عناب که در موضع مقام علی است رضی‌الله‌عنه خون سرخ جاری شد و همیشه بروز شهادت سیدالشهدا رضی‌الله‌عنه جاری می شد و خون مسطور به چشم نابینا مستعمل نماید بینا گردد و همه آزار دفع شود و همیشه بروز مسطور بدستور مذکور زیارت و تعزیه در مقام موصوف به ظهور می انجامید ـ

و مراد خان وغیره معه عبدالله یهودی دلال بصره نزد غلام علیخان و شاه نورالله خان وغیره آمده کاغذی متضمن اینکه مبلغ یک لک و سی و سه هزار قرص رومی بابت پارچات بر ذمهٔ عبدالله یهودی دلال بابت غلام علی خان و شاه نورالله خان وغیره واجب‌الادا است، به مهر و دستخط از دلال مسطور نویسانیده، به خوانین مسطور دادند، و چهار طاقهٔ زربفت به حساب فی گز هشت و نیم رومی و هشت رومی و هفت نیم رومی در سرکار بخریدی گرفتند ـ و بتاریخ سیزدهم روز شنبه شاه نورالله خان به کوتهی فراسیس نزد مراد خان وغیره رفته بسته‌های گارهای بهونگیری که
دلال واپس داده بود واز کرده، چند طاقه‌های چاک و ضایع شده برآورد، ١٣٤
باقی بدستور بسته امانت بنام خود نگاه داشته آمدند ـ

بتاریخ چهاردهم روز یکشنبه جوانان سزاول در مبلغ، که از غلام‌علی خان و شاه نورالله خان وغیره بنام حضرت امام حسین رضی‌الله‌عنه گرفته بودند، طعام پخت و پز نموده، بنام حضرت رضی‌الله‌عنه موصوف به جمیع مردمان خورانیده و فرستادند ـ و چند خلاصی وغیره بابت داو کرایه دار بابت سیف نزد غلام علی خان برای انعام خود آمدند ـ غلام علی خان از شاه نورالله خان وغیره پرسید، کسی انعام از سرکار دادن را حامی نه گردید، لاچار بست و پنج روپیه از طرف خود دهانیدند ـ

و بتاریخ شانزدهم روز سه شنبه یک اقرار نامه از محمد علی بهاتو به اقرار اینکه آینده تقاصیر بیجا و بی موقع و بدخواهی سرکار و شیوهٔ

نمک حرامی نه نماید، اگر احیاناً به وقوع رسد، وجه طلب گرفته خود از ابتدا به سرکار واپس نماید، شاه نورالله خان نویسانیده گرفتند و به غلام علی خان نمایش کردند - خان مسطور گفتند که خوب کردند، و باز به کوتهی فراسیس نزد مراد خان وغیره رفته، چند
بسته‌های گارهای بهونگیری واپس کردهٔ یهودی بنظر در آورده، از ۱۳۰
دست مصدی رقم نویسانیده باز آمدند -

و بتاریخ هفدهم روز چهارشنبه آفندی و احمد چلبی مهماندار وغیره نزد شاه نورالله خان آمده به عنوانات و قسم اقسام گفت که شما با چندین کسان پیشتر رفتن مناسب نیست، از انجاکه در راه ولایت روم از بغداد هفت صد کوه پشته و هامون درپیش است و یک آدم شما تاب و طاقت مشی و رفتن و برداشت سرما و ریزش برف وغیره نخواهد کرد و سلیمان پاشا حاکم بغداد نیز ازین جهت پیشتر رفتن نخواهد داد - درین صورت مناسب آنست که همه مردمان را روانهٔ ولایت شما نمایند و چندی کسان معتمد و کارپرداز راهی شوند - خان مسطور بجواب پرداختند که این کلام پیش غلام علی خان رفته بگویند - باز شاه نورالله خان و آفندی و احمد چلبی وغیره پیش غلام علی خان رفته به تصریح و تفسیر تمام بیان نمودند - غلام علی خان و لطف علی خان و شاه نورالله خان به آفندی وغیره به جواب پرداختند، خوب چه مضائقه، بعد دریافت و مشورت باهم انچیکه مقرر خواهد شد
بعمل خواهم آورد - آفندی وغیره بخانهٔ خود مراجعت نمودند - ۱۳۰

و بتاریخ هجدهم روز پنجشنبه شاه نورالله خان شنیدند که مراد خان وغیره وجه طلب دو ماهه جوانان رسالهٔ فقیر محمد و خلاصیان تقسیم می نمایند، خطی به نام محمد شفیع نوشتند که فکر و سبیل زر تنخواهی مایان هنوز به نظر نمی‌آید، که شما به فراغت تمام وجه طلب مردم تعیناتی وغیره خود تقسیم می نمایند، مناسب نیست، زود فکر و سبیل

زر مذکور نمایند، و به مراد خان و شمس‌الدین به آئین بهین درین
ماده بگویند، بصحابت محمد عمر چوبدار و هرکاره نزد محمد شفیع فرستادند ـ
به مجرد شنیدن مضمون خط مسطور شمس‌الدین و محمد شفیع نزد
شاه نورالله خان آمده بسیار گفت و شنود بمیان آوردند و دریافت حساب
و کتاب جمع و خرج اجناس تجارتی و ادای زر تنخواهی بابت روم
بزبانی خودها نمودند ـ آخرالامر معلوم و مقرر شد که هفت هزار هون
حیدری در زر تنخواهی کم می شود، باید که وجه طلب یکماهه به
جوانان علاقهٔ مراد خان وغیره بدهند و باقی وجه طلب آنها به بندر
مسقط رفته به عوض اجناس باقی مانده از دلال بندر مسقط گرفته بدهند ـ ۱۳۷
شمس‌الدین و محمد شفیع قبول نموده به فرودگاه خود مراجعت نمودند ـ
و شاه نورالله خان پارچهٔ سیاه بقدر دو هزار و پانصد رومی، به حساب
فی صد انکه (۱) سیزده آنه، به اسحاق یهودی، که به سرانجام آوری
بهته و خوراکی جوانان اسداللهی مامور و مقرر است، از نزد مراد خان
وغیره دهانیده، قرار نمودند که به فروخت رسانیده زر به سرکار عاید
سازد ـ

و به تاریخ نوزدهم روز جمعه یک قطعه خط از جانب مرادخان
وغیره نزد شاه نورالله خان به این مضمون رسید که مایان هر چند
خواستیم که به گفتهٔ شما به عمل آریم، درین ضمن جوانان علاقهٔ
فقیرمحمد به درخواست وجه طلب خودها بسیار شدت می نمایند و
در صورت عدم رسیدن وجه طلب آنها کمربسته اند، درین صورت شما
بنوعیکه خواهند فهمائش آنها بکنند ـ خان مسطور در جواب ان به
ترقیم درآوردند که این همه حیله و عذر و هنگامه از طرف خودها است ۱۳۸
و از طرف جوانان علاقهٔ فقیر محمد نیست، بهر عنوان نظر به امورات سرکار

۱ــ MS. آنک

نموده فهمایش آنها به عمل آورده زود به انصرام امورات سرکار پردازند ـ

و بتاریخ بست و دوم ماه حیدری سال مذکور سنه‌الیه روز دو شنبه مهماندار و حسین آغا نزد غلام علی خان و شاه نورالله خان وغیره آمده بودند ، خوانین گفتند که در سه منزل کشتی‌های شما به مردم علاقهٔ مایان کفایت نه خواهد کرد ـ نامبرده‌ها به جواب پرداختند که کفایت خواهد کرد ، مقرر گردید که فردا سرانجام به کشتی‌ها سوار کنند ، و لطف علی خان به دیدن کشتی سواری خود رفتند ـ و عبدالله یهودی و محمد شفیع و شمس‌الدین نزد شاه نورالله خان برو بروی غلام علی خان آمده گفتند که عبدالله یهودی چند عدد دوپته وغیره به سبب زیادتی انک واپس نموده است و می‌گوید که مرا درکار نیست ، اگر می‌دهند فی صد انگه بحساب یک روپیه دو آنه بدهند ، و باقی پارچه‌های سیاه هم خواهم گرفت ، و دلالی اجناس دیگر که بجای دیگر به فروخت رسانیده اند بدهند ـ شاه نورالله خان خوب دریافت نموده به گفت و شنود تمام به عنوانات مقرر نمودند که وجه
۱۳ دلالی جای دیگر دو حصه باید داد و یک حصه به دلال ثانی ، و پارچه واپس کرده را بحساب فی صد انگه یک روپیه چهار آنه و پارچهٔ سیاه را تمام به نرخ سابق به عبدالله یهودی بدهند ، راضی شده به فرودگاه خود رفتند ـ و به محمد علی بهاتو وجه طلب دو ماهه شاه نورالله‌خان به اتفاق غلام علی خان وغیره مهربان شده به عفو تقصیرات پرداخته وجه طلب دو ماهه بمحمدعلی دادند ـ و زر شش عدد پچهوری گلدار ابریشمی تارپتری منجمله بست پچهوری عنایتی سرکار به ماوجی سیتهه دلال بندر مسقط غلام علی خان داده بودند ، از سیوا گماشتهٔ دلال مذکور درخواست نمودند ، جواب داد که مرا دلال مسطور نه گفته است نه خواهم داد ـ

و بتاریخ بست و سیوم روز سه شنبه غلام‌علی‌خان و شاه نورالله‌خان

و جعفر خان یک قطعه خط موسومهٔ ماوجی دلال بندر مسقط متضمن این که بست هزار هون حیدری بابت حوالهٔ محمد حنیف و ضیاء الدین وغیره که صندل وغیره اجناس سرکار به فروخت رسانیده بودند از معرفت سیوا و پریم
گماشتهٔ دلال مسطور در بندر بصره به وصول در آمده داخل توشکخانهٔ ۱۴۰
سرکار گردید ـ نوشته به مهر و دستخط خودها نزد شکرالله وغیره مصدی سرکار دادند که بعد مواجهه و مقابله حساب و کتاب خود به اطلاع غلام علی خان و گماشتهٔ مذکور رساند ـ شاه نورالله خان در مادهٔ مهر و دستخط بر کاغذ مسطور به لطف علی خان هر چند گفتند ، خان مسطور به جواب پرداختند که علاقهٔ خود در توشکخانهٔ سرکار نیست ، مهر نخواهم کرد ـ و مقرر گردید که بتاریخ بست و هفتم ماه محرم‌الحرام پیشتر به صوب بغداد شریف راهی گردد ـ و وجه طلب یکماهه عبدالقادر منشی از سرکار دادند ـ

و بتاریخ بست و چهارم روز چهارشنبه شاه نورالله خان سه قطعه عرایض مندرجه کوایف روداد خودها وغیره نویسانیده به صحابت معلم ماستر عبدالکریم دادند که به حضور پرنور برساند، و وجه طلب یک ماهه مردم اسداللهی و سزاول دست بدست بروبروی غلام علی خان وغیره
تقسیم نمودند ـ و عبدالله یهودی دلال بصره شش عدد حقه‌های ۱۴۱
مروارید خورد مع خط خود نزد غلام علی خان و شاه نورالله خان وغیره آورد و داد که به اسلامبول به ساهوکار معتمد دادند ، شما بگیرند، خوانین در توشکخانهٔ سرکار امانت واگذاشتند ـ

و بتاریخ بست و پنجم روز پنجشنبه به جوانان بهرام وجه طلب یک ماهه تقسیم نمودند ـ و باز عبدالله یهودی دلال دوازده حقه‌های مروارید جمله بقدر پنجاه هزار روپیه آورده نزد غلام علی خان و شاه نورالله خان داد و گفت که این مروارید به حفاظت معه یک نفر گماشتهٔ خود به ساهوکار اسلامبول مع خط خود بدهند و پنجاه هزار قرص رومی

بگیرند - خوانین قبول نموده مروارید مذکور امانت به حفاظت در
توشکخانهٔ سرکار داشتند - و چند بسته‌های گارها بهونگیری و چهینت
۱۴ پامری واپس کردهٔ عبدالله یهودی به مهماندار و حسین آغا به اقرار
اینکه بعد رسیدن به بغداد زر آن به سرکار عاید نماید، شاه نورالله خان
دادند - و باز پارچهٔ چهار هزار روپیه دیگر و روغن صندل به اسحاق
یهودی دادند - و عبدالله یهودی دلال بصره چند خطوط کاغذ زر یعنی
هندوی به نام ساهوکاران اسلام‌بول و بغداد نزد غلام علی خان و
شاه نورالله خان وغیره آورد و داد - و محمد شفیع و شمس‌الدین و عبدالله
یهودی دو سه تهان سفید بابت محمودبندر و دو سه طاقهٔ سیاه ضایع و
داغدار نزد شاه نورالله خان آورده گفتند که یهودی مسطور می گوید که
یک صد و شصت طاقه‌ها بدستور چاک و ضایع و داغدار است، قیمت کم
کرده بدهند، بچه طور کم کرده آید، یهودی را شما فهمایش بکنند -
و شاه نورالله خان به عنوانات فهمایش کرده گفتند که ضابطه نیست که
بخانهٔ خود برده باز پس نمایند، بر این هم اگر باز پس می نمائی مرا
۱۴ بده که من از یک حصه زیاده واپس کردهٔ تو به دیگران به کفایت
سرکار به فروخت رسانیده‌ام، اینهم بکفایت بفروخت خواهم رسانید -
یهودی لاچار شده به خانهٔ خود طاقه‌های مسطور برد - و لطف علی خان
بر پالکی سوار شده در کوچه و بازار بندر بصره گردیده جا بجا پالکی
نهاده به خریدن چند سنگریزهٔ عتیق وغیره پرداخته حرمت سرداری و
پالکی و نام سرکار برباد دادند - چنانچه سابق ازین دو دفعه بدستور به
کوچه و بازار و هر دوکان گردیده برای کار یک فلوس تکرار از بانی و
بقال می نمودند -

و بتاریخ بست و هفتم روز شنبه سیوا گماشتهٔ دلال بندر مسقط نزد
غلام علی خان وغیره آمده چهار صد و پنجاه روپیه بابت قیمت شش عدد
پچهوری گلدار ابریشمی تارپتری منجمله بست پچهوری عنایتی خاص

به دلال مذکور در بندر مسطور داده بودند، به شدت و تردد و کاوش ۱۴۴
تمام به توشکخانهٔ سرکار رسانیده رسید گرفت - غلام علی خان نام خود
بر کاغذ مسطور نوشتند و شاه نورالله خان یک کاغذ بنام خود علحده
بنام دلال مسطور نوشتند و به دست سیوا گماشتهٔ مذکور دادند - و
یک خیمه نه گزی برای توشکخانهٔ سرکار شاه نورالله خان تیار ساختند
و چند سرانجام توشکخانه به سوار کردن بر کشتی‌ها به کنارهٔ نهر
فرستادند و به حفاظت آنها تا مد آب در نهر مسطور دو یزک از رسالهٔ
سزاول و عبدالرحمان چیلهٔ سرکار مقید شدند و دو عماری نقره مع سرانجام
آن حواله مراد خان نمودند که باز پس به حضور پرنور برساند و به
جمیع شاگردپیشه و احمد علی منشی وغیره سرداران وجه طلب یک ماهه
تقسیم نمودند - و مراد خان و محمد شفیع و شمس‌الدین برای گرفتن
رسید زر تنخواهی نزد غلام علی خان و شاه نورالله خان وغیره آمده
درخواست رسید نموده گفتند که مایان فردا به جهاز سوار شده روانه ۱۴۵
می شویم - غلام علی خان وغیره گفتند که درین ایام منحوس که قمر
در عقرب و رجال‌الغیب درپیش است، بتاریخ بست و نهم ماه محرم‌الحرام
سنه ۱۲۰۱ هجری(۱) روانه شوند، مایان هم همون روز روانه می شویم،
قبول نموده به فرودگاه خود رفتند -

و بتاریخ بست و هشتم ماه مذکور روز یکشنبه شاه نورالله خان
نزد غلام علی خان رفته به ممانعت و باز داشتن لطف علی خان از
شیوهٔ بدنامی که در بازار و کوچهٔ بندر بصره بر پالکی سوار شده
به خریدن سنگریزهٔ عقیق وغیره می پردازند، گفتند - غلام علی خان
به جواب پرداختند که این چنین بدنامی مضایقه ندارد، ازین زیاده‌تر
در بصره از تنگ دستی بدنام شدیم که به شرح و بیان راست نمی آید-

---

۱- 21 November, 1786.

شاه نورالله خان گفتند که شما دریں ماده دو هزار چهار هزار تا
ده هزار روپیه مقرر کنند، از توشکخانهٔ سرکار برآورده علحده داشته
بر این امورات می پردازم، و الامن خود به خود بدون اطلاع و تقریر ۱۴
و اتفاق شما وغیره چیزی نخواهم داد، نه شما کناره گرفته مرا بگویند
که تو این چنین کارها بکن و بدنام سرکار شو، اصلا نه خواهد شد۔
غلام علی خان بجواب پرداختند که تا الی‌الان در مادهٔ داد و دهش انعام
وغیره پرداختیم، آینده نخواهم گفت و نخواهم درآمد، شما دهند یا نه،
مانع نه شوم پسیار ازین قبیل گفت و شنود به میان آمد و لطف علی خان
هم آمدند۔ از ایشان شاه نورالله خان پرسیدند که دیروز کجا رفته
بودند که مردم این چنین می گویند۔ جواب دادند که به مقام حضرت
عباس رضی‌الله‌عنه رفته بودم، یک سنگریزه وغیره در بازار دیدم و خرید
کردم هیچ نیست۔ و در آنجا یک روضهٔ حضرت یحیی بن امام موسی
کاظم رضی‌الله‌عنه حضرت سید شعبان رضی‌الله‌عنه واقع است، غلاف باناتی
باید انداخت۔ شاه نور الله خان به جواب پرداختند که طاقه‌های
بانات حاضر است خوجه وغیره را به طلبند و غلاف دوزانند۔

و مراد خان و شمس‌الدین و محمد شفیع برای درخواست رسید
زر تنخوای نزد غلام علی خان و شاه نورالله خان وغیره آمدند۔
غلام علی خان به جواب پرداختند که حالا شام شده است فردا بیایند،
بعد رجوع و مقابلهٔ حساب رسید زر مسطور داده خواهد شد۔ و عبدالله ۱۴
یهودی نزد غلام علی خان و شاه نورالله خان آمده همه کاغذ زرو
هندویات بغداد و اسلامبول آورد و داد، اینها به توشکخانهٔ سرکار
به حفاظت نگاهداشتند۔ و مهماندار و حسین آغا نزد غلام علی خان و
شاه نورالله خان آمده بودند۔ اینها بعدم کفایت جوانان متعینات خود
در سه منزل کرایه‌دار و یک منزل آغای مسطور بسیار گفتند۔ آخرالامر
شش صد روپیه به تقرر منزل دیگر بدست مهماندار دادند۔

و بتاریخ بست و نهم ماه مذکور روز دوشنبه جمیع سرانجام توشکخانهٔ سرکار و سرانجام شاه نورالله خان برکشتی سوار نمودند مگر نقدیات توشکخانه باقی ماند ـ و مرادخان و شمس‌الدین و محمد شفیع برای گرفتن رسید نزد غلام علی خان و شاه نورالله خان وغیره آمده بودند ـ غلام علی خان بعد مقابلهٔ و مواجههٔ حساب گفتند که رسید بموجب نانیا که به توشکخانهٔ سرکار رسانیده اند خواهم داد و به تقرر هون حیدری که چندین شدند نخواهم‌داد ـ ازین جهت بسیار تکرار نمودند ـ چنانکه در جزیرهٔ خارج از سیوا گماشتهٔ دلال بندر مسقط یک هزار و هفت صد و هشتاد و پنج رومی گرفته به مردم متعینات خود
علی‌الحساب در وجه طلب آنها دادند ـ و در بندر بصره به وضع نمودن رومی ۱۴۸
مسطور یک صد و هفتاد و هشت رومی به وقوع رسیده بود از گماشتهٔ مسطور گرفتند و رسید گماشتهٔ مذکور بابت بست هزار هون حیدری که پیش از دو سه روز نوشته داده بودند واپس گرفته چاک نمودند ـ و یک قطعه رسید دیگر به دستخط خود و مهر لطف علی خان و جعفر خان متضمن اینکه، منجمله مبلغ شصت وپنج هزار هون حیدری بابت تنخواه بر محمد حنیف و مراد خان وغیره شده بود، بموجب دهانیده نامبرده‌ها بر ماوجی سیهته دلال بندر مسقط به وصول در آمده داخل توشکخانهٔ سرکار گردید، نوشته بدست گماشتهٔ مذکور دادند ـ و نیز یک قطعه رسید دیگر بدستخط خود و مهر لطف علی خان و جعفر خان متضمن اینکه، منجمله مبلغ شصت و پنج هزار هون حیدری که بر محمد حنیف و مراد خان وغیره از حضور پرنور تنخواه شده بود، مبلغ شصت و شش هزار و نهه صد و
سی و پنج رومی و شصت و پنج هزار و سه صد و بست محمودی ۱۴۹
مسقطی به موجب دهانیده نامبرده‌ها از ماوجی سیهته دلال بندر مسقط به وصول درآمد ـ و مبلغ یک لک و پنجاه و شش هزار و یک صد و پانزده رومی از معرفت مراد خان وغیره به وصول در آمده داخل

توشکخانهٔ سرکار گردید، نویسانیده به مراد خان وغیره دادند، و رسید
بست هزار هون حیدری سابق که به وقت برآمد از بندر مسقط نوشته
به محمد حنیف و ضیاءالدین وغیره داده بودند از مراد خان وغیره گرفته
چاک نمودند ـ شاه نورالله خان برای مهر نمودن بر رسید گماشتهٔ مذکور
بابت بست هزار هون حیدری گفتند که من یک قطعه عرضداشت به
مضمون اینکه رسید بست هزار هون حیدری نوشته بدست سیوا دادم باز
مهر نخواهم کرد، و برای مهر نمودن بر رسید بابت مراد خان وغیره
که رومی‌های رسانیده ایشان را هون حیدری مقرر نه کردند، من مهر
بر آن نخواهم کرد بلکه یک قطعه رسید دیگر به تقرر هون حیدری
نویسانیده مهر نموده خواهم داد ـ چنانچه شاه نورالله خان یک قطعه ۱۵۰
رسید متضمن اینکه، منجمله مبلغ شصت و پنج هزار هون حیدری که
بر محمد حنیف از حضور پرنور تنخواه شده بود، مبلغ شصت و شش
هزار نه‌صد و سی و پنج رومی و شصت و پنج هزار و سه صد و
بست محمودی مسقطی به حساب فی هون حیدری چهار رومی و فی رومی
پنج محمودی مسقطی بست هزار هون حیدری می شود، به موجب
دهانیده نامبرده‌ها از ماوجی سیهته دلال بندر مسقط به وصول در آمد ـ
و مبلغ یک لک و پنجاه و شش هزار و یک صد و پانزده رومی، که
بحساب فی هون حیدری چهار رومی سی و نه هزار و بست و هشت
و نیم هون حیدری می شود، از معرفت مراد خان وغیره به وصول در
آمده و هر دو مبلغ مسطور پنجاه و نه هزار و بست و هشت ونیم هون
حیدری می شود داخل توشکخانهٔ سرکار گردید، به مهر خود نویسانیده
بدست مراد خان وغیره دادند ـ و یک عدد دوربین سرکار نزد
غلام علی خان بود، محمد شفیع گرفتند ـ و یک جوان سزاول گلاب
نام فراری گردید ـ

و بتاریخ سلخ ماه حیدری سال مذکور سنه‌الیه روز سه شنبه ۱۵۱

شاه نوراللّه خان و غلام علی خان وغیره یک پیتارهٔ خلعت حاکم مکهٔ معظمه از مراد خان وغیره جمله هشت فرد گرفته داخل توشکخانهٔ سرکار نموده رسیدش به دستخط غلام علی خان و مهر لطف علی خان و شاه نوراللّه خان و جعفر خان به مراد خان وغیره دادند ـ و ده ضرب بنادیق معه سرانجام ان بابت جوانان مفروری سزاول و پنج ضرب بنادیق معه سرانجام بابت جوانان مفروری اسداللهی ذمه مراد خان وغیره نمودند که به حضور پرنور رساند ـ و یک قطعه عرضداشت از چهار سرداران، معه دو بارگیران سرکار، که یکی محمد اشرف دنیا ترک نمود و دویمی حسین بقلت مواجبش، نویسانیده به حضور پرنور روانه ساختند ـ و شاه نوراللّه خان یک قطعه عرضداشت در باب سفارش مراد خان وغیره نوشته به نامبردهها دادند ـ و سوای این یک قطعه عرضداشت غلام علی خان و لطف علی خان به حضور پرنور روانه ساختند ـ و نیز یک قطعه
۵۲ عرضداشت از جانب عبداللّه یهودی دلال بندر بصره از دست عبدالقادر منشی متضمن اینکه همه اجناس تجارتی سرکار به فروخت رسانید و آینده بهر اموریکه ارشاد خواهد شد به تقدیم آن ساعی و جاهد خواهد بود، و می خواست که همراه مراد خان وغیره چند سوغات و تحایف این دیار لایق ترسیل حضور لامع‌النور روانه نمایند لاکن به سبب همدستی مقصر مانده، انشااللّه‌تعالیٰ وقتی که لایق ارسال حضور همدست می شود به ارسال می درآورد، نوشته مرسول حضور نمود ـ و به وقت شب همه سرانجام جوانان سزاول بر کشتیها سوار کنانیدند ـ و یک قطعه عرضداشت شاه نوراللّه خان معه افراد جمع خرج از دست جعفر مصدی نویسانیده به مهر و دستخط خود برجمیع افراد و بدستخط و مهر غلام علی خان و لطف علی خان بر افراد حاضری نفری فقط نزد مراد خان فرستادند که به حضور رساند ـ و غلام علی خان و لطف علی خان بر افراد جمع و خرج مهر و دستخط بعدم دریافت خود نکردند ـ و غلام علی خان و لطف علی
۵۳

خان دو سبوچه(۱) روغن صندل از مراد خان وغیره بحساب فی آثار نه روپیه هفت اثار به خرید(۲) گرفتند و به دیگر ساهوکاران بندر بصره به کفایت یکروپیه به فروخت رسانیدند - و لطف علی خان هفتاد اثار حصه خود .... امانت . ... به ارادهٔ ...... بعد رسیدن به بغداد .... کفایت .... رسانیده ...... (۳) و محمد رفیق متبنای محمد حنیف سوداگر متوفی به درخواست قرض متوفی که قریب یک هزار روپیه بر ذمهٔ غلام علی خان واجب‌الادا بود، نزد خان مسطور رفته درخواست نمود - غلام علی خان و مراد خان گفتند که چند طاقه‌های بانات به حساب فی گز چلنی پنج روپیه می دهم ،همراه خود به بندر کوریال برده به فروخت رسانیده از قرض محمد حنیف ادا نمایند، اگر نقصان شود بعد مراجعت ادا نموده خواهد شد - مراد خان گفتند که اگر به حساب فی گز چلنی که شما فی گز دو روپیه دوازده گرفته‌اند به سه و نیم روپیه بدهند قبول است، اگر نفع و نقصان بر سر محمد رفیق خواهد شد، و الا من نه خواهم گرفت - غلام علی خان قبول نه کردند و زر قرض مسطور
به خان مذکور واجب‌الادا ماند، مراد خان وغیره را مرخص نمودند - ۱۵۲

و بتاریخ غره ماه طلوی سال دلو سنه ۱۲۰۰ هجری(۴) روز چهارشنبه شاه نورالله خان و مراد خان و محمد شفیع و شمس‌الدین و عبدالقادر منشی برای رخصت نزد متسلم حاکم بصره رفته بودند - شاه نورالله خان و مراد خان وغیره از متسلم پرسیدند که خطی برای آقای مایان می دهند یا نه - متسلم به جواب پرداخت که مسودهٔ خط تیار و حاضر است ، صاف کنانیده می دهم - چنانچه میر شفیع نامی مسودهٔ مذکور آورد و مسموع گردانید ، همه کوایف روداد واقعی نوشته بود -

---

۱ـ MS. صبوچه   ۲ـ MS. خریدی   ۳ـ damaged. MS.

۴ـ 29 Muharram, 1201/21 November, 1786.

و متسلم به حسین آغا داروغهٔ ارماد بصره پرسید که همه کشتی‌های سواری شاه نورالله خان وغیره تیار شده است یا نه ـ نام برده به جواب پرداخت: اگرچه همه کشتی‌ها سوار شده است لاکن کار دو سه روزه باقی است، انشاالله‌تعالی به انصرام خواهد رسید ـ من بعد متسلم به شاه نورالله خان گفت که پنج چهار روز صبر بکنند و بتاریخ هفتم ماه صفر برکشتی‌ها سوار شدند ـ خان مسطور به سبب لاچاری قبول نموده مرخص شدند و به فرودگاه خود باز آمدند ـ

۱۰۵ و محمد رفیق نزد شاه نورالله خان آمده اظهار کیفیت ندادن غلام علی خان قرض آقای خود اظهار نمود ـ شاه نورالله خان نزد غلام علی خان رفته گفتند که طاقه‌های بانات به حساب فی گز چلنی پنج روپیه اگر مرضی شما است بدهند و یک خط بنام ساهوکار آنجا بنویسند که طاقه‌های مسطور بفروخت رسانیده از قرض نامبرده ادا نماید، خواه نفع آید یا نقصان ـ غلام علی خان قبول نموده دو صد و پنجاه گز بانات از کوتهی فراسیس بطریق قرض گرفته ذمهٔ محمد رفیق نمودند و خطی بنام عامل کوریال بمعافی زکوة بانات مذکور و یک قطعه خط به ساهوکار کشور داس به مضمون ما سبق نوشته دادند ـ و شمس‌الدین و محمد شفیع نزد غلام علی خان و شاه نورالله خان آمده مرخص شدند ـ و جعفر خان یک کنیزک و یک غلام ضیاء الدین را به وقت حرق و غرق جهاز نبی بخش از رود فرات بر آورده نزد خود داشته بودند ـ مراد خان وغیره از علاقهٔ سرکار درخواست نمودند، غلام مذکور را دادند و کنیزک را ندادند ـ

۱۰۶ و بتاریخ دوم ماه طلوعی (۱) روز پنجشنبه مراد خان بست و هشت روپیه بابت خوراکی کنیزک و غلام ضیاء الدین نزد جعفرخان

۱ـ 22 November, 1786.

فرستادند ، کنیزک مسطور را درخواست نمودند ـ جعفر خان پنجروپیه از بست و هشت روپیه مسطور گرفته کنیزک را فرستادند ـ و به شب جمعه مراد خان وغیره لنگر جهاز فتح شاهی معزی و غراب سورتی برداشته به صوب بندر مسقط راهی شدند ـ

و بتاریخ سیوم ماه طلوعی روز جمعه شاه نورالله خان و عبدالقادر منشی برای دیدن کشتی‌ها رفته تاکید اکید به تیاری نموده باز آمدند ـ و یک جوان علاقه‌دار کشتی از ضرب توپ که چهار ضرب اتواب سر نمودند ، ضایع گردید ـ و محمد نتهو سرخیل و جوقدار اسداللهی برای فکر و معالجهٔ چهار جوانان بسیار بیمار اند، برای ادویه چیزی به طبیب بدهانند ـ غلام علی خان به در جواب پرداختند که نزد شاه نورالله خان رفته اظهار بکنند که همه اسباب و سرانجام وغیره بابت شماها می کنند ، برای ادویه البته ضروری خواهند داد ـ باز نزد شاه نورالله خان رفته حقیقت مسطور اظهار نمود ـ خان مسطور جواب دادند که مداوا و معالجهٔ شماها در حکمنامهٔ عنایتی خاص مندرج نیست ، اگر می بود چندین پرسش و استفسار به عمل نیامدی ، این امر را به اتفاق هر چهار سردار باید کرد ـ محمد نتهو از آنجا برگشته یک جوان بیمار را بدروازهٔ غلام علی خان و لطف علی خان و شاه نورالله خان انداخته گفت که علاج بیماری تو در اینجا خواهد شد ـ آخرالامر شاه نورالله‌خان از وقوع این کیفیت به حفاظت حرمت و سرداری خود نزد غلام‌علی‌خان آمده اظهار نمودند که این چه طور است ، شما سردار اول هستند ، انچیکه خواهند بکنند و بگویند مایان هم بجا خواهم آورد ، و این امر سوای حکمنامهٔ عنایتی خاص است ـ من بعد طبیب را پیش هر چهار سردار طلبیده بدرستگی و معالجهٔ یک یک جوان دو دو رومی مقرر نموده از چهار نفر هشت رومی دادند و به جوقدار مذکور تاکید نمودند که بار دوم این چنین زیادتی نکنند هشیار باشند ـ

و بتاریخ چهارم روز شنبه یک جوان جیونخان نام علاقهٔ سزاول که از مقام بندر مسقط مفرور شده بود در جهاز مسقطی به علاقهٔ خلاصیان بدر ماهه پنج روپیه نوکر شده به بندر بصره رسیده همدست جوانان سزاول گردید - و بتاریخ پنجم روز یکشنبه محمدامام و محمدامین جوقدار و سرخیل رسالهٔ سزاول به سیاست رسائی جیونخان جوان مفروره همدست شده معه کتاب فتح المجاهدین عنایتی خاص نزد غلام علی خان و شاه نورالله خان وغیره آمده کتاب مسطور پیش هر چهار سردار نهاده گفتند که انچیکه سیاست سلطانی در حق جوان مفروره همدست نوشته شده باشد برسانند - هر چهار سردار در کتاب مذکور سیاست جوان مسطور بدریافت آورده گفتند که در حق او قتل به ضرب گولی بندوق است و درین ملک اگر این معنی عمل نموده آید بدنامی حاصل خواهد شد، درین صورت جوان مسطور را پا در زنجیر نموده بدارند
۱۰۹ و در راه بغداد بعد طی دو سه منازل در صحرا بدستور حکم اشرف مندرجه کتاب مسطور سیاست جوان مذکور به عمل آرند - و همه خریطه های قرص رومی وغیره بابت توشکخانهٔ سرکار را شاه نورالله‌خان و جعفر خان سربمهر نمودند -

و بتاریخ ششم روز دوشنبه حسین آغا خطی از جانب شیخ سوینی عسکردار بدوی موسومهٔ خود نزد شاه نورالله خان آورده گفت که شیخ مسطور نوشته است که پنج شش روز توقف بکن، خود هم می آیم، بعد رسیدن خود به صوب بغداد شریف راهی شوند، و الا در خوف و خطر هلاک خواهند شد - شاه نورالله خان بسیار برهم شده عبدالله یهودی دلال و مهماندار را طلب داشته کیفیت مسطور اظهار نموده گفتند که حرکت شماها را انتها نیست، اگر رخصت می دهند از بندر مسقط به جده رفته از آنجا بصوب مکان مقصود راهی خواهند شد - آنها به تعذر و حیله پرداخته گفتند که در عرصهٔ دو سه روز

بهمه وجوه فراغت حاصل می شود ، بروند ـ

۱۶۰ و بتاریخ دهم روز جمعه بوقت نماز عشا حسین آغا نزد غلام علی
خان و شاه نوراللہ خان آمده گفت که متسلم عبدالله پیام نموده‌اند که
هرکارۀ سرکار خود از بغداد معه خط سلیمان پاشا آمده است، و در راه
هیچ خطر نیست ، بتاریخ چهاردهم ماه صفر سنه ۱۲۰۱ هجری که
سیزده ایام نحس اکبر هم می‌گذرند به خیریت بر کشتی‌ها سوار شده
بصوب بغداد شریف راهی شوند ـ خوانین مسطور قبول نمودند ـ

و بتاریخ دوازدهم روز یکشنبه در هر بازار و کوچهٔ بندر بصره
از افواه عوام صادر گردید که هر دو جهازات سرکار در خور بندر
بصره موضع دوسرا(۱) که از بصره بفاصلهٔ بست کروه راه واقع است به سبب
شدت طوفان بتاریخ نهم ماه طلوعی سال دلو سنه ۱۲۰۰ هجری(۲)
روز پنجشنبه بوقت شب بعد انقضای یک و نیم پاس مغروق شدند، و
به جز آفت سماوی چیز دیگر نبود، و قریب صد نفر به سلامتی جان
برآمدند ـ درین اثنا احمد چلبی مهماندار نزد غلام علی خان و شاه نورالله
خان وغیره آمده گفت که خبر وحشت اثر مغروق جهازات سرکار شما مقرر
رسیده است، باید که شماها یک آدم همراه آدم خود نزد جهازات
۱۶ مغروق روانه سازند تا کیفیت آنجا مفصل ظاهر گردد(۲) خوانین قبول
نموده دو هرکاره و یک چوبداو سرکار را همراه آدم مهماندار از راه رود
فرات روانه نمودند ـ من بعد متسلم هم چوبدار را فرستاد، بعد ادای
لوازم تسلی پیام نمود که درینجا خبر مغروق جهازات سرکار شما رسیده
است، باید که شماها یک آدم همراه آدم خود که نزد جهاز مغروق
برود روانه بکنند تا کیفیت آنجا مفصل برسد ـ خوانین گفتند آدم سرکار
همراه آدم مهماندار نزد جهاز مغروق مرسل نمود، اگرچه جهاز و اموال

۱ـ دوسرا ۲ـ MS. گردید

سرکار به اعتبار همت والا نهمت دولت لایزال حضرت خداوند امانی و امال مایان بضاعتی و قدری ندارد لاکن به سبب مغروق شدن چند اشخاص معتبر و باهوش وغیره مردم بسیار درد و الم و تحسر و تحیر بحدی رو داده است که به شرح و بیان راست نمی آید - من بعد بعد دو پاس دو نفر گوله انداز بابت جهاز فتح شاهی معزی و غراب سورتی نزد غلام علی خان و شاه نورالله خان وغیره رسیدند و کیفیت مغروق جهاز مذکور و یک بتیل رهبان بندر مسقط مفصل ظاهر ساخته گفتند که دو بارگیر سرکار و یک ماستر از غراب سورتی بیرون آمدند، و باقی
از جهاز فتح شاهی معزی، و یک معلم و ماستر و یک سرخیل و سی ١٦٢
و سه جوان علاقهٔ جیش مع دو گوله انداز و شصت و سه نفر خلاصیان مع سارنگ وغیره و دو گوله انداز جمله یک صد و سه جوان منجمله چهار صد جوان مع سرداران وغیره در هر دو جهازات بودند، از جهازات مغروق بسلامت جان برآمدند، از راه خشکی به گدائی و دریوزه گری می آیند، و غراب سورتی کشیده در مد و جذر آب فرات بدریا رسید و گم شد -

و بتاریخ سیزدهم روز دوشنبه شاه نورالله خان به صحابت آدم سرکار به متسلم گفته جهازات ارماد بصره نزد جهاز مغروق روانه ساختند، و چند جوانان خلاصی وغیره قریب پنجاه و دو نفر از جهازات مغروق نزد غلام علی خان و شاه نورالله خان وغیره رسیدند - خوانین فی نفر یک روپیه از توشکخانهٔ سرکار دهانیدند - و دو نفر خلاصی دیروزه نزد پادری فراسیس رفته بودند، دو قبا به قیمت شش روپیه دهانید -

بتاریخ چهاردهم روز سه شنبه غلام علی خان سه نفر نیم رومی و شش دست کهادی سفید از طرف خود دادند و در سرکار از معلم و ماستر و سارنگ جهاز فتح شاهی معزی و سرخیل و جماعدار رسالهٔ
فقیر محمد یک نوشته به مضمون اینکه بعد رسیدن بحضور پرنور در وجه ١٦٣

طلب خودها مبلغی که سه نفر ده رومی به خرچ خوراکی و کرایهٔ سواری جهاز تا رسیدن بندر مسقط از سرکار گرفته اند، ادا خواهم ساخت، گرفته، فی نفر سراسری هفت روپیه نقد دادند و سه روپیه به کرایهٔ کشتی بروانگی اینها به صوب بندر مسقط امانت در سرکار نگاه داشتند -

و شاه نورالله خان نزد غلام علیخان رفته گفتند که برای بر آوردن اجناس جهاز فتح شاهی معزی جعفر خان را روانه بکنند یا مرا درین جابگذارند و شماها بصوب شریف راهی شوند، من همه اجناس جهاز مغروق انچیکه همدست می شود برآورده متعاقب می رسم(۱) - غلام علی خان گفتند: در صورت بودن شما روانگی مایان بصوب بغداد غیر ممکن و در صورت بودن جعفر خان در بصره و برآوردن اجناس جهاز مغروق به بندر مسقط البته صورت خواهد بست، لاکن باز رسیدن جعفر خان به بغداد شریف غیر ممکن - آخرالامر یک معلم و ماستر را با چند خلاصی با آدم متسلم نزد جهاز مغروق روانه نمودند که انچیکه اسباب و سر انجام از جهاز مغروق برآید از معرفت متسلم فرد تفصیل نوشته به حضور پرنور به برد و نیز خطی متضمن کوایف روداد به صوب
بغداد نزد مایان به فریسد - و هرکاره و چوبدار که به دیدن جهاز ۱۶۲
مغروق رفته بودند رسیده خبر آوردند که جهاز فتح شاهی معزی و اتواپ وغیره سرانجام بنظر می آید و غراب سورتی مفقود - شاه نورالله خان نزد متسلم رفته همه حقیقت مغروقی جهازات و روانگی خود به صوب بغداد اظهار نمودند - متسلم مقرر نمود که بتاریخ هفدهم ماه صفرالمظفر سنه ۱۲۰۱ هجری بروز شنبه روانه بغداد شوند و ادمان جهاز مغروق را بعد برآوردن اجناس سرکار بابت جهاز مغروق روانه بندر مسقط کرده خواهد شد -

و بتاریخ پانزدهم روز چهار شنبه هر چار سردار به اتفاق شش نفر خلاصیان را برای کار پردازی توشکخانهٔ سرکار منجمله خلاصیان جهاز

---

۱ — .MS می رسد

مغروق گرفتند ـ و شاه نورالله خان فرد یادداشت به دستخط شمش‌الدین وغیره که نزد دلال بصره عبدالله یهودی بابت خرید و فروخت اجناس و داد و دهش بهر یک شخص معتبر به طریق خلعت وغیره نوشته داده بودند از دلال مسطور گرفته نقل آن به دفتر خود و سرکار نویسانیدند ـ

و به تاریخ شانزدهم روز پنجشنبه هر چهار سردار به مردم خلاصی
و جیش علاقهٔ جهازات مغروق موجودات دیده سه نفر ده روپیه معه ٦٥
کرایهٔ جهاز دادند و نقد هفت روپیه دادند و سه روپیه سه نفر به عبدالله یهودی برجوع و مقابلهٔ مردم مسطور بنا بر آنکه در مبلغ یک کشتی کرایه نموده به بندر مسقط رساند و معلم و ماستر و سرخیل ویک بار گیر سرکار را دوازده روسی معه کرایه دادند و نیز به مردم متعینات خود معه سرداران علی‌الحساب نیم ماهه از توشکخانهٔ سرکار دهانیده و گرفتند و به منشی عبدالقادر و محمد علی بهاتو وجه طلب برای اتمام ایام روز تیر تمام و کمال رسانیدند ـ

و بتاریخ هفدهم روز جمعه شاه نورالله خان چند عرایض و افراد جمع و خرچ و حاضری نفری وغیره به دستخط غلام علی خان و شاه نورالله خان وغیره از دست سید جعفر مصدی نویسانیده به صحابت سید ولی بار گیر سرکار که وجه طلب سه ماهه پیشگی داده معه مردم جهاز فتح شاهی معزی وغیره که به سلامت رسیده بودند سه نفر ده روپیه که جمله نهصد و سه روپیه می شد داده سپرد دلال نموده به روانگی آنها به صوب بندر مسقط تاکید نمودند ـ و چهار نفر از مردم جیش گرفته در هرکاره‌گی نویسانیدند ـ و یک ماستر عبدالکریم بابت جهاز فتح شاهی معزی را همراه خود گرفته به در ماهه معلمان همراهی وجه طلب یک ماهه از توشکخانهٔ سرکار دادند و همه سرانجام توشکخانهٔ
سرکار و سرانجام چهار سرداران بر کشتی های کرایه دار وغیره سوار نمودند ـ ٦٦
و به وقت شام یک جوان گردون نواز علاقهٔ اسداللهی مفرور گردید ـ

و حسین آغا نزد شاه نورالله خان آمده اظهار کرد که باشترده چهارده ضرب اتواپ بغیر سرب و باروت است و در راه خطر و خوف قوم خزاعل بسیار است، درین صورت باید که متسلم بگویند و الا از دست خود قدری باروت به قدر احتیاج بدهند - باز شاه نورالله خان به متسلم گفته فرستادند که باروت برای اتواپ کشتی باشترده نیست، بدهانند - متسلم به لیت و لعل گذرانید و باروت نه داد - آخرالامر شاه نورالله خان ده صندوق باروت منجمله سی صنادیق باروت که عبدالله یهودی از مراد خان وغیره به قیمت به حساب فی صندوق که سه من باروت بود دوازده روپیه گرفته در وجه قیمت آن کاغذ هندوی بر دلال بندر مسقط نموده بود حواله بر عبدالله یهودی نمودند که نامبرده بگیر و راهی شو -

و به تاریخ هجدهم روز شنبه صد رومی به عیسی نصرانی که به کارپردازی سرکار گاه گاه حاضر بود به طریق انعام از سرکار به معرفت
عبدالله یهودی دلال بصره منجمله وجه قیمت سی صندوق باروت که از ۱۶۰
مراد خان وغیره گرفته بود هر چهار سردار دهانیدند و یک قطعه عرضداشت به اتفاق هر چهار سردار متضمن کیفیت روداد جهازات مغروق نوشته بدست سید ولی بارگیر سرکار دادند که به حضور پرنور برساند - و شاه نورالله خان در طاس چهارم بر کشتی کرایه‌دار حسین آغا معه عبدالقادر منشی و محمد علی بهاتو و سه معلم و یک ماستر عبدالکریم و محمد عمر و شیخ بدهن و عبدالنبی چوبدار و شیخ مرتضی و شیخ حسین و محمد یعقوب خدمتگار و چهار نفر دهلیت سرکار و شش خلاصی توشکخانهٔ سرکار و هرکاره وغیره سوار شدند - و به وقت سوار شدن بر کشتی بخانهٔ متسلم خبر گرفتند - متسلم در خواب بود اتفاق ملاقات نه شد، از معرفت آدم متسلم به متسلم سلام گفتند - و غلام علی خان و لطف علی خان معه جوانان اسداللهی و چند جوانان سزاول و بهرام در طاس نهم

به خانهٔ متسلم رفته ملاقات کردند، و از انجا غلام علی خان و شیخ احمد علی منشی و شکرالله خان و محمد فاضل چوبدار و شیخ بدهن خدمتگار بر یک کشتی خورد تکنه نام کرایه‌دار سوار شدند و لطف علی خان بر یک کشتی خورد کرایه‌دار دیگر همون نام معه چند جوانان
بهرام سوار شدند و جوانان سزاول و سید جعفر مصدی و هر سه چیله‌های ۶۸
سرکار معه سرانجام جعفر خان بر کشتی کلان باشترده نام سوار شدند و همه کشتی‌ها لنگر برداشته تا متصل و قریب حویلی و باغ انگریز که از فاصله یک کروه راه از بصره واقع است رفتند و لنگر قایم نمودند ـ و به وقت شام غلام علی خان، حسن آغا و نعمان آغا زکوتی بصره برای دادن دوشاله به طریق خلعت که ضابطه بندر بصره و از سابق مقرر شده بود، نزد شاه نورالله خان فرستاده بودند ـ خان مسطور به درجواب آن خطی بنام غلام علیخان نوشتند که از حسین آغا گفته دوشاله به قیمت پنجاه رومی یا نقد پنجاه رومی گرفته به نامبرده‌ها بدهند ـ غلام علی خان پنجاه رومی به نامبرده‌ها دادند ـ من بعد به وقت شب در طاس دوم محمد عمر چوبدار نزد شاه نورالله خان خبر آورد که جوانان اسداللهی درو بست و جعفر خان و کنک پله ونایک هرکاره وغیره بر کشتی باشترده از راه شرارت و عدم کفایت جای به چندین کسان سوار نه شدند، و محمد نتهو جوقدار اسداللهی وغیره بسیار تکرار و گفت و شنود بروبروی غلام علی خان نمودند ـ غلام علیخان به محمد عمر چوبدار گفتند که شاه نورالله خان به جوانان اسداللهی و سزاول به اتفاق در کشتی باشترده چه طور جای تقسیم نموده بودند که حالا می گویند که جای کفایت بهر دو جوق نمی کند و فریاد می برآرند ، باید که به جوانان اسداللهی
به فهمایند ـ چوبدار مسطور به جواب پرداخت که شاه نورالله خان خود ۱۶۹
تقسیم جای نموده بودند، بلکه جوقداران و سرخیلان اسداللهی و سزاول خود به اتفاق تقسیم جای نموده بودند که حالا می گویند که جای کفایت

به هر دو جوق نمی کند غلام علي خان به چوبدار مسطور گفتند که به شاه نورالله خان این کیفیت ظاهر کند - و شاه نورالله خان پیش از وقوع این معامله بفاصله ده تیر پرتاب پیشتر رفته بودند - و غلام علي خان و لطف علی خان باوصف اطلاع به معاملهٔ مسطور جوانان اسداللهی و جعفر خان وغیره را کنارهٔ بندر بصره واگذاشته خود راهی شدند - و بر کشتی باشترده جوقدار و سرخیل سزاول از کنارهٔ بندر لنگر برداشته در اثنای راه لنگر قایم نموده اند که بجز سوار شدن اسداللهی بر کشتی باشترده پیشتر راهی نخواهیم شد - شاه نورالله خان از استماع این خبر آدم سرکار را بر کشتی باشترده فرستاده تاکید نمودند که از بندر بصره لنگر برداشته در اثنای راه ماندن چه فایده دارد باید که زود خودها را درین جا برسانند، دریافت کیفیت عدم سوار شدن جوانان اسداللهی وغیره بدریافت آورده فکر طلبیدن جوانان مسطور و جعفر خان به عمل آورده خواهد شد - من بعد به وقت سه پاس شب مردم علاقه کشتی‌ها خود بخود لنگر همه کشتی‌ها
برداشته بیشتر راهی شدند، مگر شاه نورالله خان و جوقدار و سرخیل سزاول ١٧
بدشواری و زبردستی تمام به ناخدا وغیره تعلقه‌دار کشتی‌های خودها قایم نمودند -

و شاه نورالله خان صبحی روز یکشنبه بتاریخ نوزدهم معه عبدالقادر منشی نزد کشتی باشترده رفته از جوقدارد سرخیل سزاول و مصدی سید جعفر کیفیت عدم سوار شدن جوانان اسداللهی وغیره بر کشتی باشترده و بودن به کنارهٔ بندر بصره و پیشتر رفتن غلام علی خان و لطف علی خان استفسار نموده، سه قطعه خطوط بنام حسین آغا داروغهٔ ارساد بصره و جعفر خان و محمد نتهو جوقدار اسداللهی به این مضمون که بزودی زود بریک کشتی دیگر از حسین آغا گرفته خود را سوار گردانیده درین جا برسانند، نویسانیده به صحابت شیخ حسین دهلیت به بندر بصره فرستادند، و به سبب وقوع باد صرصر در آنجا نمانده

لنگر هر دو کشتی ها برداشته پیشتر بفاصلهٔ دو کروه رفته لنگر قایم نمودند(۱) ـ

و بتاریخ بستم روز دوشنبه در طاس چهارم به سرحد فرودگاه
لشکر شیخ سوسینی عسکردار بدوی که در آنجا خیمه‌های خورد
معه افواج فرود آمده بود و از بصره چهار کروه مسافت دارد رسیدند ـ
شاه نورالله خان نزد غلام علی خان که قریب بودند رفتند ، گفتند ۱۷۱
که شیخ سوینی درینجا حاضر است باید که نام‌برده را چیزی به
طریق خلعت داده بعد ملاقات پیشتر راهی شوند والا در راه بصره خطره
و خوف بدوی بسیار است ایذا خواهد رسید ـ غلام علي خان قبول کرده
اجازت دادند ـ شاه نورالله خان معه شکرالله خان و عبدالقادر منشی و
محمد علی بهاتو و سه معلم و ماستر نزد کشتی باشترده که همه
سرانجام توشکخانهٔ سرکار برآن بار نموده بودند رفته دو دستار به آنک
هفتصد و هشتاد و هفت و نهم و دو تهان شیله به آنک یک هزار و
پانصد و دو تهان دوریه به انک یک هزار و یک صد و هشتاد و هفت
و یک گارهٔ بهونگیری بانک دو صد و هفتاد و پنج و دو پچهوری گلدار
ابریشمی تارپتری یکی به آنک یک هزار و هفتاد و پنج و دویمی
بابت بست پچهوری عنایتی خاص از توشکخانهٔ سرکار برآورده به صحابت
محمد عمر چوبدار و شیخ مرتضیٰ خدمتگار وغیره به طریق سوغات نزد
شیخ سوینی فرستادند ـ من بعد شاه نورالله خان و شکرالله خان و عبدالقادر
منشی و سه معلم و ماستر و محمد امام و محمد امین جوقدار و سرخیل
سزاول نزد شیخ سوینی رفته ملاقات کردند و از طرف غلام علي خان
به تعذر بیماری واقعی دست و پا که از بادی اماس کرده بود پرداختند
و کلام محبت انگیز متکلم شدند ـ شیخ سوینی بسیار خوشنود شده طعام

۱ـ .MS لنگر قایم و بتاریخ

١٧١ مهماندارانه(١) پیشتر از دو ساعت به اطلاع ورود خوانین به آن نواح پخت و پز نموده بود به ایشان خورانیده مرخص نمود ـ

شاه نورالله خان یک قطعه خط بنام حسین آغا و یک به متسلم حاکم بصره و یک به جعفر خان و یک به عبدالله یهودی دلال بصره نوشته به صحابت هرکارهٔ سرکار و آدم شیخ سوینی بصوب بصره روانه نمودند که زود جوانان اسداللهی وغیره را درین جا برساند و ده صندوق باروت منجمله سی صندوق مسطور از شیخ سوینی گفته به عبدالله یهودی نویسانیدند که شیخ سوینی رعایتهً از طرف خوانین برساند ـ و شیخ سوینی گفت که در اینجا توهم باد صرصر و طوفان شدید در پیش بسیار است ، باید که شماها به موضع قرنه رفته بمانند ، امروز خط جوانان علاقهٔ شما خواهند رسید ـ باز ازین جهت لنگر همه کشتی ها برداشته پیشتر راهی شدند ـ

و بتاریخ بست و یکم روز سه شنبه به وقت صبح دو دفعه‌دار و دو جوان اسداللهی لنگر کشتی غلام علي خان به هزاران دشنام و هنگامه قایم نموده نزد کشتی شاه نورالله خان ، که از مقام امام مهدی صاحب الزمان که از فاصلهٔ پنج کروه از بصره واقع است پیشتر رفته بودند ، آمده ، به هزاران دشنام و هنگامه نموده نیز لنگر قایم کنانیدند ، و هنگامه و غوغا بحدی نمودند که بیان نتواند کرد ـ شاه نورالله خان

١٧ با وصف این هنگامهٔ جوانان مسطور را نزد خود طلبیده به دلاسا و تشفی عنوانات پرداختند و گفتند که همه کشتی‌ها را نزد کشتی خود برسانند ، همه کوایف روداد شماها به دریافت آورده خواهد شد ـ باز جوانان مسطور نزد کشتی غلام علي خان وغیره رفته همه کشتی‌ها را نزد کشتی شاه نورالله خان رسانیدند ـ خان مسطور جعفر خان و

١ــ Text مهمانداریانه

محمد نتهو جوقدار اسداللهی را که با چند جوانان اسداللهی در یک کشتی خوردترین کرایه‌دار سوار شده رسیده بودند نزد خود طلب داشته کوایف روداد آنها پرسیدند ـ محمد نتهو اظهار نمود که شما پشتر راهی شده بودند و غلام علیخان و لطف علي خان برکشتی سوار شدند و مایان به اکل و شرب به کنارهٔ بندر بصره که تیار بود مشغول شده ، باز نزد غلام علي خان رسیده گفت که در باشترده جای کفایت نمی کند ، مایان را به‌نوعیکه خواهند برکشتی‌ها سوار بکنند ـ غلام علیخان گفتند که ذمه سواری شماها از شاه نورالله خان است از اوشان به پرسند و شما پیشتر رفته بودند ـ من بعد لنگر همه‌کشتی‌ها برداشته پیشتر راهی شدند ـ من بعد نزد جعفر خان که به فرودگاه خود جریده بودند رسیده اظهار این همه کوایف نموده بسیار متعجب شده به دشواری و شدت از متسلم و حسین‌آغا و عبدالله یهودی و احمد چلبی مهماندار گفته دیروز یک کشتی از سرکار متسلم گرفته
چند جوانان اسداللهی وغیره را سوار گردانید ، عنقریب خواهند رسید ، ۱۷۴
و یک کشتی خورد به‌کرایه گرفته جعفر خان خود معه چند جوانان اسداللهی سوار شده شبا شب نزد شما رسیدیم ـ و جعفر خان هم همین کیفیت اظهار نمودند و گفتند که خبر رسید که جهاز فتح شاهی معزی را مردم علاقهٔ جهازات ارماد بصره به کناره کشیده آب می برآرند ، البته چند اتواپ وغیره اجناس و هر دو عماری نقره برآورده خواهد شد ـ شاه نورالله خان به جواب پرداختند : اول خود به اعتماد آنکه همه جوانان اسداللهی همراه غلام علي خان و لطف علي خان برکشتی باشترده که پیشتر ازین اسداللهی به اتفاق سزاول جای تقسیم نموده بودند ، سوار شده خواهند آمد ، پیشتر متصدی حویلي انگیز رفته لنگر قایم نموده بودند که به وقت شب بزبانی محمد عمر چوبدار کیفیت بودن شماها در بندر بصره ظاهرگردید ، دو سه آدم سرکار و آدم شیخ‌سوینی

عسکردار بدوی نزد شما فرستاده عازم شد که به موضع قرنه(١) رساند
و انتظاری شماها نماید که بعد رسیدن شماها پیشتر روانه شود ،
خوب ، انچیکه بگذشت خوب شد ، حالا شماها به موضع مسطور مع ١٧١
جوانان عقب مانده راهی شوند ، همه بندوبست شماها به عمل خواهدآمد ـ
محمد نتهو قبول نمود و جعفر خان هم گفتند که خود بهر طور اینها را
فهمایش نموده همراه خود به موضع مسطور می آرم ـ من بعد جعفر خان
ومحمدنتهو وغیره راطعام خورا نیدند و خرمای تر به قیمت پنج روپیه از دست
خود به قیمت از خلاصی کشتی گرفته به جوانان اسداللهی دادند و گفتند
که اگر طعام پزیده می خورند برنج وغیره لازمه آن می دهانم به گیرند
و بخورند ـ محمد نتهو قبول نه کرده گفت که بعد رسیدن به موضع
مسطور پخت و پز و اکل و شرب نموده خواهد شد ـ شاه نوراللہ خان
لنگر همه کشتی‌ها را برداشته پیشتر راهی شدند ، و بعد قطع مسافت
یک کروه پیشتر راهی شده به قلت و جذر آب فرات لنگر قایم نمودند ـ
جعفر خان و محمد نتهو وغیره جوانان اسداللهی که بریک کشتی
خورد کرایه‌دار سوار بودند رسیده فرود آمده گفتند که مایان بجز
رسیدن جوانان عقب مانده پیشتر نخواهم رفت و به اکل و شرب مایل
نه خواهیم شد و لنگر برداشتن نخواهیم داد ـ و لطف علیخان با وصف ١٧٠
اطلاع خبر عدم سوار شدن جوانان اسداللهی برکشتی باشترده و به
کنارۀ بندر بصره فرود آمدن اصلا به دریافت این کیفیت نه پرداخته
پیشتر بنوعی راهی شدند که خدمتگار خاص خود را وا گذاشتند و خود
منزل به منزل گریختند ـ من بعد شاه نوراللہ خان محمد نتهو را به
فهمایش و پخت و پز کنانیدن طعام برای جوانان اسداللهی دو سه
دفعه طلب داشتند ، از راه شرارت نیامد ـ من بعد شاه نوراللہ خان

١ـ قورنه

محمد امین سرخیل سزاول را(۱) طلب داشته گفتند که شما و جوانان
اسداللهی سابق در کشتی باشترده جای تقسیم نموده قبول کرده بودند و
همراه غلام‌علیخان آمدند و جوانان اسداللهی سوار نه شدند و من پیشتر ازان
راهی شده بودم، با وصف این امروز بدشواری درین جا رسیدند - به عنوانات
فهمایش نموده گفت که تا موضع قرنه بیایند ، همه بندوبست به معاملهٔ
ایشان نموده خواهد شد ، قبول نموده حالا باوصف طلب نزد خود
نمی آیند ، درین صورت از دست خود چه می شود - محمد امین سرخیل ۱۷۷
گفت که مایان سابق انچیکه بسوار شدن بر باشترده قرار کرده بودیم به
دستور سوار شدیم بلکه اندک جای از طرف خود برای بودن جوانان
اسداللهی واگذاشتیم - من بعد شکرالله خان را از نزد غلام علي خان
طلب داشته گفتند که به غلام علي خان بگویند که محمد نتهو وغیره
را طلبیده فهمایش نمایند که درین جا به اکل و شرب مایل شده پیشتر
راهی شوند ، بعد رسیدن به موضع قرنه بندوبست شماها به عمل
آورده خواهد شد - شکرالله خان به خالی کرده دادن جای در باشترده
برای جعفر خان به شاه نورالله خان گفتند - شاه نورالله‌خان چند خلاصی
داده چند بسته‌های توشکخانهٔ سرکار برداشته علحده نهاده در کشتی
باشترده جای کرده دادند و به غلام علي خان کیفیت مسطور گفتند -
غلام علي خان به معرفت جعفر خان و شکرالله خان وغیره به فهمایش
تمام نزد خود طلب داشته فهمایش به عنوانات نمودند ، قبول نه کرده ،
همه شب لنگر همه کشتی‌ها در آن جا قایم نمودند مگر کشتی لطف علی خان
پیشتر رفت و خلاصی وغیره علاقه‌دار کشتی در غصه و غضب که مایان
درین جا نه خواهم ماند ، اگر شماها می باشند مایان کشتی خود درین
جا گذاشته پیشتر می رویم - باز شاه نورالله خان وغیره به عنوانات فهمایش
آنها نمودند -

و بتاریخ بست و دوم روز چهار شنبه کشتی بابت سرکار متسلم

۱۷، مع جوانان اسداللهی و کنک پله وغیره که پستر مانده بودند رسیدند ـ
جعفر خان همه جوانان را فهمایش کرده چیزی به اکل و شرب مایل
کنانیده بر کشتی‌های مسطور سوار گردانیده معه باشترده و غلام علی
خان وغیره به صوب موضع قرنه راهی شدند ـ و کشتی شاه نورالله خان
را به سبب کثرت سرانجام و قلت آب پاو کروه مسافت پیشتر برده
لنگر قایم نمودند ـ و در انجا دو طرف دو قلعه ویران افتاده بنا کردهٔ
برادر کریم خان والی ایران که فوج کشی نموده از همون طرف به
بندر بصره رسیده محاصره نموده به تسخیر در آورده بود واقع نمودند ـ
و به شب قدری پیشتر رفتند ـ

و به تاریخ بست و سیوم روز پنجشنبه در طاس چهارم به کنارهٔ
موضع قرنه که حصاری است کهنه و ویران و چند خانها و دکاکین
است و گوشت و روغن و گندم و جو و برنج کم همدست می شود و
یک مسجد ویران افتاده و یک مسافرخانه و چند قهوه‌خانه وغیره ویرانست
مگر چند خانها و چند دکاکین بزاز وغیره و خیاط و سه چهار قهوه‌خانها
۱۷ آباد است و یک مقام ابراهیم خلیل‌الله علیه‌اسلام متصل رود فرات و
رود عرب که در آنجا اتصال یافته اند بر کناره واقع است و نخلستان
بسیار است ـ و در آن موضع قرنه شطعرب و فرات مضموم و
متصل شده است و از راه شطفرات به موضع حله می رسد و از آنجا به
نجف اشرف و کربلای معلی و بغداد شریف که به فاصله یک دو روز
واقع است می رسد ـ و به موضع مسطور از راه شطفرات در عرصهٔ ده
یازده روز از موضع قرنه می رسد و از راه شطعرب در عرصهٔ دو ماه
بلکه زیاده به بغداد می رسد لاکن درین راه خطر و خوف تطاول قوم
خزاعل(۱) بسیار است و در راه شطعرب خوف و خطر نیست لنگر قایم نمودند ـ

---

۱ ـ MS. خزائل

و به وقت شام روز چهار شنبه لنگر کشتی غلام علی خان و باشترده
وغیره به کنارهٔ مسطور قایم نموده بودند، شاه نورالله خان به زبانی محمد عمر
چوبدار به غلام علیخان بعد خبر گیری صحت و تندرستی گفته فرستادند
که به وقت سه‌پهر بر کشتی شما می آیم باید که لطف علي خان و
جعفر خان و محمد امام و محمد امین جوقدار و سرخیل سزاول و محمد شبو ۱۸۰
و نامدار خان وغیره جوقدار و سرخیل اسداللهی را نزد خود طلب داشته
جوانان اسداللهی را بر باشترده به اتفاق جوانان سزاول سوار نمایند و
اگر قلت جای بسیار رو دهد جوانان دو سه بهره علاقهٔ سزاول از انجا
برداشته بر کشتی دیگر سوار کرده خواهد شد - غلام علي خان به در
جواب پیام پرداختند که طبیعت خود بسیار متکسل است و سواری این
اصلاً قدر و حرمت کسی از سردار نزد جوانان اسداللهی باقی نمانده،
باید که شما خوف و رعب این جانب به مردم اسداللهی نمایش کرده
بر کشتی باشترده سوار نمایند، اگر می خواهند بر این معنی لطف علي خان
و جعفر خان را نزد شما فرستاده خواهد شد - شاه نورالله خان طوعاً و
کرهاً قبول نمودند - من بعد به وقت شام شاه نورالله خان نزد غلام علي
خان رفته بودند، محمد امام جوقدار سزاول و سید جعفر مصدی هم نشسته
بودند - محمد امام قصد رفتن به مکان خود نمود، شاه نورالله خان گفتند
که بنشینید - محمد امام به جواب پرداخت که اگر شماها به ارادهٔ آنکه
از کشتی باشترده جوق سزاول را فرود آرند، از شما چه معنی بلکه ۱۸۱
فرشتهٔ از آسمان فرود آید از باشترده فرود نه خواهم آمد، برای همین
معنی می خواهند که بنشینند - ایشان گفتند نه، شما را که می گوید
که از باشترده فرود آیند - یک لحظه توقف کرد و رفت - من بعد
شاه نورالله خان در ماده سوار نمودن اسداللهی به اتفاق سزاول بر کشتی
باشترده از غلام علي خان و جعفر خان که در آنجا حاضر بودند گفتند
که تکرار و شرارت اسداللهی اظهر است و مایان بدون رسیدن حسین آغا

و احمد چلبی مهماندار پیشتر نمی رویم(۱) و دو سه روز توقف اینجا است، هر چیکه شدنی باشد خواهد شد - من بعد شاه نورالله خان به مخاطبهٔ جعفر خان و سید جعفر مصدی وغیره گفتند که به هر عنوان به انصرام امورات سرکار پردازند و الا همه امورات بر خود واگذاشته بگویند که دست خودها نمی شود، خود به هر عنوان بدرستگی امورات سرکار پرداخته خواهد شد، و حالا بسیار بیحرمتی درپیش رسید، انشاالله‌تعالیٰ بعد رسیدن به بغداد شریف در صحبت شماها نه خواهد ماند و انچیکه مناسب وقت به نظر آید به عمل آورده خواهد شد - و ازین قبیل بسیار گفت و شنود نمودند - غلام علي خان اصلا به در جواب نپرداختند و شاه نورالله خان بر کشتی خود درآمدند -

و یک قطعه خط عبدالله یهودی دلال بندر بصره موسومهٔ شاه نورالله خان نزد غلام علی خان رسیده بود دادند، متضمن این بود که منجمله سی صندوق باروت مسطوره سابق ده صندوق به حسین آغا به موجب دهانیده شما داده شد - و یک صد رومی نقد در وجه قیمت باروت باقی به عیسیٰ نصرانی به موجب نوشتهٔ شما داده شد - و نیز یک صد رومی در سه صد رومی که فی نفر سه رومی کرایه کشتی تا بندر مسقط چهار رومی فی نفر مقرر نمود، و نیز یک صد رومی به خرچ مردم روانگی داده شد - و در زر قیمت آن چیزی باقی نمانده است - و یوسف یهودی از غلام علی خان محاسبه دارد، انفصال دهند - و نیز چند زر محبوبی همدست و تیار نموده شده است، باید که کاغذ هندوی بغداد بدست آدم سرکار بفریسند، زر محبوبی به کفایت فرستاده خواهد شد - و نیز چند خطوط بنام ۱۸۰
گماشته‌های خود نوشته شده است، عنقریب خود همراه می آرد یا به صحابت حسین آغا می فریسد - و غلام علی خان یک نفر گردون نواز علاقهٔ رسالهٔ فقیر محمد که از جهازات مغروق به سلامت رسیده بود،

۱— .MS نمی روند

محمد نتهو وقت آمدن بزبردستی همراه خود به عوض یک نفر گردون نواز مفروره اسداللهی گرفته نزد غلام علی خان آورد و گفت که بنویسبند و اضافه هم نمایند - اسم نویسی کنانیده در جوق اسداللهی نگاه داشتند -

و بتاریخ بست و چهارم روز جمعه جعفر خان نزد شاه نورالله خان آمده بودند، از جعفر خان گفتند که چه طور روانگی از اینجا به عمل خواهد آمد که اسداللهی برکشتی باشترده سوار نمی شود و سرداران به چشم نمائی یا فهمایش آنها نمی پردازند - آخرالامر جعفر خان گفتند که بهر نوع شما فهمایش آنها نموده مرضی ایشان بگیرند - جعفر خان
فهایش جوانان اسداللهی نموده مرضی گرفتند که به غلام علی خان و ۱۸۴
لطف علیخان از کشتی خودها فرود آمده برکشتی باشترده سوار شوند و مایان را یک کشتی و جوانان سزاول را یک کشتی به دهند تا هر دو فریق سوار می شوند - شاه نورالله خان شنیده گفتند: خوب، چه مضایقه دارد، از غلام علیخان بگویند و راضی بکنند - غلام علی خان هم به دریافت آورده قبول نمودند و بهر دو فریق فهمایش نمودند و گفتند که مایان سردار شما هستیم یا نه، به جواب پرداختند: بلی، پس مایان بوقت برخاست ازین اینجا می گوئیم، به این نوع یا به آن نوع قبول خواهند کرد یا نه، آنها قبول نمودند -

و بتاریخ بست و پنجم روز یکشنبه(۱) غلام علی خان از زبانی شیخ محمد دوبهانسی نوملازم به شاه نورالله خان گفته فرستادند که بهر دو فریق مسطور در بارهٔ سواری اصلا چیزی نمی گویند، من فهمایش اینها کرده ام، بعد رسیدن حسین آغا اینها را سوار کرده راهی خواهم شد - شاه نورالله خان به جواب پرداختند که من از صورت هر دو فریق بیزار هستم، کدام کس می خواهد که از ایشان سوال و جواب نماید - محمد
باز گشت نمود - ۱۸۵

۱ــ شنبه It must be

و بتاریخ بست و ششم روز یکشنبه شاه نوراللہ خان یک قطعه خط متضمن تاکید نمودن به حسین آغا برسانیدن به دارالسلام بغداد و رسیدن خود به موضع قرنه و نیز در ماده تاکید نمودن به برآوردن اجناس جهازات مغروق و روانگی مردم به بندر مسقط به اهل‌کاران خود بنام متسلم حاکم بصره و یک قطعه خط درین ماده به عبداللہ یهودی و فرستادن صد من برنج و سه هزار قرص رومی گرفته همراه خود آوردن نویسانیده به صحابت یک آدم سرکار نزد متسلم و عبداللہ یهودی فرستادند ـ و بتاریخ بست و هفتم روز دو شنبه باد قوسی به شدت مانند طوفان وزید ـ و بتاریخ بست و نهم روز چهارشنبه به جوانان اسداللهی و سزاول و بهرام وجه طلب یک ماهه به وضع نیم ماهه سابق که علی‌الحساب به آنها رسیده بود دست بدست تقسیم نمودند ـ

و بتاریخ غره ماه یوسفی سال دلو سنه ۱۲۰۰ هجری(۱) روز پنجشنبه صبحی آدم شیخ سوینی عسکردار بدوی معه یک قطعه خط متضمن این معنی که زود کشتی‌های رسیدهٔ موضع قرنه را باز گردانیده ۱۸۰
به بصره رساند موسومهٔ اهلکار حسین آغا رسید ـ اهلکار به در جواب خط مسطور نوشت که حسین آغا هنوز در بصره مستقر است و خود بدون اطلاع و حکم نامبرده چه طور ازینجا برگردانم، و این همه کیفیت شاه نوراللہ خان شنیده اهلکار مسطور را طلبیده پرسیدند که این همه حرکات بیجا است ـ به جواب پرداخت که شیخ سوینی به گرفتن زکوة اجناس تجارتی که درینجا مقرر است اگر از شطفرات به بغداد رفته شود باید داد، و الا لا ، و حالا که از راه شطعرب رفته می شود و حصول زکوة مسطوره صورت نمی بندد از این جهت حرکات لایعنی درپیش می آرد، مضائقه نه دارد و امروز که روز خمیس است حسین آغا البته

۱ـ 20 December, 1786.

از بصره نزد شیخ سوینی خواهد آمد و همه مقدمات انچیکه بوده باشد
به فیصله خواهد رسانید، درین باب بی فکر باشند، انشاالله‌تعالی در عرصهٔ
دو سه روز ازین جا پیشتر به خوشی و خرمی راهی خواهند گردید ـ
و همین کیفیت به غلام علی خان رسانیدند ـ خان مسطور به شاه نورالله
۱۸۷ خان گفته فرستادند که بعد رسیدن حسین آغا همه کوایف ظاهر خواهد
گردید ـ و بوقت شام اهلکار حسین آغا نزد شاه نورالله خان آمده گفت
که چند جوان بر یک دانگ سوار شده از صوب بغداد بصوب بصره
نزد متسلم و شیخ سوینی رفتند و گفتند که از پیش سلطان روم فرمان معلی
بنام حاکم بغداد متضمن بحالی تا هفت سال و روانگی مردم هند به
ولایت روم به اعزاز تمام صادر گردید ـ از این جهت حاکم بغداد
خوش و خرم شده شش بیرقدار و چند سوار به استقبال مردم هند روانه
نموده خود را به سرعت سربعه به اطلاع این کوایف معه خط تاکید
موسومهٔ متسلم و شیخ سوینی روانه نمود ـ شاه نورالله خان از استماع
این خبر بسیار خورسند شدند ـ

من بعد آدم سرکار و هرکاره که به بصره مع خطوط موسومهٔ متسلم
و عبدالله یهودی وغیره که شاه نورالله خان فرستاده بودند مع خطوط در
جوابی رسید ـ متسلم در خط خود نوشت که غراب سورتی مفقود و فتح شاهی
معزی در وقت جذر آب رود نشانی پیدا می شود و ادمان سرکار از یک
۱۸۸ ماه هلاک و سرگردان و قریب دو سه هزار رومی به خرچ درآمد و
غواصان به سبب سردی هوا و شدت سرما غواصی کردن نمی توانند،
معهذا دو ضرب توپ و یک لنگر برآورده شد و باقی را خدا حافظ و ناصر،
و هر که به خلاف این ظاهر سازد غیر واقعی است ـ و عبدالله یهودی و
حسین آغا نوشتند که بتاریخ دوم ماه یوسفی سال دلو سنه ۱۲۰۰ هجری(۱)

۱ـ 21 December, 1786.

نزد شما می رسم و پیشتر راهی خواهند گردید و درین جا به طریق حبس مانده‌ام ، از انجا که شیخ سوینی پیشتر رفتن نمی دهد و می گوید که به بغداد خطی دربارهٔ روانگی شماها نوشته شده است، انشاءالله‌تعالی امروز فردا در جواب از بغداد می رسد البته پیشتر روانه نموده خواهد شد - و معلم احمد و ماستر وغیره بابت جهازات مغروق که نزد جهاز مغروق به دیدن اجناس جهاز مسطور که آدمان متسلم می بر آرند رفته بودند،خطی نوشتند به طریق یادداشت که حرفی آز آن اصلا معلوم نمی شود، مگر از زبانی آدم سرکار معلوم گردید که معلم مسطور می گفت که یک رسن آمار و اتواپ وغیره نقدی برآورده اند و اینها را نزد جهاز ماندن ندادند و برانیدند -

۱۸' و بتاریخ دوم ماه یوسفی روز جمعه بوقت شب باز خبر رسید که از سلطان حلب خطی به شیخ سوینی رسیده است که حاکم بغداد معزول و مبدل می شود، ازین جهت شیخ می خواهد که کشتی‌ها را روانه به صوب بغداد نمی نماید -

و بتاریخ سیوم بروز شنبه در ساعت ششم بدوی شیخ سوینی معه یک قطعه خط شیخ مسطور متضمن اینکه زود خودها را به بصره برساند، موسومهٔ شاه نورالله خان مورخه غره ماه یوسفی رسید - شاه نورالله خان به مجرد استماع مضمون خط مسطور متردد شده، می خواستند که خود را جریده نزد شیخ سوینی رسانیده به دریافت کیفیت پردازد و نیز به غلام علی خان مطلع ساختند، من بعد خواستند که آدم سرکار معه یک قطعه خط نزد شیخ سوینی روانه سازد که زود کیفیت بدریافت رسد - درین ضمن در ساعت هفتم باز یک خلاصی معرفت(۱) اهلکار حسین آغا که معه خط در جواب نزد شیخ سوینی فرستاده بود معه دو قطعه خطوط موسومهٔ

۱- .MS معرفت معرفت

اهلکار مسطور و یک نفر بدوی شیخ سوینی متضمن این رسید که زود
کشتی‌ها را به بصره رساند و آدم بدوی مسطور نزد خود آید - ازین ۱۹۰
جهت به سبب لاچاری شاه نورالله خان ازین کیفیت غلام علی خان آگاه ساخته گفتند که جوانان سزاول و اسداللهی را به اتفاق یا بنوعیکه خواهند سوار کنند، و سوای این به اهلکار مسطور گفته در یک کشتی دیگر سوار نمودن پنجاه نفر تقرر و قبول نموده شده است، بهر نوع به تفریق جوانان مسطور را سوار گردانند - غلام علی خان بجواب پرداختند که درانچیکه رضای شما بوده باشد سوار نمایند، اگر مرا می گویند کشتی خود خالی نموده در یک دانگ خورد سوار می شوم - آخرالامر شاه نورالله خان پنجاه نفر اسداللهی را بر یک کشتی دیگر سوار گردانیدند و چند جوانان مذکور را بر کشتی خورد و چند جوانان شاگرد پیشه وغیره ملازم سرکار را و جوانان سزاول تمام و کمال را بدستور سابق و نیز جعفر خان و بارگیران سرکار را بر کشتی کلان سوار نمودند -

و در ساعت نهم لنگر همه کشتی‌ها برداشته بصوب بندر بصره راهی شدند - و بعد قطع مسافت دو کروه لنگر قایم نمودند - و به وقت شب بعد انقضای سه ساعت حسین آغا از نزد شیخ سوینی آمده همه
مردم متعلقه کشتی‌ها را تاکید کرد که زود به وقت جذر آب لنگرها ۱۹۱
برداشته پیشتر بصوب بصره راهی شوند - من بعد نزد شاه نورالله خان آمده گفت که من اگرچه بدریافت عدم تخلل و تخطر در راه شما را پیشتر روانه ساخته می خواست که خود را هم عنقریب متعاقب برساند، ازین ضمن شیخ سوینی و متسلم از نزد حاکم بغداد متضمن این رسید که حاکم بغداد تا هفت سال بحال و وکلای سلطان هند را زود روانه بغداد نماید و برای ایشان پنج بیرقدار و پانصد سوار عنقریب متعاقب به استقبال فرستاده می شود، چنانچه خط عبدالله یهودی نیز درین ماده رسیده است، به شاه نورالله خان نمایش کرد و گفت که شیخ سوینی خبر

مذکور را به درجه صدق نمی رساند و می گوید که آدم خود به بغداد فرستاده قریب هجده روز است، انشاءالله‌تعالیٰ در عرصهٔ سه چهار روز می رسد، البته شما را پیشتر روانه به صوب بغداد نموده خواهد شد، باید که شماها زود به بصره متصل مقام علی مشکل کشا لنگرها قایم کنانیده انچیکه لوازمات آذقه و زادراه ضرور است مهیا سازند و مایان هم زود زادراه تیار ساخته منتظر رسیدن آدم شیخ سوینی از بغداد خواهم
شد، انشاءالله‌تعالیٰ در عرصهٔ دو سه روز می رسد، البته در عرصهٔ یک ١٩
هفته به صوب بغداد به خوشی و خرمی رفته خواهند شد - شاه نورالله خان به سبب لاچاری قبول نمودند و به وقت جذر آب لنگر همه کشتی‌ها برداشته به صوب بندر بصره راهی شده، بعد قطع مسافت پنج کروه راه لنگر قایم نمودند -

و به تاریخ چهارم روز یکشنبه صبحی در جذر آب لنگرها برداشته به اعانت اوزار و جذر آب پیشتر راهی شدند و در ساعت چهارم به مقام مهدی صاحب‌الزمان که یک قبه و میناری عظیم واقع است رسیدند - و غلام علی خان شیخ محمد دوبهانسی نو ملازم سرکار را بر مچهوه سوار گردانیده نزد شاه نورالله خان به استفسار حقیقت ملاقات حسین آغا و دریافت کیفیت روداد فرستاده بودند - شاه نورالله خان کیفیت شب مذکور من و عن گفتند که به غلام علیخان ظاهر سازد و در ساعت پنجم به فرودگاه لشکر شیخ سوینی رسیدند و خبر گرفتند، معلوم گردید که شیخ سوینی در لشکر نیست و به موضع زبیر رفته است و پیشتر به فاصله یک کروه رفته لنگرها قایم نمودند - و در ساعت یازدهم حسین آغا نزد شاه نورالله خان آمده گفت که شیخ سوینی در لشکر خود بود، تاکید به مردم علاقهٔ خود نموده بود که خود به موضع زبیر رفته است و درین‌جا
حاضر نیست، بگویند تاکه شاه نورالله خان از خود ملاقات نه نماید، و ١٩١
از حسین آغا که نزد شیخ مذکور رفته بود گفت که اگر شاه نورالله خان

درینجا آمده از خود ملاقات نماید(۱) بدنامی خود نزد سلطان روم متضمن این خواهد شد که وکلای سلطان هند را که پیشتر به صوب بغداد شریف رفته بودند از اثنای راه مراجعت کنانیده چیزی رشوت گرفت، از برای خدا از شاه نورالله خان بگویند که اصلا به خاطر چیزی دیگر راه نیابد، این همه تردد که به ظهور رسید برای خیرخواهی شما است، انشاءالله‌تعالی در عرصهٔ قریب پیشتر بصوب بغداد روانه نموده خواهد شد - شاه نورالله خان باز به چند وجوه به حسین آغا گفتند که مایان درین ضلاع بسیار هلاک گردیدیم که به بیان نمی آید، باید که بهر حال اگرچه در راه خطر و خوف باشد چند مردم را از راه دیگر جریده روانه بغداد نمایند - حسین آغا به عنوانات به جواب آن پرداخت: اگر همچنین همه طرق بغداد مسدود خواهند شد، بهر نوع شما را با چند مردم جزوی و معدوده از راه حله یا دیگر راه قریب همراه خود به بغداد رسانیده خواهد شد، خاطر جمع دارند - و یک بوزینهٔ نامیمون که از همه بوزینه و مور وغیره که بودند مردند به سلامتی جان به امان بود - حسین آغا به اظهار چند احادیث رسالت پناه و ولایت مآب متضمن نامیمونی و نامبارکی بوزینهٔ مسطور بروبروی شاه نورالله خان در ۱۹۳
صحرا از قید زنجیر و قفس رهای داده بگذرانید - و بشب لنگر همه کشتی‌ها بسبب موضع خرائب که درپیش بود قایم نمودند -

و بتاریخ پنجم روز دو شنبه صبحی شاه نورالله خان به حسین آغا گفته فرستادند که از شب لنگرها نه برداشتند باعث چیست - حسین آغا به اظهار تعذر موضع خرائب و وقوع تاریکی شب به مردم متعلقهٔ خود تاکید نمود که لنگرها بردارند، ازانجا لنگرها برداشته به صوب بغداد شریف گردیدند - و بوقت عصر بالاتر از حویلی انگریز که متصل بصره

۱— .MS درانیجا آمده از خود ملاقات بدنامی خود نزد سلطان

واقع است لنگر قایم نمودند ـ و به وقت شب از زبانی محمد نتهو جوقدار اسداللهی خبر رسیدن خطوط از بغداد موسومهٔ حسین‌آغا، شاه نورالله خان شنیده، حسین‌آغا را نزد خود طلب نمودند ـ نام‌برده رسیده خطوط بغداد از نزد تجار ذوی‌الاعتبار متضمن تکذیب خبر معزولی حاکم بغداد وغیره اخبار متوحش مورخه بست و دوم ماه صفرالمظفر سنه ۱۲۰۱ هجری رسیده بودند مسموع گردانید و گفت که انشاءالله‌تعالیٰ عنقریب در عرصهٔ دو سه روز روانگی شماها به صوب بغداد شریف خواهد شد ـ شاه نورالله خان گفتند که فردا عبدالله یهودی و جعفر خان وغیره را مع خط نزد
۱۹، شیخ سوینی می فریسم، توهم همراه رفته زود اجازت روانگی مایان بگیرد زود روانه بکن، قبول کرد و رفت ـ و لنگر باشترده که برآن جعفر خان و جوانان سزاول وغیره سرانجام توشکخانه سوار بودند و کشتی غلام علی خان به کنارهٔ بندر بصره به وقت شام رسیده قایم نمودند ـ

و به تاریخ ششم روز سه شنبه بوقت صبحی لنگرها برداشته در ساعت سیوم به کنارهٔ بندر بصره لنگرها قایم نمودند ـ و شاه نورالله خان محمد عمر چوبدار را نزد حسین‌آغا فرستادند که زود جای دیده به اتفاق حسین آغا نزد مقام علی مشکل کشا فرود آرند و نیز یک آدم سرکار برای طلبیدن عبدالله یهودی فرستادند ـ خبر رسید که دلال مسطور نزد شیخ سوینی رفته است و مردم سزاول و اسداللهی را در سرای خالی که به کنارهٔ بندر بصره واقع است فرود آوردند و حسین‌آغا نزد غلام علی خان رفته بود ـ من بعد شاه نوراللهٰ خان حسین‌آغا را طلب داشته در کشتی دیگر ملک نامبرده برای وسعت مکان مع مردم خود و منشی عبدالقادر و شاگرد پیشهٔ سرکار وغیره سوار شدند ـ

و به تاریخ هفتم روز چهار شنبه شاه نورالله خان صبحی محمد عمر چوبدار
۱۹ سرکار را مع یک قطعه خط متضمن اینکه شما روانه بغداد نموده بودند و شیخ سوینی از موضع قرنه باز گردانید، چه موجب است، معلوم نه گردید،

اگر مرضی شما باشد نزد شما رسیده مطلع کوایف مذکوره می شود، نزد متسلم فرستادند ـ و جعفر خان و محمد امام جوقدار سزاول وغیره نزد شاه نورالله خان آمده گفتند که زود فکر روانگی بغداد از راه شط عرب یا فرات یا خشکی نمایند و الا تنها کسی از سرداران(۱) پیشتر به بغداد رود(۲) و همه‌ها را زود بطلبند(۳) شاه نورالله خان به جواب پرداختند که‌من فکر روانگی بغداد بهر عنوان خوب می دانم و نیز مصمم کرده ام، باید دید که چه می شود، من بعد هرچیکه خدا خواهد به ظهور خواهد انجامید ـ

و نیز جعفر خان وغیره اظهار نمودند که چهار جوانان رسالهٔ فقیر محمد علاقهٔ غراب سورتی که منجمله هفت نفر جوانان رسالهٔ فقیر محمد و یک خلاصی و یک معلم و یک رهبان جزیرهٔ خارج بر مچهوه در حالت غرق غرّاب سورتی سوار شدند و از جذر آب به کنارهٔ سرحد چعب معه مچهوه رسیدند ـ و چهار جوانان و یک نفر خلاصی شناوری
نموده بر کناره فرود آمدند و معلم و رهبان از عدم استقامت شناوری ۱۹۷
کردن نتوانسته بر مچهوه مذکور ماندند ـ و یک نفر خلاصی مذکور در سرحد چعب نوکر گردید درین جا رسیدند ـ چنانچه عبدالله یهودی دلال سه نفر دو دو روپی داد ـ و چند لاش مردم مغروق به کنارهٔ چعب رسیدند ـ و دو خلاصی منجمله خلاصیان جهاز فتح شاهی معزی که خرچ از سرکار دهانیده مامور روانگی به صوب بندر مسقط بودند مردند ـ

و مصطفی چوبدار متسلم نزد شاه نورالله خان رسیده از نزد متسلم سلام گفته اظهار نمود که خاطر جمع دارند انشاءالله‌تعالیٰ در عرصهٔ قریب پیشتر به صوب بغداد راهی خواهند شد، و نیز خطی از بغداد متضمن

۱ــ .MS و الا تنها از کسی سرداران کسی پیشتر به بغداد

۲ــ .MS روند ۳ــ بطلبند

این رسیده است که عنقریب از بغداد پنج بیرقدار و سوار برای بردن
شماها می آیند، خاطر جمع دارند - شاه نورالله خان هم جواب سلام نموده
گفتند که زود مایان را روانه بغداد نمایند، اولی است، ازانجا که در
راه بغداد و اسلام بول امن و امان است و اصلا خوف و خطر نیست -
چنانکه خطی از نزد عثمان خان از استنبول(۱) متضمن این آمده است
که شماها زود براهی بصوب استنبول شوند و درین ماده تاکید به نام ۱۹،
حاکم بغداد وزیراعظم نوشته است، البته روانه خواهد کرد - و نیز
بدستور نزد غلام علی خان مصطفی چوبدار مسطور رفته بود -

و به وقت سه پهر به شاگرد پیشهٔ سرکار و غلام علی خان و شاه
نورالله خان و لطف علی خان و شکرالله خان و احمد علی منشی وغیره
وجه طلب یک ماهه تقسیم نمود - و محمد عمر چوبدار سرکار معه خط
متسلم بدر جواب خط شاه نورالله خان متضمن این رسید که پیشتر از دو
سه گهری چاوش را فرستاده بود البته کیفیت ظاهر کرده باشد، شماها
در کشتی‌ها چهار پنج روز متوقف شدند که مرشدالاحشام شیخ سوینی
عسکردار درین جا می رسد، به صوب بغداد روانه نموده خواهد شد - و
به وقت شب حسین آغا نزد شاه نورالله خان آمده گفت که عبدالله یهودی
دلال از نزد شیخ سوینی آمده است، می گوید که امروز فردا شیخ
مذکور برای جنگ با مخالف که از فاصلهٔ بست منزل بطرف موضع زبیر
واقع است، می رود، شماها به امن و امان بی‌فکر بصوب بغداد راهی
شوند، لاکن امروز خود نزد غلام علی خان رفته بودم گفتند که برای
فرود آمدن خود و لطف جای و مکانی در بصره خالی نمایند، قبول نموده ۱۹'
مکان هم به موجب گفتهٔ ایشان خالی نموده شد، و نیز گفتد که خود
از کشتی خود فرود آمده برکشتی دیگر وقت روانه شدن به صوب بغداد

۱- استنبول or اسلام بول

سوار نخواهم شود و خود مع چند مردم علاقهٔ خود بر یک کشتی علحده سوار خواهم شد و با فوج و افواج و مردم جیش اتفاق نمی شود - درین صورت یک کشتی دیگر به مردم شماها باید و الا کفایت نه خواهد کرد، اگر کشتی دیگر ضرور است وجه کرایه بدهند تا که زود کشتی دیگر کرایه نموده خواهد شد و الا در سرعت روانگی کشتی همدست نخواهد شد - شاه نورالله خان به جواب پرداختند که پیشتر ازین در موضع قرنه مقرر گردیده است که غلام علی خان و لطف علی خان بر کشتی باشترده و سزاول بر کشتی غلام علی خان و اسداللهی بر کشتی لطف علی خان سوار می شوند، درین صورت کشتی دیگر ضرور نیست - باز حسین آغا به جواب پرداخت که امروز غلام علی خان به این طریق گفته اند - شاه نورالله خان به غضب شدند، من بعد گفتند که خوب فردا ما هر چهار سردار یکجا جمع می شویم توهم بیا، اگر کشتی دیگر ضرور افتد البته گفته خواهد شد، قبول نمود و رفت -

و بتاریخ هشتم روز پنجشنبه شاه نورالله خان صبحی یک آدم سرکار ٢٠٠
را برای طلبیدن عبدالله یهودی فرستادند و جعفر خان و سید علی صاحب پیرزاده را برای پیام رسانیدن و فهمایش غلام علی خان به این مضمون که روانگی همه مردم از فضل ایزد متعال عنقریب خواهد شد لاکن صورت سوار شدن جوانان اسداللهی و سزاول وغیره مردم به تفریق معقول به ظهور نمی پیوندد، باید که جوانان مسطور را اگر در کشتی غلام علی خان و لطف علی خان سوار نموده خودها بر کشتی باشترده سوار شوند، بهتر است، و الا بنوعیکه درستگی و کفایت سرکار صورت بندد سوار نمایند، از کشتی باشترده طلب نموده همه کوایف روداد مذکور ظاهر ساختند که به طریق مسطور بگویند، اگر قبول نمایند بهتر است و الا خود و جعفر خان وغیره چند کس جریده به طریق زوار عتبات عالیات از راه شط فرات به بغداد می رویم - جعفر خان و سید علی صاحب نزد غلام علی

خان که حسین آغا هم درآنجا حاضر بود رفتند و همه کوایف مسطور
ظاهر ساختند - غلام علیخان به جواب پرداختند که همه امورات سرکار
بر شاه نورالله خان واگذاشته اطاعت پردازم، بنوعیکه خواهند به انصرام
امورات سرکار پردازند و برای سواری خود اگر یک تخته بدهند قبول ۲۰۱
است - من بعد غلام علی خان و جعفر خان و سید علی صاحب از زبانی
محمد عمر چوبدار سرکار شاه نورالله خان را طلب داشتند - شاه نورالله خان
مع عبدالقادر منشی نزد غلام علی خان رفتند و همه کوایف ظاهر ساختند
و مقرر نمودند که غلام علی خان و جوانان سزاول وغیره بر کشتی
باشترده و لطف علی خان بر کشتی خود بحال، و جوانان اسداللهی بر
کشتی غلام علی خان و جعفر خان وغیره بر کشتی شاه نورالله خان، و
محمد نتهو جوقدار اسداللهی را برای رضامند نمودن سوار شدن بر کشتی
مقرره طلب داشته حقیقت تقرر سواری همه مردم گفتند - محمد نتهو گفت
که در صورت بودن سزاول بر کشتی باشترده سوار شدن خودها بر کشتی
غلام علی خان غیر ممکن است، از آنجا که در صورت نفاق یکی از
هر دو فریق بر باشترده سوار نشوند و هر دو فریق بر دو کشتی علحده
باشند بهتر است - باز لطف علی خان را طلب داشته گفتند که محمد نتهو
به این طریق می گوید که غلام علی خان و شما بر کشتی باشترده
سوار شده بر هر دو کشتی خودها خالی نموده هر دو فریق را سوار
کنند بهتر است، شما درین باب چه می گویند - لطف علی خان به
جواب پرداختند که مرا هم امری از امورات سرکار اصلا معلوم نیست ۲۰۱
مگر وقتی که شماها طلب داشته می گویند معلوم می شود، چنانچه درین
روزها تا به موضع قرنه رسیده از آنجا مراجعت نمودند، چه باعث است
معلوم نه گردید، اگر برای انصرام امورات سرکار می گویند البته سخن
شماها در هر امور قبول است - من بعد مقرر بخاطر خواه محمد نتهو گردید -
و عبدالله یهودی نیز در آنجا رسید - از نامبرده کیفیت روانگی پرسیدند

که چه طور است، ظاهر کرد : انشاءاللہتعالیٰ در عرصهٔ قریب صورت خواهد بست و شیخ سوینی مرشدالاحشام نیز فردا پس فردا در اینجا می رسد و نیز آدم از بغداد خبر خیریت و خوشی می آرد البته روانگی شماها به ظهور خواهد بست ـ و الا شیخ مسطور در عرصهٔ پنج شش روز معه افواج خود که در موضع زبیر با اسباب جنگی فرود آورده است پیشتر تا بست منزل برای مقابله با مخالفی که دعوی خدائی می کند، می رود، شماها به طرف بغداد روانه شوند، کسی مزاحم نخواهد شد ـ و نیز یک
قطعه خط کهیه دیوان سلیمان پاشا حاکم بغداد موسومهٔ عبدالله یهودی ۲۰۳
مرقوم و مرسل بود نمایش کرد که مورخه بست و چهارم ماه صفرالمظفر سنه ۱۲۰۱ ھ است ، مرقوم که در عرصهٔ قریب برای طلب داشتن(۱) مردم هند پنج صد سوار از موضع بنی لام که در اثنای راه بغداد است روانه می نماید، باید که مردم و اسباب نواب را از موضع قرنه به همراهی سواران مسطور مرسل نماید تا که به حفاظت خواهند رسید و دیگر بحالی متسلم بصره و غلطی خبر معزولی حاکم بغداد مسطور بود، همه بروبروی خوانین خوانده تسلی کرد که امروز فردا آدم شیخ سوینی معه در جواب خط خیریت نمط می رسد البته روانگی شماها زود به عمل خواهد آمد ـ خوانین قبول نمودند ـ

و محمد عمر چوبدار فریاد آورد که محمد علی بهاتو اخبار متوحش و بد انجام که خدا بهر کس مبیناد هر کس می گوید و سخنهای نمک حرامی بسیار می گوید که چنانچه از دو سه روز بسیار به عنوانات به همه سرداران وغیره بلکه به ملازمان عالی دشنام داد ـ شاه نوراللہ خان و جعفر خان بسیار به غضب درآمده از یزک اسداللهی نگاهداشتند و گفتند که نام سرکار بد کرد و بدخواهی سرکار را حدی ندارد، این چنین

۱ـ .MS برای و طلب داشتن

کس را بحضور پرنور فرستادن اولیٰ است و ازو کار سرکار خراب خواهد شد ـ

۲۰۱ و شاه نورالله خان یهودی را همراه گرفته بر کشتی خود آمدند و
گفتند که اگر روانگی مایان در عرصهٔ چهار پنج روز صورت می بندد
بهتر است و الا یک بتیل خورد به کرایه بکن تا که خود و جعفر خان
وغیره چند مردم معدوده به طریق زوار عتبات عالیات از راه شطفرات
به بغداد رفته بهر طور این قافله را به بغداد طلب داشته خواهد شد ـ
یهودی مسطور قبول نمود ـ باز یک کاغذ هندوی سه هزار رومی که بر
بغداد نموده بودند به یهودی مذکور داده گفتند که زر مسطور در اینجا
نقد بدهند که به خرج ضرور است ـ

و غلام علی خان برای فرود آمدن خود یک مکان متصل مقام علی
مشکل کشا رضی‌الله‌عنه به کرایه فی روزه دو رومی گرفته همه مردم
متعلقه و شاگرد پیشهٔ خود را فرود آوردند و معلم احمد و ماستر شیخ
محمد و عبدالله سارنگ، که نزد جهاز فتح شاهی معزی مغروق رفته چند
اشیای بالای جهاز مغروق که همدست می شد، مردم متعلقهٔ ارماد
بصره برآوردند و می بر آرند، بنظر در آورده بودند، نزد شاه نورالله خان
آمده به این تفصیل اظهار نمودند که دو ضرب توپ یکی شش رطلی و
۲۰۰ دویمی چهار رطلی و لنگر دو عدد و رسن لنگر یک عدد و شمشیر شش
عدد و بنادیق قریب چهل ضرب و دو صندوق پوشاک وغیره بابت
شمس‌الدین و یک صندوق نقدی وغیره بابت محمد شفیع که در آن سی
اشرفی و چهار کاش‌شاناری و شصت و شش زر محبوب و پنج عدد
مروارید بود و یک بسته پارچه کنک پله که بهادری بست و هشت
هون و بست و یک قرص مسقطی در آن بود وغیره، چند اجناس جزوی
برآوردند ،این همه اجناس مسطور را بنظر در آورده بودند که حاجی محمد
دفتردار آفندی گفت که درین جا چرا هلاک می شوند به بصره بروند ـ به
گفتن آنها زبردستی از نزد جهاز مغروق به بصره مراجعت نمودند و

دو چادر بانات سرخ به معلم و ماستر مذکور از طاقه‌های بانات جهاز مغروق که برآوردند داروغهٔ جهازات ارماد بصره دادند - و محمود نامی عملدار خلاصی جهاز فخرالمراکب از بندر مسقط فراری شده نزد شاه
۲۰۶ نورالله خان آمده اظهار کرد که به عدم رسیدن وجه طلب خود را بندر مسطور فراری شدم -

درین ضمن عبدالقادر سکانی جهاز مسطور مع دو خریطه فرمان معلی و خطوط وغیره که کمال‌الدین ماستر جهاز مذکور از حضور پرنور رسیده بود به صحابت نامبرده بر یک منزل داو سوار گردانیده روانه بندر بصره نموده بودند که اتفاقاً در همون منزل مسطور خود هم سوار گردیده همه کوایف بدریافت آورده، چنانکه جزیرهٔ خارج رسیده بود که داو مسطور به سبب شدت طوفان مغروق گردید و همه کواغذ مسطور به غرق در آمدند - عبدالقادر سکانی مسطور از تهی دستی به بندر مسقط باز گردید و خود به بندر بصره رسید و در بندر مسقط شهرهٔ فتح و فیروزی عساکر ظفر مآثر به ظهور رسیده بود که هفت و نه قلعه‌جات علاقهٔ مرهته مقهوره به قبضه تصرف اولیای دولت قاهره درآمد و کفاران بدکردار بسیار عاجز شدند -

و نیز یک کیفیت دیگر ظاهر ساخت که در جزیرهٔ خارج نزد
۲۰۷ روضهٔ مبارکهٔ مقدسه حضرت محمد حنیف صاحب بن امیرالمومنین حضرت علی ابن ابی طالب کرم‌الله‌وجه محمد حنیف سوداگر را مراد خان و ضیاءالدین وغیره مردم متعلقهٔ جهازات سرکار مدفون ساخته بودند - حضرت موصوف به مجاور روضهٔ مبارکه خود در بشارت تاکید اکید فرمودند که زودتر لاش سوداگر مسطور از قبر بدر در آورده و دور بیندازند، و آنها را که درینجا سوداگر مذکور را مدفون ساخته‌اند عنقریب مغروق و محروق خواهم نمود - مجاور به مجرد تاکید عالی لاش مسطور را از قبر بر آورده بیرون روضهٔ متصل کنارهٔ دریا مدفون ساختند -

و بتاریخ نهم روز جمعه محمد خان نجم جماعدار سزاول وغیره نزد
شاه نورالله خان آمده اظهار نمودند که به وقت شب نه ضرب بنادیق
جوق سزاول و هر دو سرخیل که در چهار دیواری مستحکم اندرون
به حفاظت نگاه داشته بیرون بر دروازه دو یزک به حفاظت مقید نموده ۲۰
بودند و دزدان از پایهٔ دیوار سوراخ نموده اندرون آمدند، معه چند اسباب
و سرانجام جوانان دیگر وزیدند ـ شاه نورالله خان به مجرد استماع بسیار
غصه کرده گفتند: یکی نقصان مایه دوم شماتت همسایه به ظهور رسید،
خوب، آینده به حفاظت پردازند ـ

و غلام علیخان به وقت سه پهر فرود آمده به حویلی کرایه‌دار
استقامت ورزیدند ـ و نیز لطف علی خان حسین آغا را نزد خود طلب
داشته به خالی نمودن یک حویلی کرایه‌دار برای فرود آمدن گفتند ـ
حسین آغا به جواب پرداخت که چرا فرود می آیند ـ لطف علی خان جواب
دادند که درین جا در وقت بارش اصلا یک وجب جای خشک نمی‌ماند ـ
حسین آغا گفت چرا می باشند بر کشتی باشترده سوار شوند ـ لطف علی
خان قبول نموده آدم خود را نزد شاه نورالله خان فرستادند که در کشتی
باشترده جای خالی نموده یک طرف جای نمایش نمایند، البته بر کشتی ۲۰
مسطور سوار شده خواهد شد ـ شاه نورالله خان به جواب پرداختند که
شما بر کشتی مسطور رفته جای دیده فرود آیند و وقتی که غلام‌علیخان
سوار خواهد شد البته به آنها مکان خالی کرده داده خواهد شد ـ لطف علی
خان بر کشتی باشترده رفته سرانجام جعفر خان برآورده باز پیام به شاه
نورالله خان نمودند که درین جا سرانجام توشک‌خانه بسیار است و جای
اصلا نیست ـ شاه نورالله خان گفتند: خوب، چه مضایقه، من هم برای
دیدن سرانجام توشک خانه که از آسیب بارش دیروزه به ضرر رسیده است
می آیم ـ من بعد شاه نورالله خان بر کشتی مسطور رفتند و همه سرانجام
دیده در مکان خوب به حفاظت نگاهداشته به لطف علی خان گفتند که

شما چندین زودی چرا می‌کنند، انشاءالله‌تعالیٰ در عرصهٔ چهار پنج روز من خود و جعفر خان از راه شطفرات به بغداد می روم، شما را مکان‌های متعدد خالی می شود - و لطف علی خان خاموش شده بر کشتی خود
۲۱۰ سوار شدند و شاه نورالله خان بر کشتی خود آمدند - و جعفر خان و سید علی صاحب پیرزاده نزد شاه نورالله خان آمده بودند، گفتند که درین جا بیجا بودن مناسب نیست چیزی و نوعی تردد باید کرد -

درین اثنا سید عبدالرحمان که سید بزرگ و عالی خاندان است و یک موضع قریه متصل موضع قرنه آباد کرده است، نزد شاه نورالله خان برای ملاقات آمده بود ملاقات کرد و گفت که اگر به امرای یا خدمتی مامور فرمایند، البته به تقدیم آن کوشیده خواهد شد - شاه نورالله خان گفتند که اگر یک کشتی خورد کرایه‌دار نموده ما چهل و پنجاه کس را بطریق زوار عتبات عالیات از راه شطفرات به بغداد رسانند، عین احسان متصور خواهد شد و هرچیکه به کرایه کشتی مسطور افتد از دست خود خواهم داد - قبول کرده گفت که اگر شماها جریده می روند امروز فردا روانه می نمایم و الا در کشتی خود اجناس تجارتی بار کرده خود همراه شما به بغداد می رساند، خاطر جمع باشند - شاه نورالله خان و
۲۱۱ جعفر خان مد نظر به برآمد امورات سرکار نموده یک پچهوری گلدار ابریشمی تارپتری به آنک پنج صد منجمله پچهوری و شیله و گارها وغیره که در سرکار از مراد خان گرفته بودند برآورده به سید مذکور دادند - سید بسیار خوش شده گفت که امروز فردا درعرصهٔ دو سه روز شما را روانه بغداد می نمایم بلکه خود همراهی می آیم و بفرودگاه خود رفت -

و به وقت شام حسین آغا نزد شاه نورالله خان آمده گفت که امروز سه قطعه خطوط موسومهٔ متسلم و احمد آفندی زکوتی و عبدالله یهودی از بغداد به این مضمون رسید که پانصد سوار از راه بغداد و به موضع قرنه برای همراهی و استقبال و حفاظت مردم نواب روانه نموده شده است،

انشاءالله‌تعالی عنقریب می رسند، باید که به همراه سوارهای مسطور از
راه بغداد مردم هند را روانه نمایند ـ شاه نورالله خان گفتند: اگر در
عرصهٔ دو سه روز امر مسطور به وقوع رسد بهتر و الا به سید عبدالرحمان
گفته یک کشتی کرایه نموده از راه شطفرات به طریق زوار به بغداد ٢١
می روم، و فردا نزد متسلم هم می روم ـ حسین آغا قبول کرد و رفت ـ
و بتاریخ یازدهم روز یکشنبه شاه نورالله خان و جعفر خان و
عبدالقادر منشی وغیره به اطلاع غلام علی خان و لطف علی خان نزد
متسلم رفته گفتند که صورت روانگی مایان بصوب بغداد به هیچ نوع
به ظهور نمی بندد، می خواهم که به معرفت سید عبدالرحمان به طریق
زوار از راه شط فرات به بغداد رفته صورت طلب داشتن قافلهٔ متعلقهٔ
خود به ظهور رسانم ـ متسلم گفت که فردا شیخ سوینی به موضع زبیر
می آید، درین جا طلب داشته روانگی شماها مقرر نموده خواهد شد و
الا بنوعیکه شما می خواهند به عمل آورده خواهد شد ـ و پیشتر ازین
خطی متضمن خبر خیریت از بغداد رسیده بود، دیروز هم قاصدی دیگر
بیامد، انشاءالله‌تعالی در عرصهٔ قریب زودتر روانگی شما به ظهور خواهد
پیوست ـ و کیفیت برآوردن اجناس جهاز مغروق گفت که یک ماه جمیع
جهازات ارماد بصره به محنت و شدت و تردد برآوردن اجناس جهاز ٢١
مسطور هلاک اند و به تحت خرچ کثیر درآمدند، اصلا سرانجام آن
بر نیامد، مگر دو لنگر و پنج چهار ضرب توپ وغیره ـ شاه نورالله خان
خاموشی شده مرخص شدند ـ و متسلم و عبدالله یهودی و حسین آغا وغیره
اعیان بصره در درستگی امورات خودها گرفتار اند، و خوانین دربارهٔ روانگی
می گویند، به لیت و لعل می گذارند، این همه کیفیت از صورت مجالس
اعیان بصره معلوم می شود ـ شاه نورالله خان و جعفر خان وغیره نزد
غلام علی خان رفته همه صورت مسطور اظهار نموده گفتند که به معرفت
سید عبدالرحمان به تاریخ چهاردهم ربیع‌الاول جریده به بغداد روانه می‌شوم ـ

غلام علی خان به جواب پرداختند که خوب چه مضایقه فردا پس فردا شیخ سوینی می رسد، همه کوایف روانگی ظاهر می گردد، من بعد در صورت لاچاری به موجب تقرر شما به عمل آرند ـ شاه نورالله خان قبول نموده بر کشتی خود رفتند ـ

۲۱۴ و به تاریخ دوازدهم روز دوشنبه جهازات ارماد بصره از نزد جهاز مغروق به بصره رسیدند از مردم جهازات مذکور معلوم گردید که هفت ضرب اتواپ و سی و یک ضرب بنادیق و دو لنگر وغیره جزوی سرانجام از جهاز مغروق برآورده شد و به برآوردن دو عماری نقره بسیار تردد نمودند، به سبب بودن عماری مسطور در ته خانهٔ جهاز مغروق اصلا صورت نه بست، باز گردیدند و از مردم مسطور خبر دیگر رسید که پنج چهار منازل جهازات و غرابات معه سه زنجیر افیال به بندر مسقط رسیده‌اند و می خواهند که درین جا برسند، چنانکه خطی متضمن خبر مسطور در یک دانگ خورد می رسد ـ

لطف علی خان معه اسباب و سرانجام به شدت بارش و هبوب باد طوفان در کشتی بودن نتوانسته نزد مقام علی در یک حویلی کرایه‌دار فی یک ماه پانزده رومی فرود آمدند ـ و حسین آغا نزد شاه نورالله خان آمده گفت که اگر صورت روانگی قافله نه شود شما جریده بر شترها سوار شده به بغداد روند و بارش و طوفان شدید معه برق صاعقه به ظهور رسید
۲۱۵ که کشتی غلام علی خان که خالی بود معه لنگر وغیره به کنارهٔ چعب رسید ـ و بتاریخ سیزدهم روز سه شنبه حاجی جواد داووغهٔ جهازات و غرابات ارماد بصره بر کشتی شاه نورالله خان آمده یک لنگر کلان برای رفع توهم و اندیشهٔ طوفان و استحکام کشتی آورده به کناره قایم نموده از شاه نورالله خان گفت که قریب پنجاه لاش از جهاز مغروق برآمده بودند بر کناره مدفون کردم ـ شاه نورالله خان پرسیدند که چند اشیاء از جهاز مغروق برآوردند ـ گفت که به شدت و تردد تمام دو لنگر و

هفت ضرب اتواپ و سی و یک ضرب بنادیق و دو صندوق ادویات وغیره بابت محمد شفیع وغیره و چند اشیای جزوی بابت جوانان جیش وغیره برآورده شد و باقی عماری وغیره هیچ برآورده نه شد، و کیفیت خبر رسیدن جهازات سرکار مع زنجیر افیال به بندر مسقط اظهار نموده، گفت که واقعی است یا غیر واقعی معلوم نیست ـ باز به تحقیقات رسید که خبر رسیدن جهازات سرکار به بندر مسقط غلط محض مگر مردم جهاز فخرالمراکب منتظر رسیدن جهازات مغروق اند ـ

شاه نوراللّه خان محمد عمر چوبدار سرکار را نزد متسلم و عبداللّه یهودی دلال بصره برای خالی نمودن یک حویلی کلان برای فرود آمدن معه توشکخانهٔ سرکار و جوانان اسداللهی وغیره فرستاده بودند ـ متسلم مالک
۲۱۶ حویلی سابق را طلبداشته بخالی نمودن گفت ـ مالک حویلی بیت روس وکیل انگریز تعلقدار کوتهی بصره بود، ابا نمود که کرایهٔ سابق ندادند و حالا اگر به هزار عنوان بگویند نخواهم داد ـ من بعد به کوتوال تاکید کرد که یک حویلی دیگر در آبادی به کرایه خالی نموده بده ـ اگرچه کوتوال مسطور به تفحص و تجسس تمام یک حویلی به کرایه سه صد رومی به محمد عمر نمایش کرد منظور نه گردید ـ باز اسحاق یهودی که مامور(۱) سرانجام خریدن بهته و خوراکی جوانان اسداللهی است یکی حویلی کلان به کرایه چهل رومی مقرر نموده به محمد عمر نمایش کرد، منظور کرده نزد شاه نوراللّه خان اظهار کرد ـ شاه نوراللّه خان قبول نمودند ـ

و بتاریخ چهاردهم روز چهار شنبه شاه نوراللّه خان همه سرانجام و توشکخانهٔ سرکار قدری فرود آورده به حویلی مذکور روانه نموده خود بر مهوه سوار شده نزد مقام علی مشکل کشا رضی‌اللّه‌عنه رفته خواستند که از سید رحمان به تقرر روانگی خود جریده از راه شطفرات بگویند، و آدم خود را نزد سید مذکور روانه ساختند که اگر حاضر باشد، رفته

۱ـ MS. مامو

سوال و جواب در مادهٔ مذکور نماید ـ آدم مسطور نزد سید رفته خبر آورد که مقام علی بروند که خود سید هم می آید ـ شاه نورالله خان به مجرد گفتن به مقام علی مشکل کشا رفتند ـ حاجی جواد داروغهٔ جهازات
۱۷ ارساد بصره در آنجا حاضر بود و سید هم در آنجا رسید ـ شاه نورالله خان
از زبانی حاجی جواد از سید مذکور سوال و جواب تقرر روانگی می نمودند که درین اثنا یک بدوی آمده از حاجی جواد گفت که در فردهٔ زکواة یک جوقدار(۱) از بغداد معه خطوط رسیده است و خوش خبری آورده است ـ معاً شاه نورالله خان عبدالقادر منشی و حاجی جواد را نزد جوقدار فرستادند ـ حاجی جواد وغیره نزد سلیمان آغا جوقدار رفته کیفیت استفسار نمودند ـ به جواب پرداخت که به حاکم بغداد فرمان بحالی از نزد سلطان صادر گردید و یک مهماندار برای بردن وکلای سلطان هند نزد حاکم بغداد رسیده چنانکه همه سرانجام مهمانداری وغیره تیار نموده شده است، و چند صد جوانان را حاکم بغداد برای بردن مردم هند از بصره به بغداد روانه نموده است، انشاءالله‌تعالیٰ عنقریب امروز فردا خواهند رسید، و خود را برای همین معنی روانه نموده است ـ من بعد جوقدار مذکور نزد شاه نورالله خان که به خانهٔ غلام علی خان می آمده بودند، آمده خبر خیریت رسانید ـ شاه نورالله خان و حاجی جواد و سلیمان آغا جوقدار نزد غلام علی خان رفتند، جعفر خان هم حاضر بودند، همه کوایف رسیدن مهماندار نزد حاکم بغداد و صدور فرمان معلیٰ در باب فرستادند خوانین بولایت روم و روانگی پنج صد نفر به حفاظت قطاع الطریق برای بردن خوانین به بغداد
۱۸ و روانگی خود برسانیدن خبر مسطور ظاهر کرد ـ غلام علی خان و شاه
نورالله خان وغیره یک پچهوری گلدار تارپتری ابریشمی منجمله بست پچهوری عنایتی خاص و یک دستار سفید به آنک شش صد و پنجاه و سه و نیم به جوقدار مذکور به طریق انعام خوش‌خبر رسانی دادند ـ و

۱ــ .MS چوخدار

و شاه نورالله خان بر پالکی غلام علی خان سوار شده، همه سرانجام توشکخانهٔ سرکار و سرانجام خود وغیره که فرود آورده در صدد روانگی به حویلی کرایه‌دار بودند باز گردانیده بر کشتی سوار کنانیدند، نزد متسلم برای دیدن خطوط بغداد که جوقدار موسومهٔ متسلم آورده بود رفتند - متسلم نوید روانگی خوانین به سرعت بصوب بغداد گفته، نقل فرمان بحالی حاکم بغداد که از نزد سلطان روم به حاکم بغداد رسیده از آنجا نزد متسلم برای رفع توهم معزولی حاکم مسطور فرستاده بود، نمایش کرده، گفت که همه درستگی امورات شما است خاطر جمع دارند -

شاه نورالله خان از آنجا مرخص شده نزد غلام علی خان که لطف
علیخان و جعفر خان و حسین آغا وغیره حاضر بودند، رفته همه کیفیت مسطور
اظهار نموده، گفتند که محمد امام جوقدار سزاول و محمد نتهو جوقدار
اسداللهی را طلب داشته اگر قدری زر علی‌الحساب دهند اولیٰ است،
آنها سرانجام خوراکی خودها خواهند گرفت، قبول نموده جوقدار مسطور
را طلب داشته، جوقدار سزاول گفت که یک کشتی به جوانان خود کفایت
نمی کند، دو کشتی باید داد - شاه نورالله خان به غلام علی خان گفتند ۲۱۰
که اینها را فهمایش نموده بهر عنوان در چهار کشتی مقرری همه
مردم را به تفریق معقول سوار کنانند - غلام علی خان گفتند که درین
قضیه‌های مجهول خود نمی آیم، بهر عنوانیکه خواهند بکنند - من بعد
گفتند که اگر یک کشتی دیگر نمایند بهتر است و الا جای کفایت
نخواهد کرد - شاه نورالله خان گفتند که من برای کشتی دیگر اسراف
مال سرکار نخواهم نمود، شما هر چهار سردار اگر بکنند قبول است -
غلام علیخان به جواب پرداختند که نام هر چهار سردار چرا می گیرند
اگر من می کردم شما را چرا می گفتم، و این کار چندان عظیم نیست
که از دست کسی نخواهد شد، اگر من می خواهم از دست یک زنک
خواهم کنانید - شاه نورالله خان گفتند: زنک یکطرف اگر شما بکنید

قبول است از دست شماهم نخواهد شد ـ غلام علیخان گفتند : همه سخنهای شما مثل چوتیا است ـ شاه نورالله خان ازین سخن به غضب درآمده گفتند که این سخن به کسی دیگر بگویند البته خوف شما خواهد کرد، شما چوتیا هستند و شما را کسی شمار می کند ـ ازین قبیل بسیار سخنان
بدی و گرانی آمیز بسیار درمیان آمدند و غلام علی خان گفتند من ازین‌جا ۲۲۰
هرگز به بغداد نه خواهم رفت، اگر کسی نزد خود بر این معنی بیاید بر دهنش خواهم زد ـ شاه نورالله خان برخاسته بر کشتی خود آمدند ـ

و بتاریخ پانزدهم روز پنجشنبه سید عبدالرحمان نزد شاه نور الله خان آمده گفت که اگر از راه شطفرات می روند حاضرم ـ شاه نورالله خان به جواب پرداختند که به فضل ایزد متعال و یمن دعای دلی شما حالا جوقدار از بغداد رسیده است ، انشاء الله‌تعالی فردا پس فردا به بغداد روانگی به عمل خواهد آمد ـ و سید علی صاحب پیرزاده نزد شاه نورالله خان آمده پرسیدند که کدام روز می روند ـ شاه نورالله خان به جواب پرداختند که غلام علی خان تکرار بیجا دیروز نموده حرکت کرده اند ، چه طور رفته خواهد شد ، اگر شما نزد غلام علی خان رفته به اتفاق جعفر خان غلام علی خان را فهمایش نموده بر یک کشتی از چهار کشتی مقرره ، سوای یک کشتی تازه که حالا مقرر نموده شده است ، سوار نمایند ، البته روانگی به ظهور خواهد انجامید ـ سید علی صاحب پیرزاده به گفتهٔ شاه نورالله خان نزد غلام علیخان رفتند ـ درین اثنا خبر رسید که غلام علی
خان شترها کرایه نموده از راه خشکی به نجف اشرف و کربلای معلی میروند ـ ۲۲۱
و سید علی صاحب و جعفر خان به غلام علی خان به عنوانات از صبح تا شام فهمایش نمودند ، و جعفر خان قدمبوس نموده سر خود بر قدم غلام علی خان نهادند و به هزاران عنوانات فهمایش نمودند ، اصلا قبول نکرده گفتند که برای پاس خاطر شما اگر می خواهند همه زندگی سوخت نموده بر کشتی باشترده سوار می شوم و الا از راه خشکی چند نفر شتر

کرایه نموده به نجف اشرف رسیده به بغداد می رسم ـ غرض به هر عنوان بر راه راست نیامدند و فهمایش آنها قبول نکردند ـ و لطف علی خان هم حاضر بودند لاکن یک سخن فهمایش نه گفتند و خاموش بودند مثل وجود معطل و خود هم همراه غلام علی خان از راه خشکی به نجف اشرف رفتن می خواهند و می گویند ـ و محمد نتهو جوقدار اسداللهی بروبروی سید علی صاحب گفت که معه جوانان علاقهٔ خود همراه غلام علی خان بهر عنوان از فقر و فاقه خواهم رفت ـ و سید علی صاحب پیرزاده و جعفر خان بسیار آزرده خاطر شده به فرودگاه خود رفتند، این همه کیفیت از زبانی محمد عمر چوبدار سرکار ظاهر گردید ـ

۲۲۱ و بتاریخ شانزدهم روز جمعه سید علی صاحب و جعفر خان و محمد امین سرخیل سزاول نزد شاه نورالله خان بر کشتی آمدند و گفتند که غلام علی خان عجب مزاج دارند که مایان بچندین عنوان فهمایش نمودند که عنوان فهمایش در جهان باقی نماند ـ آخرالامر جعفر خان نظر به ابتری امورات سرکار و بد نامی قدمبوس نموده سر خود بر قدم غلام علی خان نهادند، اصلا فهمایش قبول نکردند و بر سر راه نیامدند ـ و جعفر خان گفتند که من نزد متسلم رفته همه حقیقت ظاهر ساخته بحضور پرنور میروم، و الا سرداران را که بر راه راست آمد، به انصرام امورات سرکار نمی پردازند فضیحت نمودند همه سرانجام سرکار همراه گرفته به حضور سلطان روم می روم ـ شاه نورالله خان گفتند آخرالامر همین علاج است که نزد متسلم رفته غلام علی خان را درین‌جا گذاشته همه مردم همراهی و سرانجام سرکار گرفته به حضور سلطان روم رفته به انصرام امورات سرکار پرداخته به حصول ماعمول(۱) در عرصهٔ یک سال مراجعت نموده می شود ـ و محمد عمر و شیخ مرتضیٰ و محمد کمال چوبدار و خدمتگار و چیلهٔ سرکار

۱ـ MS. مامول

نزد لطف علیخان رفته گفتند که همچو شما سردار خاموش نشسته این
فساد را رفع نمی سازند و به کار سرکار نمی پردازند، تعجب بسیار است،
بهرحال شما هم نزد غلام علی خان رفته فهمایش بکنند ـ لطف علی خان ۲۲۳
به جواب پرداختند که به خبر شاه نورالله خان فهمایش صورت نمی بندد،
و شاه نورالله خان می گویند که اول غلام علی خان مرا سخن بد گفتند،
من بعد به در جواب آن به عنوانیکه بود پرداختم، من فهمایش ایشان
نخواهم کرد، پس چه طور فهمایش خواهد شد ـ آخرالامر لطف علی خان
و چوبدار و خدمتگار و چیلهٔ سرکار وغیره نزد غلام علی خان رفته بودند
لاکن چیزی گفتن مناسب نه دیده باز آمدند ـ و محمد امین سرخیل
سزاول از شاه نورالله خان گفت که به کار سرکار چهار سردار آمده این
چنین نا اتفاق نمودن مناسب نیست، اگر می نمایند، خوب، فردا ما همه
مع جوانان سزاول وغیره و جمیع شاگرد پیشهٔ سرکار نزد غلام علی خان
رفته می گوئیم که بهرعنوان بر کشتی سوار شده بصوب بغداد راهی شوند
و الا کجا می روند، بگویند، و یک نوشته بدهند که من بکار سرکار نمی
آیم و امورات سرکار مرا کاری و معاملهٔ نیست، اگر بر سر راه آیند
خوب است و الا نزد متسلم رفته همه حقیقت ظاهر ساخته به حفاظت
سرانجام سرکار و سرداران دیگر که به انصرام امورات سرکار می پردازند،
پرداخته به صوب بغداد راهی خواهم شد ـ شاه نورالله خان گفتند که ۲۲۴
من بکار سرکار حاضرام ، اگر دیگر سرداران و شماها می آیند یا نه
بهر عنوان بروم رفته برآمد امورات سرکار خواهم نمود ـ و جعفر خان
و سید علی صاحب پیرزاده و محمد امین سرخیل به فرودگاه خودها رفتند ـ

و عبدالله یهودی دلال و شیخ احمد ساهوکار و حسین آغا نزد شاه
نورالله خان آمده بودند ـ شاه نورالله خان از یهودی و ساهوکار مسطور
ده هزار رومی برای خرچ ضرور است به عوض کاغذ هندوی درخواست نمودند ـ
آنها قبول نمودند ـ و برای روانگی مردم جهازات مغروق به صوب بندر

مسقط به عبدالله یهودی گفتند که زود روانه بکن - یهودی به جواب پرداخت که امروز فردا روانه می نمایم - و از حسین آغا پرسیدند که مایان بصوب بغداد به چند روز روانه می کنی - به جواب پرداخت که بروز دو شنبه تاریخ هفدهم ماه ربیع‌الاول سنه ۱۲۰۰ هجری لنگر کشتی‌ها می بردارم و به صوب بغداد روانه می شوم - و چند شاگرد پیشه متسلم نزد غلام علی خان آمده به هیا هو گفتند که مایان را چیزی ندادند - غلام علی خان به جواب پرداختند که سابق ازین صد رومی بابت حق شماها نزد متسلم فرستاده بودم ، متسلم منع کرده باز گردانید - آخرالامر غلام علی خان ده رومی به شاگرد پیشهٔ متسلم دادند -

و به تاریخ هفدهم روز شنبه شاه نورالله خان ، محمد عمر چوبدار
و عبدالرحمان و محمد کمال چیلهٔ سرکار را طلبداشته گفتند که نزد لطف علی
خان و جعفر خان و سید جعفر مصدی و محمد امام و محمد امین جوقدار
و سرخیل سزاول و محمد نتهو و نامدار خان جوقدار و سرخیل اسداللهی
رفته اینها را به آئین بهین گفته نزد غلام علی خان برده بهر عنوان ۲۲
فهمایش غلام علی خان نموده به سوار شدن بر کشتی و روانه شدن به
صوب بغداد راضی نمایند که بزودی روانگی به عمل آید - چوبدار و چیلهٔ سرکار به موجب گفتهٔ شاه نورالله خان معه محمد امام و محمد امین و محمد نتهو و نامدار خان وغیره نزد لطف علی خان رفته گفتند که به غلام علی خان بهر عنوان فهمایش نموده به روانگی به صوب بغداد راضی نمایند - لطف علی خان به جواب پرداختند که بجز فهمایش شاه نورالله خان صورت فهمایش غلام علی خان نمی بندد - آخرالامر گفتند که شما اول نزد غلام علی خان بروند من هم متعاقب می آیم - آنها قبول نموده نزد جعفر خان رفتند و گفتند - جعفر خان هم به دستور جواب دادند - همه مردم مسطور نزد غلام علی خان رفتند و نیز لطف علی خان متعاقب و به عنوانات به فهمایش غلام علی خان پرداختند - قبول نه کرده گفتند

که من از راه خشکی به نجف اشرف و کربلای معلی رفته به بغداد می آیم، شما از راه تری بروند - ازین قبیل بسیار سخنان درمیان آمد - من بعد جعفر خان و سید جعفر مصدی و محمد امام و محمد امین جوقدار و سرخیل سزاول و محمد نتهو و نامدار خان جوقدار و سرخیل اسداللهی ۲۲۶
و محمد عمر چوبدار وغیره نزد شاه نورالله خان آمده به عنوانات فهمایش نموده گفتند که بهر نوع شما نزد غلام علی خان بیایند، فهمایش غلام علی خان خود بخود صورت می بندد - شاه نورالله خان بر سید علی صاحب پیرزاده داشته نزد خود طلب داشتند و همه کیفیت ظاهر ساختند - سید علی صاحب به جواب پرداختند که اگر شما را مدنظر به انصرام امورات سرکار است بروند و الا لا - شاه نورالله خان گفتند: خوب، فردا نظر به امورات سرکار و پاس خاطر شماها نزد غلام علی خان می روم اگر از سخن سلوک متکلم می شوند خوب است و الا مناقشه دیگر برپا خواهد شد - قبول نموده همه‌ها به فرودگاه خودها رفتند -

و سید ولی بارگیر سرکار و معلم و ماستر جهاز مغروق معه یک مالک جهاز که به بندر مسقط می رفت نزد شاه نورالله خان آمده گفتند که به نودوپنج نفر با مردم جهاز مغروق برای رسانیدن به بندر مسقط هفت صد رومی می خواهد - شاه نورالله خان گفتند که نزد غلام علی خان و دیگر سرداران رفته ظاهر سازند، اگر آنها قبول نمایند مراهم قبول ۲۲۷
است - باز سید ولی بارگیر سرکار و معلم و ماستر وغیره نزد غلام علی خان رفته ظاهر ساختند - غلام علی خان به در جواب پرداختند که به همه امورات سرکار شاه نورالله خان مختار اند، نزد شاه نورالله خان بروند -

یادداشت نرخ بازار بندر بصره مرقوم تاریخ یازدهم ماه زبرجدی سال دلو سنه ۱۲۰۰ هجری(۱)

شکر فی من عطاری ۲۴ محمودی - نابات سفید فی من مذکور ۸۵ محمودی -

---

۱ — 4 October, 1786.

مصری سرخ فی من ۷۰ محمودی - مرچ سیاه فی من ۷۷ ۱/۲ فی من محمودی - الائچی فی من ۵۰۰ (محمودی) - قرنفل فی من ۸۰۰ (محمودی) - زرد چوب فی من ۱۵ (محمودی) - سونت فی من ۱۵ (محمودی) - دار چینی سیلانی فی من ۲۰۰ (محمودی) - دار چینی گوریالی فی من ۵۴ (محمودی) - کافور فی من ۱۲۰ (محمودی) - عود لوبان فی من ۱۱۵ (محمودی) - قلعی فی من ۱۰۰ (محمودی) - مس فی من ۹۰ (محمودی) - برنجی معدوم - سنگ بصری فی من ۶۰ (محمودی) - سرب فی من ۵۰ (محمودی) - صندل فی من ۸۰ (محمودی) - تنبک ماویدی فی من ۲۵ (محمودی) - رنگ قرمز فی من ۱۳۰۰ (محمودی) - ماژون پهل فی من ۳۵ (محمودی) - نیله توتیاء فی من ۶۰ (محمودی) - جوز بویه فی من ۱۲۰۰ (محمودی) - جوز معدوم - زعفران فی توله ۴ (محمودی) - پهتکری فی من ۲۲ (محمودی) - هینگ معدوم - فندق فی من بصری ۱۳۰ (محمودی) -
آهن فی من مذکور ۱۲۰ (محمودی) - پنبه فی من بصری ۱۴۰ (محمودی) - ۲۲/
بادام فی من بصری ۹۵ (محمودی) - اکروت فی هزار عدد ۱۵ (محمودی) - پسته فی من بصری ۳۰۰ (محمودی) - کشمش فی من بصری ۹۰ (محمودی) - مشک فی مثقال ۱۵ (محمودی) - خشخاش و چهار مغز معدوم - ابریشم فی من عطاری ۱۳۰۰ (محمودی) - بوند قهوه فی من ۹۰ (محمودی) - این همه اشیاء از بنادر دیگر بر جهازات میرسد و از آنجا به بندر بصره -

گوشت فی وقیه ۲ ۱/۲ (محمودی) خرما فی من بصری ۱۴ (محمودی) -

فی من عطاری بست و چهار وقیه و فی وقیه عطاری یک صد و دوازده مثقال و فی روپیه دو و نیم مثقال - وزن مقرره فی وقیه چهل و پنج روپیه اند و فی من بصری نیز بست و چهار وقیه بصری و فی وقیه بصری سه و نیم وقیه عطاری -

انگور فی وقیه ۲ (محمودی) - انار فی وقیه ۲ (محمودی) - تر کنکری ایضاً - برنج اول فی من بصری ۵۰ (محمودی) - برنج دوم فی من ۳۲ (محمودی) - و برنج

سیوم فی من ۲۸ (محمودی) - و برنج باریک مانند ولایت سرکار اصلا مفقود - گندم فی من ۳۱ (محمودی) - آرد گندم فی من ۳۶ (محمودی) - مونگ فی من ۴۰ (محمودی) - جوار فی من ۱۸ (محمودی) - لوبه فی من ۳۰ (محمودی) - عدس ایضاً - باقله فی من ۳۰ (محمودی) - نخود فی من ۶۰ (محمودی) -

و نرخ همه اجناس مذکوره وغیره هر روز بدل می شود -

پیدایش اجناس و میوه جات وغیره که در بندر بصره می‌شود این است :-

خرما انگور بہی انار گندم شالی گلاب شفتالو
مونگ لوبه عدس انجیر زرد آلو نارنگی نارنج شیرین و ترش
ترنج بادانجان کدوسفید ساگ میتھی ساگ خرفه بھندی
ترکنکری مولی پھیته پیاز کشنیز خشک و تر بیج مجیٹھه ۲۲۹
ساگ سویه ساگ انباره ساگ چولائی سیب حلوه جامون
توت جوار نخود شیرخشک -

یاد داشت اسم محله‌های آبادی بندر بصره بطرف جنوب -

مشراق کوازی مناخ میدان‌العبید -

بطرف قبله

قبله شراباتی محلة الذهب سیف که درآنجا حاکم بصره می باشد - مجموعه

بطرف شمال

نذران(۱) راس جسر محلة الجسر محلة الصبخة
مجموعه مناوی مقام علی مشکل کشا -

بطرف مشرق

جسرالعبید محله مراد پاشا محله حوش الپاشا
محله خان‌الدهن سیمر جسرالخوض -

۱- نظران

۲۳۰ یاد داشت اسمهای بازار بندر بصره -

سوق‌المزاره که درآنجا بانات وغیره سرانجام سپاه پیشه می فروشند -

سوق‌القزازه(۱) که درآنجا ابریشم وغیره سرانجام قلابتو می فروشند -

سوق‌البزازه(۲) که درآنجا پارچهٔ سفید وغیره می فروشند -

خان شتریه"(۳) که درآنجا پارچه وغیره می فروشند، و قافلهٔ شتر درآنجا فرود می آیند -

سوق‌الپهپانیه که درآنجا خیاطها می باشند -

سوق‌الهداراتیه که درآنجا کارد و قلم و اسباب آهنی و کلاه وغیره می فروشند -

سوق‌السفافیر(۴) که درآنجا مس فروشند -

سوق‌الشاباتیه" که درآنجا ظروف گلی می فروشند -

سوق‌المشراق که درآنجا سوای پارچه همه چیز میسر می آید -

سوق الحماره که درآنجا شتر و گوسفند و خر وغیره می فروشند -

سوق الذهب که درآنجا ماهی و تره‌کاری و مرغ و سبزی وغیره می فروشند -

سوق‌السیف، متصل خانهٔ متسلم خانه حاکم بصره، که درآنجا غله بسیار و گندم به وفور وغیره سوای پارچه می فروشند -

۲۳ سوق‌العطاطیر که درآنجا عطریات می فروشند -

سوق‌السیمر که درآنجا همه چیز سوای پارچه میسر می آید -

سوق‌القطان که درآنجا پنبه می فروشند -

سوق جسرالعبید که درآنجا همه چیز می فروشند -

سوق‌الهندی که درآنجا همه چیزی می فروشند، و به طرف مشرق

۱- سوق‌القزازین ۲- سوق‌البزازین ۳- خان شتریه

۴- سوق‌الصفافیر ۵- سوق‌الهنود

به کنارهٔ نهر واقع است و کسی هندوستانی آباد نموده بود ـ

یاد داشت اسم اعیان بصره ـ

متسلم حاکم بصره قاضی مفتی نقیب اشرف شیخ احمد
سید محمود شیخ معروف حاجی محمد دفتردار آفندی علی آغا
مصطفیٰ پاشا داروغهٔ جهازات ارماد بصره یعنی حاجی جواد ـ احمد چلبی
عبدالله یهودی دلال بصره ـ اسماعیل آغا یعنی زکوتی که کرک چیز می نامند(؟) ـ و حسین آغا داروغهٔ کشتی‌های ارماد بصره ـ

یاد داشت مقامات و مساجد و قهوه خانه وغیره ـ

مساجد کلان ۱۰ عدد مساجد خورد بیحساب و چند گنبد اعیان بصره و قهوه خانه‌ها هشتاد و نود آباد و سی و چهل ویران ـ

و مقام علی مشکل کشا رضی‌الله‌عنه و مقام حضرت زین‌العابدین رضی‌الله‌عنه ۲۳۲
و مقام حضرت عباس رضی‌الله‌عنه و مقام علی موسی رضا رضی‌الله‌عنه و روضهٔ یحیٰ بن موسی کاظم رضی‌الله‌عنه و روضهٔ شریف بن علی مشکل کشا رضی‌الله‌عنه و مقام علی بن موسی رضا رضی‌الله‌عنه و روضهٔ سید شعبان رضی‌الله‌عنه بیرون شهر بطرف جنوب واقع است و باقی اندرون شهر است ـ و یک روضهٔ شمس‌الدین رضی‌الله‌عنه بیرون شهر بطرف شمال واقع است و جمله تعداد خانهای خورد و کلان بندر بصره قریب یک لک یا زیاده باشد و نصف ویران بلکه زیاده ـ

و گرمابها نه عدد و دوکان حجام سی و پنج عدد و بروبروی دروازهٔ متسلم بست ضرب اتواب هفت جوش و بیتری و گرنل واقع و افتاده است ـ

و زاغ بندر بصره سیاه و ابلق یعنی بعضی زاغ سیاه و سفید است
و بعضی سیاه فقط لاکن از مردم بسیار ناآشنا به مثل ولایت هند نیست ۲۳۳
بلکه در صحرا می باشند ـ

و در بندر بصره از جهازات انگریز و فراسیس وغیره و سوداگر

چلبی و امام بندر مسقط که بوقت محاصرهٔ بندر بصره فوج کشی نموده از فوج برادر کریم خان مقابله نموده بود فی اجناس صد رومی سه رومی می گیرند و از باقی سوداگران فی صد روپیه هشت و نیم روپیه می گیرند و از سرکار فیض آثار نیز سه رومی فی اجناس صد رومی گرفتند بموجب حکم حاکم بغداد شریف۔ و شنیده شد که حاکم بصره فی سال سه هزار کیسه، فی کیسه پنج صد رومی مقرره پانزده لک رومی می شود ، به حاکم بغداد می دهد و باقی شیخ سوینی عسکردار بدوی که از باعث رعب و خوف نامبرده همه ملک آباد و در اطاعت و انقیاد است ، و علی آغا و حاجی محمد آفندی دفتردار و عبدالله یهودی دلال وغیره می خورند ۔ و وصول بندر بصره اصلا مقرر نیست و به تحقیقات مقرری اصلا نه می رسد۔ و معلوم می شود که درین ولایت بندوبست و تقید امری واحد نیست ، هر چیکه به وصول می در آید همه حکام وغیره اهلکار و سپاه پیشه می خورند و انچیکه باقی می ماند به حاکم بغداد وغیره می رسانند۔

۲۳۲ و جمله غرابات و جهازات ارماد بصره ده منزل بودند ۔ حالا یکمنزل تازه از سوداگر رزاقی به خرید آوردند ۔ و کشتی‌های ارماد بصره دو منزل ، و سوای این دو سه منزل سوداگری هستند ، این همه علاقهٔ سرکار متسلم حاکم بصره ۔ و کشتی‌های تجارتی تجاران بسیار است و کشتی‌های ارمادی و تجارتی را از کنارهٔ رود ده دوازده نفر یک رسن بسته بزور سینه می کشند ۔ و کوتهی انگریز و فراسیس و صالح چلبی سوداگر بندر سورت و امام و دلال بندر مسقط و شیخ احمد ساهوکار و سوداگر در بندر بصره واقع است ۔

و در بندر بصره قوم عرب و عجم و ترکستان و یهودی و نصرانی و ارمنی می باشند، لاکن همه‌ها لباس عرب می پوشند ، یعنی دو سه چهار پنج قبای شیله و کهادی و بانات و کملی وغیره به قدر مراتب خودها و پایجامهٔ کهادی و بانات و موزهٔ چرمی می پوشند ، و بر سر یک

کلاه باناتی و بالای آن یک شال یا دوپته یا لنگی به قدر مراتب خویش می پوشند ـ و قوم بدوی بسیار هستند ـ و لباس سرداران بدوی عبا و قبای باناتی و کملی و ازار وغیره می پوشند و برسر یک رومال ته کرده شمله‌وار می گزارند و بالای آن یک شال و یا دوپته و لنگی می بندند ـ و ادانی اینها یک رومال بر سر شمله‌وار می گزارند و یک یا دو عبا و قبای کملی فقط می پوشند ـ و لباس زنان عرب و عجم وغیره یک یا دو پیرهن و یک پایجامه و موزهٔ چرمی می پوشند و برسر چادر میگرند ـ
و لباس زنان بدوی یک پیرهن و چادر فقط ـ ۲۳۵

و خوراک عمده بندر بصره چه از قوم عرب و عجم وغیره نان گندم و پنیر و کباب، و قدری طعام می خورند، لاکن صبحی قدری نان و کباب خورده قهوه بوند می خورند و به وقت دو پهر نان و کباب و پنیر و طعام و خورش وغیره می خورند و به دستور به وقت شام ـ و خوراک ادانی بصره نان و طعام فقط، بعضی اوقات پیاز یا مولی یا کباب یا قلیه و طعام روغن‌دار می خورند ـ و بازار بندر بصره از صبح تا نماز ظهر آباد و من بعد ویران و در هر بازار و محله چوکیداران از وقت شام تا وقت صبح می نمایند ـ

و به تاریخ هجدهم روز یکشنبه شاه نوراللّه خان و عبدالقادر منشی و شیخ ابراهیم معلم و محمد عمر چوبدار سرکار وغیره به فرودگاه جعفر خان رفتند ـ جعفر خان سید جعفر مصدی و محمد امام جوقدار سزاول و محمد عمر چوبدار را(۱) به دریافت مرضی و مصالحت نزد غلام علی خان فرستادند ـ من بعد محمد عمر چوبدار به دریافت مرضی رسیده گفت که شاه نوراللّه خان و جعفر خان وغیره نزد غلام علی خان

۱ـ .MS محمد عمر چوبدار را نزد غلام علیخان به دریافت مرضی و مصلحت نزد غلام علیخان فرستادند

بیانید که لطف علی خان هم حاضراند، البته مناقشهٔ دو سه روزه سابق
از کلمه و کلام سلوک آمیز مرتفع خواهد شد۔ شاه نورالله خان و جعفر
خان و محمد نتهو جوقدار و نامدار خان سرخیل اسداللهی و بارگیران
سرکار وغیره نزد غلام علی خان رفتند و نشستند ۔ من بعد محمد نتهو و ٢٣٠
محمد امام جوقداران اسداللهی و سزاول وغیره بعد چند کلمه و کلام از
غلام علی خان و شاه نورالله خان گفتند که مایان را چندی خرچ بطریق
علی الحساب بدهانند که مایان زود زاد راه نموده تیار خواهم شد ۔ شاه
نورالله خان گفتند : حاضر است بگیرند ۔ من بعد به تقرری سواری بر
کشتی‌ها مقرر نمودند که غلام علی خان و چند شاگرد پیشهٔ سرکار وغیره
بر کشتی باشترده و جوانان اسداللهی را بر کشتی غلام علی خان و جوانان
سزاول را بر یک کشتی دیگر و لطف علی خان بر کشتی خود بحال و
شاه نورالله خان مع جعفر خان بر کشتی خود سوار شدند ۔ من بعد محمد نتهو
جوقدار از غلام علی خان پرسید که همین طور مقرر است یا نه ۔ غلام علی
خان به جواب پرداختند که من هیچ نمی دانم ، من هفت نفرشتر و چهار
راس اسپ و یک راس اشتر به کرایه مقرر نموده‌ام از راه خشکی به
نجف اشرف رفته بعد حصول شرف زیارت به بغداد خواهم رفت ۔

من بعد معلم و ماستر و سرخیل جیش علاقهٔ رسالهٔ فقیر محمد تعلقهٔ
جهازات مغروق مع شیخ سلطان نامی مالک یک جهاز که به صوب بندر
مسقط می رفت می آمدند و می گفتند که مایان را بهر نوع بر جهاز
مذکور سوار گردانیده روانه بکنند ۔ من بعد غلام علی خان و شاه نورالله
خان وغیره سه نفر برای بردن به بندر مسقط که نود و پنج نفر بودند ٢٣١
از جهاز تا پنج رومی مقرر نمودند ۔ و غلام علی خان برای تقرر کرایه
پنج رومی نقد بدست مالک جهاز دهانیدند و معلم و ماستر وغیره براضی
شد ۔ مالک جهاز به سه نفر به پنج رومی، نیم رومی دیگر سه نفر بعد
رسیدن به بندر مسقط دادن قبول نمودند ۔ من بعد جعفر خان وغیره

باز برای راضی شدن به سواری بر کشتی‌ها و همراهی قافله از غلام علی
خان سوال نمودند ـ غلام علیخان به جواب پرداختند که من هرگز همراه
شما نخواهم آمد، اگر شماها از راه خشکی می روند من از راه تری
خواهم رفت و الا برعکس آن مقرر است و من هم بسیار بیمارم و اصلا امید
زیست ندارم، اگر تندرستی می بود می بهر عنوان به همراهی قافله و امورات
سرکار پرداختمی، خوب، حالا هم از راه خشکی به نجف اشرف رفته بعد
حصول شرف زیارات مقدسات به بغداد می آیم و شریک امورات سرکار
می شوم لاکن در مقدمات مالی و داد و ستد نخواهم آمد ـ و لطف علی
خان هم چیزی نه گفته همراهی غلام علی خان قبول نمودند ـ شاه نورالله
خان گفتند: اگر مرا می گویند که در اینجا باش می باشم اگر از ۲۳۸
راه خشکی پیشتر پیشتر برو یا پستر به باش می گویند و الا من تا به
بغداد رسیده پیشتر انچیکه از دست من خواهد شد بجا خواهم آورد ـ
و از آنجا جعفر خان وغیره را همراه گرفته بر کشتی خود که طعام تبرک
نام مبارک حضرت رسالت پناه پخت و پز نموده بودند رفتند ـ و جعفر خان
و شکرالله خان و احمد علی و عبدالغفار منشی و سید جعفر مصدی و
بارگیران سرکار و محمد نتهو جوقدار و نامدار خان سرخیل و جوانان سزاول
و اسداللهی وغیره را طعام مذکور خورانیدند و بخانهٔ غلام علیخان و
لطف علی خان وغیره طعام نیز فرستادند ـ

و شاه نورالله خان و جعفر خان وغیره ملازم سرکار سواری غلام علی
خان و لطف علي خان وغیره مقرر نمودند که غلام علیخان و
لطف علیخان از راه تری به بغداد نمی آیند، خوب، دفعه دیگر
اطلاع نموده پیشتر رفتن مناسب است ـ ازانجا که امورات درپیش، و
سید ولی بارگیر سرکار برای روانگی خود به صوب بندر مسقط و نوشته
دادن عرضداشت به حضور پرنور متضمن رفتن مردم روانگی روم تا مواضع ۲۳۹
قرنه و برگردیدن از موضع به بندر بصره به سبب اختلاف اخبار متوحش

و باز درپیش شدن روانگی به صوب بغداد به غلام علی خان گفت - غلام علی خان به عبدالقادر منشی که حاضر بود گفتند که یک قطعه عرض داشت متضمن مضمون مسطور از طرف هر چهار سردار نوشته نزد خود بفریسند، بر عرضی مهر نموده داده خواهد شد - و باز شیخ ابراهیم معلم همراهی برای روانگی شرف‌الدین معلم که از عارضهٔ پیچش بسیار بیمار بود به صوب بندر کوریال از غلام علی خان گفت - غلام علی خان نیز به عبدالقادر منشی گفتند که اگر مرضی هر چهار سردار باشد یک عرضداشت متضمن اینکه معلم شرف‌الدین را از عارضهٔ پیچش بسیار بیمار بود روانه بندر کوریال نموده از طرف هر چهار سردار بنویسند و بدهند - عبدالقادر منشی قبول کرد و رفت - و عبدالقادر منشی هم از غلام‌علیخان برای انصرام امورات سرکار به اتفاق هر چهار سردار و روانگی به صوب
بغداد به اتفاق از راه تری بسیار گفت و شنود بمیان آورد اصلا قبول نه ٢٤٠
کردند - شاه نورالله خان به جوانان اسداللهی و بارگیران سرکار وغیره قدری زر علی‌الحساب از توشک خانهٔ سرکار دهانیدند و سید ولی بارگیر سرکار را که برای روانگی به حضور پرنور معه عرائض خودها مقرر نموده بودند وجه طلب یکماه دادند -

و بتاریخ نوزدهم روز دوشنبه عبدالله یهودی دلال بندر بصره نزد شاه نورالله خان مع یک قطعه خط ساهوکار بندر سورت متضمن اینکه مروارید مرسلهٔ عبدالله یهودی به سبب هنگامهٔ فوج کشی حضرت نواب مستطاب فلک جناب خلدالله ملکه همه تجاران وغیره از بندر مسطور فراری گردیدند به فروخت نرسیدند، موسومهٔ عبدالله یهودی رسیده بود آمده گفت که فوج آقای شما تا سرحد رود کشنا رسیدند و مرهته مقهوره را بسیار مغلوب ساختند - شاه نورالله خان از استماع این خبر خوش و خرم شدند و پنج‌هزار روپی از عبدالله یهودی مسطور گرفته داخل توشک خانهٔ سرکار نمودند -

و بتاریخ بیستم روز سه‌شنبه شاه نورالله خان و جعفر خان و عبدالقادر

منشی بر سه راس اسپ سوار شده نزد متسلم رفتند ـ شاه نورالله خان از متسلم گفتند که پنج چهار منزل کشتی کرایه‌دار برای رفتن به بغداد
از راه شط فرات که بزودی رسیده خواهد شد از معرفت سید عبدالرحمان ۲۴۱
نموده شد ، باید که مایان را مرخص نمایند ـ متسلم به جواب پرداخت که در راه شط فرات هنوز خوف و خطر باقی است ، اعتماد کلی نیست و وقتی که شماها از راه مسطور روند و نوعی دیگر خوف و خطر درپیش رسد ، حرف بدنامی عاید حال مایان خواهد شد و بنام شما بسیار است ، که همراه خود خیلی جواهر و زر و نقدیات بی شمار از هندوستان می دارند ـ شاه نورالله خان گفتند : خوب چه مضایقه ، برکشتی های کرایه‌دار مسطور سوار شده از شط عرب به موضع کوت که از آنجا بغداد از راه خشکی فاصلهٔ سه منزل دارد و از راه تری بست و پنج منزل رسیده به بغداد رفته خواهد شد ، کشتی‌های حسین آغا مایان را درکار نیست که نامبرده بسیار دروغگو است و بوعده امروز فردا کار سرکار ابتری نماید و به صوب بغداد راهی نمی شود ـ متسلم به جواب پرداخت که کشتی باشترده و دومنزل دیگر از علاقهٔ سرکار است ، یک و دومنزل دیگر کرایه نموده آدم دیگر همراه گرفته بروز شنبه تاریخ بست و دوم ماه ربیع‌اول سنه ۱۲۰۱ هجری بصوب بغداد راهی شوند ـ شاه نورالله خان قبول نمودند که اگر بروز مقرری مسطور به
عمل آید ـ متسلم گفت والله‌بالله راست است و درین هیچ خلاف نیست ـ ۲۴۲

من بعد متسلم کیفیت بندر کوریال از نام منگلور پرسید و از دست خود نوشت به طریق یادداشت که محصول و زکواة بندر مذکور چه قدر است و دیهات چند دارد و کدام کدام اجناس و اقمشه پیدا می شوند و در شهر و بیرون شهر نهر و چاه‌های آب شیرین هست یا نه و عسکر متعلقهٔ بندر مذکور چه قدر است و به طرف مشرق و مغرب و شمال و جنوب کدام کدام ولایت است و نام آن ولایت ها چیست و درانجا جهازات تیار می شوند یا نه و از بندر مسقط جهازات به بندر کوریال در عرصهٔ

چند روز می رسند و دارالسلطنت پتن از بندر مسطور فاصلهٔ چند منازل دارد - شاه نورالله خان وغیره به جواب پرداختند که محصول بندر کوریال نه لک روپیه و زکواة سه لک روپیه و زکواة جهازات تجاران که از بنادر دیگر می رسند هشتاد هزار روپیه - و دیهات خورد و بزرگ مرتب هفت صد و پنجاه - و صندل و الایچی و فلفل گرد و آهن و برنج باریک و نارجیل وغیره و پارچهٔ سفید وغیره از هر قسمی سوای بانات و شال در آنجا پیدا می شوند - و در شهر نهرهای آب شیرین موفور - و یک‌هزار
و هفت صد جوان جیش و سه صد سوار در قلعه همراه قلعه‌دار و همراه ٢٤١
عامل یک هزار نفر پیاده می باشند وبست و هشت قلعه‌جات متعلقهٔ بندر کوریال اند و فی قلعه یک صد نفر پیاده بلکه زیاده متعین اند - و بطرف قبلهٔ دریا و به طرف مشرق دارالسلطنت پتن بفاصلهٔ دوازده منزل و به طرف شمال خوشحال پور به فاصلهٔ سه منزل و به طرف جنوب بندر کلیکوت(١) بفاصلهٔ هشت منزل واقع اند و بسیار جهازات در انجا تیار می شوند - و از بندر مسقط تا بندر کوریال جهازات بعضی اوقات در عرصهٔ یک هفته و بعضی اوقات در عرصهٔ دو هفته تا چهل روز می رسند -

ازین صورت معلوم گردید که پیش از سلطان روم خطی متضمن دریافت کیفیت بندر کوریال موسومهٔ حاکم بغداد رسید و از آنجا به حاکم متسلم رسیده باشد - و کیفیت داد و ستد بندر کوریال و بندر بصره به سلطان ظاهر گردیده باشد - چنانچه در نقل فرمان سلطان روم که موسومهٔ حاکم بغداد رسیده نزد متسلم حاکم بصره از صحابت جوقدار رسیده بود ، مرقوم بود که وکلای سلطان هند را که بسیار معتبر و معتمد اند و برای سوال و جواب داد و ستد بندر کوریال و بندر بصره وغیره رسیده اند، زود روانه ولایت روم نمایند -

شاه نورالله خان وغیره از نزد متسلم مرخص شده به فرودگاه

١- کالیکٹ

جعفر خان آمدند و منتظر رسیدن عبدالله یهودی دلال بصره که فرار نموده
بود شدند ـ درین اثنا سید جعفر مصدی سرکار وغیره نزد شاه نورالله خان ۲۴۴
آمده برای رفتن نزد غلام علی خان و فهمایش و همکلامی با ایشان
بسیار به عنوات گفتند ـ شاه نورالله خان گفتند که پیش ازین نزد غلام
علیخان به گفتهٔ جعفر خان و شماها رفته وغیره چند سخنهای بابت امورات
سرکار درمیان آورده اصلا به امری از امورات سرکار متوجه نه شدند و
قبول نه کردند و قصد رفتن خود از راه خشکی به نجف اشرف مصمم
ساختند ، باز رفتن مناسب نیست ، اگر لطف علیخان و جعفر خان
می گویند که غلام علی خان را به انصرام امورات سرکار به موجب
حکمنامهٔ عنایتی خاص متوجه و راضی نمایند من فردا نزد غلام علی خان
رفته از چند کلمات سلوک آمیز متکلم می شوم ـ سید جعفر مصدی نزد
لطف علی خان رفته همه کیفیت مسطور ظاهر کرد،نزد شاه نورالله خان که
به فرودگاه جعفر خان بودند لطف علی خان را آوردند ـ شاه نورالله خان
از خان مسطور گفتند که پریروز نزد غلام علی خان بروبروی شما رفته
کلام بچند عنوانات در امورات سرکار نمودم، اصلا متوجه نه شدند و
کلام بر ضد نمودند ، حالا چه طور رفته می شود ، باید که شما و
جعفر خان و سید علی صاحب پیرزاده وغیره فردا نزد غلام علی خان رفته ۲۴۵
مرضی خان مسطور متضمن این که به موجب ارشاد مندرجه حکمنامهٔ
عنایتی خاص امورات سرکار بجا می آرم و از حکم حکمنامه بیرون
نمی روم و به جمیع امورات سرکار متفق می باشم، گرفته خود را طلب
دارند نزد غلام علی خان خواهم آمد و از کلام سلوک آمیز و امورات
سرکار متکلم می شوم و الا پیش غلام علی‌خان نخواهم رفت و در عرصهٔ
دو سه همراه مردمانیکه می آیند به بغداد می روم ـ لطف علی خان
قبول نمودند و درین باب ازین قبیل بسیار سخنان به میان آمدند ـ و
شاه نورالله خان وغیره بر کشتی خود آمدند و از متسلم هفت ضرب

بنادیق منجمله سی و یک ضرب بنادیق برآورده جهازات مغروق گرفته حوالهٔ جوقدار و سرخیل جوق سزاول نمودند ـ

و بتاریخ بست و یکم روز چهار شنبه سید جعفر مصدی معه آدم لطف علی خان صبحی نزد شاه نورالله خان آمده گفتند که غلام علی خان می گویند که همه سرداران مقرر کنند که به موجب حکم حکمنامهٔ عنایتی خاص به انصرام امورات سرکار پردازند یا نوشته بدهند که به موجب حکم هر چهار سردار بجا آرند و حکمنامهٔ عنایتی خاص را یک طرف دارند، شما نزد غلام‌علی‌خان بیایند البته همه مقدمات انفصال خواهند یافت ـ شاه نورالله خان به جواب پرداختند که سید علی صاحب پیرزاده از غلام‌علی و خود آزرده شده اند، درین‌جا طلب دارند به اتفاق رفته خواهد شد ـ ٢٤
سید جعفر وغیره نزد سید علی صاحب رفتند ـ

و عبدالله یهودی نزد شاه نورالله خان آمده گفت که اگر همراه حسین آغا نمی روند من از متسلم گفته سوای سه منزل کشتی سرکار دو کشتی دیگر بابت یک سید معتبر به کرایه گرفته شماها را در عرصهٔ دو سه روز روانه می نمایم ـ شاه نورالله خان قبول نموده حسین آغا را طلب داشته گفتند که به تاریخ بست و چهارم می روی یا نه ـ حسین آغا گفت که مقرر به تاریخ مسطور بصوب بغداد راهی می شوم ـ شاه نورالله خان به عبدالله یهودی گفتند که به حسین آغا تاکید نموده زود روانه بکن ـ یهودی مسطور گفت که حالا نزد متسلم رفته همه حقیقت ظاهر نموده، می گویم که اگر حسین آغا زود راهی می شود خوب است و الا دو کشتی دیگر از معرفت سید معتمد کرایه نموده شماها را روانه نمایند ـ شاه نورالله خان قبول نموده محمد عمر چوبدار و عبدالرحمان چیلهٔ سرکار را همراه یهودی مسطور نزد متسلم روانه ساختند که زود کیفیت دریافت نموده بیایند ـ خبر آوردند که متسلم گفت که فردا حسین آغا را طلب داشته مقدمهٔ شما را فیصله داده همراه حسین آغا یا سید معتمد

شما را روانه می سازم فردا بیایند ـ

من بعد شاه نورالله خان و سید علی صاحب و عبدالقادر منشی و سید ۲۴۷
جعفر مصدی وغیره به فرودگاه جعفر خان رفتند و از آنجا نزد غلام علی خان به اتفاق جعفر خان رفتند و لطف علي خان را هم طلب داشتند و به کامهٔ و کلام سلوکِ آمیز متکلم شدند ـ و شاه نورالله خان همه کیفیت دیروزه سوال و جواب متسلم ظاهر کردند ـ و یک قطعه عرضداشت متضمن کوایف روداد و روانگی محمد علي بهاتو به سبب ظهور شرارت و شرایط نمک حرامی و شرف‌الدینِ معلم همراهی را به سبب عارضهٔ پیچش و ترسیل فرد حاضری وصول سید ولی بارگیر سرکار و نامبرده‌ها به حضور پرنور هر چهار سردار به اتفاق نویسانیده سر بمهر هر چهار سردار سپرد سید ولی نمودند که به حضور پرنور برساند ـ و نیز یک قطعه خط از جانب هر چهار سردار موسومهٔ ماوجی سیته دلال بندر مسقط متضمن اینکه نود نفر معلم و ماستر و خلاصی و جوانان جیش ملازم سرکار متعلقهٔ جهازات مغروق که به سلامتی جان بر آمدند بر یک منزل داو کرایه‌دار سلطان ابن حاجی محمد بحساب سر نفر پنج رومی مقرر نموده دو صد و هفتاد رومی نقد داده سوار نموده روانه بندر مسقط کرده شد ، باید که بعد رسیدن مردم
مذکور یک صد و هشتاد رومی از نزد خود داده از سلطان ابن حاجی‌محمد رسید ۲۴۸
بگیرد و مردم مذکور معه مردم جهاز فخرالمراکب به بندر کوریال روانه سازد ، نویسانیده به نامبرده دادند و به خلاصیان و جوانان جیش وغیره مردم جهاز مغروق سر نفر دو رومی به خرچ آنها دهانیدند ـ

و محمد علی بهاتو نزد غلام علي خان و شاه نورالله خان وغیره آمده گفت که مرا به حضور چرا روانه می سازند ـ شاه نورالله خان به جواب پرداختند که تو هر بار به ملازمان عالی بدی گوئی(۱) و دشنام می دهی(۲)

۱ــ .MS می گوید   ۲ــ .MS می دهد

و به هرکس اخبار متوحش ولایت خود می گوئی(۱) و از خود ظاهر می نمائی(۲) هر چند که ترا بارها نصیحت نمودند هرگز شیوهٔ نمک‌حرامی و بدگوئی و بی‌غیرتی نمی گذاری ،(۳) همراه بردن مناسب نه دانسته روانه حضور می کنیم ـ محمد علي بهاتو قسم اقسام خورده انکار نمود و دست بر زمین مالید ـ شاه نورالله خان از روبروی خودها بیرون کنانیده در یزک نهادند و قدری زر علی‌الحساب به محمد علی بهاتو و معلم شرف‌الدین وغیره دهانیدند ـ

و غلام علی خان از شاه نورالله خان و لطف علی خان و جعفر خان و سید علی صاحب پیرزاده مخاطب نموده گفتند که آینده یا به موجب حکنامهٔ عنایتی خاص به انصرام امورات سرکار پردازند و یا یک نوشته بکنند که
۲۴۱ بموجب گفتهٔ هر چهار سردار غلام علی خان به انصرام امورات سرکار پردازد، از هر دو مقدمه یک مقدمه مقرر نمایند ـ همه‌ها قبول نمودند ، لاکن نوشت و خواند به ظهور نرسید ـ و شاه نورالله خان و جعفر خان به فرود گاه خود رفتند ـ من بعد غلام علی خان از لطف علي خان و سید علی صاحب و عبدالقادر منشی و سید جعفر مصدی گفتند که اگرچه شاه نورالله خان آمدند لاکن نوشت و خواند به ظهور نه انجامید ، اگر بهمین طور بگذرد آینده خلش و فساد در پیش است ، باید که یک نوشته شما هر چهار سردار بکنند که بموجب حکم هر چهار سردار عمل نماید یا به موجب حکمنامهٔ عنایتی خاص ـ لطف علی خان به جواب پرداختند که نوشته از جانب مایان به مضمون اینکه شما به موجب گفتهٔ مایان به عمل آرند هرگز نخواهد شد مگر شما نوشته بدهند که به موجب گفتهٔ خود به اطاعت پردازند قبول است ـ آخرالامر لطف علی خان از سید علی صاحب وغیره به شاه

۱ــ .MS می گوید

۲ــ .MS می نماید

۳ــ .MS نمی گذارد

نورالله خان درین ماده گفته فرستادند که درین ماده به مضمون مسطور غلام علي خان یک نوشته درخواست می دارند ـ شاه نورالله خان به مجرد استماع گفتند که یک نوشته هر چهار سردار به اتفاق به این مضمون
بنویسند که هر چهار سردار به اتفاق بموجب حکمنامهٔ عنایتی خاص به ٢٥٠
انصرام امورات سرکار پردازند ـ اگر امری از امورات سرکار سوای امر مندرجه حکمنامهٔ عنایتی خاص اتفاق هر چهار سردار به اتفاق به انصرام آن پردازند، نوشته در توشکخانهٔ سرکار نگاه دارند و دیگر نوشته درکار نیست ـ سید علي صاحب به وعده فردا برکشتی خود رفتند ـ

و مهماندار احمد چلبی نزد غلام علي خان و شاه نورالله خان و لطف علی خان علحده علحده رفته دوصد رومی برای خرچ خود رعایتاً درخواست نمود، همه‌ها حواله بر شاه نورالله خان نمودند، خان مسطور به لیت و لعل گذرانیدند ـ و روانگی بصوب بغداد شریف به تاریخ بست و هفتم یا بست و نهم ماه یوسفی سال سنه ١٢٠٠ هجری به ظهور خواهد انجامید ـ

تحریر فی‌التاریخ بست و یکم ماه یوسفی سال‌دلو سنه ١٢٠٠ هجری مطابق نوزدهم ماه ربیع‌الاول سنه ١٢٠١ هجری ـ (١)

نقل عرضداشت علی راجه بتاریخ بست و هفتم حیدری سال کلان سنه الیه ٢٥١
موافق ماه ذی حجه سنه ١٢٢١ هجری(٢) رسیده است ـ

درین ولا تبرک حضرت بیت‌الله شریف سر بمهر ارسال حضور است، امید که از راه خداوندی قبول یابد ـ وکیلان که از جانب والا بسمت روم مرخص گردیده بودند به فضل‌الهی از پیش گاه قیصر به خوشی و خورمی رخصت شده همراه قافله معه خلعت فاخره وغیره سرانجام و جواب مکتوبات روانه شد، به خیریت داخل مدینهٔ منوره گردیدند ـ و شاه نورالله

١ــ 19 Rabi 1, 1201/9 January, 1787

٢ــ Incorrect date.

بسبب بیماری همانجا ماندند و وکلای دیگر به بندر جده آمده و در آنجا یک مرکب داو یعنی کشتی باجوره مقرر کرده بران سوار شده معه سر انجام روانه مسقط شدند انشاءالله عنقریب به بندرکوریال خواهند رسید ـ و بعد رخصت وکلای سرکار سلطان حمید خان قیصر روم انتقال نمود و سلطان محمودخان برتخت قیصر جلوس نمودند ـ و در ماه شوال بروز جمعه در وقت خطبه در جماعت یک شخص هندوستانی خطیب را برخنجر شهید کرد و مردمان نیز او را کشتند ـ و سوای این در ملک عرب از ابتدای ماه ربیع‌الاول تا آخر ماه شوال در بندر مخا و بندر هوویدا(۱) و بندر لجا(۲) و بندر لبان و موضعات بیت‌القصیر(۳) در بیت هندی و ابوعریش در یک روز دو دفعه سه دفعه زمین از قدرت الهی می لرزد و عمارتها و خانهامی افتد، ازین باعث تمام عالم حیران و پریشان هستند، و ازین یک موضع زمین شگافته شد از آنجا آتش پیدا شده چند موضعات آتش گرفته جلا وطن(؟) ساخت، بنابر اطلاع بعرض پرداخت ـ

۱ــ or حویزه ۲ــ Probably ام‌لج ۳ــ بیت‌القصر

فهرست اسماء الرجال و القبایل والاماکن

(ح)

(خ)

(د)

(ش)

(ص)

(ض)

(ط)

(ع)

(ن)

غلطنامه

صفحه	سطر	غلط	صحیح
۱۰	(حاشیه ۲)	خورفگان	خورفکان
۱۱	(،، ،،)	رنام	ریام
۱۵	۲۱	وایر ملاکی	واپر ملاکی (؟)
۱۶	۲۱	برد او	بر داو
۱۹	۷	یزداشته	برداشته
۲۷	۱۹	تنبا کو	تنبا کوی
۳۱	۸	خورد و بر دیوار	خورد بر دیوار
۳۴	۱	دومامه	دو ماهه
۳۴	۱۲	بد کنارهٔ	به کنارهٔ
۳۹	۸	کفیت	کیفیت
۴۱	۱۱	همد سیت	همد ست
۴۲	(حاشیه ۴)	فاد	فاو
۴۴	(حاشیه ۲)	الحجیر	العجیر
۴۹	۴	شیح بدهن محمد حسین	شیخ بدهن و محمد حسین
۵۴	۹	دررو	درر و
۵۵	۱	وهی	وصی
۸۰	۲۵	نزو	نزد
۸۲	۲۴	بسیا	بسیا ر
۸۸	۱۹	عتیق	عقیق
۹۸	۱۸	چوبداو	چوبدار
۹۸	(حاشیه ۱)	دوسرا	دواسر
۱۲۹	۹	امرای	امری
۱۳۲	۲۲	سوق الهندی	سوق الهندی (ص)
۱۵۱	۵	شماها رفته وغیره	شماها وغیره رفته
۱۵۵	۱۸	ذی حجه	ذوالحجه